ECHAD 5:

The Global Anthology of Jewish Women Writers

general editors —

ROBERT & ROBERTA KALECHOFSKY

Library of Congress Cataloging-in-Publication Data

The Global Anthology of Jewish women writers/general editors, Robert and Roberta
Kalechofsky
      p. cm.---(Echad : 5)
   ISBN 0-916288-29-3
1. Jewish literature--Women authors. 2. Women, Jewish--Biography.
I. Kalechofsky, Robert. II. Kalechofsky, Roberta. III.. Series.
PN6067.G5   1990   90-6231
808.8'00082--dc20   CIP

Printed in the U.S.A.

Typeset by Beverly A. Hower

Acknowledgements: Yeshayahu Leibowitz, Rochelle Furstenberg "Of Thorns, Idols
and Prophecy," Hadassah Magazine, May, 1990, 17. Leah Shakdiel and report on
International Jewish Feminist Conference: Roselyn Bell, "Wide-Awake Dreams,"
Hadassah Magazine, Feb., 1989, 24-27.
Hannah Arendt, "Jewess and Schlemihl," Rahel Varnhagen: The Life of A Jewish
Woman, Harcourt Brace Jovanovich, 1974.
Bernice Rubens, excerpt from Brothers, Abacus, Sphere Books Ltd., 1984. Author's
perm.
Fredelle Brusar Maynard, "The Silk Umbrella," Raisins and Almonds, Paperjacks,
1973. Perm. S. Bacon.
Anzia Yezierska, "College," Bread Givers, Persea Books, Inc., 1975.
Shulamith Hareven, excerpt from The City of Many Days, tr. H. Halkin, New Writing
from Israel, ed. J. Sontag, Corgi Books; Doubleday, 1977. Author's perm. Amalia
Kahana-Carmon, "N'ima Sassoon Writes Poetry," tr. Arthur Jacobs, Meetings With
the Angel, ed. B. Tammy & L. Yudkin, Andre Deutch, 1973. Author's perm.
Peggy Parnass, "Childhood," Konkret Literatur Verlag, tr. Iris Wesselman and
author. Author's perm.
Marianne Walter, "An Encounter." Author's perm.
Fay Zwicky, "Hostages," Coast to Coast, ed Frank Moorhouse, Angus & Robertson,
Sydney, 1973; "Tiananmen Square. Author's perm.
Angelina Muñiz-Huberman, stories from Enclosed Garden, The Latin American
Literary Review Press, 1988.
Bat Ye'Or, Dhimmi Peoples: Oppressed Nations, Editions de l'Avenir, 1978.
Author's perm.
Esther Cameron, excerpt from C or The Autoanalysis of a Golem. Author's perm.
Emma Goldman, "The Role of Women in The Spanish Revolution," Visions on Fire, ed.
David Porter, Commonground Press, 1983, perm. Ian Ballantine.

Nancy Keesing, "Ladies Only," "Half English, half something else," <u>Lily On The Dustbin</u>, Penguin Books, 1982. Author's perm.

Cynthia Ozick, "Virility," <u>The Pagan Rabbi and Other Stories</u>, Schocken Books, 1976, perm. Random House - Alfred A. Knopf, Inc.

Roberta Kalechofsky, <u>Meditation on an Animal</u>, Between The Species, Vol 3, no. 3, Summer, 1987.

Barbara Mujica, "Don Bernardo's Second Death," from <u>The Deaths of Don Bernardo</u>. Author's perm.

Luisa Futoransky, excerpt from <u>Son cuentos chinos</u>, ediciones albatros, 1983. Author's perm.

Shirley Eskapa, excerpt from <u>Blood Fugue</u>. Quartet Books Ltd., 1981. Author's perm.

Eugenia Ginzburg, excerpt from <u>Within The Whirlwind</u>, tr. Leila Vennewitz, Harcourt Brace Jovanovich, 1982.

Liliane Atlan, excerpt from "The Carriage of Flames and Voices," <u>Modern Literature Annual</u>, vol 1, general editor, Bettina L. Knapp, tr. Marguerite Feitlowitz. Trans' perm.

Shelley Ehrlich, "Naamah and The Ark," from <u>Dreaming The Ark</u>, Juniper Books 49, 1985. Perm: Dr. Frederick Ehrlich.

Nelly Sachs, "O the Chimneys," "Now Abraham has seized the roots of the winds," "If the prophets broke in," "The Night of the Weeping Children," <u>O The Chimneys</u>, Farrar, Straus & Giroux, 1967. "In the Land of Israel," "This land," "Women and Girls of Israel," "We Mothers," "O you Animals," <u>The Seeker and Other Poems</u>, Farrar, Straus & Giroux, Inc. 1970.

Else Lasker-Schüler, poetry from <u>Hebrew Ballads and Other Poems</u>, tr. & ed. by Audri Durchslag and Jeanette Litman-Demeestere. Jewish Publication Society, 1980. Original source: Else Lasker-Schüler, <u>Gesammelte Werke in drei Banden</u>. Perm. Kosel-Verlag, Munchen.

Elaine Starkman, poetry from <u>Love Scene</u>, Sheer Press, 1980. Perm. author.

Raquel Jodorowsky, poetry from <u>Woman Who Has Sprouted Wings: Poems by Contemporary Latin American Poets</u>, ed. by Mary Crow, 1988.

Carol Adler, poetry from <u>First Reading</u>, Northwoods Press, 1984. Author's perm.

Naomi Doudai, "The Myth of The Morning of the World." Author's perm.

Clarice Lispector, stories from <u>Family Ties</u>, tr. Giovanni Pontiero, University of Texas Press, 1960.

Nora Glickman, "The Jewish White Slave Trade in Latin American Writings," <u>American Jewish Archives</u>, vol 34, no. 2, Nov., 1982, 178-89.

Fran Katz, "Dinah Shore, Where Are You Now When We Need You?" <u>Cimmaron Review, Best American Short Stories of 1971</u>, Houghton Mifflin. Author's perm.

Teresa Prozecanski, "Dying for Love," Ciudad Impune, Monte Sexto S.R.L., 1986. Tr. Patricia Greene. Author's perm.

Nadine Gordimer, "Sins of The Third Age," <u>Something Out There</u>, Viking, 1983.

Cover Design, <u>Old Fashioned Flora Borders on Layout Grids</u>, ed. Carol Belanger Grafton, Dover Publications, 1989.

INTRODUCTION

In November, 1988, the First International Jewish Feminist
Conference was held in Jerusalem. It was a milestone on the road
from a Jewess like Rahel Varnhagen, who lived in the first generation
of Jews freed from ghetto life, to the modern Jewish woman. The
conference was also noteworthy for the kinds of Jewish women who
attended, from South America and South Africa, from Australia, New
Zealand, the United States and Israel, orthodox and secular,
exemplary of Jewry in the modern world, a polyphony of traditions,
cultures, languages, races, ideas and ideologies. Yet a conscious
commonality brought them together in Jerusalem.

This anthology explores what the modern world has made of the
Jewish woman, and what the Jewish woman has made of modernity. Our
chronology begins with the diary of Rahel Varnhagen, and involves
two of the most tumultuous centuries in Jewish history, doubly
tumultuous for the Jewish woman, who has lived through these
historical changes seeking a double enfranchisement.

The Women's movement is now a cultural force almost everywhere,
and it has become a similarly shaping force in modern Judaism, among
religious as well as secular Jewish women. But it would be puerile
to rate such changes among the varying kinds of Jews, as if cultural
forces were horse races to be won with specific goals in mind.

For westernized Jewish women, we chart a change in personality,
and assert that personality is an historical factor, noting the
difference between the timidity of the immigrants in the fiction by
Fredelle Brusar Maynard and Anzia Yezierska, whose stories deal with
the Jewish woman first experiencing college and intellectual
excitement, and the revolutionary dexterity of Emma Goldman or the
brash cool of Luisa Futoransky. The "liberation" is in tone and
sensibility, expectations and assumptions. From the diary of Rahel
Varnhagen (1771-1833) to the fictional diary of a trip to China in
Luisa Futoransky's Son cuentos chinos, we trace the emergence of the
modern Jewish woman from ghetto to world traveller, revolutionary,
or suburban housewife - participants in the social experiments and
social constructs of modernity.

Rahel Varnhagen was among the first Jewish women to confront the
Enlightenment. Liberated from the ghetto with little financial means,
no special talents, no beauty, she survived by wit and shrewd
intuitions to become the mistress of a famous salon. An avowed social
climber, she remained poised in hesitation between assimilation
and embrace of her "inescapable Jewish destiny," writing letters to
her nieces in Yiddish at the end of her life, and demanding that
they respond similarly.

Her life was most certainly an obsession for Hannah Arendt, who wrote in her preface to the 1956 edition of the diary:

> The German-speaking Jews and their history are an
> altogether unique phenomenon; nothing comparable to it is
> to be found even in the other areas of Jewish assimilation.

It was her aim to study, through Rahel Varnhagen, "the complex problems of assimilation" and "the manner in which assimilation to the intellectual and social life of the environment works out concretely in the history of an individual's life, thus shaping a personal destiny." Except for the last two chapters, Hannah Arendt took with her the manuscripts of Rahel Varnhagen when she left Germany in 1933, surmising that an extraordinary cultural history was coming to an end, one which had included the presence of Jews in Germany for over a thousand years, and whose greatest lyricists, Heine, Nelly Sachs and Else Lasker-Schüler, wrote in the German language.

The Nazi era must remain pivotal in an understanding of modernity, and of evil in the modern guise. The Holocaust holds one key to the structure of modern evil, whose fundamentals of radical utilitarianism are very much part of modern intellectual and moral equipment. The works which treat the Holocaust in this anthology present a spectrum of reactions: Marianne Walter's semi-autobiographical work, "An Encounter," deals with the difficulty of passing judgment on those who were not evil themselves, yet were participants in an evil work; Fay Zwicky's short story, "Hostages," speaks for Jewish children encompassed by "normal childhoodness," who have to wait to grow up to understand the abnormal adult world. The "I" in this story is remote from the "I" in the work by the German writer, Peggy Parnass, a child who already knows that the adult world is sinister, and for whom the future suggests no reprieve. The pain is unlyrical, stripped of intellectual recompense. The "I" defies the adult world to make poetry of this pain.

The work by Esther Cameron is the biographical account of an extraordinary reaction to the Holocaust. Influenced by Celan's poetry, and in search of those contiguities between herself as Gentile witness and the need for spiritual shape, Esther Cameron entered a yeshiva in Israel and converted to Orthodox Jewry. Her autobiography recounts the 60's in the United States, and its trajectory into her path from hippie to Bat Shem. In sharp contrast, Nadine Gordimer's circumspect story, "Sins of The Third Age," underlines the difficulty of merging the Holocaust with the beatitudes of middle class life.

Some omissions were necessary, since we desired the anthology to present a fair geographical representation, and to publish new writers. Israeli women poets were admirably anthologized in Burning Air and A Clear Mind (Ohio University Press, 1981), but there is no similar representation of Israeli women who write fiction. Hence we chose work by Shulamith Hareven, whose excerpt from her novel, The City of Many Days, is a sly slice of life from the mandatory era and the story, "N'ima Sassoon Writes Poetry," by Amalia Kahana-Carmon, also set in the mandatory era, is about the growing poetic conscious-ness of a young child; while the first generation Israeli writer, Naomi Doudai, reflects the Jewish woman who has gone abroad from her native land (in this case, Scotland) to Israel and elsewhere to discover the tense myths and misbegotten misperceptions of east and west.

Some writers, such as Nancy Keesing, inevitably evoke place by the nature of their interests. Ms. Keesing, who relates in her autobiography, Riding The Elephant, that she is "descended from Jews who settled in Australia and New Zealand in the eighteen-forties and eighteen-fifties," is a sharp and amusing observer of the anthropo-logical and linguistic currents in her culture; while the writings of Teresa Porzecanski from Uruguay and Angelina Muñiz-Huberman from Mexico are disembodied themes, verbally and philosophically intricate; and Clarice Lispector's story, "The Daydreams of a Drunk Woman," suggests that class, rather than country, influences personality.

The excerpts from work by Eugenia Ginzburg, Bat Ye'Or and Emma Goldman are examples of the influential participation of Jewish women in political life and political movements: Rosa Luxemburg, Helen Suzman, Ida Nudel, the "angel" of the Jewish refusenik movement in the Soviet Union, Golda Meir, Renee Epelbaum, who helped found the Mothers of Plaza de Mayo in Argentina and expose the appalling episode of the "desaparacidos," and, of course, Betty Friedan.

Eugenia Ginzburg, who was arrested at the age of thirty for an inexpressibly trivial reason, and who did not emerge from prison until she was almost fifty, was among the first to write in that genre later made famous by Solzhenitsyn, ". . . of that terrible and absurd cosmos, which begins approximately at the 130th meridian, the archipelago of prisoners and detainees." She was also among the first to sense the sinister in Stalin, whose autocracy led to her eighteen years of imprisonment and forced abandonment of the two sons she adored, one of whom later died of starvation in Leningrad, and the other, Aksyonov, who is now one of Russia's famous poets.

The two volumes which tell of her prison experience, Journey Into the Whirlwind and Within the Whirlwind, breathe with her forceful intelligence, her omnipresent struggle to retain her dignity, and her joy in intellectual life. They chart her progression from astonishment that she, a teacher and intellectual, "an ordinary Communist woman during the period of the personality cult," could be imprisoned for eighteen years to an adjustment to prison life which involved other astonishments about the human race, such as the excerpt here which reveals to her that romance can take place under the most desperate circumstances, and that the force of motherhood in her supports her intellectual life. The need for poetry and for children rival her need to eat. These starvations come from the deepest reaches of her nervous system.

Bat Ye'Or is the pen name of Giselle Littman, who was born in Egypt and knows the history of Jews, as well as of other minorities, in Arab lands. Her scholarly book on this subject, The Dhimmis, is considered a major study of the ways in which the religion of Islam shapes the behavior of Moslems to minority groups, known as "dhimmi," whose status is often that of a despised caste. Her work illuminates the insufficiently understood fact that, in Islamic countries, the political and religious realms are not separable and that western expectations of political solutions, in such circumstances, are exercises in cultural cross-purposes. Her analysis of the Arabic perception of Israel as a "dhimmi" state is central to this problem, and to the divergence in the dialectical languages between east and west.

The Jewish woman writer, social commentator and activist is involved with every aspect of modernity, with questions of social injustice and racism, as in the selection by Shirley Eskapa from South Africa, with the inequities of enormous wealth and poverty in South America, as in the excerpt from Barbara Mujica's novel, The Deaths of Don Bernardo, with the horrors of animal abuse, as in the story, "Meditation Upon An Animal," and, of course, with the movement which is affecting her life and everywoman's. Cynthia Ozick's story, "Virility," is a wonderful spoof, in her inimitable style, on that spurious literary category of gender writing. Very different in style but equally concerned with the new assumptions of womanhood, the excerpt from Liliane Atlan's play, "The Carriage of Flames and Voices," is mystical and poetically strenuous. Her editor, Bettina Knap, characterized the play as ". . . both modern and ancient in scope . . . the latest theatrical techniques are put to use to exteriorize and concretize the pain felt by a woman who is cut off from Divinity, from herself - from life itself . . . . The Carriage of Flames and Voices is a drama of Creation. It is the trauma of the severed human being (Louli-Louise) . . . ."

iv

The act of emerging is one that is being undergone by Jews everywhere, as cultural transformations take place in transit from medieval ghetto to modern statehood and historic homeland; and in the consequent need to redefine the relationship of the diaspora to Israel, of Judaism as a religion to Judaism as people and nationhood; of Sephardi to Ashkenazi, of Oriental Jew to western Jew; and of Jewish female to Jewish tradition.

Yeshayahu Leibowitz, one of Israel's influential thinkers, has said that:

> Today's woman is a different human species than the woman halakha (traditional Jewish law) recognizes. Legally, professionally, educationally, culturally, she has nothing in common with the woman halakha addresses. I have a daughter who works in physics and is the mother of seven children. Did such a situation exist for halakha?

Forces of change are at work, and many voices are shrill in their effort to control the direction of these forces. Global concerns regarding famine, environmental decay, the ubiquity of weapons merchandizing, the ambiguities of genetic control, the transformation of animal into machine and its consequent cruelties, the potential for subversion of all biological life by technology, will impinge on the Jewish future. A new Jewish culture is in the making, and it will be shaped by forces from within and without. Two of these changes exhibit a describable direction: Rabbi Arthur Green, in his inaugural address at Reconstructionist College, said that he believed that vegetarianism would be the new kashruth of the Jewish people; Leah Shakdiel, an Orthodox woman living in a small town in Israel became the first woman to sit on a local religious council. "It is possible," she declared, "to have a religious revolution that innovates while it restores what was lost." Change must come with conscience and responsibility for the Jewish past and the multi-voiced nature of the Jewish present.

This anthology is dedicated to Anne Frank,
and the silenced Jewish women of her generation.

Roberta Kalechofsky
May, 1990

v

TABLE OF CONTENTS

emerging

from *Rahel Varnhagen*

JEWESS AND SHLEMIHL
(1771-1795)

"What a history! – A fugitive from Egypt and Palestine, here
I am and find help, love, fostering in you people. With real
rapture I think of these origins of mine and this whole nexus of
destiny, through which the oldest memories of the human race
stand side by side with the latest developments. The greatest
distances in time and space are bridged. The thing which all my
life seemed to me the greatest shame, which was the misery and
misfortune of my life – having been born a Jewess – this I should
on no account now wish to have missed." These are the words Karl
August Varnhagen von Ense reports Rahel to have said on her
deathbed. It had taken her sixty-three years to come to terms
with a problem which had its beginnings seventeen hundred years
before her birth, which underwent a crucial upheaval during her
life, and which one hundred years after her death – she died on
March 7, 1833 – was slated to come to an end.

It may well be difficult for us to understand our own history
when we are born in 1771 in Berlin and that history has already
begun seventeen hundred years earlier in Jerusalem. But if we do
not understand it, and if we are not outright opportunists who
always accept the here-and-now, who circumvent unpleasantness
by lies and forget the good, our history will take its revenge,
will exert its superiority and become our personal destiny. And
that is never any pleasure for the person affected. Rahel's history would not be curtailed because she had forgotten it, nor
would it turn out to be any more original because she, in utter
innocence, experienced the whole of it as if it were happening
for the first time. But history becomes more definitive when (and
how rarely this happens) it concentrates its whole force upon an
individual's destiny; when it encounters a person who has no way
of barricading herself behind character traits and talents, who
cannot hide under moralities and conventions as if these were an
umbrella for rainy weather; when it can impress something of its

1

significance upon the hapless human being, the *shlemihl,* who has anticipated nothing.

"What is man without his history? Product of nature – not personality." The history of any given personality is far older than the individual as product of nature, begins long before the individual's life, and can foster or destroy the elements of nature in his heritage. Whoever wants aid and protection from History, in which our insignificant birth is almost lost, must be able to know and understand it. History bashes the "product of nature" on the head, stifles its most useful qualities, makes it degenerate – "like a plant that grows downward in the earth: the finest characteristics become the most repulsive."

If we feel at home in this world, we can see our lives as the development of the "product of nature," as the unfolding and realization of what we already were. The world in that case becomes a school in the broadest sense, and other people are cast in the roles of either educators or misleaders. The great trouble is that human nature, which might otherwise develop smoothly is as dependent upon luck as seed is upon good weather. For should anyone's life fail in the few most important things that are naturally expected of him, his development is stopped – development which is the sole continuity in time that nature recognizes. Then the pain, the grief, is overwhelming. And the person who has no recourse but nature is destroyed by his own inexperience, by his inability to comprehend more than himself.

German literature offers only a single example of real identity between nature and history. "When I was eighteen years old, Germany had also just turned eighteen" (Goethe). In case of such an identity, indeed, the purity of a person's beginnings may immediately be transformed, materialized as it were, and "stand for" something impersonal, not to be sure for some defin- ite notion or concept, but for a world and history in general. It is his singularity not to need experience to know a world and a history which he contains in himself. Confronted with this kind of identity, with so great, well-known and deeply loved an exemplar, persons wiser and more gifted than Rahel could find themselves losing their hold on standards; those even more sen- sible and cultivated than she could be deluded into excessive demands upon life, excessive susceptibility to disappointment. In such a fortunate case, to be sure, the person's initial purity is transformed; his function becomes to "stand for" – not for anything particular, anything different, but for himself. And then the person in whom history is embodied can know the world even without experience.

In those days Jews in Berlin could grow up like the children of savage tribes. Rahel was one of these. She learned nothing, neither her own history nor that of the country in which her family dwelt. The earning of money and the study of the Law — these were the vital concerns of the ghetto. Wealth and culture helped to throw open the gates of the ghetto — court Jews on the one hand and Moses Mendelssohn on the other. Nineteenth-century Jews mastered the trick of obtaining both wealth and culture. Rich Jewish parents sought an extra measure of security by having their sons attend the university. In the brief and highly tempestuous interval between ghetto and assimilation, however, this practice had not yet developed. The rich were not cultured and the cultured not rich. Rahel's father was a dealer in precious stones who had made a fortune. That fact alone decided the complexion of her education. All her life she remained "the greatest ignoramus."

Unfortunately, she did not remain rich. When the father died, the sons took over his business, settled a lifetime allowance upon the mother, and determined to marry off the two sisters as quickly as possible. With the younger sister they succeeded; with Rahel they failed. Left without any portion of her own, she was dependent upon her mother's allowance, and after her mother's death upon the dubious generosity of her brothers. Poverty, it seemed, would condemn her to remain a Jew, stranded within a society that was rapidly disintegrating, that scarcely existed any longer as an environment with a specific self-awareness, with its own customs and judgments. The only ties among German Jews of the period seemed to be that questionable solidarity which survives among people who all want the same thing: to save themselves as individuals. Only failures and "shlemihls," it would seem, were left behind within this German-Jewish society.

Beauty in a woman can mean power, and Jewish girls were frequently not married for their dowries alone. With Rahel, however, nature went to no great trouble. She had about her something "unpleasantly unprepossessing, without there being immediately apparent any striking deformities." Small in body, with hands and feet too small, a disproportion between the upper and lower parts of her face, she had, below a clear brow and fine, translucent eyes, a chin too long and too limp, as though it were only appended to the face. In this chin, she thought, her "worst trait" was expressed, an "excessive gratitude and excess of consideration for others." These same qualities struck others as a lack of standards or taste. This, too, she was aware of. "I have no

3

grace, not even the grace to see what the cause of that is; in addition to not being pretty, I also have no inner grace . . . I am unprepossessing rather than ugly. . . . Some people have not a single good-looking feature, not a single praiseworthy proportion, and yet they make a pleasing impression. . . . With me it is just the opposite." So she wrote in her diary when she had occasion to think back upon a succession of unhappy love affairs. Although this was written fairly late in life, she adds in explanation: "I have thought this for a long time."

In a woman beauty creates a perspective from which she can judge and choose. Neither intelligence nor experience can make up for the lack of that natural perspective. Not right, not cultivated and not beautiful — that meant that she was entirely without weapons with which to begin the great struggle for recognition in society, for social existence, for a morsel of happiness, for security and an established position in the bourgeois world.

A political struggle for equal rights might have taken the place of personal struggle. But that was wholly unknown to this generation of Jews whose representatives even offered to accept mass baptism (David Friedländer). Jews did not even want to be emancipated as a whole; all they wanted was to escape from Jewishness, as individuals if possible. Their urge was secretly and silently to settle what seemed to them a personal problem, a personal misfortune. In Frederick the Second's Berlin a personal solution of the Jewish problem, an individual escape into society, was difficult but not flatly impossible. Anyone who did not convert his personal gifts into weapons to achieve that end, who failed to concentrate these gifts toward this single goal, might as well give up all hope of happiness in this world. Thus Rahel wrote to David Veit, the friend of her youth: "I have a strange fancy: it is as if some supramundane being, just as I was thrust into this world, plunged these words with a dagger into my heart: 'Yes, have sensibility, see the world as few see it, be great and noble, nor can I take from you the faculty of eternally thinking. But I add one thing more: be a Jewess!' And now my life is a slow bleeding to death. By keeping still I can delay it. Every movement in an attempt to staunch it — new death; and immobility is possible for me only in death itself. . . . I can, if you will, derive every evil, every misfortune, every vexation from *that.*"

Under the influence of the Enlightenment the demand for "civil betterment of the Jews" began to advance toward realization in Prussia. It was spelled out in detail by the Prussian official

Christian Wilhelm Dohm. Excluded for centuries from the culture and history of the lands they lived in, the Jews had in the eyes of their host peoples remained on a lower stage of civilization. Their social and political situation had been unchanged during those same centuries: everywhere they were in the rarest and best case only tolerated but usually oppressed and persecuted. Dohm was appealing to the conscience of humanity to take up the cause of the oppressed; he was not appealing for fellow citizens, nor even for a people with whom anyone felt any ties. To the keener consciences of men of the Enlightenment, it had become intolerable to know that there were among them people without rights. The cause of humanity thus became the cause of the Jews. "It is fortunate for us that no one can insist on the rights of man without at the same time espousing our own rights" (Moses Mendelssohn). The Jews, an accidental and embarrassing hangover of the Middle Ages, no longer throught of themselves as the chosen people of God; equally, the other no longer viewed them as suffering condign punishment for resisting Christianity. The Old Testament, their ancient possession, had in part become so remote, in part entered so completely into the body of European culture, that the Jews, the contemporary Jews, were no longer recognized as the people who had been its authors. The Old Testament was an element of culture, perhaps "one of the oldest documents of the human race" (Herder), but the Jews were merely members of an oppressed, uncultured, backward people who must be brought into the fold of humanity. What was wanted was to make human beings out of the Jews. Of course it was unfortunate that Jews existed at all; but since they did, there was nothing for it but to make people of them, that is to say, people of the Enlightenment.

The Jews concurred in this and similar emancipation theories of the Enlightenment. Fervently, they confessed their own infer- iority; after all, were not the others to blame for it? Wicked Christianity and its sinister history had corrupted them; their own dark history was completely forgotten. It was as if they saw the whole of European history as nothing but one long era of Inquisition in which the poor good Jews had had no part, thank God, and for which the must now be recompensed. Naturally one was not going to cling to Judaism — why should one, since the whole of Jewish history and tradition was now revealed as a sordid product of the ghetto — for which, moreover, one was not to blame at all? Aside from the question of guilt, the fact of inferiority secretly hung on.

Rahel's life was bound by this inferiority, by her "infamous birth," from youth on up. Everything that followed was only confirmation, "bleeding to death." Therefore, she must avoid everything that might give rise to further confirmation, must not act, not love, not become involved with the world. Given such absolute renunciation, all that seemed left was *thought*. The handicaps imposed upon her by nature and society would be neutralized by the mania "for examining everything and asking questions with inhuman persistence." Objective and impersonal thought was able to minimize the purely human, purely accidental quality of unhappiness. Drawing up the balance sheet of life, one needed only to think "in order to know how one must feel and what is or is not left to one." Thinking amounted to an enlightened kind of magic which could substitute for, evoke and predict experience, the world, people and society. The power of Reason lent posited possibilities a tinge of reality, breathed a kind of illusory life into rational desires, fended off ungraspable actuality and refused to recognize it. The twenty-year-old Rahel wrote: "I shall never be convinced that I am a Schlemihl and a Jewess; since in all these years and after so much thinking about it, it has not dawned upon me, I shall never really grasp it. That is why 'the clang of the murderous axe does not nibble at my root'; that is why I am still living."

The Enlightenment raised Reason to the status of an authority. It declared thought and what Lessing called "self-thinking," which anyone can engage in alone and of his own accord, the supreme capacities of man. "Everything depends on self-thinking," Rahel remarked to Gustav bon Brinckmann in conversation. She promptly added a thought that would hardly have occurred to the men of the Enlightenment: "The objects often matter very little, just as the beloved often matters far less than loving." Self-thinking brings liberation from objects and their reality, creates a sphere of pure ideas and a world which is accessible to any rational being without benefit of knowledge or experience. It brings liberation from the object just as romantic love liberates the lover from the reality of his beloved. Romantic love produces the "great lovers" whose love cannot be disturbed by the specific qualities of their sweethearts, whose feelings can no longer be rubbed raw by any contact with actuality. Similarly, self-thinking in this sense provides a foundation for cultivated ignoramuses. Being by birth exempt from obligation to any object in their alien cultural environment, they need merely, in order to become contemporaries, peel off old prejudices and free themselves for the business of thinking.

Reason can liberate from the prejudices of the past and it can guide the future. Unfortunately, however, it appears that it can free isolated individuals only, can direct the future only of Crusoes. The individual who has been liberated by reason is always running head-on into a world, a society, whose past in the shape of "prejudices" has a great deal of power; he is forced to learn that past reality is also a reality. Although being born a Jewess might seem to Rahel a mere reference to something out of the remote past, and although she may have entirely eradicated the fact from her thinking, it remained a nasty present reality as a prejudice in the minds of others.

How can the present be rendered ineffective? How can human freedom be so enormously extended that it no longer collides with limits; how can introspection be so isolated that the thinking individual no longer need smash his head against the wall of "irrational" reality? How can you peel of the disgrace of unhappiness, the infamy of birth? How can you – a second creator of the world – transform reality back into its potentialities and so escape the "murderous axe?"

If thinking rebounds back upon itself and finds its solitary object within the soul – if, that is, it becomes introspection – it distinctly produces (so long as it remains rational) a semblance of unlimited power by the very act of isolation from the world; by ceasing to be interested in the world it also sets up a bastion in front of the one "interesting" object: the inner self. In the isolation achieved by introspection thinking becomes limitless because it is no longer molested by anything exterior; because there is no longer any demand for action, the consequences of which necessarily impose limits even upon the freest spirit. Man's autonomy becomes hegemony over all possibilities; reality merely impinges and rebounds. Reality can offer nothing new; introspection has already anticipated everything. Even the blows of fate can be escaped by flight into the self if every single misfortune has already been generalized beforehand as an inevitable concomitant of the bad outside world, so that there is no reason to feel shock at having been struck this one particular time. The one unpleasant feature is that memory itself perpetuates the present, which otherwise would only touch the soul fleetingly. As a consequence of memory, therefore, one subsequently discovers that outer events have a degree of reality that is highly disturbing.

Rousseau is the greatest example of the mania for introspection because he succeeded even in getting the best of memory;

in fact, he converted it in a truly ingenious fashion into the most dependable guard against the outside world. By sentimental- izing memory he obliterated the contours of the remembered event. What remained were the feelings experienced in the course of those events – in other words, once more nothing but reflections within the psyche. Sentimental remembering is the best method for completely forgetting one's own destiny. It presupposes that the present itself is instantly converted into a "sentimental" past. For Rousseau (*Confessions*) the present always first rises up out of memory, and it is immediately drawn into the inner self, where everything is eternally present and converted back into potentiality. Thus the power and autonomy of the soul are secured. Secured at the price of truth, it must be recognized, for without reality shared with other human beings, truth loses all meaning. Introspection and its hybrids engender *mendacity*.

"Facts mean nothing at all to me," she writes to Veit, and signs this letter: "Confessions de J. J. Rahel" – "for whether true or not, facts can be denied; if I have done something, I did it because I wanted to; and if someone wants to blame me or lie to me, there's nothing for me to do but say 'No,' and I do." Every fact can be undone, can be wiped out by a lie. Lying can obliterate the outside event which introspection has already converted into a purely psychic factor. Lying takes up the heri- tage of introspection, sums it up, and makes a reality of the freedom that introspection has won. "Lying is lovely if we choose it, and is an important component of our freedom." How can a fact mean anything if the person himself refuses to corrobate it? For example: Jews may not go driving on the Sabbath; Rahel went driving with the actress Marchetti "in broad daylight on the Sabbath; nobody saw me; I would have and would and shall deny it to anyone's face." If she denies it, nothing remains of the fact except one opinion against other opinions. Facts can be disintegrated into opinions as soon as one refuses to consent to them and withdraws from their context. They have their own peculiar way of being true: their truth must always be recognized, testified to. Perhaps reality consists only in the agreement of everybody, is perhaps only a social phenomenon, would perhaps collapse as soon as someone had the courage forthrightly and con- sistently to deny its existence. Every event passes – who may claim to know tomorrow whether it really took place? Whatever is not proved by thinking is not provable – therefore make your denials, falsify by lies, make use of your freedom to change and render reality ineffective at will. Only truths discovered by

reason are irrefutable; only these can always be made plain to
everyone. Poor reality, dependent upon human beings who believe
in it and confirm it. For it as well as their confirmation are
transitory and not even always presentable.

That facts (or history) are not acceptable to reason, no
matter how well confirmed they are, because both their factuality
and their confirmation are accidental; that only "rational truths"
(Lessing), the products of pure thought, can lay claim to validity,
truth, cogency — this was (for the sophistries of the Assimilation) the most important element of the German Enlightenment that
Mendelssohn adopted from Lessing. Adopted and falsified. For to
Lessing history is the teacher of mankind and the mature individual recognizes "historical truths" by virtue of his reason. The
freedom of reason, too, is a product of history, a higher stage
of historical development. It is only Mendelssohn's version that
"historical and rational truths" are separated so finally and completely that the truth—seeking man himself withdraws from history.
Mendelssohn expressly opposes Lessing's philosophy of history,
referring slightingly to "the Education of the Human Race, of
which my late friend Lessing allowed himself to be persuaded by
I do not know what historian." Mendelssohn held that all realities
such as environment, history and society could not — thank God —
be warranted by Reason.

Rahel's struggle against the facts, above all against the
fact of having been born a Jew, very rapidly became a struggle
against herself. She herself refused to consent to herself;
she, born to so many disadvantages had to deny, change, reshape
by lies this self of hers, since she could not very well deny
her existence out of hand.

As long as Don Quixote continues to ride forth to conjure a
possible, imagined, illusory world out of the real one, he is
only a fool, and perhaps a happy fool, perhaps even a noble fool
when he undertakes to conjure up within the real world a definite
ideal. But if without a definite ideal, without aiming at a definite imaginary revision of the world, he attempts only to transform himself into some sort of empty possibility which he *might*
be, he becomes merely a "foolish dreamer," and an opportunist
one in addition, who is seeking to destroy his existence for the
sake of certain advantages.

For the possibilities of being different from what one is are
infinite. Once one has negated oneself, however, there are no
longer any particular choices. There is only one aim. always,
at any given moment, to be different from what one is; never to

assert oneself, but with infinite pliancy to become anything
else, so long as it is not oneself. It requires an inhuman
alertness not to betray oneself, to conceal everything and yet
have no definite secret to cling to. Thus, at the age of twenty-
one Rahel wrote to Veit: "For do what I will, I shall be ill,
out of *gêne,* as long as I live; I live against my inclinations.
I dissemble, I am courteous . . . but I am too small to stand
it, too *small. . . .* My eternal dissembling, my being reasonable, my yielding which I myself no longer notice, swallowing
my own insights – I can no longer stand it; and nothing, no one,
can help me."

Omnipotent as opinion and mendacity are, they have, however,
a limit beyond which alteration cannot go; one cannot change
one's face; neither thought nor liberty, neither lies nor nausea
nor disgust can lift one out of one's own skin. That same winter
she wrote: "I wish nothing more ardently now than to change
myself, outwardly and inwardly. I . . . am sick of myself; but
I can do nothing about it and will remain the way I am, just as
my face will; we can both grow older, but nothing more. . . ."
At best , then, there remains time which makes everyone older
and carries every human being along, from the moment of birth
on, into constant change. The only drawback is that this change
is useless because it leads to no dream paradise, to no New
World of unlimited possibilities. No human being can isolate
himself completely; he will always be thrown back upon the world
again if he has any hopes at all for things that only the world
can give: "ordinary things, but things one must have." In the
end the world always has the last word becasue one can introspect
only into one's own self, but not out of it again. "Ah yes, if
I could live out of the world, without conventions, without
relationships, live an honest, hard-working life in a village."
But that, too, is only possible if the world has so arranged
matters, whereas: "But I have nothing to live on."

Relationships and conventions, in their general aspects, are
as irrevocable as nature. A person probably can defy a single
fact by denying it, but not that totality of facts which we call
the world. In the world one can live if one has a station, a
place on which one stands, a position to which one belongs. If
one has been so little provided for by the world as Rahel, one
is nothing because one is not defined from outside. Details,
customs, relationships, conventions, cannot be surveyed and
grasped; they become a part of the indefinite world in general
which in its totality is only a hindrance. "Also, I fear *every*

change!" Here insight no longer helps; insight can only foresee and predict, can only "consume" the hope. "Nothing, no one can help me."

Nothing foreseeable, and no one whom she knows can help her, at any rate. Therefore, perhaps the absolutely unforeseeable, chance, luck, will do it. It is senseless to attempt to *do* anything in this disordered, indefinite world. Therefore, perhaps the answer is simply to wait, to wait for life itself. "And yet, wherever I can get the opportunity to meet her, I shall kiss the dust from the feet of Fortune, out of gratitude and wonder." Chance is a glorious cause for hope, which so resembles despair that the two can easily be confounded. Hope seduces one into peering about in the world for a tiny, infinitesimally tiny crack which circumstances may have overlooked, for a crack, be it ever so narrow, which nevertheless would help to define, to organize, to provide a center for the indefinite world — because the longed-for unexpected something might ultimately emerge through it in the form of a definite happiness. Hope leads to despair when all one's searching discovers no such crack, no chance for happiness: "It seems to me I am so glad not to be unhappy that a blind man could not fail to see that I cannot really be happy at all."

Such was the inner landscape of this twenty-four-year-old girl who as yet had not actually experienced anything, whose life was still without any personal content. "I am unhappy; I won't let anyone reason me out of it; and that always has a disturbing effect." This insight rapidly became a final one, unaffected by the fact that Rahel went on hoping for happiness almost all her life; secretly, no matter what happened to her, Rahel always knew that the insight of her youth was only waiting to be confirmed. Suffering disadvantages from birth on, unhappy without having been struck down by destiny, without being compelled to endure any specific misfortune, her sorrow was "greater than its cause . . . more ripely prepared," as Wilhelm von Burgsdorff, the close friend of Caroline von Humboldt, wrote to her during those years. By renouncing — without having had anything definite to renounce — she had already anticipated all experiences, seemed to know suffering without having suffered. "A long sorrow has 'educated' you; . . . it is true that a trace of suffered destiny is visible in you, that one see in you silence and reticence early learned."

11

from *BROTHERS*

It must have been snowing.

Whatever else we know about Czarist Russia, whatever events
punctuated its history, we can be pretty sure that it was snowing
at the time. Snow fell on almost every Tolstoy page. Gorki's
childhood was grievously gloved. Alexander Nevsky subdued the
Teutonic knights in a celluloid battle on ice. The sun shone on
the Odessa steps only because snow could not provide those
stricken shadows. So we can safely assume that, on the day that
the milk—brothers were born, it must have been snowing.

In fact, we know with absolute certainty that the temperature
was well below freezing. We know it because it was historically
recorded. Not that the birth of the milk—brothers merited a
chronicle of any kind, but they chose to make their debut on that
very day in the winter of 1825 when Czar Nicholas the First succeeded to the throne of Russia. On his inaugural way to the Palace of St Petersburg, it is recorded that one of the many horses
drawing the royal carriage stumbled and fell on a mound of snow
that had carelessly been left on an otherwise cleared highway.
As a consequence, the royal carriage was delayed, a delay that
did not improve the new Czar's habitually sullen temper. The
negligent shoveller, leaning on his spade, was stationed by the
wayside along with crowds of other pageant—fanciers, excited at
the prospect of pomp and ceremony. When he saw the carriage
falter, and realised its cause, he slunk away, with a haste and
a tool that marked him as undeniably guilty. Poor Ivan Vassile-
vitch was the first casualty of the many thousands that littered
Nicholas's reign and, before the royal carriage had reached the
Palace, his power—peppered body had been shovelled away to the
side of the road together with the mound of snow that he had so
dearly neglected. By evening, a vulture — at that time there
were many such birds in the Russian skies — would gnaw poor Ivan
out of recognition.

No Czar had ever been good news for Jews, and Nicholas the
First upheld that tradition. He was a military man, with an
unsurprisingly narrow vision and, in the course of his inaugural

speech that day, he made reference to that time—honored irritant to the Russian soul. 'The Yids run everything here,' he said. 'They are merchants, contractors, publicans, mill—owners. They are regular leeches, and suck our unfortunate provinces to the point of exhaustion.' So it would have seemed audacity, to say the least that on that very day, and in the very echo of his words, yet two more affronts surfaced on the Russian soil to vex the Czar's mighty person.

The milk—brothers were born in snow—bound Odessa with ten minutes and one rickety storey between them. The first appear-ance was that of the only male offspring of Jakob and Esther Bindel, that partnership having already produced four daughters. Esther was forty when the boy was born. Her husband, two years her senior, who all his married life had prayed for a son, cursing God behind his hand every time a girl dropped from Esther's fertile womb, now felt himself entitled to the status of Patriarch and, in keeping with his forefather, whose name he bore, he ordered the boy, this last child of his, to be called Benjamin, 'the son of my right hand.' He kissed his wife and left her bedside, making his way to the front part of the house, to that section which served as his tavern. It was five o'clock in the morning. Only one customer sat here — Faivel, the insomniac, Jakob's closest friend.

'Nu?' Faivel said as Jakob entered. There was little hope in his voice. A woman like Esther Bindel did not have the sinew for a man—child.

'Benjamin,' Jakob said softly, and he poured two glasses of kvass.

A tear fell from Faivel's eye. It might have flowed from sheer fatigue or from the two glasses of wine he had already consumed. But whatever its source, he meant it for joy. 'Mazel-tov,' he said. *Le'chaim.*'

Jakob raised his glass. 'To Benjamin,' he said.

Esther Bindel put little Benjamin to her breast, and listened to her daughter Miriam's labouring cries from above. Sofia was with her, her oldest, still unmarried child. Esther began to sing softly, a song of joy and celebration, as much to welcome her own son, as to herald the arrival of her first grandchild. Then she heard a piercing cry, and she knew that the Bindel line had nudged itself a little further into continuity.

At the moment of her grandchild's birth, the child's father, Leon Wolf, was in the shed behind the tavern milking Devorah, the family cow. When Miriam had gone into labour, her sister

13

Sarah had volunteered to replace him at milking–time. But the
cow had kicked and whined at the touch of an unfamiliar hand.
Leon was happy enought to be called away from the thrashing
bedside. He could not bear his wife's pain, or his own embarrassment. Leon Wolf was a shy man, and he was happier alone, his
head resting on Devorah's warm flank as he pumped her teats to
relieve her. When he heard his wife's piercing scream and shortly
afterwards, the undeniable cry of a new–born child, he quickly
finished the milking, nuzzled Devorah's nose, and returned to
his wife's bedside. Miriam had borne him a son and, as his
father–in–law had called the last of his line by the traditional
Benjamin, in that same manner Leon's first–born was to be named
Reuben, which translated means, 'Behold a son.' So, whether it
is the first or last born, it is the maleness of the child that
is proclaimed and celebrated. Leon kissed his wife and went to
join Jakob in the tavern. Man's work it was to toast one's sons.

Sofia ran to tell her mother of her new grandson, and returned to Miriam with the news of her baby brother. Both children, oblivious of their strange and almost synchronized kinship,
sucked happily at their mothers' breasts.

Or at least did Reuben. Downstairs little Benjamin was having
a tougher time. He sucked a little and then he stopped. He sucked
again, and again he paused. Young as he was, he had an instinct
for the notion of supply and demand, and there was no doubt in
his mind as to a certain imbalance in that assumption. His mother
was aware of it too, and without surprise. With her last child,
Zena, she had heard the hollow cries of a dried–up well. She
clasped her new–born tightly to her breast, kissing him on his
puckered bewildered brow, then she wrapped him in a blanket.
'Your sister will suckle you,' she whispered. She handed the
bundle to Sarah who took it to the room above.

Miriam put her brother to her breast where he suckled till
his brow was smooth. His nephew fed on the other side. Both
children's eyes were closed. They neither saw each other, nor
did they touch. Between them there was no sibling blood, but
the bond of milk that coupled them was secured by an enduring
and compelling love, a bond that was to remain unbroken throughout their lives.

*

On the eighth day the children were to be circumcised, and
Jakob, who had never before been granted the privilege of such a

14

ceremony, was determined to make of it some celebration. He was, too, and for the first time, a grandfather, a cause which on its own account called for commemoration. So he sprinkled sawdust on his tavern floor, set up sundry wines and schnapps on his counter, and fussed about the stove as his daughters baked cinnamon cakes, honeyed rolls, and pots of peach and raspberry jam.

'Can we dance, Papa?' little Zena asked. 'Is it allowed?'

'We shall dance,' Jakob said. 'The Bindels shall dance and the Wolfs shall dance. Whether it is allowed or not,' he whispered to himself. There were enough restrictions on their daily lives, enough from the rigid tenets of their own faith. More and more Jakob Bindel resented the restrictions that the elders of community forced upon the ghetto congregation. Their taboo on the learning of anything but the scriptures, their insistence on speaking Yiddish, their sheer contempt for the Russian tongue. But he must refrain from argument. Esther got very nervous if he aired his views. They would be coming to the ceremony, some of those black-robed men of God. Jakob Bindel would hold his tongue. But, nevertheless, he would dance. And so would the women.

'Will you dance with me, Sofia?' he said. Sofia was his favourite. Of all the daughters, she, being the first, was the only one whose gender was forgiven. He wished he could see her married. But there were impediments to that, terrible obstacles that he dared not think about. She was different from the others, headstrong, like himself. She would be no man's lackey. Besides, she was cleverer than any young man he knew. She spoke and read Russian. She dreamed of getting out of the Pale. She even dreamed about Palestine. 'Russia isn't home,' she told her father once. 'It's exile.'

'Will you dance with me?' he said again.

'Dance with an old grandfather?' she teased him and, although she hugged him, pulling playfully at his beard, he felt her separateness for the first time.

Although it was not the Sabbath, the guests had put on their Sabbath clothes. The custom of circumcision, of cutting a covenant with the Lord, was a deeply religious act which called for appropriate attire. The men wore long black caftans with their brushed sable hats, and the women wore silk shawls under their woollen wraps. Reb Schlomovitch was the first to arrive, his wife three respectful paces in the rear. Crooked in her elbow, she carried his bag with the tools of his trade, his prayerbook

15

and shawl, his knife and his roll of lint. Reb Schlomovitch was also the cantor in the synagogue, with a voice of operatic splendour, whose dulcet sonorous tones were occasionally at odds with the duties that were part of his calling.

Reb Schlomovitch sat down heavily on a corner bench and eyed the kvass on the counter. But Jakob made no offer. Reb Schlomovitch was getting old. His hands were already shaky.

'Afterwards, Reb Schlomovitch,' Jakob said. 'We'll drink like Czars.'

Then he went to the door to welcome Faivel. His friend's eyes were red-rimmed, athirst for the sleep that forever eluded him. His wife walked in his stooping shadow. One earful of Raisl explained Faivel's insomnia. It wasn't that she was an incessant chatterer. In fact she spoke little. But it was the tone of her voice. Its sound was of measured, monotonous, soporific tedium. It was like a continual drip which, given time, would wear away rock. Poor Faivel, Jakob thought, and he dragged him behind the counter and slipped him a measure of kvass.

From his stand, he caught sight of Mendel Meisels as he negotiated his large ungainly body through the tavern door. As always, when seeing Meisels, Jakob's spirits were clouded with foreboding. He did not like the man, and for good reason. Jakob owed Mendel a favour. And not just any favour. The nature of Mendel's pay-off was quite specific, though Mendel himself had never detailed it. But he would drop hints at every meeting and usually with a lecherous grin, so that it was clear to Jakob that there was only one means of squaring the debt. And that means was very costly. Sofia. Jakob owed Mendel Sofia, and nothing less than Sofia would satisfy him.

Mendel Meisels was the head of the Jewish Community Organization, the *Kahal*. This body acted as liaison between the government and the ghetto and was responsible for collecting the crippling taxes and executing the sundry restrictions that the government thought might help efface that ubiquitous eyesore on their landscape. Some years before, Alexander the First, the then Czar, had ordered that Jews could no longer be licensed as tavern-keepers. Many lost their homes and livelihood. But Mendel Meisels had turned a blind eye on the Bindel holding. Government officials were always bribable. Part of the *Kahal*'s funds were earmarked precisely for that purpose. On his occasional visits to the Bindel tavern, Mendel Meisels had caught sight of Sofia. And for many years, since the death of his wife, and even before, if he were honest with himself, he had coveted her. But he had

to admit to hmself that he had little to commend him in Sofia's
eye. He was older than her father. His body was ungainly. He
had nothing but money and position and she would be attracted
by neither. He needed Bindel in his debt. He needed Bindel
beholden. Sooner or later he would have to pay his due. Neither
man ever referred to the nature of the pay-off. Jakob was totally
silent on the subject, but Mendel skirted around it from time to
time, voicing his paternal concern with Jakob's daughters and
inquiring as to their marriage prospects. 'Now that eldest one
of yours,' he would occasionally say, with positive non-reference
to her name, 'she's not getting any younger, you know.' And Jakob
would cover with a smile, as his heart soured with the thought
of what Meisels had in mind.

So when he saw him standing at the tavern door, he looked
quickly around the room for Sofia, as if with his glance he could
protect her. And she, ignorant of the sacrifice that was expected
of her, was approaching the door to welcome him, as she would
any guest, with her smiles and greetings. Mendel eyed Jakob behind
the counter. Sofia took his hand. She led him to her father.
Jakob stared at Sofia's fingers, willing them to be disjoined
from his guest's. The look was not lost on Mendel.

'How's business, Bindel?' he said, which, sub-titled, was a
reminder that he was beholden to him to be in business at all,
whether his profits were large or small.

'Business is good,' Jakob said, 'and today even better. For
I have two heirs who will make it prosper.' He thought it as well
to remind Meisels of the purpose of the gathering.

'As long as the tavern remains in Bindel's name,' Meisels said
with a smile. He tightened his grip on Sofia's hand, and Jakob
saw how she pulled it away, giggling a little to hide her embarrassment.

'Are we all ready?' Reb Schlomovitch sang from his corner.
His eye had fallen on a dish of cinnamon rolls that Zena had
carried to the counter. He was anxious to get on with the job
and let the festivities begin.

'We're waiting for the Pinskis,' Jakob said.

'Then we'll wait for ever,' Reb Schlomovitch groaned.

The Pinskis were notorious for their lack of punctuality. But
for the most part they were forgiven because, as Jakob pointed
out, they were artists, and were therefore licensed to find the
notion of time irrelevant except in so far as it referred to
immortality. The Pinskis were music teachers, Dov of the violin,
and Rosa of the piano. Almost every child in the ghetto had, at

one time or another, passed through their kitchen/studio, and most of them without payment. Many of them were talented, but there was little in those days that a Jewish performer could achieve outside the teaching profession, and often the Pinskis regretted that they had unstopped a talent that had been better left dormant and at peace. The Pinskis were much loved in the ghetto, and pitied too, because they were childless, which was why many mothers were happy to share their children with them. Little Zena ran to the door and looked down the street.

'They're coming,' she shouted, excited. 'And somebody else is with them.'

'It must be that nephew of theirs,' Raisl's tubular voice tunnelled through the tavern, turning the room into a vast echo chamber. 'He was driven out of his village.'

It took a little while for Raisl's reverberations to subside, by which time the Pinskis and their companion had reached the tavern door. Jakob caught sight of Sofia's face, as she herself caught sight of the stranger's in the doorway. It was as if two stars had glided into her eyes and, in an instant, had burned out her childhood. He knew then that he would lose her, but he felt no sorrow. At least, not until he caught Mendel's eye and then his knees trembled. He looked to the tavern door.

Yosif Pinski was probably Sofia's age with a beauty that matched her own. In the restless line of his eyes and mouth there dwelt an equally unquiet spirit. The magnet that coursed between their two glances was almost tangible. Sofia did not move from the counter, nor Yosif from the door, even when the Pinskis moved into the tavern apologising for their tardy arrival.

'Dov was giving a lesson,' Rosa explained. 'The Bok's little girl. So talented. We didn't notice the time. This is Yosif,' she said, almost in the same breath, and looked around for him. 'Yosif,' she called, 'why don't you come in?'

And so Yosif was obliged to move and he lowered his eyes as if their mutual and compelling gaze could not contend with his mobility.

'This is Dov's brother's boy,' Rosa said.

'God rest his soul,' Reb Schlomovitch put in his kopek's worth. The boy's father was a no-good, a drunk and an idler, who'd been stupidly killed in a tavern brawl. But villain as he was, Reb Schlomovitch thought that he was still entitled to some blessing, perhaps even more so than those who had led a virtuous life, insuring their souls along the way. 'How's your poor mother?' he asked.

'She's not well,' Yosif said. 'The journey was hard for her.'

When Sofia heard his voice, she lowered her eyes for the first time. Its gentleness was almost unbearable.

'On Shabbos they did it. Of all days.' Raisl's pneumatic drill was at it again, and its whine shattered the caress of his voice that still echoed across the tavern.

'In the middle of the Shabbos service,' Dov Pinski said, 'they stormed into the *shul* and told everybody to leave the village. Just like that. No warning. Nothing. They walked out of the *shul* and took to the road.'

'It's getting worse and worse,' Faivel said. 'Where do they expect them to go? The ghettoes are overcrowded already.'

'What do you do for a living, young man?' Jakob said, and Sofia blushed for it was the time-honoured question of a father to a possible son-in-law. But Jakob had only meant it for con-versation and he realised too late how others might interpret it.

'You lose no time,' Reb Schlomovltch laughed.

'I'm a farrier by trade.' Yosif said.

'In Odessa we have more farriers than horses,' Jakob said smiling. 'You'll have to look for something else.'

'I know Russian,' Yosif said. 'I could teach it.'

'Russian?' Mendel Meisels sneered. 'Yiddish isn't good enough for you? To learn Russian is the first step to baptism.'

'I don't agree,' Yosif started, but Jakob quickly interrupted him. You didn't argue with Mendel Meisels.

'Go and get the children, Sofia,' Jakob said loudly. And, for the first time since Yosif had arrived at the tavern, Sofia moved from the counter. Her step was unsteady. Her knees were trembling, and she stiffened them, walking slowly, her head bowed, andxious to hide the rapturous confusion in her heart. But once out of the tavern, she held her head high. 'He is for me,' she almost sang. 'Yosif is the man I shall marry.' She repeated it over and over again, until she reached the back room, then paused at the door to whisper it to herself yet again.

She opened the door. Her mother was holding both children who were sleeping, blissfully unaware of the price they were about to pay to be one of the chosen. 'You look so beautiful, Sofia,' her mother said, catching the glow on her face. 'I've never seen you more beautiful,' she whispered. Then Leon came and gathered the children in his arms, and still they were not disturbed. Sofia opened the door for him, and stayed behind with the women, while the men got on with man's work of going about God's business. Suddenly Miriam began to cry and rushed

to her mother's side for comfort, but Esther, for all her mothering years behind her, was new herself to this man's game, and
was holding back her own tears. It was Sofia who embraced them
both with the strength and the love with which Yosif had word-
lessly and remotely flooded her.

Leon carried the babies into the tavern. Benjamin who was
the elder of the two, was the first to be initiated. Leon was
to hold him as Reb Schlomovitch performed the rite. It was
considered an honour to present a child in such an offering, but
Leon could have done without it. It seemed to him to be a fruit-
less act of mutilation. He was a God-fearing Jew but he couldn't
understand that his God could seriously demand such dire payment
for His friendship. But he had never voiced any opposition. He
cradled Benjamin in his arms, and he shut his eyes. He felt that
if he was not a witness to such a procedure, he could not be held
responsible. 'God forgive me,' he whispered to himself, though
it sounded ridiculous to ask forgiveness for obeying a commandment. So he amended his prayer. 'I forgive You, God,' he said,
and he held the child in his outstretched arms.

Reb Schlomovitch the baby's lips with a little kvass, his
small concession to anaesthesia. Then, holding his knife in a
surprisingly steady hand, he sang a prayer and did what had to
be done. Benjamin woke with a scream of affront, and as they
linted his wound, he squirmed with reproach. He had been initiated, not so much into Judaism, as into the concept of pain,
which, as he was to learn during the course of his life, added
up to much the same thing. Leon gathered him into his arms and
moved away, not wishing to see his own son submit to the ordeal.

Rueben had already awoken, warned no doubt by Benjamin's
cries. He struggled a little in Jakob's arms, sniffing Benjamin's
blood, and knowing the pain that was now his due. Jakob took a
gulp of kvass, and kissed his grandson on the lips. Then, with
joy, he held him out for the sacrifice. Reb Schlomovitch wielded
his knife once more, accompanied by the same prayer. Reuben was
silent. Not a whimper escaped him. Benjamin had wept for both
of them, as Reuben would have done had he been first on the
knife.

And so it was done. The knife was put away and the children
removed to their mothers. It was in order for the festivities to
begin. Leon returned from the back room behind the tavern with
his accordion. Sofia and Jakob poured the wine, and Zena and Sarah
handed around the cakes. Jakob held his glass high. 'Le'chaim,'
he shouted, and he looked around for his friend Faivel with whom

he shared everything. But Faivel, who had with half an eye witnessed the first cutting, had closed it with disgust and desolation. He would rather die than witness another. And at that
moment God gave him sleep.

Jakob leaned over the tavern counter. Faivel was sprawled on
the sawdust floor, his arm crossed over his chest, and blowing
through his parted lips a gentle childlike snore.

'A miracle,' Jakob whispered. 'Faivel is sleeping.'

'It's a good omen,' Raisl rasped, staring at her man with
abject astonishment.

'Sh,' Jakob said. The last thing Faivel would want to hear,
and possibly the only thing that would wake him up, was his wife's
voice. 'We'll have some music,' he said. 'A lullaby.'

And as Leon stretched his concertina into a gently spread
chord, Yankel, the *schnorrer,* as if on his music cue, appeared
at the tavern door. His arrival was greeted with warmth and a
certain relief, for no Jewish ceremony was complete without its
attendant *schnorrer.*

There were four professional beggars in the Odessa ghetto,
and Yankel was the doyen of them all. He was well over sixty,
and his years, if not his calling, provoked a certain respect.
The other operators were relatively newcomers to the district,
and to the trade as well. Over the past years, they had been
expelled from their villages and from their livelihoods and, out
of necessity, and with a certain initial shame, they had taken
to begging. Until their arrival, Yankel had a clear field, and
their poaching posed a positive threat. Moreover they tarnished
his profession. He had been a regular and highly trained *schnorrer*
all his life. So had his father and his father before him. It
was a calling that demanded qualifications, skill and apprentice-
ship. But Yankel was a generous man and he could not deny others
a living. But it had to be orderly and non-competitive. So
Yankel called them all to a meeting and together they formed what
might loosely be called a *schnorrer's* union. They debated whose
beat belonged to whom, and the rules pertaining to trespass. But
most important of all was the principle that, whatever charity
was offered, no services must be rendered in return. That code
was unbreakable. A good *schnorrer* was one to whom it was a
privilege to give, and that privilege, and that alone, was the
only permitted feed-back. In view of Yankel's age and experience,
he was accorded the larger slice of the charity cake. He was
allowed to take his choice of weddings, barmitzvahs, circumcisions
and funerals. The others could pick up on those that Yankel did

not think worth his while. It was a good arrangement, for he very rarely went to funerals, and there were good pickings to be had at the graveside. And in those days in Odessa, there were more burials than nuptials. Besides, as a long-time professional *schnorrer*, Yankel had made his pile. In his line of work, there was always demand. Whatever the political or economic climate, wherever a Jew celebrated or mourned, wherever joy dwelt or sorrow, guilt was its eternal bedfellow. The most convenient and handy outlet for guilt is charity, and Yankel was always on the spot for the purposes of mitigation. A Jew in joy will always question what he had done to deserve such happiness, and that same Jew, in sorrow, will often blame himself. Guilt in the ghetto was a ubiquitous shadow. Even without the excuses of joy or sorrow, in the simple day-by-day grind of ghetto life, there lurked the self-reproach of survival itself.

'Welcome, Yankel,' Jakob shouted from the counter. 'Take a glass of wine with us and drink to our sons.'

Yankel kept his stand at the door. A glass of wine would be brought to him. He knew his place, and it was part of his professional skill to keep it at all times. Socialising was no part of a *schnorrer's* pursuit. And the guests knew their place too. Apart from the initial welcome, there would be no further conversational exchange. A *schnorrer* after all, was almost a divine messenger, a broker from God as it were,, sent for the relief of them all, and his calling would brook no familiarity. Yankel would stand sentry at the door till the festivities were at an end.

Leon struck up an old Chassidic folksong, and Jakob rose to his feet. He was a tall man, of rock-like stature, and as he spread his arms to invite his guests to dance, it was as if he would embrace them all. He clasped Reb Schlomovitch's shoulder and danced him to the centre of the floor. Dov Pinski joined them, and Yosif, unaware of Mendels's hostility, took his rival's ungainly arm, and linked the circle. Then each man took out a white handkerchief and waved it to the rhythm of the song. The women sat around the circle and clapped their hands. That, according to ritual, was the limit of their participation. Sarah, Zena and Sofia stood at the counter, their feet itching for the sawdust. If they'd been alone, with just their parents and the Pinskis, they could have danced too. But the presence of Reb Schlomovitch and, even more forbidding, of Mendel Meisels, chained their feet to the floor. Leon was playing his heart out and the singing grew louder as the dancers were transported in the love-

—words of the song, and, at its dizzy circling height, Dov Pinski waved his arm in Sofia's direction. 'Come,' he said. 'Join the dancing.'

Suddenly the circle lost its momentum. It was Mendel Meisels who skidded it to a halt. He stood stock still, horrified at Dov Pinski's suggestion, and he made to withdraw, not only from the dancing, but from the tavern itself.

'But it's not every day we have two sons,' Dov protested, looking to Jakob for some support.

Had it been anyone else but Meisels who had taken offence, Jakob would have stood by his friend. But to Meisels he was beholden, and today the presence of Yosif Pinski was a sad reminder of that debt.

'It's not done, Dov,' he said quietly, begging his friend to understand.

But Dov did not know of Jakob's obligation and he was more bewildered than hurt. He shrugged his shoulders and made to get on with the dancing. But now the music had stopped too, and Jakob rushed to the counter to refill glasses. He sent the girls around with the trays of cakes, anxious to rekindle the light of good cheer that till that moment had filled the tavern.

'Play,' he shouted to Leon, but Leon was already drinking. It took very little wine to render Leon incapable. Jakob looked at his concertina shrivelling on the floor, and he knew that Leon would not play again that day. He looked over the counter and saw that Faivel was still sleeping. He wished he would wake up. Suddenly Jakob Bindel felt very alone.

At the tavern door Yankel had missed nothing of the proceedings, and had overheard Dov Pinski's outrageous suggestion, and in view of that he counted on a little extra from Pinski's pocket.

'Where are the mothers?' Rosa suddenly asked. Jakob went out. He was sad at the turn that the festivities had taken. He hated Meisels. The thought of him brewed an implacable rage in his heart. He wished him dead, and quickly, and he did not even ask God for forgiveness. Meisels's demise would be just and honourable. There were others in the ghetto who were bound to him in misery. The thought even passed through Jakob's mind that he might kill him himself. He shuddered. He went into the back room and gently embraced his wife. Hers was a cleansing love and it soothed his troubled spirit.

'Is Meisels still there?' she whispered.

He nodded.

'Has he said anything?' she asked.

'No.'

'What should he say?' Miriam asked.

'Nothing,' Jakob said quickly. No one except himself and Esther knew of Meisels's blackmail. And Faivel. Jakob kept no secrets from his friend. 'Come,' he said. 'The guests are waiting.' He led them back to the tavern.

All the women had gathered together and Jakob led the mothers to their table. Their arrival was an excuse to propose another toast, and Jakob welcomed it, for it might well sweeten the scowl on Mendel's face and soften the bewilderment in Dov Pinski's eye.

'To Esther and Miriam.' Jakob raised his glass.

Reb Schlomovitch's mouth was full of cinnamon cake and he could only raise his glass to his lips. He swallowed quickly, coughing and choking on his mouthful of food. His wife slapped him on the back until he recovered, and when his mouth was empty he gave another toast to cover his embarrassment. He caught sight of little Zena with her tray of cakes. her name would do as well as another. 'To little Zena,' he shouted, wanting to be part of the festivities once more. Then Dov raised his glass and gave a toast to Reuben and Benjamin who at that moment were nursing at Miriam's breast. Then there was a pause, while the guests scratched in their minds for someone else yet to be toasted.

Then Mendel Meisels coughed and raised his glass. Jakob trembled.

'To Sofia,' Mendel said.

There was silence. No one echoed his words, for they were all mystified by his choice. Only Jakob understood, and Esther too, and she lowered her head into her lap. For in that toast both of them heard his undisguised proposal of marriage.

Sofia laughed. She thought it ridiculous that such an old and ugly man should toast her, but she thanked him out of kindness and pity.

Mendel took her thanks as a sign that she was not entirely indifferent to his person, and he translated her laughter as an embarrassed girlish giggle. He sat down and took another glass of wine. Let that Yosif feast his eyes on her, and she on him. Sofia was his, or she, with all the Bindel tribe, would be out on the streets, the tavern-door closed firmly behind them. No, he would not be moved by pity. Solomon Zemach, another innkeeper on the edge of the ghetto, was also beholden. It is true that he already handed over to Meisels a large proportion of his monthly profits, but Zemach also had a daughter. Not as young as Sofia, and certainly not as pretty, but a woman for having children. But as he looked at Sofia, he knew that no one could ever match her, and that he could settle for nothing less. He would even offer to take her without dowry. He raised his glass once again. 'A toast to our future,' he said, addressing the company in general, then slowly edging his glass in Sofia's direction.

At the tavern door, Yankel made note of the movement. He did not like Mendel Meisels and his hypocritical piety. He was a foreigner to the Meisels type of orthodoxy and, like a foreigner, he read the sub-titles of Meisels's ambivalent toasts. They spelt out nothing but his lechery. If men like Meisels heeded their conscience, men like Yankel would be millionaires. He hoped that the festivities, such as they were, would soon end. He had a wedding that afternoon, a rich wedding, a timber-merchant's daughter, and it was a long and tiring walk across the ghetto to the house of the bride.

'To our future,' the guests were responding to Meisels's toast, and Dov picked up Leon's accordion and once again music filled the tavern. But there was no longer any dancing.

'Sofia, sing a little,' Dov shouted. He knew she had a good voice. when she had come to Rosa for piano lessons they had discovered it and now he played what he knew was her favourite folk-song. Sofia blushed and lowered her head. Normally she would have sung without any shyness. She was always singing. An audience made little diference to her. But Yosif's presence unnerved her. Yet she couldn't refuse for fear of betraying the secret in her heart. So she went over to Dov's side, turning her back on Yosif, singing to Dov's melody as if she were singing for Dov and Dov alone. When they reached the chorus of the song, Dov urged the rest of the company to join in. But only one voice obliged, a voice as beautiful as Sofia's. Dov caught Rosa's eye and they smiled at each other. At the tavern door, Yankel translated the smile. 'They are made for each other,' it said. Dov and Rosa Pinski, the match-makers.

When the song was finished the company cheered, and Sofia felt obliged to turn to her singing partner and acknowledge him. But her cheeks were on fire, and she dared not reveal to him such ardour. It was he who came to her. 'Thank you,' he said to her back.

Then she had to turn or else appear rude, and make a public issue of that very thing she wished to hide. But now everyone in the tavern knew how Sofia's heart was beating, and Sarah and little Zena didn't even bother to stifle their giggling. And all were happy for them both, except for Jakob and Esther, who knew the perils of such an encounter, and Mendel Meisels, who knew them too.

'We must be on our way,' Reb Schlomovitch suddenly stood up, shamelessly stuffing what was left of the cakes into his large cape pocket.

'For the children,' Mrs Schlomovitch explained, as she did at the end of every function. She had been saying it for so many years that she had overlooked the fact that her children had long since left home and had children of their own. She waited as Reb Schlomovitch extracted a few kopeks from another pocket to pay his exit money to Yankel. Farewells were given all round, and Yankel straightened his back for his first customer of the day.

'I must wake Faivel,' Raisl rasped, and made for the counter. But Jakob barred her way. He had an omen of an impending Meisels confrontation, and he needed his friend about him, even if his presence was a sleeping one. It would be a comfort to him, a silent support.

'Let him sleep,' Jakob said. 'He gets little enough. I'll send him home when he wakes. I'll bring him myself,' he reassured her.

Nevertheless, Raisl insisted on at least looking at her man. Faivel in a state of sleep was such a rarity that it gave cause for anxiety: that perhaps it was something more than sleep, that Faivel had decided that there was nothing left in his life to keep him awake at all. Raisl knelt down beside him and stroked his forehead. Then she bent over and kissed him on the lips. Faivel did not stir. Jakob thought he saw a faint smile on his lips and he was convinced that behind those still-closed eyes his friend was as wide awake and as tired as ever.

As Raisl left the tavern, Yankel bowed to her, letting her pass without payment. It was a principle of his never to take alms from a woman. Women had other ways of squaring their guilts. Harder ways. Money, as long as you had it, was the easiest thing in the world to give. Women tended to acknowledge their guilt and attempt to do something about it. It took longer, sometimes a lifetime, and its cost was often blood, and always it was tears. Yankel looked to his next customer.

Mendel Meisels was putting on his coat. 'Have another glass,' Jakob said, anxious to delay his departure and the whispered demand that might well accompany it.

'No,' he said. 'I have business, and a little with you too, Bindel,' he said, 'if we could have a private word.' He motioned him to a quiet corner of the tavern.

Esther trembled. She watched Jakob as he followed Meisels to the darkened corner. Meisels's back was turned to the room and Esther could only see her husband's face. It was clear that Meisels was doing the talking. At first there was a great deal of it, for Jakob said not a word. As he listened, his face was grave, and his lips parted, wider and wider, as Meisels had his say. Then he spoke a few words and it looked to Esther like a timid and futile protest. She hoped she would never see begging in his eyes. Then he was shaking his head, not with adamant refusal, but as a signal of total disbelief. Suddenly Meisels turned and made for the door. He nodded a polite farewell to Esther, but the smile on his face she knew was not for her, but for himself and his envisaged future.

As Meisels approached the door, his face beaming with confidence, Yankel had the distinct impression that he had it in mind to walk straight past him, so gently he shoved his foot forward and barred the way. Then he put out his gnarled hand. To his surprise, Mendel had his money ready, and big money it was too, as a first downpayment to insure his future. He put a rouble into Yankel's hand, neatly stepped over his foot, and went out into the falling snow.

Esther looked at her husband. His face was grey. At his feet lay Leon, stirring slowly out of his drunken sleep. Jakob squatted and lifted him gently to his feet, leaned him over the counter and pushed a beaker of water into his hand. Then he pulled back Leon's head, and his face wore the beginnings of a smile. But the smile was not for Leon. It was for himself, that he had overcome a desperate desire on seeing Leon prone on the floor to kick him violently into some kind of sensibility, to vent his terrible spleen on anyone near to hand. Yet he had refrained. He looked at Esther and shook his head with despair. Sofia was collecting the glasses and the empty cake-dishes. He dared not catch her eye. He would never tell her. If she were to know the debt he owed, the debt for which he had never volunteered, she would settle it for him. She would not see him lose his livelihood. She was that kind of girl, his Sofia. So she must never know. He smiled at her as she looked across at him. He saw the glow on her face, and her happiness broke his heart.

Dov Pinski took his arm. It was a gesture of good will to show that he held no grudge against his host for his lack of support against Meisels.

'I can explain,' Jakob said, scratching in his mind for some excuse.

'It's not necessary,' Dov said, 'though I'd like to ask a favour of you.'

'Anything,' Jakob smiled, grateful for his friend's trust.

'It's about Yosif,' Dov said. 'You were right. There are more farriers than horses in the ghetto. D'you need help in the tavern? He's a good hard-working boy. If only for his meals. That would help. Times are hard.'

Jakob shook his head. It hurt him deeply to refuse his friend, especially as he had, only that morning, considered taking on another hand. What with his growing family, he could do with another cow, and some chickens perhaps, and even a vegetable plot, all too much for Leon to handle. But Yosif was out of the question. He must not see Sofia again. Perhaps if she married no one else, he might keep Meisels at bay. God forgive me, he whispered as he realised what pain such a suggestion would cause her. He knew that he could not do it. Again, and without any plea for forgiveness, he wished Meisels dead, and quickly, unmourned, unpardoned and a relief to them all.

'I have nothing,' he said to Dov Pinski and his voice was gruff and hostile, and once again Dov was bewildered, not so much at his friend's refusal, but as to its manner.

Jakob put his hand on Dov's shoulder. 'One day I'll explain everything,' he said.

'Is there anything I can do?' Dov said.

'Keep Yosif away from the tavern.'

The two friends stared at teach other. 'I can't tell you why,' Jakob said after a while.

'I think he loves her,' Dov whispered.

'And she him,' Jakob said.

Dov moved away. 'Neither of us can do anything to change it,' he said.

Jakob watched and saw the Pinskis take their leave. He stood by and saw Yosif take Sofia's hand in farewell. He spoke words to her and she smiled at him. He was possibly requesting to see her again. Jakob looked on, helpless. He knew that if he had to choose between his livelihood and Sofia's happiness, he would not hesitate. But he had to consider the rest of his family who would be homeless and without means of support. He watched the Pinskis leave the tavern paying their exit dues into Yankel's outstretched hand. Then he himself went to the tavern door.

'You had a good day, I hope?' he asked, pressing money into the beggar's hand.

'Good enough to insure a long life for your children,' Yankel said. Then, like a courtier, he bowed, and stepped backwards to take his leave.

Jakob returned to the counter. The tavern was empty now. The women had gone to their quarters and only Faivel remained, sleeping peacefully on the sawdust floor. Jakob watched him. He remembered the stories they would tell each other as children, impossible stories which stretched one's belief. The story that was even now unfolding itself in his life would not have reached the heights of their boyhood fantasies. For it was as banal and as predictable as any hackneyed fairy-tale. But it was actually happening under Jakob's roof, and its happy ending was in no way guaranteed.

FREDELLE BRUSAR MAYNARD

THE SILK UMBRELLA

Snow fell in May the day my father died. I had expected,
really, not to care; he had been such a long time dying, and the
manner of his going shadowed us all. Was it ten years before
that he began to drift away? It is hard to say exactly, we paid
so little attention. Not that we didn't love him. But ours was
a matriarchal household, intensely female. "You are the captain,"
my paternal grandmother told my mother after the wedding. It was
that way from the beginning. Mother made the decisions, charted
the course; my sister and I sat on deck, planning how to amuse
ourselves at the next port and admiring the view; and my father
kept the engines running. No, even that is not the right metaphor.
He was never good with things complicated or mechanical. On a
ship he would have kept the decks clean, the paint sparkling.
And no task would have seemed to him menial if it contributed to
our comfort. He felt himself privileged to serve.

My father was an infinitely gentle man. When I see him — as
I do often, now that the death of that sad invalid has liberated
my true, my real father — it is alway in the posture of tender
protection. What was it Hamlet said of the dead king? "So loving
to my mother That he would not beteem the winds of heaven Visit
her face too roughly." My father was like that. If he could
have carried us through the world on his shoulders, he would
have done so. One of the few conflicts of his life, I think (he
was a man simple and straight, not vexed by division), was the
pull between the desire to give us everything and the need to
keep us safe.

"Papa, I want a cap gun!"

"What for, darling? You should hurt yourself?"

"Scornful, impatient, I stamped my Buster Brown shoes
(oxfords, for the sake of my arches). "You can't get hurt with a
cap gun. Everbody else has one!"

So I got my pistol, and the little red roll of paper caps to
carry. When the moment came — wait until Sammy Horton sees *this!*
— I handed Papa the weapon and he fired. For Halloween, he
scooped out the thick-ribbed pumpkin, carving its features with

a pearl—handled knife, and through the dark streets he swung the
jack—o'—lantern lit with its candle flame. I skipped beside him,
a broadcloth witch, collecting candy that Papa would next day
distribute to other, less exquisite children. (Who knew, after,
where such candy came from, how it had been handled?) In winter
he longed for me to skate — a healthful exercise, and with friends
— but there was danger to consider. What if I should turn my
ankles? Or, God forbid, fall? He met the problem by ordering a
special pair of skate boots with laced inner supports and metal
outer clamps to brace my ankles. Toqued, mittened, muffled,
cocooned in wool, I shuffled across the ice, flinging myself
periodically against the walls of the rink for balance. And
beside me in galoshes, an ocean liner among the darting tugs,
ready for rescue or praise, my father.

No single word will conjure up the quality of my father's
generosity. It was not permissiveness: a feeling for what one
did and did not do was strong in our household. It was not indulgence in any ordinary sense. I think of it, rather, as a special
sensitivity to need. When, as a child, I waked crying because
the dark got in my nose, he was beside me in an instant. Then
he would light the lamp and sit at the foot of the bed, singing
softly:

> *Lule, lule luinke*
> *Shlof nu shlof meyn meydele,*
> Sleep now sleep my little girl,
> *Ah, ah, lulinke,*
> *Lule, lule, lulinke. . . .*

When I wriggled about, unable to sleep, he understood. "You want
I should take you to the toilet?" Nonsense, Mama said. There
was a chamber pot in my room, no need to go outside in zero
weather. But Papa knew how the pot offended my dignity. Kneeling
by the bed he buckled on my galoshes, tumbled me into my coat
and tied the knitted cap under my chin. Then out into the
frosty night, feet crunching on the fresh snow. I always left
the door of the privy open. That way I could look out at the
silhouettes of pine trees, dark under the northern lights, and
hear the distant yapping of coyotes. Paper stood comfortably
close, rolling and crushing in his hands the tissue wrappings
saved from crates of oranges. Most people had to use newspaper
or pages torn from old catalogues.

31

In the store, he tried to enforce Mama's rule against eating between meals, but the desire to give pleasure overcame scruple. "A fresh fig bar?" he would ask. Or, "Look, this is a new kind!" (breaking open a chocolate marshmallow puff to reveal, at its quaking center, a jelly heart). Though he had never learned to say NO, he hesitated a little the day I asked for a second box of popcorn. "What would Mama say? So much sweet an hour before suppertime?"

"But, Papa —" I gave his hand a conspiratorial squeeze. "I won't even eat it. I just want the prize."

"Friedele, you want another kewpie, we get one from the toys. No need to open popcorn."

"But I didn't want this kewpie doll. Hazel got a ring with a rubber bulb and it squirts water." I put my arms around his neck. "Please, Papa, I want a ring."

"All right. We try another box." He spilled the popcorn onto the counter. A tin whistle rolled out.

"Oh, I wanted a ring!"

"Now then, we try one more, just one."

But the next box produced a mirror, the one after that a toy compass. It became a game. Papa slit open the tops of the boxes, I shook out the popcorn. And that was how Mama found us when she came to say supper was burned already — Papa busy with the broom and I on the counter, queen of the popcorn mountain.

My mother, in memory, is always moving, blurring the camera image with swift energy. Baskets of clothes to the line, wax on the floors, blintzes in the pan, ruffles spinning out under the sewing machine needle. . . . My father is a still picture. At the store, he sits on a high stool, copying out accounts (mostly uncollectable) in his elegant embellished script, or leans over the counter talking. At home, the chair and the book. One moment I remember especially, a spring scene. Exhilarated by the first mild days of May, with maples dropping pink tassels and the world greening over, I am dashing off to school bare-legged and bare-armed. Papa cautions, "Take a coat, dear heart. I see clouds." "It won't rain!" I call over my shoulder. An hour later, during arithmetic class, the storm breaks. Shivering, I watch hail pellets bounce off roofs and slatted side-walks. How will I get home in my organdy dress, my taffeta hair bow? (Most children eat lard pail lunches, but Mama likes us to have hot meals at noon.) I think of tapioca pudding. . . . Maybe knishes with sour cream. . . . I will have to make do with my recess apple. I stare miserably out the window, careless now of multi-plication tables. And then I see my father. He has left the store, in the middle of a business day, and stands there motion-less, waiting, holding high his black silk umbrella.

My mother acted, my father thought. My mother talked, my father read. *Der Tog,* the Jewish newspaper from New York, copies long outdated by the time they reached us in Birch Hills; the Talmud and its many commentaries; the stories of Sholem Aleichem. Often he laid aside the book to share a folk tale that delighted him. "A *yolde,* a foolish fellow, wishes to go courting. But he has no words. 'Papa,' he asks, 'what shall I say?' 'Easy,' says the father. 'First, you discuss love. Then, family. And afterwards, a little philosophy.' The son goes, happy, but ten minutes later he is back. 'What happened?' asks the father. 'You didn't do like I told you?' 'I did,' says the *yolde.* 'First, love. I said, "Do you like noodles?" and she said, "Yes." Then, family. "Do you have a brother?" She said, "No." That left only philosophy. So I asked her, I said, "Well, if you did have a brother, *would* he like noodles?"'"

I did not much enjoy Papa's Jewish stories. The landscape was unfamiliar, a world peopled by rabbis, starving *melameds* (teachers), matchmakers, grandfathers with earlocks, and long caftans. Their concerns, too, were utterly foreign. What to me was the concept of *derech—eretz,* respect to parents, on which so many punch lines depended? Or *yikhus,* honor, an abstraction passionately sought by these bizarre characters? Perhaps only an Eastern European Jew, accustomed to the fantastic intricacies of Talmudic interpretation, could have appreciated the logic chopping of these folk tale heroes. (I recall happily, however, simpler thrusts of logic. Like the story of two guests whose hostess offers, at tea, a plate with two *kichlach,* egg cookies. One cookie is a touch bigger than the other. The Jews eye the plate. "You first," says Jacob. "No, you," says Isaac. So Jacob takes — the larger *kichl.* Isaac is indignant. "How come a Jew has no manners? You took the big one!" "And if you had been first, what would you have done?" Jacob inquires mildly. "I would have taken the smaller!" says Isaac. "Then," says Jacob, "why do you complain? *You have it!"*) The life pattern which alone could have made these tales comprehensible was mysterious to me. My father would laugh delightedly at the story of the Jewish six-year-old reproved, by a passing elder, for playing in the street barefoot and without trousers. "Why are you not in school?" asks the elder. "Because yesterday I got married," says the boy. "A married man and no trousers?" The sage is scandalized. "Well," says the boy, "yesterday I got married, I wore, the trousers. Today my brother gets married, *he* wears the trousers!" "But why is the boy married?" I would ask. I could not read, in my father's warm brown eyes, the poverty of the ghetto Jews, their desperate strategems to save children from the Czar's Army.

"It's nothing. Just a foolishness." He would have liked to pass on the heritage of Judaism, only without its harsh, fearful knowledges — as if there could be a Passover *seder* without *maroses,* bitter herbs. And then he would tell me another story about Goodie and Baddie. Sitting in his lap, my head against the blue shirt that smelled like sunshine and flatiron steam, I surrendered again to the comforting predictableness of these heroines. Goodie was just like me — she had curly hair, loved her Mama and Papa, and did as she was told. Baddie was always going into the dark forest, where her Mama had distinctly for- bidden her to go. I pictured her as having straight hair like my sister's. Dragons, giants, elves, monsters, wicked kings. . . they were all vanquished by bedtime, and Baddie turned good. In my sophisticated twenties I recalled these stories, with their Manichean dualism, as evidence of my father's simplicity. I have wondered, since, whether his understanding was not more complex than it seemed. Was I not Baddie too?

I see my father in the context of domestic life. The friend- liest of men, he had no friends but us. Would it have been different in the city, in a Jewish community? I don't know. But certainly, marooned on the prairies, an island of Jewishness in a barbarian sea, he never formed ties beyond the limits of his business life. In the store he was sociable, and on a variety of levels. He talked crops with farmers, theology with the local minister, household matters with women. But he would no more have thought of accompanying a farmer to the beer parlor than, years before, he could have joined a Cossack for a gallop across the steppes. The feeling was not snobbishness in the sense of "I am better than you" or "My position is above you." It was a pride without vanity, the exclusiveness of the *shtetl* Jew who has learned to say, of walls or barbed wire, "Fences keep them out. They do not keep me in."

Though money and social position played no part in Papa's ambitions for his children, he shared the traditional Jewish

concern with *naches*. It is difficult to translate into English
this elusive term. *Naches* is pride, but pride in spiritual or
intellectual attainments, and so illuminated with loving joy.
Naches accrued when my sister played in the piano festival, when
I won a scholarship to the university. Papa's first happiness
in my academic honors, however, was modified by a growing anxiety.
A B.A. was fine, splendid, qualifying me, in the marriage market,
for a world of Jewish doctors and lawyers. An M.A. – probably all
right still. A doctor likes an educated wife. The Ph.D., however,
gave him pause. "With a Ph.D., you don't marry just an ordinary
intelligent person. So how many Yiddishe boys have a Ph.D.?"
Learning and family life, those two great primary goals, warred
in him now. *"Freidele zoll kennen lernen Torah. . . ."* What
if the studies he had urged should, in the end, destroy my
Jewishness?

I think he was not surprised when I told him I had fallen in
love with a gentile. Devastated, but not surprised. The curse
of the evil eye awaits those whose happiness is too great. (Had
he not told me how, in the old country, women covered the faces
of infants lest general admiration invite disaster?) And so
there began the passionate, unequal struggle. I was young,
confident, a city intellectual certified by the university; my
father was a failed painter, an unsuccessful country merchant.
Such authority as he might have exercised he had abrogated will–
ingly years back. ("A wise head," he used to say, introducing
me to strangers. "Nine years old, already she knows more than
her Papa.") He was like the unwary knight who, pursuing a quest,
relinquishes one after another his sword, his lance, his shield,
only to find he stands defenseless when the dragon roars. My
father did not argue or threaten. (I had known girls who, after
marriage to a gentile, were pronounced officially dead. Their
families sat shiva, in ritual mourning for the departed.) Papa's
response was characteristic. He invoked my mother – "This kills
her" – and he told stories. Now, for the first time, I heard
tales of pogroms. "Every gentile is a barbarian at heart," he
would say. "I know. In Russia we had friends, peasants, drank
tea in our kitchen daily. When the Cossacks came, they took
sticks and guns, these friends, and fell upon the Jews. One, a
neighbor, dragged from a cart a young Jewish woman, was nursing
a child. The woman he took by force on the dirt of the barnyard.
And when the child cried – I saw with my own eyes, I lay hidden
in my father's grainery – the child he struck on the head with a
stone, and threw to his pigs. Three days later, when the Czar
said, 'Enough,' back comes this *goy* to our kitchen. For tea."

35

When he saw I was not to be moved, he wrote me a letter. "Once upon a time," he began, "there lived a young man, a scholar and a good son. And it came to pass that he fell in love with a beautiful girl. Now this girl was a witch. Flowers, fruits, jewels he brought to her, and still she refused him. 'What can I do,' he cried, 'that you should love me?' The witch smiled and said, 'Bring me your mother's heart.' Now this young man's mother was dear to him. But he was in love. He took a knife and cut out his mother's heart and ran with it, still warm and bleeding, to the witch. In such a hurry, he tripped and fell. The heart slipped from his hand. He was frightened. His gift, maybe, spoiled? But as he picked it up, the heart spoke. "O my dear son, I hope you have not hurt yourself."

My marriage did not kill my mother; she was made of sterner stuff. A pragmatist, she started from the premise given. It placed my father, however, in an extraordinary position. Central to his whole being were the principles that his child could do no wrong, and for a Jew to marry a gentile was wrong. Even God cannot will a contradiction; my father was forced to rise above the shuddering clash of axioms. He did so, not by feats of casuistry, but by a kind of gentle distancing. He became no less loving, but more remote. Perhaps we had never talked seriously after I moved into the university world and a set of heterodox opinions. Now, when I came home for visits, we spoke only of domestic matters. His fears — and they must have been many — appeared only incidentally, as when, observing that I walked barefoot in summer, he said, "But when you go to bed, you wash well the feet, yes?" I laughed. "My husband doesn't check my feet." Papa looked grave. "Now he doesn't. But an old wife with dirty feet, this is another matter. You remember that story, the Jew who complains, 'I married a young *shiksa*, now I have an old *goy*'?" A *shiksa* is a nubile stranger, sensual and passionate; the *goy* is the enemy. Did his imagination leap ahead to those classic scenes in which the husband call his wife *Jew*? Or the children turn anti–Semite and forswear their mother?

Always a demonstrative man, my father embraced me very seldom after I married. In this new reserve, there lay no hint of reproach. I remained his own dear child. Whatever had gone wrong, the fault must be his. If he had given me a proper Jewish education . . . if he had taken us earlier to the city, to be among our own kind. . . . He sighed heavily, reading the paper, and I would look up from my book. "What's the matter, Papa?" "It says here that Ted Williams, a baseball player, makes for the year fifty thousand dollars. And my daughter, a college graduate, scholarships and medals you can't count them, gets twenty-five hundred." "That was last year, Papa. Now that I'm not teaching, I get seventy-five cents an hour marking papers." Given at last a suitable target, he raged. "What kind of world? Where is justice, where? An ignoramus with a baseball bat – and Gelber's daughter, a nothing, a head a potato, is engaged I hear a Jewish professor!"

"Annie Gelber's not stupid, Pa." I tried tactful diversion. "She's at the university this year. Do you know what she's taking?"

"Taking?" A melancholy smile. "Sandwiches, that's what she's taking!" He looked at me, eyes full of tears at the thought of the Jewish professor who would never marry me now. Then, very quietly, "I don't want you should mark papers for seventy-five cents an hour. I give you a dollar an hour *not* to mark them."

One morning, opening a jar of raspberry jam I had made the summer before – the last summer I carried his dreams – he stood scraping a delicate fingernail on the paraffin seal.

"Has it gone moldy?" I asked.

He held the wax wafer to the light and I saw, struck to the underside, a strand of black hair.

"I'm sorry. I should wear hair nets when I cook. Let me fix that."

But he had deftly disengaged the single hair. He walked to the dining room china cabinet and unlocked it. All that visit I saw my hair in the crystal candy dish. It was not a ritual burial; my father loved my life. No, it was rather a ceremonial guard, behind the cabinet's glass doors, of Sleeping Beauty. The prophecy had been fulfilled, the wicked fairy had struck, and all the joy of the household had sunk into heavy sleep while thorns tangled the palace gates. But who was to say that the future might not still be bright and that somehow, triumphing over appearances, the prince might not yet come?

World War II did for my father what no amount of industry has every accomplished; it gave him a measure of success. Wages rose and job openings multiplied, farmers grew rich, and money flowed into small towns hungry for decades. Goods were scarce. A merchant with a substantial stock was bound to prosper. Papa repriced his pre-war woolens, observing, as he changed "2's to 3's." "You see, it is not lost, that training from the art school. I make at last money with my pencil." Faces not seen in years reappeared at the grocery counter. "You got sugar, Bruser? Raisins?" Papa reported wryly new developments in the human comedy. "Guess who comes back today? Mrs. Dreyba, has had here a bill from three

Christmases back and passed by the store like a blind woman.
Now she tells me Johnson is no good, keeps the dried apples for
special customers. I sold her a tin strawberry jam and she
says, 'You're a real white man, Bruser.' Such friends are good
to have."

Papa took on another clerk, had the store painted, met his
bills on time. But these evidences of financial security did not
delight him. He moved more slowly. Talking to customers, he
seemed the aging actor in a long-run play, a man who, having
wearied of the role, produces lines and gestures he can no longer
feel. His manner with children, even, suggested an edgy impatience, the orange given not so much affectionately as to keep
the child quiet so he might conclude the transaction, get back
to the house, and rest. "He falls asleep all the time," I reported
on a summer visit to Grandview. "I've seen him sit down at the
store desk and suddenly drop off." "He's tired, Mama said.
"Overworked." He returned from a buying trip to Winnipeg with
an alarming tale, presented as a joke. He had fallen in the
street — I don't know what happens, all of a sudden I'm dizzy, I
go down like a stone" — and had been picked up by the police as
a drunk. A doctor, consulted hastily, said, "Inner ear disturbance. Nothing serious." But the sky darkened. He would forget
to lock up, mislay the bank book. One evening, after a particularly brisk Saturday, he asked, "Where's the money?" "In the
register?" Mama said. It wasn't there. We looked in drawers
and on tables. "Think, Boris," Mama urged. "Where did you put
it? The register tape shows over five hundred dollars we took
in." Papa shielded his eyes with his hand. In the last few
months dull red blotches had spread over his white indoor skin.
"I don't know," he sad. "I remember nothing. Nothing." We
found the money, neatly rolled, in the rice bin. It was decided:
the store must be sold.

In forty years of marriage, my parents had never taken a
holiday together. They had never taken holidays at all, only
traveled separately to see relations or conduct business. Now,
with the store sold, my mother laid plans. What does a Jewish
storekeeper do when he retires? In the old country he would have
bought his wife a Sabbath dress and pearls. In the new world he
buys her a fur coat and goes to Florida. My mother frowned over
the coat, but that was clearly a part of the ritual, evidence to
the world that Boris Bruser had made the grade at last. We saw
them off in a scene like a stage set, or a travel agent's folder:

Mama flushed and overheated in her mink jacket, bought wholesale; Papa in a straw hat and two—color suede oxfords. Mama sent us accordian—pleated postcards (flamingoes, cabanas, tropical foliage, hotel lounge) and then, two weeks after their arrival in Miami, a telegram. My father had been struck by an out—of—control car that veered onto the traffic island where he stood awaiting a red light.

If it is true that life approximates to the condition of art, then Papa's was the perfect life – unified, consistent, whole. Lying on his hospital bed, with two broken legs and a compound fracture, he repeated wonderingly, "But I am standing the whole time on the safety island." The negligent driver was penniless and uninsured. Medical bills poured in – often from totally unfamiliar doctors who claimed to have been consulted, or present at the accident site. Six months in that Florida hospital consumed a decade's savings; he came home on crutches and was never well again. Mama wept, "Where is justice?" but Papa shrugged. He stood with Tevyeh the dairyman: "The Lord is good to all – and suppose He forgets somebody now and again, good Lord, hasn't He enough on his mind?"

My father's last illness came slowly on. There was never a moment on which you could place your finger, saying, "He has lost touch," never a clear line crossed. Retired, settled now in Winnipeg, he simply became quieter, less mobile. ("It is the accident," we said to each other. "His legs hurt.") He read for longer periods, turning the pages a little too slowly – but he never held a book upside down. His emotions, always easily touched, were triggered now by cruder stimuli. He would weep, sitting before the television. "How can you get worked up over such trash?" I would say, snapping the channels. I was impatient, too, when he asked once again for my sister's address. Hadn't he written to her, to the same house in Toronto, for twenty years? She lives in Alaska," I would say. Or, "Timbuctu." He smiled. "This I know. But in Timbuctu what street!" Only occasionally I felt a leap of fear. He would look out the window, freshly interested and then puzzled. "When did they build so many new houses? Already you can't see the grain elevators." "Papa!" (Keep it steady, don't frighten him.) "You are in Winnipeg, not Grandview!" And he was my familiar father again, motioning away the foolishness with a wave of his hand. "Of course, I know. I was asleep a little minute, and waking I forgot." His paths contracted. Stairs were an effort, streets treacherous. Now he scuffed the rug in a cautious trek from bed to bathroom to chair.

I would have thought him helpless, except that sometimes, when
Mama and I went out for a walk around the block, someone had made
it to the kitchen with remarkable speed and cleaned out the
cookie jar. Questioned, he shook his head. "Reading the whole
time. Mice, maybe." Though the doctor recommended a strict diet,
I urged indulgence. Surely, in a shrinking life, he might enjoy
the pleasures of pastry! He is too heavy," Mama said. "If he
falls, who will lift him?"

There is a special sadness that comes with reversal of roles
in the life between parent and child — when the child literally
becomes father of the man. I grew accustomed to that sorrow.
Still I cannot think without pain of the day I bathed my father.
It was such a logical task to assume; my mother had trouble with
her shoulder, I was younger and stronger. But I had always
temporized. "I'll put dinner on while you bathe Papa." This
time, Mama ill with a headache, the apartment hot and steamy, I
took his arm and persuaded him to the tub. He had been silent
for days; he did not speak as I fumbled with buttons and zipper,
easing him out of his clothes. I knew the procedure. "Here —
feet on the rubber mat, so you don't slip. Now, hang on to the
shower curtain bar. Both hands."

When I was a child, I often tried to see my father naked. I
remember hanging about the kitchen door on bath nights, but for
all his earthiness he was careful about that. It was no good,
trying not to look. His skin was whiter than I would have
believed possible, and strangely smooth — the skin of a man who
has lived indoors and never used his body except for love. Even
now, in age, his sex hung enormous. I remembered his telling us,
years ago, how women had admired him. Why, a prostitute, with
all *her* experience, said she had never encountered a man so
magnificently endowed. Standing awkwardly crouched in the tub —
he was too tall for this arrangement — my father met my eyes. He
began to stutter, as he did, sometimes, in the days when he had
speech and grew excited. "T–t–t–t–t. . . ." "What is it, Papa?"
He shook his head, frustrated, and I saw that he was crying, but
then the cry became a laugh, a strange hysterical mirth that
filled the small room with its shrill despair. "I shouldn't
bathe him," I said to my mother, leading him, terry–robed, back
to the chair. "It's humiliating." "Does he know?" she asked.
"He just doesn't like baths." I knew she was wrong. Drifted
away he was, lost and confused and wandering, but that brief
indignity had summoned him back to protest. A woman does not
look upon her father's nakedness.

It does not seem to me that we ever *decided* to move my father
to a nursing home – only that a current carried us towards that
sad inevitability. In the process of *not* considering, we exchanged
cheerless assurances of progress – at least, of holding ground.
"Yesterday he recognized Weintraub," my mother would say. "Think
of it – a man he hasn't seen for twenty years." (But of course
we all knew that the shreds of memory clung, like smoke, to a
distant landscape. It was now, ten minutes ago, last week, that
escaped him.) "We had a long discussion about Uncle Colman," my
sister said. "Dad said Colman was a wonderful fellow, a prince."
(I had heard that discussion. Cecely talked, my father listened
with soft, unfocused gaze. And when she prodded, "Don't you think
so, Dad? Isn't Colman a prince?" Papa said, "Yes.") Reality
was the frightening difficulty of moving a large man whose limbs
no longer seemed part of him. "Right now," the social workers
said, "you could still get him into one of the better places. I
mean, Mr. Bruser looks pretty good, and he's got some control.
Later on – well, have you seen the King Edward?"

We had seen the King Edward Hospital for Incurables. We found
a nursing home. My father wore his best suit for the journey (by
ambulance; he had difficulty getting in and out of cars), and he
did indeed look good. He said not a word the whole time. A nurse
flicked a cold eye over his possessions. "You can take back the
pajama bottoms," she said. And then, looking at his old chinchilla
coat, which Mama had cleaned and brushed that morning, "He won't
need *that* again." We stayed just until supper was served ("We
feed them at four, that way they're ready for bed by seven"),
and my father spoke at last. Supper was mashed potatoes,
unnaturally loose and milky, with a slice of plastic–foam bread,
a thick pool of gravy, and sausages. Papa had told me, once,
how the Czar had dragooned Jewish boys into his Army and defiled
them with pork. Now he took up his fork. *"Wait for Sabbath
bread and you lose the plain."* My mother moved away so that he
should not see her face, and he startled a minute. "Where is
Mama going?" "Shopping," I said. "Eaton's has a sale."

I saw my father only summers, when I made the long trip from
New Hampshire to Winnipeg. The surprising thing was that, on the
surface, the changes were so slight. Seated in his wheelchair or
propped on pillows, he remained a handsome man, his face unlined,
his hair still dark at the roots. "He looks younger than I do,"
my mother sighed. "He has no worries." Increasingly, though,
there were two faces: my father's, and that of a dull–eyed
stranger, slack–jawed, unstrung. He was almost always able to

41

summon himself for the moment of greeting. (Names would not come
to him, only, "Hello, *dear*.") Then he would begin to drift.
Normal conversation being impossible, we devised a game, the kind
of quiz one gives children to explore their skills. "What's my
name, Papa?" He waved this one away. Impossible to tell whether
he had forgotten, or merely felt the query demeaning, ridiculous.
One day, when he had not spoken at all, I teased him with questions. "What do I do, Papa? Am I a musician?"

Silence.

"Am I a dentist?"

A smile. Whatever I might be, I was not that.

"A lawyer?" He shook his head. "A nurse? An engineer? A
teacher?" He hesitated, then frowned *No*. "A doctor, a scientist,
a judge. . . ."

He spoke suddenly with absolute clarity. "I know, dear,
whatever you do, you do *well*."

He kept now strange company. The room, technically semi-
private, accommodated three other beds, and through those beds
moved a lamentable procession of the helpless and senile. A leg-
less man with the unnerving habit of removing his prosthetic legs
when he had climbed into a wheelchair; a profane French Canadian
who filled the room with bi-lingual obscenities; old men who
fought and complained and wept and emptied their bowels freely.
. . . My father stared them all down. He seemed unaware of the
others until a more than ordinary disturbance attracted his
attention and then, looking very much like De Gaulle confronting
his critics, he would ask, "Who is that hooli*gan*?" (He pronounced this word Russian style, with accent on the final syllable.)
Something invincibly aristocratic shaped his features till the
end; the orderlies who addressed him in familiar style — "Eat up
now, Ben, that's a good boy!" — seemed merely absurd, the bump-
kins of *Midsummer Night's Dream* transported onto the wind-swept
heath of *Lear*.

The last time I saw my father he lay high on pillows under a
white sheet. (The nurses had given up dressing or moving him
into a chair. Windows and doors all one to him now.) His mouth
hung partly open, revealing the smooth gums. (He had eaten away
his teeth, and how could he be fitted for dentures?) His eyes
were filled with the haze of advanced glaucoma and his arms, out-
lined under the cover, lay straight at this sides, as if arranged
by someone else. He looked at me without change of expression.
"Papa," I whispered, "it's me." Then, using the name he called
me when I was little, "It's Freidele." I felt, as if it were a

physical thing, the slow tremendous effort to gather himself together. Intelligence and recollection gradually suffused his face, the way light flushes through a neon tube. "Freidele," he repeated wonderingly. "Dear child." He drew one hand out from under the sheet and placed it, palm down, on mine.

I had always admired his beautiful hands. Mine are stubby-fingered, suggesting a certain peasant coarseness; he had long, delicate fingers with oval nails, crescent-mooned – the hands of a Bronzino portrait. That day a brown stain showed under the nails. He watched as I scrubbed with a soapy cloth. "Am I hurting you, Papa?" "No, dear, how could you hurt me?" A last ambiguity from a most unambigous man.

I learned from a stranger that my father was dying. Three thousand miles away a voice said, "If you want to see your father alive, come at once." I packed slowly, without tears, and on the plane I had a long conversation with a Saskatchewan farmer about new methods of grain production. I worried about not being able to cry at the funeral. How could I explain that his passing was a relief, that I had been waiting for death to give me back my father?

To know what one really feels is a lifetime's learning. It seemed to me, leaving for the funeral, that the day's ceremony merely recognized what had occurred years before. Why then be upset? And indeed, I could have protected myself against any-thing said in English, for English is the language of my rational life. How could I know the *shamas* would ask me, before the service, to repeat a Hebrew prayer? "Boruch atoy adenoy elohenu, Blessed art thou, O Lord our God, King of the Universe. . . ." I learned it on a summer afternoon forty years ago, the day I came home crying after boys called me a kike. "They made fun out of bitterness," Papa said, stroking my hair. "Because God has chosen the Jews, from all nations in the earth." *Boruch atoy adenoy elohenu,* my father chanting *kaddush* over the winking wine. . . my father telling me how Moses led his people out of bondage in Egypt, the Lord before them by day in a pillar of cloud, by night in a pillar of fire ("And Moses stretched out his hand over the sea, and the Lord . . . made the sea dry land, and the waters were divided.") Passover matzo, the heavy–sweet *hamantashen* of Purim bursting with honey and poppy seeds, green boughs at Sukkos and the dizzy–spinning *dreydel* at Hanukkah. . . *Boruch atoy,* the surprise of my temperate father wine–flushed at the *seder*, singing our favorite song, *Chad Gadyoh,* and then the always stunning stroke by which a familiar nursery–rhyme pattern

("Then came a dog and bit the cat that ate the kid. . .!") was transformed into a shout of trimph, the ancient Hebrew ecstasy: "Then came the Holy One, blessed be He, and slew the angel of death that took the butcher that killed the ox that drank the water that quenched the fire that burnt the stick that beat the dog that bit the cat that ate the kid My father bought for two *zuzim!*"

At the cemetery, six young men who had never known my father carried the coffin to the grave's edge. The rabbi stood there under a canopy, hunching into his upturned coat collar. (Was it the same *chupah* that arches over a bridge and groom?) A mat of artificial grass, like the straw lining Easter baskets, lay rolled to one side, ready. The rabbi approached, blinking rain from his glasses. "Will you say *Kaddish* for your father?" he asked. "I can't," I said. "I don't know how." As he turned away, a wild gust of wet wind tore at my umbrella, straining the bright shaft.

Father, I write your name in tears: Dov Ber, the son of Chaim.

ANZIA YEZIERSKA

from *Bread Givers*

COLLEGE

That burning day when I got ready to leave New York and
start out on my journey to college! I felt like Columbus
starting out for the other end of the earth. I felt like the
pilgrim fathers who had left their homeland and all their kin
behind them and trailed out in search of the New World.

I had stayed up night after night, washing and ironing,
patching and darning my things. At last, I put them all together
in a bundle, wrapped them up with newspapers, and tied them
securely with the thick clothesline that I had in my room on
which to hang out my wash. I made another bundle of my books.
In another newspaper I wrapped up my food for the journey: a
loaf of bread, a herring, and a pickle. In my purse was the
money I had been saving from my food, from my clothes, a penny
to penny, a dollar to a dollar, for so many years. It was not
much but I counted out that it would be enough for my train
ticket and a few weeks start till I got work out there.

It was only when I got to the train that I realized I had
hardly eaten all day. Starving hungry, I tore the paper open.
Ach! Crazy-head! In my haste I had forgotten even to cut up the
bread. I bent over the side of my seat, and half covering myself
with a newspaper, I pinched pieces of the loaf and ripped raven-
ously at the herring. With each bite, I cast side glances like
a guilty thing; nobody should see the way I ate.

After a while, as the lights were turned low, the other passengers began to nod their heads, each outsnoring the other in
their thick sleep. I was the only one on the train too excited
to close my eyes.

Like a dream was the whole night's journey. And like a dream
mounting on a dream was this college town, this New America of
culture and education.

Before this, New York was all of America to me. But now I
came to a town of quiet streets, shaded with green trees. No
crowds, no tenements. No hurrying noise to beat the race of the

hours. Only a leisured quietness whispered in the air: Peace. Be still. Eternal time is all before you.

Each house had its own green grass in front, its own free space all around, and it faced the street with the calm security of being owned for generations, and not rented by the month from a landlord. In the early twilight, it was like a picture out of fairyland to see people sitting on their porches, lazily swinging in their hammocks, or watering their own growing flowers.

So these are the real Americans, I thought, thrilled by the lean, straight bearing of the passers-by. They had none of that terrible fight for bread and rent that I always saw in New York people's eyes. Their faces were not worn with the hunger for things they never could have in their lives. There was in them that sure, settled look of those who belong to the world in which they were born.

The college buildings were like beautiful palaces. The campus stretched out like fields of a big park. Air — air. Free space and sunshine. The river at dusk. Glimmering lights on passing boats, the floating voices of young people. And when night came, there were the sky and the stars.

This was the beauty for which I had always longed. For the first few days I could only walk about and drink it in thirstily, more and more. Beauty of houses, beauty of streets, beauty shining out of the calm faces and cool eyes of the people! Oh — too cool. . . .

How could I most quickly become friends with them? How could I come into their homes, exchange with them my thoughts, break with them bread at their tables? If I could only lose myself body and soul in the serenity of this new world, the hunger and the turmoil of my ghetto years would drop away from me, and I, too, would know the beauty of stillness and peace.

What light-hearted laughing youth met my eyes! All the young people I had ever seen were shut up in factories. But here were young girls and young men enjoying life, free from the worry for a living. College to them was being out for a good time, like to us in the shop a Sunday picnic. But in our gayest Sunday picnics there was always the under-feeling that Monday meant back to the shop again. To these born lucky ones joy seemed to stretch out for ever.

What a sight I was in my gray pushcart clothes against the beautiful gay colours and the fine things those young girls wore. I had seen cheap, fancy style, Five- and Ten-Cent Store finery. But never had I seen such plain beautifulness. The simple skirts and sweaters, the stockings and shoes to match. The neat finished quietness of their tailored suits. There was show—off in their clothes, and yet how much more pulling to the eyes and all the senses than the Grand Street richness I knew.

And the spick—and—span cleanliness of these people! It smelled from them, the soap and the bathing. Their fingernails so white and pink. Their hands and necks white like milk. I wondered how did those girls get their hair so soft, so shiny, and so smooth about their heads. Even their black shoes had a clean look.

Never had I seen men so all shaved up with pink, clean skins. The richest store—keepers in Grand Street shined themselves up with diamonds like walking jewellery stores, but they weren't so hollering clean as these men. And they all had their hair clipped so short; they all had a shape to their heads. So ironed out smooth and even they looked in their spotless, creaseless clothes, as if the dirty battle of life had never yet been on them.

I looked at these children of joy with a million eyes. I looked at them with my hands, my feet, with the thinnest nerves of my hair. By all their differences from me, their youth, their shiny freshness, their carefreeness, they pulled me out of my senses to them. And they didn't even know I was there.

I thought once I got into the classes with them, they'd see me and we'd get to know one another. What a sharp awakening came with my first hour!

As I entered the classroom, I saw young men and girls laughing and talking to one another without introductions. I looked for my seat. Then I noticed, up in front, a very earnest—faced young man with thick glasses over his sad eyes. He made me think of Morris Lipkin, so I chose my seat next to him.

"What's the name of the professor?" I asked.

"Smith," came from his tight lips. He did not even look at me. He pulled himself together and began busily writing, to show me he didn't want to be interrupted.

I turned to the girl on my other side. What a fresh, clean beauty! A creature of sunshine. And clothes that matched her radiant youth.

"Is this the freshman class in geometry?" I asked her.

She nodded politely and smiled. But how quickly her eyes sized me up! It was not an unkind glance. And yet, it said more plainly than words, "From where do you come? How did you get in here?"

Sitting side by side with them through the whole hour, I felt stranger to them than if I had passed them in Hester Street.

47

Wasn't there some secret something that would open us toward one another?

In one class after another, I kept asking myself, "What's the matter with me? Why do they look at me so when I talk with them?"

Maybe I'd have to change myself inside and out to be one of them. But how?

The lectures were over at four o'clock. With a sigh, I turned from the college building, away from the pleasant streets, down to the shabby back alley near the post office, and entered the George Martin Hand Laundry.

Mr. Martin was a fat, easy-going, good-natured man. I no sooner told him of my experience in New York than he took me on at once as an ironer at fifty cents an hour, and he told me he had work for as many hours a day as I could put in.

I felt if I could only look a little bit like other girls on the outside, maybe I could get in with them. And that meant money! And money meant work, work, work!

Till eleven o'clock that night, I ironed fancy white shirt-waists.

"You're some busy little worker, even if I do say so," said Mr. Martin, good-naturedly. "But I must lock up. You can't live here."

I went home, aching in every bone. And in the quiet and good air, I so overslept that I was late for my first class. To make matters worse, I found a note in my mailbox that puzzled and frightened me. It said, "Please report at once to the dean's office to explain your absence from Physical Education I, at four o'clock."

A line of other students was waiting there. When my turn came I asked the secretary, "What's this physical education business?"

"This is a compulsory course," he said. "You cannot get credit in any other course unless you satisfy this requirement."

At the hour when I had intended to bo back to Martin's Laundry, I entered the big gymnasium. There were a crowd of girls dressed in funny short black bloomers and rubber-soled shoes.

The teacher blew the whistle and called harshly, "Students are expected to report in their uniforms."

"I have none."

"They're to be obtained at the bookstore," she said, with a stern look at me. "Please do not report again without it."

I stood there dumb.

"Well, stay for today and exercise as you are," said the teacher, taking pity on me.

She pointed out my place in the line, where I had to stand with the rest like a lot of wooden soldiers. She made us twist ourselves around here and there, "Right face!" "Left face!" "Right about face!" I tried to do as the others did, but I felt like a jumping-jack being pulled this way and that way. I picked up dumbbells and pushed them up and down and sideways until my arms were lame. Then she made us hop around like a lot of monkeys.

At the end of the hour, I was so out of breath that I sank down, my heart pounding against my ribs. I was dripping with sweat worse than Saturday night in the steam laundry. What's all this physical education nonsense? I came to college to learn something, to get an education with my head, and not monkeyshines with my arms and legs.

I went over to the instructor. "How much an hour do we get for this work?" I asked her, bitterly.

She looked at me with a stupid stare. "This is a two-point course."

Now I got real mad. "I've got to sweat my life away enough only to earn a living," I cried. "God knows I exercised enough, since I was a kid -- "

"You properly exercised?" She looked at me from head to foot. "Your posture is bad. Your shoulders sag. You need additional corrective exercises outside the class."

More tired than ever, I came to the class next day. After the dumbbells, she made me jump over the hurdles. For the life of me, I couldn't do it. I bumped myself and scratched my knees on the top bar of the hurdle, knocking it over with a great clatter. They all laughed except the teacher.

"Repeat the exercise, please," she said, with a frozen face.

I was all bruises, trying to do it. And they were all holding their sides with laughter. I was their clown, and this was their circus. And suddenly, I got so wild with rage that I seized the hurdle and right before their eyes I smashed it to pieces.

The whole gymnasium went still as death.

The teacher's face was white. "Report at once to the dean."

The scared look on the faces of the girls made me feel that I was to be locked up or fired.

For a minute when I entered the dean's grand office, I was so confused I couldn't even see.

He rose and pointed to a chair beside his desk. "What can I do for you?" he asked, in a voice that quieted me as he spoke.

I told him how mad I was, to have piled on me jumping hurdles when I was so tired anyway. He regarded me with that cooling steadiness of his. When I was through, he walked to the window and I waited, miserable. Finally he turned to me again, and with a smile! "I'm quite certain that physical education is not essential in your case. I will excuse you from attending the course."

After this things went better with me. In spite of the hard work in the laundry, I managed to get along in my classes. More and more interesting became the life of the college as I watched it from the outside.

What a feast of happenings each day of college was to those other students. Societies, dances, letters from home, packages of food, midnight spreads and even birthday parties. I never knew that there were people glad enough of life to celebrate the day they were born. I watched the gay goings—on around me like one coming to a feast, but always standing back and only looking on.

One day, the ache for people broke down my feelings of differerence from them. I felt I must tear myself out of my aloneness. Nothing had ever come to me without my going out after it. I had to fight for my living, fight for every bit of my education. Why should I expect friendship and love to come to me out of the air while I sat there, dreaming about it?

The freshman class gave a dance that very evening. Something in the back of my head told me that an evening dress and slippers were part of going to a dance. I had no such things. But should that stop me? If I had waited till I could afford the right clothes for college, I should never have been able to go at all.

I put a fresh collar over my old serge dress. And with a dollar stolen from my eating money, I bought a ticket to the dance. As I peeped into the glittering gymnasium, blaring with jazz, my timid fears stopped the breath in me. How the whole big place sang with their light—hearted happiness! Young eyes drinking joy from young eyes. Girls, like gay-coloured butterflies, whirling in the arms of young men.

Floating ribbons and sashes shimmered against men's black coats. I took the nearest chair, blinded by the dazzle of the happy couples. Why did I come here? A terrible sense of age weighed upon me; yet I watched and waited for someone to come and ask me to dance. But not one man came near me. Some of my classmates nodded distantly in passing, but most of them were too filled with their own happiness even to see me.

The whirling of joy went on and on, and still I sat there watching, cold, lifeless, like a lost ghost. I was nothing and nobody. It was worse than being ignored. Worse than being an outcast. I simply didn't belong. I had no existence in their young eyes. I wanted to run and hide myself, but fear and pride nailed me against the wall.

A chaperone must have noticed my face, and she brought over one of those clumsy, backward youths who was lost in a corner by himself. How unwilling were his feet as she dragged him over! In a dull voice, he asked, "May I have the next dance?" his eyes fixed in the distance as he spoke.

"Thank you. I don't want to dance." And I fled from the place.

I found myself walking in the darkness of the campus. In the thick shadows of the trees I hid myself and poured out my shamed and injured soul to the night. So, it wasn't character or brains that counted. Only youth and beauty and clothes – things I never had and never could have. Joy and love were not for such as me. Why not? Why not? . . .

I flung myself on the ground, beating with my fists against the endless sorrows of my life. Even in college I had not escaped from the ghetto. Here loneliness hounded me even worse than in Hester Street. Was there no escape? Will I never lift myself to be a person among people?

I pressed my face against the earth. All that was left of me reached out in prayer. God! I've gone so far, help me to go on. God! I don't know how, but I must go on. Help me not to want their little happiness. I have wanted their love more than my life. Help me be bigger than this hunger in me. Give me the love that can live without love. . . .

Darkness and stillness washed over me. Slowly I stumbled to my feet and and looked up at the sky. The stars in their infinite peace seemed to pour their healing light into me. I thought of the captives in prison, the sick and the suffering from the beginning of time who had looked to these stars for strength. What was my little sorrow to the centuries of pain which those stars had watched? So near they seemed, so compassionate. My bitter hurt seemed to grow small and drop away. If I must go on alone, I should still have silence and the high stars to walk with me.

*

Never before or since in all my life had I worked as hard as during that first term. I was not only earning a living and

51

getting an education, I was trying to break into this new college world.

Every week, I saved a bit more for a little something in my appearance – a brush for the hair, a pair of gloves, a pair of shoes with stockings to match. And now I began to work still longer hours to save up for a plain felt hat like those college girls wore. And the result of my wanting to dress up was that I was too tired to master my hardest subject. In January, the blow fell. On the bulletin board, where everybody could see, my name was posted as failing in geometry. It meant taking the course all over again. And something still worse. Two weeks later, the bursar sent me a bill for the same old geometry course.

I hurried to his office and pushed myself in ahead of the line of waiting students. "I want my money back for the geometry course that you didn't teach me," I cried. "I paid to learn, not to fail."

The man gaped at me for a moment as if I had gone mad and then paid no more attention to me. His indifference got me into such a rage that I could have broken through the cage and shaken him. But remembered the smashed hurdle and the kind dean. With an effort, I got hold of myself and went to this more understanding man.

"I didn't smash any hurdles, but I'm ready to smash the world. Why should I pay the college for something I didn't get?" And then I told him how they wanted to cheat me.

This time, even the dean did not understand. And I had no new hat that winter.

I flung myself into the next term's work with a fierce determination to wring the last drop of knowledge from each course. At first, psychology was like Greek to me. So many words about words. "Apperception," "reflex arc," "inhibitions." What had all that fancy book language to do with the real, plain every day?

Then, one day, Mr. Edman said to the class: "Give an example from your experience showing how anger or any strong emotion interferes with your thinking."

Suddenly, it dawned on me. I jumped to my feet with excitement. I told him about Zalmon the fish-peddler. Once I saw him get so mad at a woman for wanting to bargain down a penny on a pound of fish that in his anger he threw a dollar's worth of change at her.

In a flash, so many sleeping things in my life woke up in me. I remembered the time I was so crazy for Morris Lipkin. How I had poured out all my feelings without sense. That whole picture of my first mad love sprang before my eyes like a new revelation, and I cried, "No wonder they say, 'All lovers are fools'!"

Everybody laughed. But my anger did not get the better of me now. I had learned self-control. I was now a person of reason.

From that day on, the words of psychology were full of living wonder. In a few weeks I was ahead of any one else in the class. I saw the students around me as so many pink-faced children who never had had to live yet. I realized that the time when I sold herring in Hester Street, I was learning life more than if I had gone to school.

The fight with Father to break away from home, the fight in the cafeteria for a piece of meat — when I went through those experiences I thought them privations and losses; now I saw them treasure chests of insight. What countless riches lay buried under the ground of those early years that I had thought so black, so barren, so thwarted with want!

Before long, I had finished the whole textbook of psychology.

"I'm through with the book," I said to Mr. Edman. "Please give me more work. I've got to keep my head going."

He gave me a list of references. And I was so excited with the first new book that I stayed up half the night reading it on and on. I could hardly wait for the class to show Mr. Edman all I had learned. After the lecture, I hastened to his desk.

"I'm all ready to recite on this new book," I cried, as I handed it to him.

"Recite?" He looked puzzled.

"Ask me any questions. See only how much I've just learned."

"I'm late to a class right now. I'm busy with lectures all day long."

"If you're busy all day, I'll come to you in the evening. Where do you live?"

He drew back and stared at me. "I'm glad to tell you what to read," he said stiffly. "But I have no time for recitations out-side of class hours. I'm too busy."

God! How his indifference cut me! "Too busy!" The miser. Here I come to him hungry, starving — come begging for one little crumb of knowledge! And he has it all — and yet pushes me back with, "I'm too busy!"

How I had dreamed of college! The inspired companionship of teachers who are friends! The high places above the earth, where minds are fired by minds. And what's this place I've come to? Was the college only a factory, and the teachers machines turning out lectures by the hour on wooden dummies, incapable of response?

53

Was there no time for the flash from eye to eye, from heart to heart? Was that vanishing spark of light that flies away quicker than it came unless it is given life at the moment by the kindling breath of another mind — was that to be shoved aside with, "I'm too busy. I have no time for recitations outside class hours?"

A few days later, I saw Mr. Edman coming out hurriedly from Philosophy Hall. Oh, if I could only ask him about that fear inhibition I had read about. How it would clear my mind to talk it over with him for only a minute. But he'd maybe be too busy to even glance at me.

"How do you do, Miss Smolinsky!" He smiled and stopped as he saw me. "How are you getting on with those references I gave you?"

My whole heart leaped up in grattitude. "Oh, perhaps I bothered you too much."

"No bother at all. I only wish I had more time."

That very evening I overhead two tired-looking instructors in the college cafeteria.

"Maybe I was a fool to take this job. No sweatshop labor is so underpaid as the college instructor.

"How do they expect us to live? I get a thousand dollars a year and I teach sixteen periods a week."

"And look at Edman. He teaches eighteen periods and his pay is no more than ours."

So that was it! And I had thought I hated Mr. Edman for being so aloof, so stingy with his time. Now I understood how overworked and overdriven he was. How much he had taught me in that one little class! What a marvellous teacher he was! *Ach!* If one could only meet such a man outside of class, how the whole world would open up and shine with light!

Summer came. And when the others went home for their vacation I found a canning factory near the town. And all summer I worked, stringing beans, shelling peas, pulling berries. I worked as long hours as in the New York laundry. But here, it was in sheds full of air.

And as I worked, I though of Mr. Edman and all he had taught me. His course in psychology had opened to me a new world of reason and "objectivity." Through him, I had learned to think logically for the first time in my life.

Till now, I lived only by blind instinct and feeling. I might have remained forever an over-emotional lunatic. This wider understanding of life, this new power of logic and reason I owe to Mr. Edman.

How could I ever have been so crazy for a little bit of a poet like Lipkin? If I worshipped Mr. Edman, there would be some *reason* in my worship. Edman is not a silly poet like Lipkin. He is a thinker, a scientist. Through him I have gained this impersonal, scientific attitude of mind.

I returned to college a week before the new term started. I went to the post office to buy some stamps. There was Mr. Edman! He was giving the postman his new address. Tanned with the summer sun, he looked more wonderful, more distinguished than ever. "Eighteen Bank Street." So that's where Mr. Edman lived.

Turning from the postman, he looked up and saw me.

"Hello! What have you been doing?" was his friendly greeting.

"Working in a canning factory. But my head was going over and over everything you taught me."

"That's splendid," he smiled. "I'm glad to find a student who takes psychology so seriously."

How kind, how wonderful he was! For a long time after he went away, I could only look and look after him. How that little bit of friendliness had changed the world for me! How I could be filled to the brim with happiness by the sound of a voice, the smile of a face!

Before I knew how or why, I found myself walking up and down the sidewalk of the house marked Eighteen Bank Street.

All at once I noticed the sign, "Room To Let."

My heart gave a sudden jump. I stopped still, almost without breath. Then I walked up the steps and rang the bell.

"May I see the room to let?" I asked of the woman who opened the door.

She led me up to the third-story hall bedroom. It was a dollar a week more than I could afford to pay. But even if I had to starve, I had to rent that room. What matter if my body starved as long as my soul would be fed!

"All my roomers are from college," she said, as I paid her a week's rent in advance. "Miss Porter, the art teacher, has my front parlor. And right below you is Mr. Edman, the teacher of psychology."

And people doubt that there's a God on earth that orders all the events of our lives? Why was I so driven to get an education? Why did I pick out this college of all colleges? Was it not because here was the man who had the knowledge that I had been seeking all my years?

That very afternoon, I moved in. On the way up the stairs, a suitcase in my hand, I bumped right into him. "Think only!" I cried with uncontrolled gladness, "I live now in the same house you live."

"Oh, is that so?" he said, in his quiet voice. And then I wondered if his voice was so extra quiet because my own voice was so loud with gladness.

The next morning I was wondering what hour he went to class. So as not to miss him, I was waiting for him on the doorstep from eight o'clock on. *Ach!* I thought. To walk and talk with him for the few minutes to college, what a feast of joy to begin the day!

At last he came out.

"Good morning," he said, and walked on.

"Oh, Mr. Edman, I'm going to college, too," I cried, catching up with him. I had a thousand questions that I had in my mind to ask him. But only after he bowed and I saw him walk up the steps to Philosophy Hall did I realize that I had forgotten everything that I had meant to talk to him about.

In the evening, as I passed his door, on the way up to my room, I heard him cough. I tried to go on with the lesson, but the repeated sound of his cough went through and through me so that I could not concentrate on my work. And before I knew what I was doing, I was in the delicatessen store, buying a pint of milk. I hurried back to my room, heated the milk on my gas jet, and with the hot saucepan in my hand I knocked at his door.

"Hot milk is good for your cough," I stammered, as he opened the door.

He look in surprise at me, and then slowly smiled. "Oh, you shouldn't have done this." He poured the milk into a glass. "Thank you," he said, handing me the saucepan and closing the door.

Because of the rain, I couldn't wait for him on the doorstep the next morning. I didn't hear him go out till the front door slammed. Through the window, I saw him walk quickly, with his head bent, through the rain. Quick as lightning I seized my umbrella and ran after him, crying, "Mr. Edman – Mr. Edman! You mustn't get wet. Remember, you have a cold. Here's my umbrella."

He stopped. He turned around. "Miss Smolinsky, you mustn't bother so about me. I don't like it."

His tone of annoyance hit me like a blow. I remained standing in the rain and let him go on. He hurried along the drenched pavement, and over him the quiet elms poured their cooling drops steadily.

As I watched him disappear down the street, I knew with sudden terrible clearness that he was going out of my life for ever.

Oh, Morris Lipkin! Was it all for nothing? God! Must I always remain such a fool! Such a fool! Will even the hurts and shames of my life teach me nothing? O God! Give me only the hard heart of reason!

A thousand years older I was by the time I dragged myself up the stairs to my room. I threw myself on the bed. My whole body ached with the bitterness of it all. Insane I've been — reaching for I know not what and only pushing it away in my clumsiness.

I want knowledge. How, like a starved thing in the dark, I'm driven to reach for it. A flash, and all lights up! Almost I seem to touch the fiery centre of life! And there! It was only a man. And I'm left in the dark again.

What was that flash of light that lured me into this blackness? Was it desire for the man, or desire for knowledge? Why does one kill the other and make everything that was so real nothing but an empty mockery?

For hours I lay listening to the breathing of the elm leaves in the rain.

Slowly, the clouding numbness left me. Work to be done. Work to be done. That's why I came to college.

Stupid *yok*! Always wasting yourself with wild loves. I'll put a stop to it. I'll freeze myself like ice. I'll be colder than the coldest. I'm alone. I'm alone.

Little by little, I began to get hold of myself. If I lost out with those spick-and-span youngsters like Mr. Edman, I won with the older and wiser professors. After a while, I understood why the young men didn't like me. I knew more of life as a ten-year-old girl, running the streets, than these psychology instructors did with all their heads swelled from too much knowing.

With the older men I could walk and talk as a person. To them, my Hester Street world was a new world. I gave them mine, and they gave me theirs. What could such raw youth as Mr. Edman know of that ripened understanding that older men could give!

As time went on, I found myself smiling at the terrible pain and suffering that my crush for Mr. Edman had cost me. That affair, like the one with Morris Lipkin — all foolish madness which, though it nearly killed me, made me grow faster in reason than if I had no such madness in me.

Each time, after making a crazy fool of myself over a man, I was plunged into thick darkness that seemed the end of everything, but it really led me out into the beginnings of wider places, newer light.

Gradually, I grew up even to be friends with the dean. His house was always open to me. Once, while we were chatting in his library, I asked him suddenly, "Why is it that when a nobody wants to get to be somebody she's got to maker herself terribly hard, when people like you who are born high up can keep all their kind feelings and get along so naturally well with everybody?"

He looked at me with the steady gaze of his understanding eyes.

"All pioneers have to get had to survive," he said. He pointed to a faded oil painting of his grandmother. "Look! My grandmother came to the wilderness in an ox cart and with a gun on her lap. She had to chop down trees to build a shelter for herself and her children. I'm more than a little ashamed to realize if I had to contend with the wilderness I'd perish with the unfit. But you, child – your place is with the pioneers. And you're going to survive."

After that I could not go back to my little room. For hours I walked. I needed the high stars and the deep stillness of the night to hold my exaltation.

*

The senior year came, and with it a great event. The biggest newspaper owner of the town, who was a rich alumnus of the college, offered a prize of a thousand dollars for the best essay on "What the College Has Done for Me." Everybody was talking about it, students, instructors, and professors.

What had the college done for me? I thought of the time when I first came here. How I was thrilled out of my senses by the mere sight of plain, clean people. The smashed hurdle in the gymnasium. The way I dashed into the bursar's office demanding money for my failed geometry. Yes. Perhaps more than all the others, I had something to write about. Maybe they wouldn't understand. But if truth was what they wanted – here they had it. I poured it out as it came from my heart, and sent it in. Then I had to put it out of my mind because I was so buried deep in my examinations. Everything was forgotten in this last fight to win my diploma.

It was Commencement Day at last. Glad but downhearted I was – glad because I'd won, but so sad I was to leave the battlefield! The thing I had dreamed about for so many years – and now it was over! Where I was going now, will I be able to find these real American people again – that draw me so?

With all the students and professors, I sat in the big assembly room and listened to the long speeches that seemed never to end.

At last a man came up to announce the winner of the contest. "The student," he said, "whose essay the judges found the best is a young lady. Her name is –" God in the world! Who? Who was it? They were clapping to beat the band. I only heard him say, "Will she please come forward to the platform?"

I heard the clapping louder and louder. Then I saw they were all looking at me. "Sara Smolinsky, it's you. It's you! Don't you hear? They're calling for you."

How my paralyzed feet ever got me to the platform, I don't know. So exciting it was! It was I, myself, standing there before the sea of faces!

The man handed me an envelope and said things that flew over my head. How could I have the sense to hear or think to say something?

Then all the students rose to their feet, cheering and waving and calling my name, like a triumph, "Sara Smolinsky – Sara Smolinsky!"

SHULAMITH HAREVEN

from *"CITY OF MANY DAYS"*

Sara's father had never met morality in person and so could be forgiven his neglect of it. Even in the Jerusalem of those days, which was a passionate city of passionate quarters, Don Isaac Amarillo was considered an exceptionally passionate man who was unable to resist the general sweetness of things, such as the pure breeze that whistled down the oboes of the alleyways when a heat wave suddenly broke, driving before it sun-bronzed women, all colours of children, the smell of jasmine crying out in Arab courtyards from an overdose of evening, a dusty shepherd returning from the city's fields with a lamb on his shoulders, a fragrance of arak, thyme and repose. At such times his defences were down! Tears of utter helplessness flooded his good-natured, nearsighted eyes; he grew weaker than a baby; and he was capable of taking every cent that he had, his own soul had anyone requested it, tying it in one of his not always immaculate hand-kerchiefs, and giving it away. One might compare him then to a big, kind Gulliver with a horde of children perched on his hat brim, tweaking his ears to make him run and stamping their feet on his forehead for the fun of it. And when summertime came, bringing the wild red rut of watermelons piled high in the market by the Jaffa Gate, along the path that led down to the Hebron road from the Old City wall, he was at the mercy of the first woman who came along.

Perhaps it was just such a time, at the break of a heat-wave, when life began to flow again through the narrow streets as though blown out of a bellows, that saw him drying the face of Hannah, a young socialist pioneer from Russia who had come to live in Jerusalem, in the new part of Beth Israel. As her tears proved too much for him, he came back again and again, until she bore him a son whom she named Tanhum. Don Isaac Amarillo promptly acknowledged his paternity. Indeed, he might have acknowledged it if he hadn't been the father too, for how was a man like him to abandon an unclaimed baby, and a little boy at that? A white

tropical hat on his head, he stood proud and penitent in the doorway of Hannah's room holding a bouquet of flowers. For a while
he felt obliged to live with her in Beth Israel, so as to stand
by her when she was taunted by the neighbours over the shameful
consequences of his too fond heart. But the neighbours too were
young socialists: they went about unkempt, wore tattered Russian
blouses, worked at their printing press until all hours of the
night, and couldn't have cared less about the origins and ancestry
of Hannah's squalling child.

Three months after Hannah gave birth to Tanhum, Don Isaac
was summoned home, where his wife, Gracia, had given birth too,
to a second daughter, named Ofra. Once again he stood proud and
penitent in a doorway with a bouquet in one hand. This time it
was his own wife's tears that proved too much for him. He moved
back home.

Eventually Hannah took Tanhum and went to live in a village
near the coast, where she taught school for a living – whereupon
Don Isaac's escapades might have come to an end, had not a
strange young woman turned up in Jerusalem several years later.
A small, slender thing surrounded by bundles and suitcases, she
arrived in a gigantic hat that resembled a wagon wheel, and a
white muslin dress, chattering away in loud French. Rumour had
it she was the daughter of a French count and countess. Since
Don Isaac was one of the heads of the Jewish community, she
appeared before him in his office one morning with a roll of
pictures under one arm, looking like a starched hornet. The
story she told was a strange one. The pictures, she said, had
been painted by her late mother, and her one desire was for Don
Isaac to help her *arranger une exposition,* that is, a public
showing, in Jerusalem. Dipping her lips in a little coffee, she
explained, seated opposite him, that she was the daughter of a
French count and countess who had travelled to Lebanon and lived
there for a while until, compelled one day to return to France
on family business, they left her behind with their Arab servant
and his wife. The two of them tragically perished at sea and
she became an orphan.
Don Isaac was so overcome with compassion that his tongue
clucked unconsciously in his mouth. The more it clucked, the
less he was able to stop it, for the tale went from bad to

worse. The servant and his wife brought the girl up, but they were vulgar, common people with whom it was impossible for her to live any longer. Not only that, it was just her misfortune that, as she matured — and her benefactor, Don Isaac, could see for himself that she wasn't exactly unattractive — her servant guardian began making advances to her until she didn't have a moment's peace. She packed up a few of her belongings, just a smattering of what she owned, took her mother's paintings, which were her most precious possessions, and fled.

Don Isaac wiped his eyes. He would be only too happy, he declared, to come to her aid as best he could, even *arranger une exposition* of her mother's paintings in Jerusalem, though in fact no one in the neighbourhood knew what *une exposition* was, or how it might be arranged. In this and all other possible ways he could think of, he would help her raise the money to trace her legal kin in France. He was so carried away by his desire to be of assistance that he hardly bothered to listen to the rest of her story, which included such things as stock companies in Panama, diamonds her guardian had made off with, and various other financial details that could make a man's head spin round.

The exposition was never held. One one occasion the countess wasn't feeling well; on another she feared that there weren't enough paintings for a proper show; on still another she cancelled because not enough guests were invited, or because they weren't the right sort of people. Finally, when a hall had been rented and Don Isaac had taken care of everything down to the smallest detail, guaranteeing the presence of just the right number of just the right sort of guests, she sent him a messenger the morning of the opening with a note to inform him that the paintings had been stolen that night. And that was that.

Don Isaac Amarillo was not one to abandon a countess in distress. He himself was a man of some means, and he spared no effort to see that she was properly looked after, with lawyers for her stocks, pawnbrokers for her jewellery, doctors for the mysterious attacks of illness that periodically befell her, and maids to iron her dresses. Eventually he became her slave. She sent him messages over every little thing, until he found himself devoting half his time to her and her affairs, and ultimately the whole of it. Before five months were out Don Isaac disappeared from Jerusalem one fine summer day along with the Countess

Claudine – who, it was rumoured, was not really a countess at all, and was perhaps half–an–allegorical–figment of Don Isaac's imagination to begin with.

Sara was seven at the time. "An evil beast hath devoured Zaki," her grandfather declared, as Jacob had of Joseph in the Bible. The members of the family didn't officially go into mourning; but they did mourn Zaki none the less, that is, Don Isaac, their pride and their joy, of whom it was difficult to say whether he had cast them out of his life or himself out of theirs. One way or another, he had suddenly ceased to be a husband, son–in–law, father and son, and had become as good as dead.

Sara was sick with a fever that week, covered all over with the chicken pox, which itched and itched, and she simply couldn't believe that her father could desert her at such a time. He had always been so nice to his daughters whenever they chanced to intrude on that invisible ballet of which his days were composed. Why, just the other evening, standing by her bedside after return- ing from his day's affairs, he'd gently wiped her moist brow and promised that if she didn't scratch the blisters and scar her face for life, he'd invite the Turkish army band to serenade her beneath her window on Saturday night. He'd promised in so many words – and now he was gone for good. In Jerusalem he was never seen again. It was said that he was in Panama. Or perhaps, like Elijah in his chariot, he was carried off in a storm to Brazil. Sara's mother kept a stiff upper lip and never mentioned his name. In all likelihood she had hated him down all the years, with a dark and ponderous hatred, for his stupid, compassionate heart. Indeed, now that he was gone it was remarked on in Jerusalem that somehow one's contacts with Don Isaac Amarillo had always ended in disappointment. This feeling was well put by a local porch–sitter named Nissim Misrahi, known slyly to the neighbours as Mirácolo Orientale because of his dandyish ways. "It's as though," said Mirácolo, a thin slip of a man who drove a wagon for the burial society, "Zaki was always promising to take you to heaven in a speeding coach, and you trusted him so much that you didn't even look where you were going, and then suddenly, wham–bang, he reins in the horses and out of the wagon you fall!"

And yet he had been a good man.

63

In purely practical terms, nothing changed very much. The
role of Sara's grandfather, Elder Amarillo, became even more
clearly defined as that of pater-familias. The family continued
to live in one house with him and Sara's grandmother, mean old
woman who spent all her days bed-ridden in her alcove, from
where she issued orders to the household. Grandfather Amarillo
was a strong and taciturn man, strict and pious in his habits;
he never patted the cheeks of the children and always met his
obligations. He considered it his duty to look after Tanhum,
whose grandsire he had been made by his idiot son – nor was Sara
unaware of the fact that he frequently sent money to a certain
village near the coast, much to her mother's displeasure.

One day Sara met Tanhum. Hannah came with him to Jerusalem.
A dry, bespectacled woman, she shut herself up with grandfather
in his office, and its big, black, intricately carved safe. It was
shortly after the Turks had left the country, and Hannah had come
on hard times. Gracia retired at once to her room, whose curtains
were drawn and well-tied, and lay there groaning with a headache,
a handkerchief soaked in eau de cologne on her forehead, muttering *tranquil, tranquil* to herself in French as though it were
a magic charm. Bukas, the cook, made a tomato omelette for
Tanhum, who sat silently in the kitchen and refused to eat.

Sara saw him when she entered the kitchen: he was only a
little shorter than herself, thin and intense, with electric,
bristly hair. She sat without a word by his side and cut up
everything on his plate into little bites, though he was at least
nine years old and could have done it himself; yet he took the
food from her hands and ate. "Eat, Tanhum, eat," she urged him
on quietly, a lump forming in her throat. He didn't even shy
away when she stroked his wiry hair. His arm was black-blue all
over, because, Bukas said, that *pigsada* of a pioneer was always
pinching it. The two of them sat on the window sill, swinging
their legs; though they didn't talk, they were already fast
friends. Afterwards Sara wasn't sure whether they really hadn't
exchanged a word that day. She would have given anything to
remember, for within the year they found out that Tanhum was
dead of diptheria. If Don Isaac Amarillo had any other son left,
he could only be growing up in Panama, watered daily by his
father's contrition. And if he didn't, he had only his two
daughters.

Grandfather Amarillo prayed hard all week long; Bukas wiped
her eyes in the corners of the house; and even Sara's mother was

heard to remark, *"Pobro chico,* to think such a good-looking boy
could come from such an ugly old thing!" The day of her unbearable migraine, it appeared, she had sneaked a good look at the
two of them through a crack between the curtains.

Hannah moved soon after to a kibbutz, several of whose
members she knew from her old neighbourhood in Jerusalem. In
time she married a pioneer from Germany, a fanatical socialist
who was bald and loved sports. Grandfather Amarillo stopped
sending her remittance, and even gifts for the holidays. The
family lost touch with her.

The holidays were the worst times of all. On the first night
of each, her mother's quarrels with her grandfather invariably
came to a boil, frothing up like one of Bukas' pots that were
always seething and simmering crossly like the cook herself.
Gracia wanted a divorce in order to be able to remarry. Grandfather Amarillo wouldn't hear of it. "Some day," he would say,
"Zaki will come back. What will they say of you then? Shall we
make a harlot out of you?" "Then find him for me so that he can
divorce me thimself," Gracia would scream in a desperate, drawn-
out, up-and-down wail. "You have no pity!" She knew perfectly
well that Don Isaac was not to be found. There wasn't an agency
through which Elder Amarillo hadn't tried to trace him; he had
even turned to the British Government, whose tentacles were all
over the world. Privately he was of the opinion that Zaki was
no longer alive. "The boy is crazy," he admitted, "that's true.
And he's weak, that's true too. But it's still inconceivable
that he would abandon his wife and family, just like that. If
he could write, he would write. Chances are that he's dead."

Sometimes Grandfather Amarillo was brought lists by Captain
Tony Crowther of His Majesty's army. In them were the names of
all sorts of men whose bodies had been found, murdered perhaps
in some violent brawl in one of the port cities of the world:
under smoky, flickering lights, amid the smells of cheap alcohol,
fish, seaweed and salt, astride rotting, slippery planks, in
docks and piers licked by the ocean tides, in the shadows of
mouldy warehouses greasy with petrol and tar, they had gone to

65

their deaths. There were lists of the dead in railway accidents too, descriptions of men missing, of curious fatalities in India and Abyssinia, Turkey and British Guiana, of circumcised corpses of whom nothing else was known. Good Lord, how many weird, anonymous, footloose Jews there are in Your world!

None of the descriptions fitted. The names on the lists were strange, even comical, each a joke in itself. Sara and Ofra would sit in a corner and repeat them one by one, roaring with laughter. Their lives seemed made up to them of the names and fragments of names of the anonymous dead. Men put on and took off names like clothing, changed them, threw them away like used rags, had them come to life again in some office in Jerusalem like a balloon blown gloriously up for a minute, for the sake of some document, clarification, only to be punctured again and discarded like bits of old scrap. None of them was Don Isaac, neither the official Isaac ben Rabbi Moses Amarillo of the record books, nor the Zaki whom everyone knew. One day Captain Crowther brought a faded, yellowed photograph of a man in a white hat, dressed in a white tropical suit and white shoes. Sporting a thin mustache, he stood leaning on a column in the patio of some villa against a background of palms. It was hard to say whether the villa was real or a painted backdrop in some photographer's studio. Elder Amarillo, his daughter-in-law, his children and grandchildren inspected this snapshot for three or four days through a magnifying glass until they returned it to the captain with a mixture of heartbreak and relief: no, it wasn't he. The Englishman, who happened to be in dress uniform with a diagonal belt on his chest and a swagger-stick under one arm, sipped his arak on ice, the cloudy complexion of which may have reminded him of London fogs, and said: "Pity!" He looked searchingly as he spoke at Sara's mother, who was the most romantic-looking woman he had seen in his life.
That evening Gracia wailed until midnight:
"I can't stand it any longer! May God strike me dead; If He's going to let the likes of him live, then let Him kill me instead!" Sara and Ofra stopped up their ears in their room and put their dolls to sleep with a lullaby.

> Daddy's work is far away
> He'll come back at close of day
> He'll bring games for us to play-a-y.

In the course of time Gracia's suffering became ritualized. With the approach of every holiday or feast, the family braced itself for her screams, her migraines, her slamming of doors, her drawn-out wails that faded away in the end to an incantatory *tranquil, tranquil,* her appeals to God in Hebrew, French and Ladino. Glancing up at the grandfather clock that hung in the kitchen, where she was busy straining steamed wheat to make noodles, her sleeves pushed back and her arms caked with flour, Bukas would grumble:

"Look how late it is! Why hasn't she started yet?"

The whole neighbourhood awaited Gracia's screams: they gave everyone the chance to say pityingly *miskenika,* poor little one, allowed the women to despise their husbands and remind them of all their sins, and the men to congratulate themselves for not acting like that fool of a Zaki, who left his wife high and dry, despite their little peccadillos. At such times a kind of communal atonement took place, a ritual of purification that reaffirmed what mattered in life and made everyone feel his self-worth. The important thing, the neighbourhood held, was what went on behind a family's doors, not in front of them – and so strengthened in their convictions, all sat down to eat, penitents if not perfect angels, poured the children a drop of wine, and made sure that they drank no more.

Once when Sara was sitting in the kitchen with Bakas, kneading a small ball of dough which she had plucked from the bowl, she inquired:

"Bukas, why doesn't grandfather let my mother get married again?"

"Who said she wants to get married?" said Bukas crossly. "Just because you scream, does that make it so?"

Sara jumped up and hit her. Grandmother Amarillo banged with her cane on the floor of her room. Bukas went to complain. It ended with angry tears.

"Don't you ever tell me again my mother's a liar!"

"She's not only a liar, she's cross-eyed too," said Bukas, as she left the room.

Little by little, however, Sara began to think that perhaps Bukas was right. There was something put on about her mothers' holiday tantrums. Once Sara went up to her room before the Passover *seder* and saw her burning a piece of cork in order to blacken the already dark circles beneath her eyes. She and Ofra

stopped paying attention to her attacks. Only Grandfather Amarillo
still paced back and forth in his room, troubled and ill-at-ease:
back and forth, back and forth, while his daughter-in-law wailed,
until, spying Sara in the doorway, he would motion her inside
and hand her a bill from the safe.

"Go buy yourself something, *miskenika*."

There was an air of trumpery in grandmother's room: ancient,
cunning trumpery, yet also brazen, improperly concealed. Grandmother was full of a malicious energy. She rambled querously on
and on, whether to herself or someone else no one knew.

"I'm sixty years old. That's a fact. Of all the neighbours
only Luna Cardozo *no tiene* any shame, she says I'm seventy-two.
What a lie, what a lie; God strike me dead if there's a word of
truth in what she says. They've all become liars, *kazzabe'eva*.
It's impossible to live with them. That Bukas is the biggest
liar of all. *Mentirosa*. She told me she paid four mils for my
handkerchiefs, but I saw it say five on the label with my own
eyes. Why does she lie to an old woman? What for? When I don't
get out of bed, nobody knows how I suffer. Everyone cheats me
to my face. Gracia's a liar *también*."

The business of prices was anything but simple. Grandmother
Amarillo refused to believe a word about prices going up. The
merchants, she insisted, were cheats, and the family was stupid
enough to be cheated. To keep on her good side, it was a household rule never to tell her the real price of anything. Even
this didn't satisfy her, though, and she would begin to mutter
to herself, chewing the price with her ancient teeth. The family
had been deceiving her in this way for years, doing everything
to avoid her wrath, until one day she decided that it wasn't
enough for prices to stay the same: the family deserved a discount.
Propped up in all her trumpish magnificence in her huge bed,
which resembled a taut-sailed schooner that never raised anchor,
she demanded a discount. The family obliged her and knocked
prices down even further. In grandmother's room bread now cost
a quarter of what it did in the market. But Grandmother Amarillo
still didn't believe them. Playing a cunning game of her own,
she secretly sent Sara or Ofra to ask what things really cost.
In their innocence the girls did as they were told. *Grandmother,
he said half a piastre a rotel. He said a piastre and a half a
bottle, grandmother.* The old woman nearly had a stroke each
time. Stubborn, senile and stinking of pee, she would scream at
Bukas until she was red in the face:

"You're a liar! A cheat! There's no God in your heart! I swear to God there's no God there!"

It would end with her groaning:

"It was never like this when I was *en mi cama matrimonial.*"

She meant her big double bed. Ever since she had left it for her alcove kingdom full of chamberpots, trumpery, pistachio nuts, muslin nightgowns, shawls and Turkish-delight, the world had never been run properly.

Grandmother Amarillo played cards with the girls and cheated with a straight face. They played rummy in her room, which always smelled of medicine and urine, the cards scattered over her bed. Grandmother Amarillo ate candy while she played. She refused to offer it to the girls and boastingly won every hand. Sara caught her cheating once or twice, but got a box in the face when she mentioned it. Ofra, on the other hand, either didn't or pretended not to notice, for the only way to get one of grandmother's sweets was to lose.

"How well you play, grandmother," twittered Ofra, looking up with her baby blue eyes, while Sara whispered venomously in her ear: "Asslicker!"

Once Grandmother Amarillo cheated so openly that it was impossible not to react. Sara screamed. Grandmother Amarillo screamed too. Grandfather Amarillo came to the room.

"Que se pasa aqui?"

Grandmother Amarillo said that Sara was a snake: that's right, a snake, whose head should be crushed before it bit everyone. Grandfather Amarillo took one look at the cards, gathered them up, and threw them out of the window.

"Sodom and Gomorrah!" he said out loud, and left the room.

Ofra picked up the cards in the street and returned them to her grandmother.

Once Gracia sat on the terrace with a friend while Sara did her homework inside. Though she couldn't see her mother, she did see her long brown taffeta dress that hung down to the splendid floor tiles, the black tassels that dangled from it, and, above them, a black knitted shawl. She saw her mother's hand, too, which held a purple Japanese paper fan, and the railing of the terrace, which was beautifully worked into a pattern of lilies, acanthus and horse-drawn carriages, all held together by long,

formal ropes of ivy that were also black grille work. In the
spaces between the bars the smith had made a kind of anchor that
hung suspended in air, over nothing.

"For giving them money, I forgave him," Gracia said to her
friend. "What he did *con son cuerpo,* I forgave him too. Everything I forgave him, except what he whispered in their ears. I
could have torn his eyes out for that."

"Yes," said her friend. "You're right about that, Gracia.
They can be forgiven everything except the whispers."

One day a pleasant-looking, unassuming Arab arrived in the
lane and asked for Elder Amarillo. It was the last house on the
corner. Beyond the border that it marked lay an empty field,
and then the great unknown. The Arab entered the house and shut
himself up with Grandfather Amarillo in his office, talking
Arabic with a Lebanese accent.

He was, it turned out, the father of the countess. He lived
in a village not far from Beirut and was a fez-cleaner by trade.
In his shop, he related with modest pride, he had a special steam
press: Judge Amarillo would scarcely believe what pleasure he
got from adjusting a wrinkled fez on the machine and seeing how
clean, smooth and ready-to-wear it came out, its tassel newly
sparkling and springy. He had ten children, of whom one, his
daughter Claudine, was never quite right in the head. The paintings for the exposition that she claimed were her mother's were
actually her own, while the jewels, begging Elder Amarillo's
pardon, were all stolen. This wasn't the first time she had run
away from home or found some man to fall for her story. He was
genuinely sorry that she had done such a thing to the Amarillos.
The news had come as far as his own village when he had already
given up hope of finding her. He had simply come to the Judge,
as he put it, to help him shoulder the misfortune. Her madness
had struck both their families, not just one of them, he said.
Should Elder Amarillo ever visit Lebanon, he and his family must
stay with them. As for Don Isaac Amarillo's children, he considered them his own.

Elder Amarillo insisted that the visitor stay for awhile.
They dined together, conversed till late in the night, and parted
on friendly terms.

That evening Ofra asked with perfect nonchalance:
"What happened, have they found father?"

"They haven't and they never will," said Bukas. And Gracia added:

"One lie has met another."

Sara and Ofra broke into hysterical laughter in their room. They jumped on the beds, threw pillows at each other, and shouted at the top of their lungs:

"No Panama! No Nicaragua! No India! No England!"

And when the family tried to quiet them, with cajoling and threats, they screamed till they were hoarse:

"No father! No mother! No grandfather! No grandmother! No nothing!"

In the end a pillow broke open and feathers flooded the room. Sara started to bite them. Ofra fell on the bed and hurt her hand. Imperceptibly they passed from shrill laughter to tears. Bukas refused to sweep up the feathers until morning. They fell asleep among them, exhausted by the sensation of a bitter and all-knowing victory.

Translated by Hillel Halkin

AMALIA KAHANA-CARMON

N'IMA SASSOON WRITES POEMS

'Do tears know who sheds them?
And hearts know who tills them?
They are tilled by light entering the turf
And the turf does not know what's within.'

('Lament' – Yehuda Halevi, 1075–1142)

Our teacher, Mr Havdala, said, among other things: 'Our pupil N'ima Sassoon has given us great pleasure with her splendid poem, "Dear Teacher", which is at the top of the latest issue of our wall–newspaper.'

Now, our whole school, the Tent of Sara School for Orthodox girls, would read the poem.

We went up to our classrooms in pairs. I passed teacher Ezekiel, who was standing with the headmistress. I did not know what they were discussing. I could hear him saying in his unique voice, a voice that was full of pith though it was broken, like Louis Armstrong's, 'There's nothing to it,' and her replying, 'Let's see you do it, then,' while he answered, 'What do you want me to do? Leap about on one leg?' and she replied, 'Look who's talking!' And as I hear him being spoken to like that I feel torn.

Teacher Ezekiel is our form teacher. We have learned that a man should not be joyful among those who are weeping, or weep among those who are rejoicing, nor should he keep awake among those who are sleeping or sleep among those who are awake, etc. Yet teacher Ezekiel sits all day at his desk on the little plat- form in front of the blackboard, and never raises his eyes from his worksheets, his books, and his registers. Mid–morning break. How was it, for an instant, a dream come true – by chance, was it, or was it absent–mindedness – that he noticed me again for a moment, that the green eyes rested on me. And I could not contain myself. I approached. The sun was beaming through the window, and I was wearing a new summer frock which I thought was

full of promise. Teacher Ezekiel was now sitting motionless.
As though he was trying to turn his annoyance into good humour.
And, I told myself, as though he was braced to receive a blow,
and I realized again that all was lost. I walked right past
him, at full tilt. I tumbled the stones of the blue plums into
the wastepaper basket, as teacher Ezekiel, over there at his
post, unwrapped a sandwich and began eating. Reflected in him,
sitting there, I see the most handsomely dressed young man of
his day, languid, a ballet prince, with the profile of Ivor
Novello. And then I understand, no, neither is it like that;
but that you are a hard man with an extraordinary gentleness.
And I am a silly girl. Sick all year. With a kind of blind
determination I have brought on myself, let us say, a certain
type of cold. A cold with a high fever. And I don't want to be
cured. And I no longer have the power to decide. And I am not
happy any more. Not happy. Or sensible any more. Not sensible.
And because of you, twice a day, I take the wrong bus.

On two occasions there was no vacant seat, except the one
beside him. I sat down beside him.

At the first stop he got up. He offered his seat to a woman,
who was not young, yet the wrinkled skin on her sun—tanned chest
and arms was quite attractive. She sat down, opened her bag,
and took out a packet of cigarettes. She struck a match, like a
man. One of those feeble matches that snap when you strike
them, shoot off at all angles, and drop back to burn a hole in
your trousers. But since then, whenever I catch sight of her, I
don't take my eyes off her, so as to relive the scene once more:

I turned my head towards him. Teacher Ezekiel is standing
clutching the leather loop hanging from the bar above. Other
people can see a dark moon of a face; green eyes shine clearly
out of the face. And none of these people could imagine what
strength this young man has stored up in him. But he is like a
boxing champion who wouldn't hurt a fly.

'I'll hold your briefcase for you,' I tried to stammer out.

Teacher Ezekiel put his briefcase down on the floor between
his shoes, stood over me, and the air between us quivered.

And there was another time. And by then he would no longer
talk to me.

In front of us sat Mr Havdala, the teacher whom the girls
called Mr Abdullah behind his back. I see him in my mind's eye
shaped in the image of Hillel the sage, a pastor of Israel. Next
to Mr Havdala, a man was sitting upright, looking as though he
was asleep, reading a newspaper propped up in front of him. Mr

Havdala, fussily self-important, turned to me and kept up a
conversation the whole way:
'You're lucky to have curly hair,' he said, 'you don't need
to comb it.'
And then: 'What do you do when you get home?'
'Nothing. Read.'
'Read. What do you read?'
'Nothing. Daddy's books.'
'How's your Daddy been doing lately?'
'Nothing. He's ill.'
'So what will happen?'
'Nothing. We're selling the business.'
'And what are your plans, little lady?'
'I shall study.'
Throughout this conversation teacher Ezekiel was looking out
of the window. When we came to his stop, I took a chance. I
got up and left the bus.
Teacher Ezekiel stayed in his seat and did not get off.
As I stood on the pavement I could see Mr Havdala, and as he
yawned his face looked as it must have done when he was a baby.
The man asleep was still sleeping seated. But teacher Ezekiel
was no longer looking outwards.
Having gone past his proper stop, he must now really be going
home, I tried unsuccessfully to cheer myself up. And I reflected:
he will get home. He will put on comfortable clothes. His
slippers. His wife will be in her chair by the window. Sometimes
when I pass by there I see her. She is older than he is. She's
got a dog. She is tiny and fragile, with a mouth drawn in pink,
only her throat reveals age, and she sits viewing the street.
She takes up half the window, a curtain fills the rest. It is
elaborately patterned, and if you look at it closely, you can
make out among the netting and webbing the shapes of birds in
flight like bats, or birds of paradise at rest. And below their
flat is a workshop that specialises in embroidery, drawn-work,
and plissé. I saw her once coming out of a shoe shop. On her
breast she was wearing a locket with a photograph set in it.
Was it teacher Ezekiel's photo? A photo of the dog? Now she
will probably get up from her chair, and go to put on her locket
for teacher Ezekiel. Only the curtain will be left.
Yet I, however, am still here. The mirror sky is shimmering
over the city like a sheet of water. It is brighter now than at
any time of day. Zion Square looks as though it is resting on
the bed of a calm, translucent sea. Civilians, soldiers. Through

74

this hour made his by the poet Lebensohn the neon–signs fire their cheerful flashes of light: Have you managed to get home all right, teacher Ezekiel? You deserved to break a leg on the way, teacher Ezekiel. And there are the alternating hues of the traffic lights. Even on the flanks of passing vehicles there are multi–coloured lights gleaming like precious stones. It's uncanny, how such brisk movement is possible underwater. Only I, with the weight of that transparent sea in my breast, am choking. 'Are you tired, N'ima Sassoon?' he once said to me. 'So many mistakes in one maths problem.' 'July. Called after Julius Caesar.' There was all the explicitness in the world, in his wonderful, broken voice, and in his look. Together with the pleading, the hopeless- ness. Which is also a token. But I no longer knew if even that still existed. Now, that was all I asked to know.

Women were driving their cars, women who had beautiful jaws, arched necks. They all had a hard kind of charm, selfish and sharply whetted. A big embassy car, driven by a uniformed chauffeur, went past, with only a child in it. And the lights in the square, up Ben Yehuda Street, and along Jaffa Road, like those of great cities and seaports that never yet existed, shining seven times more brightly In this twilight hour, in electric splendour, an alien scarlet of wanton jubilation and thriving prosperity smelted into a red river, in untempered orange of sulphur and gold ore, in untempered green, in pellucid sapphire which shone like the terrible ice, in blue and in deep purple, constantly proclaimed the power of red, green and blue worlds, to which one need only find the path. And perhaps none of it is serious. Perhaps it is just meant to enhance the brief life–span of the pearly evening. It is, the evening, like a transparent leaf, etched with thin tracings of coloured veins, the first to fall in the autumn, flitting about like a butterfly a long while. An evening which will never be matched in clarity or purity. Or in its quintessential anguish. And there is this vicious circle: I performed an act, offered a gift. And the gift was declined. Why does he never reprove me for my imperti- nence? Perhaps he has not yet found the words. Perhaps there is some natural reticence: after all, who is one to tell others what to do. Perhaps he lacks the nerve, hopes it will all sort itself out. Perhaps he hasn't the heart to do this to me. Perhaps he is thinking of himself, and is afraid to lose me. But in my heart I knew it was none of these things. It was simply this: there are those who, without meaning to be, are torches to show others the way.

After that evening he was careful not to sit near me. Or ask me questions. Or look at me. What else had he left to deny me, I asked myself.

And it is already the end of the school year. The last few days. Days like weak winter flies, that you could touch even while they are flying around. There is the usual commotion and din of the girls. Desk lids are slammed shut noisily. Benches are dragged along. Yet the air is filled with a slow poison, as though the walls have been smeared with arsenic. The accustomed drabness has some new element in it. Like acrid ammoniac fumes dispersing. Something is draining away. And the girls, who look suddenly overgrown in their blue, childish pinafore uniforms, write keepsakes in each other's albums, prepare in groups for the finals hanging over us, get together on Friday nights at this or that one's home, and then go out together, arms linked, dreaming aloud their visions of what is to come.

None of this has anything to do with me. I take no chances. All my evenings I reserve for teacher Ezekiel, sitting at the iron table on our back verandah. At night the blades of the Eucalyptus look like tin leaves. In the dry exhalation of the pine tree leaning over from our neighbours' yards, there is some vague, scented guaranty, cool and quickening like the taste of licorice. Beyond the fence is a stony, rocky slope. The nights are lukewarm. In the housing estate on the shoulder of the hill across the wadi, dogs are barking. Its lights are like holes punched out so that you can peer at the fire under the earth's thin rind. Teacher Ezekiel does not come. He never comes. I draw closer to the fence. Some other teacher Ezekiel begins ascending into the space that is between the heavens and the earth. He gazes everywhere, cloaked in a blazing garment. And every night, as I read out the terrible letters inscribed on the crown of his forehead, my heart fails within me, as I know the moment has come, and I can hardly keep from falling into a swoon. Teacher Ezekiel vanishes behind the curtain of the sky. He has reached the place where glory is the bread of the dead. And grief is their water. Streams of suffering, that bear affliction and sorrow like myriad huge leaves in their currents, form their boundaries. All this, I, N'ima Sasson, have written in the exercise book of my poems, from which I submitted the poem called 'Dear Teacher' to the wall-newspaper of our school.

Yet all day, blear-eyed, it seems, I keep muttering to myself. All day I am in his presence, at a distance. It is a teacher Ezekiel of flesh and blood. As though in a dream, he comes in, sits down, gets up at the bell, leaves, comes back with the bell, sits down again. Moving with the conviction of a sleepwalker, with the astonishing trust of a piece of seaweed flung around by the flow. I for a long time now have been unaware of what is happening to me. Teacher Ezekiel comes towards me. He stops at my desk:

'N'ima Sasson, the bell has gone. Lessons are over,' he says, about to leave.

'Teacher Ezekiel,' I cry out to him, abasing myself for the millionth time, though the first in weeks. 'I wanted to tell you. Something odd happened to me yesterday.'

One elbow is resting on the windowsill, and his other arm hugs its opposite shoulder. Teacher Ezekiel stands still, as though he is observing the window frame, or the exposed electric wiring, or the distempered walls. Or is it at the hills, the misty eventide hills, like traces of tidemarks, layer upon layer and against the sky, while a distant road winds and rises in the mist as into a future.

But Alfandary, the school janitor, comes in to ask for keys. Teacher Ezekiel does not linger to hear what happened to me yesterday.

Teacher Ezekiel does not turn back to me. Over there by his desk he squats. His pale-blue shirt is taut on his back, his belt almost snapping, as he slips a wedge of folded wastepaper under one of the legs of the desk, to stop it wobbling. And for some reason, seeing him so young, so well-knit, that which I have discovered in him flashes out and pierces me afresh. The wild cub fastened to my heart for many days now, whose claws are in my flesh, frets to rub, and strains at its ropes.

Last try. I went and stood beside him.

Teacher Ezekiel continues staring complacently at his desk's firmness. Fly, o bird, away to your mountains. But instead: 'Yesterday I was walking down the street,' I say, with lips that seem to be groping, to the back of the neck of the man pretending to be occupied with some meaningless task.

Teacher Ezekiel rests his hand on the flap of his desk, and straightens himself, non-committally.

But illusion has a sham sweet taste:

'I was wandering along the street,' I continued, and having
had no sign of encouragement I wasn't sure how to, 'and there
was a woman there, all untidy. Her head had recently been shaved,
and the hair was just starting to grow again, her clothes were
all in tatters, and her lips were very swollen. She was trying
to strike up a conversation with two small children, who looked
as though they were terrified of her. "I'm mad," she said to
them, like in confidence. "And she's mad, too." She pointed to
me, and I was amazed. I asked myself how she could have known.
But in fact, I was asking you. Because I had this urgent
feeling, the sense that this was in direct line with something
that turned topsy-turvy,' that how is it that I am here, for you
to notice me, and you don't, I wished to say but didn't, or did
I make it all up.'

'Make it up, make what up, little girl?'

'You ask make what up. That shows it is all made up.' My
spirits drooped.

And so the school year might have ended: teacher Ezekiel
clutching at the sides of his desk, his face the face of an enemy,
'I asked what you made up to avoid the question. You didn't
make it up,' he says, and I stare at him thunderstruck.

From that day onwards teacher Ezekiel has behaved as though my
place in class were empty. It would never have occurred to me,
not even in a dream, to tell him about my poem 'Dear Teacher'.
But it has happened, like this. It is during a lesson and I am
sitting listlessly, on my own in my place at the back of the
class. 'Rabbi Sa'adya Gaon was a very strong-headed man, which
did not make for an easy life,' teacher Ezekiel was declaring.
Idly, I try to sketch his features: the ears that seem attached
not quite in place, the lovely green eyes, clear, with a darker
rim round the iris. I try to capture them and fail. I give up
in despair. But to leave no room for doubt, I have written at
the top of the page 'Teacher Ezekiel,' unaware that the lesson
has ended, and that teacher Ezekiel has approached and is
standing over me.

'N'ima Sassoon, the bell has gone. Lessons are over.'

He had not spoken to me for many days, and now he was
speaking softly, leaning on the back of my chair, and on my
desk, inclining forwards a little, to look at my exercise book.
Hurriedly, I covered up my sketch, my handiwork, with both
hands. But teacher Ezekiel straightened up, reached out for the

exercise book and my hands fell away. Then, all shattered – and only because I felt all shattered – without knowing why or wherefore, I said:

'I submitted a poem to the school paper.'

Teacher Ezekiel, still examining the sketch, asked preoccupied: 'Was it accepted?'

'Mr Havdala liked it. The headmistress, too, stopped me and praised it. But, Teacher, the credit should not go to me. I had a very special subject. I called the poem "Dear Teacher".

At once teacher Ezekiel dropped my exercise book. He went back to his desk and gathered up his worksheets, his books and his registers, without lifting his head.

I followed him.

'And if you care to read the poem, you will see you are wrong about me,' I whispered.

I do not know whether it was my whispering which moved him. I do not know, indeed, what he meant when he answered: 'Maybe it's you who are wrong.'

'I wish it were,' I whispered, as he picked up his briefcase and fled.

A raised threshold, extended arches, each with the verse, 'For thy Law is my delight', in iron open–work, over an elongated Star of David, rivets in the shape of large–petalled flowers, fluted rods, and a kind of butcher's hook shaped like a clenched fist, as a knocker: the massive gate of our school. One of the doors in the gate, incredibly, is fitted with a hatch, that has a peephole. Like a toy broody hen, with a broody hen inside it, and, inside that, an egg.

We were standing, both of us, the next day, which was a Friday, at the bus stop by the gate. Teacher Ezekiel could not have known. As I watched him going out, striding, as he did, rather like a sailor, I summoned up my courage and went out in step with him. Now teacher Ezekiel had assumed the impatient look of someone waiting for the bus to arrive, and was lightly tapping his briefcase against his knees. But it looked as though a shadow was hovering round the edges of his mouth. He must have caught it from me. I was possessed, and my heart was pounding so much:

'Teacher,' I said, 'ever since yesterday I have talked nothing but rubbish to you, and I can only regret it. But now I would like to ask you a question. Just one. And you will tell me the truth, won't you?' And I let cross my lips the notion over which in class, and in my bed at night, I have been eating my heart out:

teacher Ezekiel is no longer concerned about me, he is concerned with Bathsheba. He always treats her so well. (The idea! Bathsheba is as black as the devil. And it wasn't Bathsheba that I wanted to talk about.)

Teacher Ezekiel looked quite taken aback.

'A new caper. Bathsheba Hayun is it? Why Bathsheba Hayun, of all people? What a surprise. As if things aren't complicated enough without that. No one gets special treatment. Neither Bathsheba Hayun, nor anyone else. Get this clear: there's no special treatment for anyone.'

'Why Bathsheba Hayun? I must be having hallucinations now. It must be my imagination.' I sighed and teacher Ezekiel gave me a brisk look. But I added, 'I've got another recurring hallucination. Generally, I know you're like everyone else, but sometimes – and this is the hallucination – I think you are different. Apart. Singled out. One more question. Please, just one. Tell me, teacher Ezekiel, are you really singled out?'

The last girls to leave were passing us. 'Yesterday I went to the pictures. All of a sudden, a tiger. It sees Jane. Jane starts saying, "The Lord–is–my–shepherd–I–shall–not–want. He-maketh–me–to–lie–down–in–green–pastures. He–leadeth–me–beside–the–still–waters . . ." Then suddenly: Tarzan. Leaps from the treetop on to the tiger's back. Strangles it. Jane puts her hand on the dead tiger, and says, "This fur coat." Tarzan says, "Coat. What–that?" Jane says, "Never mind. A barbarian trimming." Tarzan says. . . .'

As usual teacher Ezekiel, takes his time before answering.

'I don't think I'm singled out. But everyone is unique to himself. So I probably don't qualify as a witness.'

What was the spell cast over us at that moment. Like the innocent moon, waxing and rising. Generosity and goodwill surround us like shield–like. The heart rests from its battering. What was devoured is made whole. And for a moment it is as thought I too come near the secret which makes the faint–hearted heroic.

A street urchin blowing pan–pipes made of slate went past, stuffed the instrument in his pocket, and bent to pick up a cigarette end from the gutter. He stuck it in his mouth with a very grown–up air. In the distance we could see the bus approaching, lurching from side to side. And I said,

'Teacher, special treatment or not, for me you will always be, how shall I put it, one, unique, and I am so happy that I am lucky enough to know that someone like you exists. I don't know how to say it in words. So I tried to express it in writing.'

Till that moment I did not know whether I dared show him my exercise book of poems which I had brought for him. Now I propped my satchel against one of the doors in our school-gate, against the identical copies of a rabbinic proclamation, laid out in thickly clustered lines of print, like samples of type-face, all ranges, all sizes. A manifesto denouncing some distraceful conduct, terrible enough to make ears ring at the sound of it. And a condemnation: 'Their house is rich and nothing lacks/But mice will dance upon their backs.' I tried to unfasten the catch but could not manage it. I felt ashamed that he might notice my fingers trembling. Teacher Ezekiel smiled a little smile, and assuming I meant to take out my purse, rested his briefcase between his shoes, and opened my satchel for me. A joint enterprise. Like two people with a common purpose. But I took out the exercise book, and proffered it to him without looking at his face.

A father, on his way home, got off the bus, and halted. His small offspring was running to greet him, baring his chest that was spotted and scrawled over with a ball-point pen, exclaiming proudly, 'Look, tattoo!' I parted from teacher Ezekiel, and started making my way home on foot. The toddlers had moved on to the pavement out of the way of the bus, abandoning their dust castles that had matchbox balconies, and date-stones instead of flags, and approaches made out of wooden splinters laid out crookedly. One infant in a wooden crate was making believe it was a motor car, and his lips were working at the speed of electric fan blades. A schoolboy was bowling a hoop along, running after it. A young bride, in thick stockings, sleeves down to her elbows, her hair tied up in a kerchief, passed by, carrying a basket on her arm. Her face was freckled, and like milk. There was a light shining in her eyes. A little girl was carrying a broad tray on her head, with two Sabbath loaves and assorted pieces of dough on it, towards the bakery. She was taking a short-cut across an empty building site, that had only some derelict foundations on it, a signpost that a Talmudical College was shortly to be erected there, and piles of rubbish. A newspaper was fastened to the side of a kiosk by a drawing-pin, and a man drinking orange juice was standing reading it. Above the newspaper was pinned an announcement of a most sorrowfully arousing oration to be delivered at eight o'clock, European time, by an exalted member of the rabbinical court, at a memorial service for a distinguished rabbi who had been killed in a road accident. There was a sign saying, 'Ice Cream — Family Size — To Take Away.'

And on the marble counter, a picture of a red water melon, cut
in half. Beside it, like a reflection, a real red water melon,
halved. Behind my back I could hear: 'I met him on the street.
He said, "What's this, going about now without a hat?" So I
answered, "Just show me where in the Bible it says you must keep
your head covered." "Heretic!" he screamed', In a backyard
children were jeering, 'Run–away–cowardy–cow,' and a tearful
babyish voice cried, 'I'm not a cow.'

A delicatessen with cuts of cured beef, minced meat, potato-
salad, and borsch in tureens, in the open, sloping fridge in the
shop window. A small sign with an arrow, pointing to the public
baths. A large sign with an arrow, pointing to the charitable
institution of Rabbi Meir the Miracleworker. A greengrocer's.
Crates outside. Spinach leaves. The aroma of over–ripe bananas
with a hint of vanilla in it. The aroma of ripe melon and guava,
like sweat. A dumpy woman, holding a brown paper bag with pears
in it, and counting her money as though she were telling slanders.
Then suddenly workmen pounding at the pavement with pneumatic
drills. Their muscles jerking, as though in the throes of
seizures. And suddenly they break off. Men shouldering a load
that is visibly dear to them: an Ark of the Covenant. 'And
I'll tell you this: the boundary line between the tribe of
Benjamin and the tribe of Judah must have run along Jaffa Road,'
asserts one first lieutenant to another first lieutenant, 'that
is to say along King David Street, past Rosh Rehavia and the
Bezalel buildings, Mazkeret Moshe, Mahane Yehuda market, and
Jaffa Road as far as Mei Naphtoah. Romema was the highest point.
The Tenth Roman Legion, "Arteniz", was stationed where the
national Assembly Hall is now.' Through a barred window can be
seen a mysterious hall, looking most fitting for an orthodox
Burial Society. There is a black varnished grandfather clock in
there, with Hebrew letters instead of numbers, and a copper
pendulum.

A labyrinth of human nesting places. On lower, middle and
upper levels. With countless partitions, and outside stairways,
as steep as ladders. A burnished frying–pan rests on a window
sill. Hard, green tomatoes are ranged on a window sill. A
starched curtain is fastened with a light–blue ribbon. In the
darkness of a corridor gleams the red eye of an electric boiler.
An upper beam of a door with a plant pot hanging from it in a
cascade of violet–coloured leaves. On a sofa by a wall, a woman
is lying, with medicine jars and a glass and spoon on the radio
beside her. One door of the wardrobe is not shut properly, and

the girl at the table doing her homework is tucking her hair behind her ear. On a bench in front of a doorway a big girl is feeding a baby, who is darting out his lips like a baby bird. And now there is the Yemenite synagogue in a cellar: carpets striped in many colours, benches, cushions, and an old man snoozing, with a scrap of paper sticking to his cracked lip, while under the pierced beaten tin chandelier a small boy is waiting with infinite patience.

And I reflected: pick any street. Add some indefinable quality to it. Is it only by the power of sight – the vision of aspiration in eyeless things, humble things, struggling to be realised? I shall atone for them. And I reflected: an enchanting life. All in all, a mountain. Swarming with people, coming in and out like ants, making their living in the bowels of the earth. But each one of them knows: Jerusalem, thou that art builded as a city that is compact together – and it is Jerusalem where I am. How singular, how wondrous, how privileged. To be so close to the central pivot of things. What a rare privilege, indeed. Everyone senses the miracle in his heart. But I, please God, when I grow up, will find out how to describe this miracle, all the miracles, in writing. I have to. Otherwise, my life is no life.

On Sunday I set out early for school.

Coming through the wide, vaulted entrance hall, with its marble plaque in everlasting memory of the charity of the virtuous Mistress Estella Assa, blessed shall she be above women in the tents, who laid the foundations of and established this house as a sacred memorial to her righteous mother Mistress Sarah who perished in the earthquake, at Kirkagac, near the town of Ismir, there was my teacher Ezekiel at the other end of the corridor coming through a side door.

Seeing me, he veered into a small side corridor, and did not appear till the bell. Perhaps he had something to attend to there.

Lessons were over. Each girl had up-ended her chair on her desk. Everyone had gone.

'Teacher, about the poems. Forgive me, I did not know. This morning you seemed shocked, so to speak.'

Teacher Ezekiel turned to look at me, and stayed silent. And as if he had counted to ten, replied, like an actor who had rehearsed his part.

'Your poems. I started to read them. I must have read about two pages and then I fell asleep.'

I am not here, I told myself. I am on the distant road that
winds up to the hills. A pool of stagnant water, like a grey
lake, the colour of olive leaves. Rocks at the roadside.
Clefts in a tree trunk. Olive trees. The meagre strips of land
at the base of the hill are narrow furrows of ploughed, curving
lines. Low fences of heaped-up stones. Heavy clusters of dark
grapes swelling in the lap of the outspread, emerald leaves,
clinging to the wire. A mulberry tree. Dark cypresses. And it
is already autumn. The air is laden, glittering. There is a
mercury sheen on every thing. On the skyline there is a row of
aged pines, dishevelled, drooping. Their foliage touches the
sky. In the valleys the numbers of the turned-over fields
increase. I shall not see the standing corn. For I shall not
pass this way again. I shall no longer see Jerusalem. The road
winds up and up. Now there is a grey sky, with torn strips of
red and very dark grey in it. I am carried, as on an escalator,
towards a city. At the end of the street the sun was setting.
People were hurrying towards it. People were coming away from
it. As though they were coming away from a fire. I who am
being swept along at the edge of the pavement, have my hands
over my breast, like someone who has lost her child. Gradually,
the sky grew all lit up, spilling over the earth its blood-like
radiance. The radiance of the End of Days. Its thick glow
lasted a long time. Only the needling rows of the street lamps,
spaced out at neat intervals, like a coiling serpent of light,
pierced and wounded the russet glow. Until nothing remained
except the cloud stallions, galloping on two legs, across the
orange horizon. Now people's faces are draped with knotted
cloths to screen their eyes that have been watching. Then there
are no more people. Only the stallions of darkness, stallions
of the valley of the shadow, stallions of great gloom, stallions
of hail, stallions of iron, stallions of mist. The road ran
through winter, emerged and reached the bridges. It is noon.
And flames are rising and leaping from bridge to bridge, with
great smoke and swirling of hot ash. My hands are over my eyes.

By chance, was it, or was it absent-mindedness. Teacher Ezekiel
is sitting there eating his sandwich. Since morning, some of
his hair has shifted to the wrong side, and he looks as though
he's playing one of the early pioneers of the American West.
And in this novelty is an unlooked-for-freshness, charm. The
handsome cheekbones, the chin, look as though they have been
newly carved.

Someone comes up to him with her book. She tells him: 'Can't get the hang of this.' He takes out his pencil. Points to an earlier passage. 'And this, you get? Read it. See if you get this.' The patience, the impermeable remoteness. A man totally detached, governed only by hidden, unknown summons. How long ago had I once plucked up courage and said to him, blushing and helpless, 'Teacher, you should tell your barber from me to make a better job of it next time,' and he felt the back of his clipped head awkwardly and gave a little smile. Long, long ago. When he could still say, passing among the desks, and catching sight of the towering palace I had drawn in the margin of my exercise book: 'In an excellent neighbourhood. Comfortable three-roomed flat. Easy terms.'

I finished tumbling out the plum stones. I went back to my seat. Through the window came the counting up voices of the little girls, playing with skipping-ropes. Bathsheba came into the classroom, and began conferring secretly with the other girls. My heart flutters. It's about my poem. The chestnut, apricot and peach faces are assessing, examining, murderously. Now it occurred to me, even the headmistress had been speaking to me with great compassion, as though I were ill. And this morning, as she stood there with teacher Ezekiel, as I passed by them, she stared at me and at teacher Ezekiel, and again at me and at teacher Ezekiel. Only Mr Havdala is colour-blind. I folded my napkin. 'No, the wormwood tree is not a tree with worms', teacher Ezekiel was replying in the even-tempered voice. 'It's a kind of bitter herb. Well, then, why precisely worm-wood? I don't know. He is a writer. He writes what he feels like.' And he went on, 'We are concerned only with the idea.'

In the corridor I passed dear old Mr Havdala. Mr Havdala put his hand on my head. 'We must, and please God we will, send the poem to the papers, to the *Blast of the Ram's Horn*,' and talking to someone over my shoulder, he said with pride, 'The whole staff-room agrees. N'ima Sassoon is going to be a poet.' Now I could see who had been coming up behind me. It was teacher Ezekiel. But teacher Ezekiel did not reply, and walked on.

As soon as Mr Havdala let me go, I hurried after him. 'Teacher, I would like to talk to you.'

Teacher Ezekiel shook his head, refusing. He strode on, laughed, and said wildly gesticulating, unusually for him: 'What a morning. Like nothing on earth.'

'What does it matter, teacher,' I pleaded. 'Look. Just now when you laughed and talked with your hands, I didn't recognise you. You were like Bathsheba and the rest of the girls. You were like a man who is shown a picture of, let's say, a statue of Venus, and he giggles and points and says, "look, Venus isn't wearing anything." But that doesn't matter, either. And I told you, Mr Havdala and the headmistress spoke well of the poem. And that doesn't matter, either. It was nice to hear. But I only wanted your opinion, because, "they are tilled by light entering." Still, I'm not asking.'

'N'ima Sassoon. A girl, who is altogether too clever for me.' Now he stopped. Like a man carved out of chalk, like a pillar of salt, with white lips, and the shadow settled round his mouth, he said, 'Cleverness is a real virtue. But it's only one of many. And not one of the most important. And another thing, it isn't always easy to tell, even for you, when or why a man laughs. Besides, you keep pressing me to tell you something. You must see that I can't. I can't,' and here he rebelled, 'and I don't want to.'

Hurt and humiliated, my self-respect means nothing to me.

'Why?'

'Because it is not done,' he concluded. He pursed his lips.

A hard man. With an extraordinary gentleness. A hard man. Even in hell you would not burn.

'Fine,' I said. To my own astonishment, I pointed to the staff-room. 'You can go. You're free to go.'

'I go this way,' he said quietly, and pointed angrily in the opposite direction.

I did not stir. Teacher Ezekiel walked away. But then he stopped, turned his head, shot me a ferocious look, and walked on.

'Teacher,' I hurried after him, again, '"They are tilled by light entering the turf/And the turf does not know what's within." Oh, teacher.'

I do not know if he heard. Because while I was still speaking, he turned to me:

'Today, it's school. Tomorrow, life. Listen, and bear this in mind. Limits are set. We are not living in the days when there was no King in Israel, and every man did that which was right in his own eyes. A certain N'ima Sassoon, a certain Ezekiel Da Silva. Will they please stick to the rules. That's how it is here. And that's how we want it.' And he turned away.

Oh, my heart seethed within me. Oh, I told myself, if he should bring me my exercise book I would tell him, 'Do you see that dustbin over there — fling it in there.' Oh, I wish I had never written the poems, I told myself, and I couldn't hold back my sobs. The title of a play I had once seen advertised on a hoarding came back to me, *The Taming of the Shrew.* And the sleeve of a record album in a shop window, a picture of a whip decked with roses. Then, all at once, I was in alarm at a sudden recognition, as though plucked up by my hair and lifted on to another plane, my eyes struck by flashes of light. It has been spoken. The secret that makes the faint-hearted heroic. I already knew it. I have always known it. How could I not have known I knew it.

'And the Lord answered Job from the whirlwind . . . where wast though when I laid the foundations of the earth? declare, if thou has understanding. Who hath laid the measures thereof, if thou knowest . . . for who shut up the sea with doors, when it brake forth . . . the cloud the garment thereof, and thick darkness a swaddlingband for it. And brake up for it my decreed place, and set up bars and doors. And said, Hitherto shalt thou come, but no further: and here shall thy proud waves be stayed. . . . Where is the way where light dwelleth? and as for darkness, where is the place thereof. . . . That's how it is here. And that's how we want it.' With the terror of soaring, which for an instant was touch and go, the light that had once begun to break forth like the innocent moon, waxing and rising, now became a blinding glare.

Halfway along teacher Ezekiel stopped in his tracks. Swung round. Came back towards me.

What are the strings that keep tugging at us. He walked. I hurried towards him. He walked. Stopped. Walked. I did not stir. Hurried towards him. He stopped. He walked again. I stood still. He walked, then spun round again. Started coming back. What is the flute we dance to? Now he was standing still, not knowing what to say. Nor did I know what to say. I rubbed my eyes with my fist. Teacher Ezekiel looked at my new frock. 'You have got thinner N'ima Sassoon, you've lost weight,' he finally let out in a wretched voice, making for the staff-room, crest-fallen. I stood where I was, and saw him go in and sit down at the big table covered with a velvet cloth. He sat alone, apart, underneath the oil-painted mural, which showed the biblical tree that was pleasant to the sight with a scroll saying 'It is a tree of life for them who put their trust in it,' drawn like a curling ribbon below its roots. Someone was describing something. Someone said, 'Aspera Bré.' The books are locked up in a bookcase delicately wrought with iron: *The Duties of Hearts, the Book of Principles, The Correction of the Soul, Examination of the Universe.* Does anyone read them? on his own, teacher Ezekiel was toying aimlessly with the large, square, china ashtray, the one with the crest and inscription of the 'Palace Hotel' stamped on it in blue. He sat like someone on whose head the blow has finally fallen. His hair shifted to the wrong side now had a touch of mockery in it. Alfandary came in, bringing him a demi-tasse of Turkish coffee. Asleep among those who were awake, awake among those who were asleep, teacher Ezekiel worked his lips in Alfandary's direction, and without looking drew the demi-tasse towards him. But his hand did not let go of the ashtray, did not stop. Oh, don't dear teacher, please don't. There is an enormous wall of water sus-pended before the event, any event. Now suspended, now falling, this way or that. Which way has it fallen? A moment of birth. What has been born? And if all the sky were parchment, the whole world scribes, and all the forest quills, they could not write down all I have learned from my teachers. 'Albert, called the headmistress to teacher Albert, though she turned to look at the door. I quickly slipped away to avoid being seen. And the flute is still blowing. The spirit strives to follow, comprehend, the melody. My ring is in your nose, the bit is between your teeth, and still the spirit can only yearn.

He never gave back my exercise book. I do not know what became of it. Perhaps he burned it.

I bought a new one.

In the evening I draw a chair up to the iron table on the verandah. A most precious moon is travelling across the sky. Jerusalem slumbers. In me alone phantoms perform. Flying, they reel and wheel: image after image rises, and alters without sound, only with movement and gesture. They plead for their lives, for the stress, the dazzle, the glowing halo, the breath of life of the living, bleeding moment. To rescue it. To redeem it. In safe-keeping. Before everything vanishes, departs from the region of light to the region of darkness.

We have learned, over the bed of King David a lyre hung, and when midnight came the north wind blew and caused it to play by itself. And King David rose and immersed himself in the study of the Law till the morning star appeared in the sky.

But I, with a faltering pen, scribble down and stumble and start again.

'Our teacher, Mr Havdala, said among other things . . . .'

Translated by Arthur Jacobs

I take

shape on

the loom of

history

PEGGY PARNASS

CHILDHOOD

Of course I immediately said yes when asked to write about my childhood experiences. The way I always say yes too quickly when I feel tempted by the theme. Only afterwards did it occur to me that I never was a child. Probably now I've finally become one. Sometimes.

So, now I only have to consider this. Up to what point is one still officially a child? As long as one's mother is alive? Until one enters school? Until one sleeps with someone the first time? Until one carries responsibility for oneself and others?

I had to find some way to feed myself, and to some extent, my brother, since I was 14. Let's say I was a child until then. But, of course, that's nonsense.

My memories change from day to day, depending on my state of mind. Sometimes only a chain of nightmares. Or my heart is gripped with longing and desire and tears draw into my eyes. Either way, every memory is connected to Mommy. With her presence or absence. Unfortunately, in this area, nothing changes. Funny. On the one hand, never a child. On the other hand, never an adult.

*   *   *

She was small. With tousled curly black hair. Lots of hair. Usually in a knot, in order to look more mature and tidy. Gigantic grey eyes. A big nose. And lots of mouth. She always had nice smelling skin, because she always washed herself. We were very poor, and because of this, she had to wash herself at an ice cold sink, standing in the kitchen. Stone tiles. There she stood every morning and scrubbed herself from head to toe. And in spite of being so overworked, she had hands like lilies, because she greased them with Vaseline. Not even a cut on her fingers, even though she worked as a house cleaner. Her skin was soft all over her body. Her breasts too. Because there was meat on them. Quite round. Whenever I was especially good, I

90

was allowed to sleep with her, hiding away between her nice smelling breasts. I can remember no other feeling of security.

Mommy always thought that she wasn't pretty. Even though she was beautiful. Everyone who knew her says this. But it's not captured so well in pictures. Because you can't hear or smell her then. She would say, "I have legs like stovepipes." And she thought her nose was too big. I was supposed to be prettier. Mommy said, "Push your nose up so it doesn't become crooked." Which I did, but it didn't help. And my chicken breast chest from rickets, she couldn't manage to cure either.

Her laughter and her voice. We lived downstairs. Even from far way one could recognize our window sill. The only one in town which was scrubbed. Not at all like "dirty Jews." And you could hear her laughter even out in the street. A contagious lust for life filing the air, the way music from other apartments often floated outside. When I was outside and heard her laughter, I knew just how she looked. Her mouth was very big, from ear to ear, and her big eyes, small. And she cried just as loudly as she laughed. Only not that often. I probably only knew about it when it was loud. She didn't want sympathy.

Whenever Pudl failed to come home, she would always say that he'd be home any minute. And the next morning, that he'd already gotten up and left early. Even if he hadn't come home at all.

She was so soft and acquiescent. But once, when he stayed away three days and nights playing poker, she had a nervous breakdown. Lay on the couch for hours, on her belly, yelling and crying, and beat her feet and fists on the cushions. I knew I couldn't help her because it was HIM that she wanted. After that, I hated him for what he had done to her. When, finally, she nabbed him somewhere, I was there. He was ashamed as always and I said, "Pudl, you're a pig." I still regret it to this day. I insulted her love.

Pudl was a gambler. Poker was his main passion. Once he won a big goose. His face was beaming when he brought it home. That was a feast! But that, of course, didn't make up for his losses. Without effort, he ruined himself and everyone he knew. Like every gambler.

Pudl was a Pole. Even before he, as a Jew, was not wanted here – he, as a gambler, was labeled as an unwanted foreigner. He was small, slender, with many black curls. And an elegant moustache the entire length of his mouth. Not like Hitler's. A beautiful narrow face with high forehead and laughing eyes.

Nearly 30 years older than Mommy. A boy at heart, always with silly ideas in his head. Colorful and adventurous. Always ready for jokes. The hands so slender and sensitive, one would conclude that they were accustomed to instruments other than cards. But he was absolutely tone deaf. Sang heart-renderingly off-key.

An elegant figure, erect like a dancer.

He was very proud of me. Made me his accomplice in order to have a chance to show off with me. For example, when he did magic. At all the children's parties I was his assistant. But always, as if it weren't planned, but an act of God. With my help, he played tricks on all of our relatives and friends. He taught me to recognize the "letter-pictures" which were on all the cans in the kitchen. Whenever the house was full of visitors he would say off-handedly to me, "What have you read today?" When the others responded with, "That kid can't read!" he would say, "Of course she can!" And he proved it extensively in the kitchen.

We had a nice small front yard and somewhat bigger backyard. With homegrown flowers and a swing. Stupidly, Pudl had built a concrete sidewalk which passed under the swing. One summer day when he was out there swinging, as he liked to do, he fell over backwards on his head. Mommy threw herself over him crying as he lay there as if he were dead. When he finally regained con-sciousness, we had to swear not to tell anyone how the accident had happened. "I am a grown man. Just say that I fell from the shed."

I liked him the most when he came home. Mommy always waited for him feverishly. Even if he were gone for only two hours, or even one, she would tear open the door when he showed up and jump upon him with passion. She embraced him with arms and legs and they kissed and kissed until they were breathless. I liked that.

One night I slept with Mommy in the big wide bed. I cuddled myself up to her. We talked. We always talked. For some reason, I asked her where babies came from. She told me that everything was arranged nicely. That when two humans love each other, they want to be as close to each other as possible. And that it is very nice, because the man fits into the woman just like puzzle pieces fit together. She explained to me how the semen comes out and how it may or may not become a baby. I thought this was magnificent. And I saw a connection between what she told me and the affectionate kisses between Pudl and her. The next day,

on a walk with Uncle Heinerle, Uncle said, "Storks!" I looked.
"Those are the ones that bring little babies." Mommy and I
grinned at each other. We knew better. After a while, I couldn't
keep my mouth shut, as usual, when I happen to know something.
I said, "You know, Uncle Heinerle, you're a bit dumb and childish.
I can explain how it really is. It's not the stork at all." I
felt proud and happy.

I was also always a step ahead of my cousin, Ursel. I discovered the lies about the Easter bunny, Santa Claus and the
stork. I was able to disprove the lies of the adults. Because
she was like a twin sister to me, I was always in a great hurry
to rob her of illusions. But since I now know what effect this
had on her — I first learned of this as an adult — I'll be damned
if I'll talk people out of their beliefs.

When I was little, and still believed in God myself, my evening prayer was, "Dear God, make me stupid. It hurts so much
to think." Even now, I wish more and more often that I could
just stop thinking for awhile.

I'm sure my parents tried to protect me like other parents
do. Both of them loved me. And they wanted the best for me.
But they both failed. Pudl blessed me very day, putting his
hands on my head. And told me, every day, that a Jewish girl has
to be clean, upright and honest. And smarter than all the others.
And that when I grew up I had to marry a Jew, not a Gentile.
When it came out in the open that a "molester" had touched and
caressed me with my permission (I agreed, if he would tell me
all his experiences with women), Pudl wanted to beat me to death.
Mommy threw herself between us. Then Pudle tore up a portrait
of me instead. The one of me in a poodle–cap which he had always
said was "so life–like." When my brother, Buebchen, wanted to
kiss me, Pudl said, "Don't. She's poisoned."

Mommy always wore very soft dresses. From the smooth fabric
one can find again today at second–hand stores. Over this, she
always wore a white starched apron. On a daily basis, I drove
Mommy into despair with my unwillingness to eat, my inability to
eat. An hour before mealtime, I already had cramps from fear.
Every meal lasted forever, because I didn't finish it. Afterwards
I always threw up. The skinnier I got, the more butter she put
in. She would sit beside me at the edge of the table and sigh,
"The poor children in China would be happy to have a quarter of
your nice meal." Then I would respond, just as sadly as she,
with, "Me too, Mommy. Me too."

Over and over again I was sent to recovery homes. At one

place I was terribly homesick. There I threw up into my plate, because I was not allowed to leave the table. The nurse then forced me to eat my vomit. Like a perpetual motion machine – eat–vomit–eat–vomit – until even the pedagogue tired of this tactic. Another time I was hospitalized for six week with whooping cough. There they taught me not to throw up anymore. But before this was successful, I hid the chamber pot full of vomit far under the bed in terrible fright. I don't remember how they got rid of my addiction to throwing up. But until this day, despite how sick I feel, I can't bring myself to throw up. Not even with a finger down my throat.

I was then sent to a children's hospital in order to regain my strength. It was like a Zauberberg for kids. Everyone was nice. On a thin slice of butter bread they put chocolate chips as an enticement. I could see through their methods, but I didn't mind because I like sweets. And still do. The nurse was very proud when, in front of Mommy and Pudl, I could be seen eating bread and chocolate.

Mommy also found work as a cook in Jewish summer camps. Almost everything was fun there. Except for when it was time to eat. When all the other kids were done and gone, I would still sit there and cry into my dish. Again, a professional decided to intervene and I was locked in the dressing room with my full plate of casserole. Mommy was weak and outranked. She didn't let me out. She didn't knock in the door to free me. She only cried loudly outside while I cried inside. She sobbed, "My kitten I beg you, eat, so they let you out again."

I wished she had been stronger. But if she had been, she probably wouldn't have been so nice and soft. Later, when she was more mature, she put herself on the spot for others. I know this from a few Warsaw survivors. Anyway, today I really like to eat. Since a couple of years. But before, I was always proud to be able to survive without food, sleep or john. Felt independent because of it. In times of no money it was an advantage for me. It's good not to miss what you haven't got.

My jealousy stayed a problem. Because of my brother, Buebchen, I nearly had a fit. He lay there bald–headed and ugly and kicking his legs. "How cute, how cute!" yelled the relatives, in spite of knowing that he had messed up Mommy's breast, it was inflamed and Mommy screamed like hell from the sharp pain. So I lay beside the crib and kicked my legs too. "Get up, what is this nonsense!?" my aunts said then. I would have liked to smash my brother against the wall.

When we and Pudl were arrested, my pretty Aunt Bertie was
allowed in for a last visit. I couldn't believe my eyes. She
said goodbye to Pudl with a real kiss. Very long and right on
the mouth. And her eyes were closed as she squeezed right up
next to him. I still resent her for that. Recently, I asked her
if they had been in love with each other. She said no. But that
kiss was too long!

Mommy was allegedly kissed in similar manner. When she was
fifteen or sixteen in a youth group. By Uncle Heinerle, the pig!!
He did it to show off. Was already 18 and had a girlfriend.
That's what one likes!

Later she was kissed by another. When she was eighteen. He
was married and never heard from again. Mommy stuck her head in
the oven with the intention of killing herself. Was saved, let
herself be seduced by Pudl, and had me. And then, she died with
him. She didn't really get arrested, because she wasn't registered. She strongly insisted to be taken too. I think what she
did was right. Even though it would have been better if they
had resisted.

Mommy, who was released again against her will, read Pudl's
letters to me. There was a lot about a 13-year old girl on the
long transport to Poland. And that she was allowed to talk to
Pudl the whole time. That she was a pretty girl. And very
smart.

I could never forgive that girl for being able to talk constantly to Pudl. Especially, when Mommy cried for him. Even
when Mommy read to me that she did not arrive in Poland alive.
She, like so many others of this transport, was killed at the
border.

The Nazis were all around us. I can't understand how Kies-
inger and others could overlook them. Every day I saw something
and was scared stiff. Uncle Leo came home from prison, his whole
head covered with a white bandage, like a mummy. It was horrible,
but I would really have liked to know just what they had smashed
under it. But we were not allowed to ask, because he was not
allowed to talk. When Buebchen turned two, the other kids threw
him down on the street and jumped up and down on him. Punishment
for being a Jew. At the time, he had an abundance of white-
blond curls and was a hundred times lovelier than all the others.
Once they taught him a poem against Jews. He proudly recited it
for Mommy. The kids pulled me into an unfamiliar stairwell,

pushed me against the wall and yelled in a chorus something about Jews' blood, which spurts from a knife. Until grandfather rescued me.

In summer, every day was a nightmare. There were signs everywhere about what we were not allowed to do, but we did it anyway. Sat on a park bench even though "Forbidden for Jews" was printed right on it. Then sat there as if our behinds were baked on to it. Too scared to get up again. Went with Mommy to get ice cream in a double waffle. Also forbidden. Unable to lick, because of fear. With Mommy, Buebchen, Ursel and Guenther to the swimming pool in Fuhlsbuettel during a heat wave. Getting in was easy, as everyone was pushing forward. Ursel and Guenther were redheads anyway. Buebchen and I blond. And then toward closing time it became emptier and emptier. We could only think about Mommy's black curls and that everyone could see that we were Jews. Mommy became very pale and was too scared to go through the exit. The fear grew and grew, because we knew that sooner or later we would have to go out right past the restriction sign. Nothing happened to us. But we felt sick the rest of the night and wished we hadn't gone swimming at all.

I was sent away again for a few weeks. Our teacher walked with us through the forest. Through some bushes we discovered a gang of boys in the Hitler Youth. The kind we knew from the city, where they often threw stones at us. We and the adults threw ourselves to the ground and hid, as in a jungle war. I nearly choked from lack of air – I was too afraid to breathe.

When there was a violent knocking at our door in the darkness of late autumn around five in the morning, even I knew it was the police. I couldn't bear to see how Pudle tried to show those idiots his WWI medals. There were so many medals. He kept them in a wooden box. He opned it and displayed it to them. He couldn't believe that it didn't change anything. It hurt me to see how they treated him. Oddly enough, my fear had disappeared.

It hurt me even more when the milkwoman slapped Mommy's face. Only because she wanted to get something for us to eat. I got slapped too. Then she and her husband lifted Mommy up and shoved her up and out the stairs. I felt responsible for her and was very ashamed because I was unable to help her.

I am also ashamed because she is dead.

*　　*　　*

I can't recall that I played very much. Except for marbles,
which I knew how to play very well. And rollerskating. Bent
down with one leg pushed out. It was called drive-a-cannon. But
my favorite game was "story-ball." You stand against a wall and
throw a ball against it. With the head, breast, behind the back
and under the leg. There were some kids who could do it again
and again with their head, without touching the ball with their
hands. Your turn lasted until you missed the ball. The whole
time one would tall a story which one made up on the spot. I
was allowed to drop the ball very often, because I told such
exciting stories. Usually about love. I always wanted to become
a journalist and an actress. Would call myself Chaplina, because
I loved Chaplin so much.

Pudl always promised me a piano and a pony "as soon as I
win." Of course, nothing ever came of it. But I thought it was
very nice that he wanted to give me these presents anyway. Yet,
where would we have put the pony in our small, clammy apartment?

I also like to play run-away. To run away with Buebchen and
my cousin Ursel without knowing where. And very far away, until
we reached a meadow. We would lie there amidst the wild flowers
and invent horror stories. That is, I would make them and the
others would cry out of fear. When Buebchen and I were new in
Stockholm we really got lost. Without wanting to. We didn't even
know one word of Swedish. Only toward evening did some people
bring us back to our foster parents, whose address we didn't even
know. Only their names. They were Danish Jews. A loud man,
who squeezed me – just for fun – until I turned blue, and a tall
woman with shiny red hair. An opera singer. She constantly played
"Fur Elise," dadadada-dada-dada-dam .... I thought they surely
would have called the police and that they had been looking all
over for us. That when we returned they would yell and scold
and maybe even beat us. But it was even worse. They hadn't
noticed that we were gone. It was then I knew that we were alone.
Once and for all.

My fear of separation almost drives me crazy. There are so
many memories I can't suppress. First. In a hospital once. Mom
and Pudl were not allowed in when they visited me. Could only
press their noses flat against the separating glass of the
window. The danger of being contagious. When they left I couldn't
run after them. And we couldn't touch each other.

Second. The separation from Pudl. After our arrest we were
loaded onto an animal truck along with other Jews. Were slowly
driven through the streets. People looked out of their windows.

People looked away. People walked behind us laughing. Pudl says, "Stand as much as you can on the outside. They must see what happens to children here." "I am not at all embarrassed, I am not at all embarrassed," I told myself from checkpoint to checkpoint. One policeman cried. Head on the table. With a banana beside him. Then we were unloaded into a gymnasium, where most of the Jews fell to their knees and prayed to God. I thought the grown-ups were really rather stupid. It was clear to me that a dear God would never let something like this happen. Wished I were a grown-up. Though then I would resist. Because there were many more of us than there were guards. At some point Pudl told me to say Papa to a stranger, to walk out naturally with him, to look cheerful and not to turn around. If only I would have turned around. I never saw Pudl again. The SS guards at the exit were obviously kid lovers. They lifted me up and wanted to know what the name of the cute little girl was. Once again, I feared I would throw up. Directly down on them. And thus reveal myself. The stranger gave me tram money, put me on the tram and said, "Go to the next Jewish orphanage."

There was a reunion. Cousin Ursel, my innocent twin, lay in bed like a stone when I crawled up to her two days later. She constantly repeated, "I know you're not here, you're dead."

Third. When Pudl remained under arrest and we were back home again. We knew he was in Poland. But still, whenever a bicycle rang out on the street, Mom nearly fell apart. Pudl always rode a bike and rang when he was home.

Fourth. How we were sent to Sweden along with other children. Mom brought us to Hamburg's main train station. Ever since, I hate this particular station even more than all the others. I can't look at trains without feeling sick. Mom said she would follow in six months, but that was nonsense, of course. Even though she knew she would never see us again, she stood there and laughed. Her beautiful laugh with the wide open mouth. She waved until we could no longer see her. So the goodbye wouldn't be so hard on us. Didn't make much difference. No, not true. Did make a difference.

Fifth. When Buebchen and I were separated after our first common foster families. Buebchen stopped eating all together. If he hadn't been only four years old, one would have called it a hunger-strike. When, after four months, we met again, he had lost his speech too. Where he was staying no one spoke German, and no one bothered to teach him Swedish.

Sixth. I stayed with 12 different foster families. Buebchen, first with four different families, and then, five years at a Catholic orphanage. That was really the shits. I was only allowed to visit him every second Sunday for two hours, and I loved him desperately. I received 20 Oere a week pocket money, which added up to about a nickel. I mostly spent it on bonbons. I cut them into four pieces so there would be plenty, and brought them along. I was always on the verge of exploding when I sped up those stairs to the fourth floor. I never knew if I would be let in. There she stood, as big as a house — this woman of Satan — with her arms stretched out to each side. That is, she held onto both sides of the door jam in order to block the way. And stared down at me as I shrank smaller and smaller under her glare. I was already very small anyway. She always kept up this torture for at least five minutes. Only then would she open her mouth and coldly ask, "What do you want?" Then, I had to respond, "I want to visit my brother." By then Buebchen was already in the hall-way crying and calling my name. She would then very slowly step aside, or say, "It is not possible." "But why?" Triumphantly, she would then say, "He's sick." "What do you mean, he's standing right there." "You heard what I said, he's sick."

Seventh. When Buebchen and I were new in London. I already knew English. But he didn't know a word. I took him with me into the Hades of the underground. We enjoyed every second we were able to be together. But here too, at first, we didn't live together, but in separate Jewish orphanages. Only later could we be together. Uncle's house was still in ruins from the bombings. We held onto each other very tightly when we were together. But in the shoving and pushing at the subway, he was pushed in and I was shoved out. The doors closed. I saw Buebchen, so tiny, eyes open wide in fear. Under the blonde curls, his open mouth. I pan-icked. Ran crying from one supervisor to the next. They called around and I was able to embrace him again at another station. You wouldn't believe how we cried. What luck that he didn't fall out of the train. Or hadn't gotten lost in the city of millions. These panes of glass which separate people. Like in court. Later, I had to deal with even more unbreakable glass.

Eighth. In Stockholm I kept everything which was holy to me — all letters and pictures of Mom — in a shoebox. Also the five postcards from the Warsaw Ghetto. All written on the same day. When they had to leave for Auschwitz. It was like one-last-call-from-the-window during a fire. Written in gigantic letters: GOOD BYE. SHALOM. WE LOVE YOU. WE ALWAYS THINK OF YOU. BE

BRAVE AND NOT SAD. Often during the day I would pet and kiss
everything in the box. Then our gardian, Farbror Sigge, said,
"You're becoming depressed," and burned the box and all its
contents.
Alarmed by this loss, for years I carried all my pictures around
with me from morning to night — first in big bags and later in
suitcases.

*   *   *

    I was also a frequent cause of embarrassment to Mom. The
first time was when Urselchen made me mad. It wasn't her fault.
She didn't do anything. It just infuriated me that everyone
thought she was so nice. No wonder. She really was nice. And
my best friend on top of it. I blamed her for the naivete which
always made her more cheerful than me. Happy, round face. She
hated her beautiful red hair. In order to pull a fast one on her,
and God, I begged in my most charming voice, "Dear God, poor
Urselchen is so unhappy because of her ugly red hair. Because
she's my favorite cousin, I want to free her from this burden.
Dear God, give me her ugly red hair forever and give her my
beautiful hair." Only I knew about this hypocrisy. But after
waiting and waiting in vain for my hair to turn red, my rage
only grew toward the innocent Urselchen. The adults laughed and
talked in the other room. Urselchen and I were playing as darkness fell in the kids' room. It was then my evil plan took form.
I went pee-pee in the chamber pot, as much as I possibly could.
Took the beautiful new ball and said, "Urselchen, throw the ball
into the air, no not there. No, here!" And Urselchen said,
"but then it will fall into the pot."
    "Who cares, Urselchen, maybe it will, maybe it won't — hurry
up, come on, throw it!" When I failed to get the proper Urselchen
to go along, I angrily snatched the ball from her hands, dunked
it to the bottom of the chamber pot, and yelled, "Eeek, Mommy!"
With outstretched arms, holding the ball disgustedly with only
my fingertips, I walked towards the grown-ups, "Eeek, Yuck, how
disgusting, look what Urselchen did." And because she denied
it, everyone got on her case. She was scolded, spanked and sent
out of the room. Mommy was the only one who didn't believe me.
"Tell the truth, Kitten. If you tell a lie, a light lights up
your brow and shines right through the keyhold of the locked
door." In a dark room with the door closed, Mommy went on as if
conjuring up spirits. "Tell the truth and nothing will happen

to you." I confessed then and there, because I believed in the glow of the magic light and because I always wanted the truth. Mommy kept her word, but Pudl beat me for the first time. Because of this sordid incident, I felt ashamed throughout my whole child- hood, and still later, and I tried hard to iron things out.

Then my first day of school turned out to be a disaster for Mommy. She had given me a dress for my birthday. When I came into my room it was hanging on a cord as a surprise. This is what I wore. She put my long hair into ponytails. And I wore glasses. All of a sudden I had become cross-eyed. But she cured me with the glasses. I have a picture of it. I really look like a four- year-old professor.

All the parents and children were in the classroom. Soon the teacher asked, "Can one of you children sing a little song?" Immediately, I was at the front of the class, in a good mood and singing bass, "A fart fell from the roof top, and broke its back today. A lot of farts came running, and took the Stinker away." The teacher said, I'm sure you must know some other songs, my child." So I sang, "This is the love of the sailors, in the long run for love I thirst, oh my dear, my pants will burst." And when the teacher tried to stop me again, "Don't Sail into the Wide World Sailor," and "A Voyage on the Sea is Fun," . . . "And the cook in his cabin, was a hell of a swine. He spit in the veggies, and vomited in the wine." I knew these songs from my half-brother, Herli, who was a sailor. In fact, an officer. He had just left for Palestine. Mommy was so embarrassed, she ran out of the class- room. I was sorry I had disappointed her so much. I knew many other songs which she had taught me and I could have sung some of them. "Have you up there forgotten me and my heart that LONGS for love?" . . . and the tango, "Oh Donna Clara I saw you dancing and your beauty drives me insane" . . . and "Father, mother, sister, brother — I have got no more." Mommy had such a beautiful voice. And then this.

She was also good at writing poetry. Especially for birth- days. She was able to do a lot. Even delivering newspapers at night. Sometimes, I was allowed to accompany her. As I've already said, she had house cleaning jobs. These people naturally, were quite wealthy, and, I'm sure they were quite nice. In Sweden, I was invited once to the birthday party of a very dear lady, who had emigrated there. She had a beautiful, spacious apartment and the most delicious food to eat. A guest asked me, "Hey kid, how did you end up here?" Just as I responded very happily, "I was invited. This is a friend of my Mommy's," the hostess was

101

standing right behind us. She corrected me with a frosty smile, "Your Mommy was not my friend, she was my housekeeper."

As if one excludes the other. The party was spoiled from that moment on. Because she had slighted Mommy in front of the others.

*   *   *

I also hated a lot of people. First, the offenders. Then, the victims who didn't resist. In Sweden, all 12 foster parents. Their kids. Their different habits and intimacies. Their friends and relatives. I still don't know what was worse — their indifference or their occasional odd attempts at showing an interest in me. They were a motley group — Russians, Danes, Swedes, Jews, Nazis — it didn't matter. I hated them all. Because they were not my Mommy. And they acted as if they could take her place. My most intense hatred was for the director of Buebchen's orphanage. And my skin crawls even when I think of her. Aunt Lisa was her name. What a gentle name for such a tough woman. Whenever I was allowed inside the orphanage, we tried to hide ourselves away. Then we would tell each other everything that had happened in the meantime. And for telling me what went on, he was often beaten. Three times I was able to kidnap him. Said insolently that we had an appointment with our guardian. One time we watched Snow White at the children's performance. By Walt Disney. And once a man invited us both into a coffee house. For a piece of real cake. Another time we went to the amusement park. Someone invited us to go on a merry-go-round ride.

And there was a DANSBANA, a wood dance floor built out in the open air, where people danced to the music of a band, even during the day. We danced so wildly with each other that we became dizzy. Every time we got caught. And every time Buebchen was beaten. Even though I was the instigator. And every time I swore to kill that dirty sow, as soon as I was big enough. I saved my money for a long time in order to buy Buebchen a red fire engine for his birthday. He had never seen anything that nice in his whole life. It had a very long ladder, and was big and unbelievably red. I gave it to him. He couldn't believe it. I couldn't believe it either. We were both enraptured. And then the dirty old hag came and took the fire engine away, saying, "This is too good for you." Then she put it on top of a wardrobe closet. Visible. For two years he could see it there, but was never allowed to play with it. One day he came home from school.

During the day the orphanage also served as a kindergarten. She
had taken down the fire engine and given it to the kindergartners
to play with. They demolished it immediately. Oh! It was awful.
All those years, I only waited to grow up and take revenge on
this woman. Then I came back, grown up, impressive, a world
traveler in the meantime, London–Hamburg–Paris, experienced and
chic. No one could get in my way. I was as hard as steel. I saw
the old woman. Wrinkled, bitter. Saw her loneliness. Thought,
she was probably already menopausal even back then. Never loved,
for good reasons. And I couldn't do anything to her. Just
turned and walked away. With weakness in the knees and unrequited
hate.

It was the same with the milkwoman who had slapped me and my
mother in Eimsbuettel. I hated her too and wanted revenge. I
forced myself into her store. The woman stood there. In earlier
years she had had shiny red hair — the only thing beautiful about
her. I just stood there leaning against the wall so I wouldn't
fall over. Didn't say a word. Just looked at the woman. Non
stop. And she served one person after another. Finally, things
just dropped out of her hands. Grey in the face, she said she
thought she was seeing a ghost. She thought I was Mommy. And
after she recovered she was finally realizing I was the child,
and no ghost, she said, "And how often, how often, have I thought
about your dear mother. Oh. Oh God, I've thought, such a dear
woman."

Yes, even then, I walked out. Wretchedly sick. But not even
these two times was I able to throw up.

Translated by Patricia Estrada and Iris Wesselman

AN ENCOUNTER

At Tubbs, Duncan and Osburn we had a rota for working on Saturday mornings, so that there were always two architects in the office. On this Saturday I had just finished my work and walked down High Holborn looking for an Italian restaurant where you could get a big helping of Spaghetti Bolognese quite cheaply. I sniffed the slightly dusty air and relished the atmosphere. Everything in London was new, very interesting and hopeful. I did not in least expect the extraordinary encounter that was to happen. There were the rambling half-timbered buildings and the shabby little bistros. There were the newspaper vendors who would go off for a drink or a snack whilst customers left their pennies for the papers on a box. There were the little horse-drawn carts with their carved, brightly painted wheels. The fruit and vegetables were laid out on green 'grass' matting. The men walking beside their little horses would call out their wares in melodious calls that differed little from the 'Street Cries of London' of the 16th Century. There was dust, there was untidyness, there were some shabby buildings, but High Holborn was on a human scale. The Prussian militarism was absent.

Outside the little Italian restaurant that I was aiming for, there was a newspaper vendor who sold papers in many languages. I studied the headlines, but did not buy a paper. With my weekly salary of three pounds and an uncertain future I had to be very careful with money. I was on the point of going in when a gaunt man in a well worn, long, German-looking raincoat barred my way. He stood with his back to me in the doorway of the crowded, dark and noisy eating place evidently trying to find an empty table. His coat pockets were stuffed full with newspapers, English and German. He turned around and I saw a face that was familiar. I knew him, but could not place him. The face was thin and pale. Then suddenly I recognized him. The man I had known in another world had had a full, healthy face, he had been well fed, well dressed in a smart uniform, holding himself very erect and wearing highly polished black boots. He recognised me at once:

"Marianne, Marianne Löhnberg! What are you doing in London?"

"And you?" I did not address him by his Christian name, "What you doing in London?"

"Marianne, have you eaten? No? I was just going to have some spaghetti. . . ."

"So was I."

"Can you, would you care to join me? Would you mind? Would you sit at the same table as I? But maybe you were meeting someone?"

"Thank you very much, I will — if we can find a table, but there is no need to invite me, I will join you all the same."

He laughed.

"And I will not get into trouble for being seen with you!"

"I notice you are laughing," I said, "I don't think I have ever seen you laugh before. . . ." His face fell, he sighed.

"My problems are not over yet. . . ." He sighed again as we found a small, rickety table in a corner. Still amazed, I studied his face. It was Christopher Alberts all right, but he had changed. Sharp lines were running down beside his mouth, he looked thinner, his skin greyer, less healthy, his suit hung loosely about him, his coat was shabby and not quite clean. Yet he seemed more relaxed.

We had known each other in another world, when I had been a student of architecture in Berlin in 1934. The professor of Building Construction, Jobst Siedler, had appeared with a swastika on his lapel the day after Hitler had come to power, yet, to my surprise, he was one of the two professors who continued to greet me. No one else dared to acknowledge me any more in 1934; only Professor Hans Poelzig and Professor Siedler continued to greet me, even when other staff or students were present.

One day, I met Siedler in the corridor. He looked around to make sure no-one was in sight, and then beckoned me to follow him into his own room.

"Tell me, Fräulein Löhnberg, are you allowed to continue with your studies?" I could feel my throat tightening. Clutching the corner of his desk, I tried to prepare myself for the blow that would follow.

"All right," he said, "I won't bite you, I only wanted to know whether you had been allocated a place to work at your thesis?"

"No, I haven't, I did not like to ask for one especially."

"Your people don't live in Berlin, you live in digs, don't you?"

"Yes, I have digs in Uhlandstrasse."

"Well look," he said, "I have a nice studio, plenty of room, plenty of books. You can let me know what further books you want from the library and I'll get them for you. You can work in my studio in peace until you have finished your thesis."

"Run along now," he added as I seemed to sniff from a sudden cold, "And no word to anyone, mind you."

A few days later I entered the cool, dark ground floor of Siedler's house. He opened the front door himself, a dark thick-set man with a fleshy face, and greeted me without shaking hands. He explained the way to the studio on the top floor, where I was to work on my thesis for the next few months.

"You will find my assistant working there," the professor told me. "He's a quiet man and will not bother you. He will give you the necessary drawing materials, and you may also borrow any of my books in the studio." I thanked him and walked up several flights of stairs, my books and rolls of drawings under my arm, grateful to Siedler for offering me this facility. The room I rented at the time did not have a desk big enough to accommodate a large drawing board, nor was the chair of the right height. In the winter it was never warm enough and there was not enough room to lay out drawings.

Siedler had written a very good book about building materials but he was not a good lecturer. Hearing his monotonous voice drone on and on during the warm weather made it very hard for his audience not to fall asleep. What would have happened if, one fine summer's day, he had found his entire audience asleep? My thesis did not concern him, but final year students were usually allowed special working facilities in the college. By now I found it unbearable to live in complete isolation, for wherever I went or sat in a lecture theatre there was a silent empty space around me. In the college, none of my former friends and associates dared to speak to me, or even smile or be seen near me. No one had told me where I might work in the college, nor had I asked for a place. I avoided lectures and seminars as far as I dared, and worked on my own as far as possible.

On the fourth floor there were two adjoining studios. The door between them stood open to let air pass through. In front of me a beautiful large drawing board was set out, freshly covered with clean white paper. Beside it was a set of fine drawing instruments. One other place at the far end of the light, spacious attic was occupied by a tall solid-looking fair-haired man, who just glanced at me, grunted something and continued to work in silence. There was quite a good library along one of the walls, which included Siedler's own books on building construction.

I was deeply immersed in my work, when the man got up, glanced at me without curiosity, threw on his jacket and cap and left for lunch. I realised now why he had not said a single word to me — he wore the uniform of a high ranking officer of the S.A.

Coming back from lunch, he just cleared his throat and then went over to his drawing board. I could not afford a restaurant lunch and had bought some rolls and milk in a shop nearby, which also saved me time. I was anxious to complete my thesis as soon as possible for the doors of the college might be closed to me at any time. They had already closed on all non-Aryan students, except for Liesel Oppenheimer and myself.

I worked in complete silence in the studio for a week or more. Neither Professor Siedler nor any member of his household ever came up. The telephone and his own studio were on the ground floor. Only occasionally would he speak to the S.A. officer on the house telephone, and the man would quickly put his jacket on, clear his throat and go down to the ground floor for a consultation.

On his return he had to pass my drawing board and on one occasion I was busy mounting some ink and wash drawings of village churches. He stopped and looked at my drawings with sudden interest. He looked at me, obviously very embarrassed. I looked at him and could not help grinning at his embarrassment, it all seemed so ridiculous. He grew crimson, swallowed hard and went back to his drawing board without a single word. An hour or so later he suddenly turned round and asked me in an unnecessarily loud voice what I had made those drawings for. I explained that I had made a study of the development of village churches in Western Germany. I had given lectures about it and was going to submit a set of my drawings with my thesis. As it turned out, he too was very interested in village churches and had made a similar study of the brick-built churches in Mark Brandenburg. The following day he brought me his notes to read and a set of quite first-class photographs of gothic brick churches. He came over to my drawing board, spread his photographs on it, and we were engaged in a very lively discussion, when Professor Siedler suddenly stood behind us. He joined in my admiration of the fine photographs and disappeared as suddenly as he had come. The S.A. man went back to his board, but the silence was broken. We both worked hard, but now we also talked. We talked a great deal. After a few days,when he had put his jacket on to go to lunch, he suddenly clicked his heels together, made a smart bow

and introduced himself as Christopher A...... I told him my
name was Marianne Löhnberg. Again blushing crimson, he asked me
whether I would do him the honour of being his guest for lunch.
This was extremely awkward for me. I had been given notice of
the withdrawal of the scholarship I held: Jews were no longer
eligible. The scholarship had also entitled me to free lunches
and teas at the Academy of Fine Arts and I had had to surrender
my free tickets: Jewish and Negro students could no longer eat
there. I rarely had a proper meal, and was usually hungry. I
would have loved a good meal, but I shuddered to think what might
happen to an S.A. officer if he was discovered to have invited a
Jewess for a meal.

In June that year (1934) Roehm, a leader of the S.A. together
with his political friends, other Nazi party members, members of
the Reichswehr and hundreds of people who were regarded by the
S.S. as dangerous, unreliable or simply as inconvenient, had
been rounded up during the night and shot on Hitler's personal
orders. I had been an unsuspecting witness of some of these
executions one early morning – the shots were still ringing in
my ears. I apologised to Christopher A. for not accepting his
lunch invitation. It would be too risky for him, I said, if we
were seen together in a restaurant. He stared at me with a very
odd expression, as if he was seeing me for the first time and
could not believe it. He threw on his officer's cap, turned
smartly and left the studio without another word.

When he returned in the afternoon, he seemed changed.

"I had some wine," he said, "wine, women and song, what else
is there left in this damned, bloody, lousy life."

"I am not a woman," I said, "I am a Jewess – what you call
vermin."

"Don't talk to me like that." He barked at me. I suddenly
flared up in a rage I could not control.

"I am responsible for all the unemployment, I am responsible
for the treaty of Versaille, I am responsible for every single
crime committed in this country – isn't that what you say?"

"Well," he said, still annoyed, "There are quite a few Jews
in Germany, you are not the only one."

"No," I retorted, "I am not quite alone, there are a million
or so Jews in Germany, but there are 65 million Germans and you
tell me that the Germans are the most superior race there is,
and yet those few Jews are responsible for 6 million unemployed,
for all the misery, crime and violence there is in Germany. If
I have committed a crime, if any other Jew has committed a crime,

why don't you put us in court and give us a proper trial? Let everyone hear the evidence, let everyone hear the prosecution, let everyone hear the defence." He tried to interrupt me, but the torrent of words would not be halted.

"I am a young girl and have to read every day the vilest insinuations and accusations against me and my fellow Jews. But there is never a proper trial in a court of justice such as every civilised country accords to the worst criminals. Why not? What is happening in the Law Courts, why are judges escaping from Germany? Why has a distinguished German judge committed suicide?"

"Wait a moment," he called out, "Surely that is not true. I have never heard of a Germany judge committing suicide."

"Oh yes, it is true, remember Dr. Arnold Freymuth, president of the Senate, a leading lawyer? You know the name? Well, he was a close friend of my father. He and his wife fled to Paris and there they committed suicide. He left letters to say that he despaired of the possibility of justice in Nazi Germany." (The Senate was one of Germany's highest Courts, and Freymuth was famous for his absolute impartiality and wide learning.)

"I know several artists and scientists, who have left Germany for good, although they are not Jewish, because as one writer put it, 'Germany is sinking into barbarism.'"

"I didn't know that, I haven't heard anything about that." He sounded disturbed.

"Whatever I do," I went on, "It will be misinterpreted. All my actions are supposed to have evil motives. I am supposed to want to destroy Germany. Why should I? Why? My ancestors have lived in Germany for many centuries, so why should I or any other Jew wish to destroy his country? You are an educated grown-up man and you allow people you have not even met to dictate to you what books to read and what books to burn! How are you going to find out the truth, if you ignore all the evidence that is not convenient?" He wanted to cut in, but I was so furious, I could not stop.

"If a client called you in, Mr. A...... to advise you on the structure of a building in danger of collapse, you would make a proper investigation, and not behave in this senseless way. Because you know very well that if you did, the building might collapse around your ears. Don't you see that if you continue to ignore opinions or facts that run counter to the party line, you cut yourself off from understanding what is going on in the world? You will misunderstand people, you will misjudge events and one day your structure will collapse around your ears.

"If you study village churches, it will be regarded as a contribution to culture, but when I study village churches It Is with destruction in my heart. You are meant to believe that. I believe in striving after the truth and I know from the knowledge of my own self that your accusations are all lies, lies, lies!"

Somehow I knew that he was not going to have me arrested or make trouble for what I had said. The tensions of the last year, my growing isolation, the insecurity, the recent frightful experience of the shootings, it had all exploded in me. But after my outburst neither of us said another word for a very long time. I thought that he had relapsed into his former silence. Suddenly he turned round from his drawing board and said in a very quiet voice:

"Marianne, on the 30th of June this year, they shot my very best friend. They said that he was one of Röhm's boys, that he had been a cissy and a traitor. But he was not a homosexual and neither was he a traitor. He had nothing at all to do with Röhm. He was an honest, brave German boy. What they said about him was all lies. He was born in Gardelegen, where I was born, we knew each other all our lives, we were like brothers. He had no trial either and I know he was innocent of all that they accused him of."

"Herr A.," I said, although I had noticed that he had addressed me as 'Marianne! "Herr A., I am so deeply sorry."

"You are sorry, Marianne? Do you realise whom you are sorry for? He was a Nazi, as good a Jew-baiter as any of us. When he tortured a Jew, he could make him confess to any crime he liked. He has killed some Jews too, have you heard his name?" He mentioned the well-known name of one of the S.A. leaders and a friend of Gregor Strasser who, for a brief moment, threatened to outshine Hitler. But try as I may, I cannot remember his name any more.

"And keep in mind," Christopher A. went on, "That this man was my best friend. You have talked to me about your childhood, your parents, your interests as though I was an ordinary decent man whom you could trust. You know nothing whatever about me. I noticed that you never asked me a question about myself. What do you know about who I am? What I have done? You talk in the same way about Professor Siedler. You are grateful to him because he has been kind to you. You think he is an honest, decent man. Do you know that he was a member of NSDAP (Nazi Party) for many years before they came to power? He carefully concealed it from his colleagues during the Brüning Government – he was not going to give himself away, if Hitler's bid for power failed. But after the burning of the Reichstag when the power of the Nazis was really confirmed, Siedler came out with a low party number, about No. 10,000, so he must have been a member for years. You think he is kind to you, well, what do you think he does it for? How do you know what crime he is atoning for? Or perhaps he's keeping a back door open for himself through you. Perhaps he thinks that you will get on in life, you will go abroad and who knows what the future holds in store. Do you remember how he suddenly came up to the studio when we talked together for the first time?" I nodded as he pointed to the speaking tube or 'house-telephone,' – I remember how you could hear on my father's speaking tube when there was a conversation at the other end.

"He knows that you and I have been talking together and that because of it, he will be safe from me." He got up and looked down at me, his face set and grim. Horror-struck, I was unable to say anything at all. He was wearing the mud-colored S.A. shirt, his hair was cropped Nazi fashion, he had a large full face, blue eyes, he was a big, athletic, very Germanic-looking man. And as I stared at him I suddenly saw behind the grim surface of his set face the face of a young boy who was completely bewildered, a child's face almost. A child who was yearning for kindness, who was yearning to be allowed to be kind and decent himself. A young boy who was blinking back his tears.

I felt like taking his hand and saying a word of comfort to him, but then it came to me who his friend had been, and what his friend had done, and that he himself was an officer of the S.A., who used every kind of deceit, every kind of cruelty to increase their power. It was he and his friends who were responsible for all the suffering and persecutions that all liberal thinkers, socialist writers, progressive artists and Jews were suffering. It was he and his friends who wanted to militarise and re-arm Germany, so that one day it would dominate the whole of Europe. I thought of the growing police terror of the S.S., who wore a death's head as their emblem, whom I had seen beating up innocent people, and of that horror when one early morning I had been walking in a park at the other end of Berlin.

I was looking for a bench I had been told about. Some Jewish people who were about to leave Berlin had commissioned me to do a water-colour of it, to take away with them as a souvenir. I sometimes got such commissions from people about to emigrate. The park was bounded on one side by a high brick wall. The birds were singing in the tall trees, early morning sunshine fell through their irridescent leaves and lit up bright green patches on the grass covered ground, which was still glistening with dew. I was walking on a wide shadowy asphalt path towards a bench I had just spotted, when I heard loud military barking from behind the dark wall. The birds scattered in all directions. There was some rhythmic stamping, loud staccato barking and then a sudden burst of two series of rifle shots, perhaps fifty each. They were followed by complete silence. I did not dare to move, nothing else seemed to move, only a blue glittering beetle began to cross the asphalt path into the sunlight. Then there was a subdued noise of people walking about, hushed voices, the sound of a motor. It seemed to move away, then there seemed to be several more suddenly cut off. Then more stamping, marchers standing still, more, even louder barking and again a salvo of rifle shots, followed by another. Again silence, again noises of movement and of motors approaching, moving away, and this time I could hear moaning, a rifle shot and more subdued quick talking. This procedure was repeated again and again. I stood there, my feet nailed to the ground by terror and yet I did not fully realise the awful meaning of those noises, until in the evening I heard what had been happening. I had heard the execution of people, how many I never knew, for the shootings were going on in many places. I had been separated from the scene only by a high wall.

Standing there in Siedler's studio, I thought that Christopher A.'s best friend could have been those men, whose last moments I had witnessed. I do not know how long we stood there, glaring at one another.

* * *

Mrs. Levkoff, a Jewish widow from eastern Prussia, brought my supper on a tray and put it on my desk in front of me. She was a large untidy-looking woman, with an enormously long face, always shuffling in carpet slippers and very fond of telling me the details of her various ailments. Despite her own somewhat slovenly appearance she kept the flat, which she shared with a son, impeccably clean and tidy. She always did more for me than I had paid for, and since the loss of my scholarship she often made me accept her suppers, which were not included in the rent. When I tried to refuse, she would burst into tears and beg me not to make her so unhappy. On one such occasion her bosom heaved so much that I was afraid she was going to have stroke.

Yet I did not fully appreciate her warm—hearted unselfishness until one day when she was ill, and doing some shopping for her and seeing her pantry, I realised on how very little she had managed for herself, whilst giving the best that she had to me, who was young, healthy and strong and far more able to with— stand deprivations than her own aging body. I don't know what happened to her after I left Germany. . . .

It was some time after I had finished working in Siedler's studio that one evening, back at my room in Mrs. Levkoff's apartment, I found a large bunch of white roses in a big water jug on my writing table and a visiting card from Christopher A. It contained no address, but a politely worded request that he might come and see me. I did not know how to take this and was a bit alarmed. Mrs. Levkoff looked at me very curiously, but said nothing. A few days later he called again, when I was in — of course in his S.A. uniform — and asked whether he could stay a little and talk. Feeling uneasy, I agreed. Mrs. Levkoff, who had opened the door for him, fled, but a little later returned with a tray with coffee and home—made cake. She did not bring the tray into the room but passed it to me through the door and disappeared.

"Well, we were never treated like this in Siedler's studio," he commented cheerfully, but the ice was not broken. "Look here," he continued, "Dont misunderstand my motive for coming here. First of all, let me reassure you, you have nothing to fear from me, remember that. Secondly, I want to talk to you about myself and ask you a great favour, if you can trust me sufficiently. You see, I have a very low party number, I joined the party during my last year at school, together with my friend whom they shot in June. I have been brought up on Nazi literature, I have learned whole sections of Hitler's *Mein Kampf by heart. We read and discussed Rosenberg and Streicher's articles In Der Stürmer.* My father is a Lutheran Vicar at Gardelegen and now he has to keep a copy of *Mein Kampf* next to the bible on the pulpit and read from it during the service. I assure you that he hates having to do that. I have no brother — my friend was like a brother to me and his father was my father's best friend. My friend's mother had died and he often spent the whole of his holidays in our house. We did everything togther, we joined the Hitler youth together and then the party. Ever since I can remember, I have been ordered what to do and what to believe. Father was the general in command at home. My mother was gentle, but very quiet. She did everything for my father and for me. She was always working and looking after us. All the friends who came to our house were father's friends. After a meal father and his friends would have their coffee and brandy in the *Herrenzimmer* (gentlemen's room) whilst mother continued about the house. My friend and I were always busy with party activities. And then in June this year they shot him, on Hitler's orders."

He paused for a long while.

"Then I met you. I have never talked to a Jew before. I have never known a Jewish person before. When you refused the lunch invitation out of consideration for my safety, for me, an S.A. officer, something snapped in me. Siedler noticed that you only bought rolls and milk and never went into a restaurant for lunch. I suddenly remembered that in the bible it is said that Jesus was a Jew, and so was Mary, and so was Joseph. All the disciples of Jesus were Jewish people and he lived amongst them, and they were his friends. I could not get that thought out of my mind. Your behaviour was altogether a great shock to me."

"You are quite unlike anything that the Jews are supposed to be. I want to ask you a question: Are there other Jews like you, are you and your parents very different from other Jews? If not, please can you introduce me to some of your Jewish friends? I must know what your people are really like. I must know whether I have been told a lot of lies about this and other things. I must try to discover the truth for myself. If I want to know the truth, I suppose I must begin with the truth about myself."

He got up and started walking about in the confined space of my room. Then he sighed and sat down again and continued, whilst staring out of the window.

"I am not a nice man, you see. When I first joined the party, I believed in Hitler as the saviour of Germany. Everything was different then. I was full of ideals. About men and about women. But the brown-clad Hitler girls we met did not accord with my ideal of women. Any man six foot high, any officer, can have any of them, any time. I don't like to talk about it to you, they disgust me. They were my first disappointment. Then I started, secretly of course, to read many of the books that we had to requisition.

"I was supposed to supervise the burning of books in Gardelegen at the time, but I rescued quite a number and hid them in my father's library. I did not dare to tell even my friend about this, he was so loyal to the party." He got up again, turned his back to me and went on speaking. His hands were twitching behind his back but he was not aware of it.

"Then came the people in the S.A. cellars. We were told that they were recalcitrant, hardened criminals. We were told about horrible things that they had done. Please try to understand," he suddenly turned round and looked at me, "All of us believed what we were told about them. The things they had done, it was quite awful what we were told. Then we got a lot of Schnapps to drink. And then. . . . I helped to torture them. I helped to beat them, I can't tell you the details, it is too horrible. Some of them died, I was there, I saw them die. Oh, my God." He stopped and after a long silence he added, "Some of my party pals enjoyed it even, and perhaps it was all lies, perhaps they did not even commit crimes we were told they had committed. I wonder what the officer who gave orders to have my friend executed was told about him? What were the men who were given orders to shoot him told about him?

"I have come to realise that there have been lies. I can't believe anything any more. How many lies have we been told? How much is true? Perhaps the people in the S.A. cellars were just people like you, people like any others, perhaps they were not those awful criminals at all? Who made these lies up? Who passed these lies on? And why? Why? Oh my God, what have I done?"

He was pale and shaking all over.

"For the sake of all you hold holy, tell me the truth, are Jewish people 'vermin' as we are told, are Jewish men out to degrade Aryan girls? Do the Jews want to corrupt and destroy Germany? Tell me the truth — the worse it is, the less guilty I shall feel. Only tell me the truth!"

I was shaken to my depth. But despite my anguish I realised that whatever awful things he had done, he was sincere in his desire to know the truth, even if it condemned him. When at last I managed to speak, I said:

"You asked me what Jewish people are like. You know it already. They are like me, they are like any other people. You have sent me white roses and you ask me what I am like, you ask me to tell you the truth. You do not ask your party about me, not Mr. Rosenberg. You don't ask Julius Streicher what young Jewish girls are like, because you know it. The answer is in your heart already. Jewish boys and girls are neither worse nor better than any other people. But they have suffered a great deal more. For two thousand years they have suffered from the antagonism of people with whom they would be friends, they have been excluded from the crafts and from many professions. In time of epidemics and hardship they were accused of having poisoned the wells. The tradition of that suffering has helped young Jewish people to understand things earlier than Aryan boys and girls. It has also often made them more neurotic. No doubt it is the tradition of that suffering that is responsible for a Jewish passion for justice."

* * *

One of the people who agreed to meet Christopher A. was Nina. Nina was half Jewish and an orphan. Her father had been a noted chemist and had left her a beautiful house in the most exclusive part of Berlin—Dahlem. The garden adjoined one of the spacious fir forests to the west of Berlin. Nina lived in the big house with her sister, a house—keeper and a large sheepdog. Nina was plain, with straight rather mousy hair. She was slim and long-legged and had a lovely shy smile. Her voice was quiet and melodious and she had a tinkling laugh, rare in those days in Germany.

Nina's sister was beautiful. She had black, slightly frizzy hair, large blue eyes with enormous black eyelashes, the finest of eyebrows, full red lips, colours like milk and roses. This hauntingly beautiful head sat on a body no larger than a child's. Except for her head, hands and arms, she was completely paralysed. The sisters were devoted to each other and their house—keeper to both of them. Nina was a librarian, she earned reasonably well and had not yet lost her job. She was not classed as 'Jewish' but as 'Non—Aryan.' At that time 'Non—Aryans' were still usually allowed to continue with their work.

I took Christopher to Nina's house. Nine met us at the last underground station with her large sheepdog, her short straight hair flowing in the wind. She looked beautiful as she stood there in the fading light at the edge of the forest, tall, slim, smiling shyly. With Christopher and Nina it was love at first sight. They were at once completely at ease with one another and forgot there was anyone or anything else in the world. As they walked together ahead of me along the grassy edge of the woodland, the sheepdog licking the man's hand, they looked as if they had been created for each other.

A week or so later Nina rang me up: "Christopher sent me a bunch of red roses, Marianne. You don't mind, do you?"

"Of course I don't mind, why on earth should I?"

"Well, I just wanted to make sure, I didn't really think so, but anyhow I'm glad it is all right."

"Nina, dear, I knew as soon as you two met. I wish with all my heart that things will be all right for you both."

"Oh, Marianne," she said, "I am so happy." I had other pre-occupations and sorrows at the time and I left the telephone feeling far from happy, wondering uneasily what the future would hold for the storm-trooper and the half-Jewish girl.

*   *   *

Even the most awful powers that be
give place in their succession. Snow-massed winter yields
to summer with her fruits.
The gloomy circle of the night stands back, gives place
to Day with her white horses and her kindled light.
There is the blast of dread winds that lets the sea
sleep after clamour, and there is the strong wrestler, sleep
who slips his chancery nor ever holds what he has gripped.
How then shall we not recognise what our place is?
I myself only now have come to understand
How I must hate my enemy only so much
as one who yet shall love him. . . .

Sophocles, 'Ajax'
transl. by R. Lattimore

All this had been three years ago in Berlin. I was in London now, and there opposite me in the little Italian eating place sat Christopher A., ordering two portions of Spaghetti Bolognese for himself.

"Well, what you doing here?" I repeated my question. "Tell me about yourself, surely, you are not a refugee?"

"Well, yes and no," he answered, "I am on holiday actually."

"On holiday?"

"I left Professor Siedler shortly after you left. I got a job with Göring. I worked for the Air Ministry. You probably saw the beginning of the building." I nodded. "It's an enormous building and it had to be designed, detailed and carried out in

record time." He stopped and looked round him to see whether anyone was listening. 'The German look,' we used to call it.
In London people were not so desperately anxious about someone else overhearing your remarks, but I did the same, of course, as did all the other refugees I knew. I kept doing it for years . . . . But Christopher A., why should he? As if he had read my thoughts, he leaned forward and told me:

"There are central heating radiators in the whole block, but they are not under the windows as usual. The panels below the windows slide back and there are guns under the window sills. From there you can dominate the streets – in case of a revolution or street fighting."

"You mean to say that from Göring's Air Ministry you can shoot the German people?" I asked.

"You most certainly can! Herrmann isn't going to take any chances. You can't imagine the equipment, you never saw such luxury in all your life. Well, when the roof was up and we were celebrating, there was Herrmann Göring, drinking beer with the building contractors. He slapped everyone within reach on the back and strutted about in his white uniform with decorations all over it." (It is an old German custom to celebrate a build-ing contract, when the roof is on a building. A tree with many coloured ribbons is put on top of the roof, and the client, in this case the Air Minister, supplies beer and sometimes sausages to all the workmen and the architects who worked on the con-tract.)

"Herrmann was at his most expansive, so when he came round to where I was sitting, red in the face and sweating, I took the opportunity to ask him for a holiday. I got a slap on my back and my holiday. Three weeks. But they don't know I shan't be coming back. Germany won't see me again ever. Not whilst I am alive."

"And Nina?"

"Nina has been all right, up to now, she has a different job in the book trade. Where she works now, no one knows that she is not an Aryan. She is excused from party service because of her sister."

"But what of the future? Aren't you going to see her again, then?"

"I am trying to get a visa to go to New Zealand and I hope to get Nina and her sister over as well. It will not be easy."

"Will Nina's sister be able to get a visa?" I was doubtful about that.

"I have an uncle who is the director of the Liverpool Zoo-
logical Park and Gardens, he has trade connections with New
Zealand, and he's trying to help me to get a visa for the three
of us. . . ." "Yes, Marianne, I want to marry Nina, I want to
read what I want and say and think what I like — and I don't
want to see those murderous faces around me again. Not ever.
This is my idea of paradise."

I talked to him almost as though in the past he had been a
personal friend of mine. But I remembered too vividly the things
he had told me he had done. He had been a torturer and a murderer. No regret on his part could undo these deeds and restore
the lives he had helped to destroy. He had been lied to and he
did not know that at the time. But he knew that what he did was
not part of a civilised judicial process, there had been no
trial, the 'accused' had no means of defending themselves, they
had no access to legal assistance.

He had worked as an architect for Herrmann Göring's new Air
Ministry. He had managed to get official permission to go abroad.
He must have continued as a good party member to obtain such con-
cessions. He must have acquiesced in the ever-growing cruelties
against those who now or in the past had opposed Hitler, against
'Non-Aryans,' against Jews. And yet I also knew that he could
not do anything at all to prevent the torturing and killing of
ordinary, innocent people in German. If he had dared to oppose
these things in Germany at that time, he would have been done
away with himself.

And I? What had I done to stop the inhumanity? I had known
from the start, what Christopher with his background could not
have known, and did not know, until his friend was killed, that
the Nazis' were lying, that they were corrupting Germany so as
to obtain absolute power. It was easy for me: from my father
and his friends I knew what true nobility was; I was not taken
in by the Nazi's mystical claptrap.

But how would I have behaved if I had lived in Germany as a
German Aryan? I did not imagine that I would have been sufficiently strong to oppose the NSDAP and live in the knowledge,
that if this was discovered, acid might be spilled into my eyes,
my fingers broken. Anyone can have courage for a brief heroic
moment. (In the spring of 1933 I had voted against Hitler whilst
a uniformed Nazi stood behind me, looking over my shoulder.) I
certainly would not have been able to do that. You cannot live
a decent life in a country corrupted by terror. On the surface
of a sphere all straight lines become curved. Like everyone else,

like Christopher A., I would have played safe. But while talking to him I could not forget that he had been a torturer.

To quit was for him no doubt the only way out of the dilemma, nor could it be easy for him to leave his parents behind, probably never to see them again. He was an only son. He was loyal to Nina and willing to take on Nina's sister. But wherever he went, he would have to bear the awful knowledge of himself. He could never be as free as I was. And had he ever told Nina the whole truth about himself? Would he have to conceal his awful deeds from her? And if he ever told her what he had done, would she, could she, continue to accept him as before?

As we sat in the little Italian bistro, we talked between long silences, each occupied with our own past and with our own future. I wished him and Nina every success in their plans, but I continued to feel an inner reserve — almost a recoil— when we met once more to say goodbye. I wish I could add that he succeeded in finding a new life in New Zealand, but I do not know, for I never saw him or heard of him again.

FAY ZWICKY

HOSTAGES

I think I began to hate when I was twelve. Consciously, I
mean. The war was then in its fourth year, there was no chocolate and my father was still away in Borneo. I barely knew him.
Till then I had learnt to admire what my mother believed to be
admirable. Striving to please with ascetic rigour, I practised
scales and read Greek myths. Morality hinged on hours of piano
practice achieved or neglected. I knew no evil. The uncommon
neutrality of my existence as a musical child in wartime was
secured in a world neither good nor malevolent. My place among
men was given. Did I have feelings? I was not ready to admit
them for there seemed to be rules governing their revelation
which I either could not or would not grasp. Nameless, passion-
less, and without daring I repressed deepest candour. But *tout
comprendre c'est tout pardonner*; what was once self-indul-
gence is now permissible revelation. Why, then, should shame
crimp the edge of my reflection so many years after the event?

It all started with the weekly visit to our house of a
German refugee piano teacher, Sophie Lindauer-Grunberg. Poor
fat sentimental Sophie, grateful recipient of my mother's pity.
I was to be her first Australian pupil.

'But why me?'

'Because she needs help. She has nothing and you, thank
God, have everything. She's been a very fine musician in her
own country. You have to understand that this is someone who
has lost everything. Yes, you can roll your eyes. *Everything,*
I said. Something I hope, please God, will never happen to you.
So you'll be nice to her and pay attention to what she says.
I've told Mr Grover he lives too far away for me to go on taking
you to lessons twice a week.'

Suddenly dull and bumbling Mr Grover in his music room smelling of tobacco and hair oil seemed like my last contact with the
outside world. I was to be corralled into the tight, airless
circle of maternal philanthropy.

The day of my first lesson a hot north wind was tearing at
the huge gum tree in front of the house. Blinds and curtains

were drawn against the promised heat. The house stood girded like an island under siege. My younger brother and sister had gone swimming. I watched them go, screwing up my eyes with the beginnings of a headache, envying their laughter and the way they tore sprigs off the lantana plants lining the driveway. I awaited my teacher, a recalcitrant hostage. The rooms were generous and high–ceilinged but I prowled about, tight–lipped, seeking yet more room. A deep nerve of anger throbbed in me and I prayed that she would not come. But she came. Slowly up the brick path in the heat. I watched her from the window, measuring her heavy step with my uneasy breath. Then my mother's voice greeting her in the hallway, high–pitched and over–articulated as if her listener were deaf, a standard affectation of hers with foreign visitors. 'Terrible day . . . trouble finding the house . . . Helen looking forward so much. . . .' I ran to the bathroom and turned on the tap hard. I just let it run, catching sight of my face in the mirror above the basin.

Could I be called pretty? Brown hair hanging long on either side of high cheekbones, the hint of a powerful nose to come, a chin too long, cold grey eyes, wide mouth, fresh colour. No, not pretty. No heroine either. A wave of self–pity compensated me for what I saw and tears filled my eyes. Why me? Because she has to have pupils. Am I such a prize? No, but a Jew who has everything. 'Be thankful you were born in this wonderful country.' My mother's voice sounded loud in my ears. 'They're making them into lampshades over there.' I had laughed but shrank from the grotesque absurdity of the statement. Why the dramatics? All I remember is the enveloping anger directed at everthing my life had been and was. I wanted to be left alone but didn't know how or where to begin. 'She has lost her whole family. Taken away and shot before her eyes. . . .' So? Now she has me.

My mother and Miss Grunberg were talking about me as I stood in the doorway. My own hands were clammy as I moved forward to the outstretched unfamiliar gesture. Hers were small, fat and very white, surprisingly small for such a tall, heavily built woman, like soft snuggling grubs. She herself looked like some swollen, pale grub smiling widely and kindly, a spinster of nearly sixty. Her little eyes gleamed through thick, round spectacles. On the skin beneath her eyes tiny bluish vessels spread their nets.

'So here is *unsere liebe Helene*!'

I raised my eyebrows insolently as the girls did at school
after one of my own ill-judged observations. It was essential
to the code governing the treatment of victims. But this time
I had the upper hand and didn't know how to handle my advantage.
The cobbles of Köln and Cracow rang hollow under my boots. The
light from the pink shaded lamp fell on my new teacher. The wind
blew in sharp gusts outside.

'Helen, this is Miss Grunberg.' My mother with a sharp look
in my direction. 'I've been telling her about the work you've
done so far with Mr Grover. Miss Grunberg would like you to
have another book of studies.'

'Perhaps you will play *ein Stück* for me. Liszt perhaps?'
She nodded ponderously at our Bechstein grand that suddenly took
on the semblance of some monstrous piece of abstract statuary,
out of all proportion to the scale of the room. 'Lord no. I've
never done him.' I fell into uncharacteristic breeziness. 'I'm
not really in practice. Hardly anything going at the moment and
I'm pretty stale on the stuff Grover had me on for the exams.'
Deliberately fast, consciously idiomatic, enjoying, yes, *enjoying*
the strain of comprehension on my victim's round, perpetually
smiling face. 'You can *still* play those Debussy "Arabesques",'
said my mother, her neck flushed. 'I put the music on the piano,'
and she gave me yet another warning look.

I opened the lid noisily and sat down with elaborate movements,
shifting the metronome a few inches to the right, altering the
position of the stand, bending to examine my feet fumbling
between the pedals. The 'Arabesques' moved perfunctorily. I
kept my face impassive, looked rigidly ahead at the music which
I didn't see. Even during the section I liked in the second piece,
a part where normally I would lean back a little and smile. I
had begun to learn how not to please. But the process of self-
annihilation involved the destruction of others. *Tout pardonner*
did I say?

Miss Grunberg arranged with my mother to return the following
week at the same time. 'Why are you behaving like this?' asked
my mother, red and angry with me after she had left in a taxi.
The young blond driver had tapped his foot noisily on the brick
path as Miss Grunberg profusely repeated her gratitude to my
mother for the privilege of teaching her talented daughter.
Moving rapidly away from them I conversed with him, broadening
my vowels like sharks' teeth on the subject of the noon temperature. I was desperate that the coveted outside world and its
tranquil normality should recognize that I was in no way linked

with the heavy foreign accent involved in demonstrative leave-taking on our front lawn.

'Behaving like what?'

'You know what I mean. You behaved abominably to that poor woman.'

'I played for her, didn't I?' She came closer to me with a vengeful mouth.

'You could call it that. I don't know what's got into you lately. You used to be such a good child. Now you know the answers to everything. A walking miracle! What terrible things have we done, your father and I, that you should behave like a pig to a woman like that? We've given you everything. *Everything!* And because I'm good to an unfortunate refugee who needs help wherever she can find it, you have to behave like that! I'm sorry for you, *really* sorry for you!'

'Spare your sympathy for the poor reffos!' The taxi driver's word burst savagely out of my mouth. She flew at me and slapped me across the face with her outstretched hand.

'One thing I do know,' she was trembling with rage, 'the one thing I'm sure of is that I've been too good to you. We've given you too much. You're spoilt rotten! And *one* day, my girl, one day you too may be old and unwanted and. . . .'

'A lampshade perhaps? So what.' I shook with guilt and fear at the enormity of what I'd said, terrified of the holocaust I'd shaken loose and my mother's twisted mouth.

But the revolution didn't get under way either that day or that year. The heroine lacked (should one say it?) courage. Sealed trains are more comforting than the unknown wastes of the steppes. The following week Miss Grunberg toiled up our front path and I sat down to a new course of Moscheles studies and a movement of Mozart concerto. *Her* music. Scored heavily in red pencil, the loved and hated language dotted with emotional excla-mation marks. Her life's work put out for my ruthless inspection. She moved her chair closer to my stool to alter the position of my right hand. 'Finger *rund, Kleine,* always *rund.* Hold always the wrist supple, *liebe Helene.*' I shrank from the alien endear-ment and her sour breath but curved my fingers, tight and delib-erate. Her smell hung over me, a static haze in the dry air. Musty, pungent and stale, the last faint reminder of an airless Munich apartment house. Her dress, of cheap silky fabric, rustled when she moved her heavy body. Breathing laboriously she tried to explain to me what I should do with the Mozart. She couldn't get used to the heat of the new country and was

beginning to find walking difficult. But I didn't practice
between her visits and gave only spasmodic attention to her
gentle directions. I was shutting myself off from words and
from music, beginning a long course in alienation. I seldom
looked my mother in the eye in those days. I quarrelled bitterly
with my sister, ignored my brother.

About six months after my lessons with Miss Grunberg started
I was not much further advanced. I spent a lot of time reading
in my room or just looking out of the window at the garden which
was now bare. Squalls lashed the gum tree and drove the leaves
from the weeping elm skittering across the grass. Miss Grunberg
now had several pupils amongst the children of the Jewish community and even one or two gentiles from the neighbouring school.
She lived in a very poorly furnished flat in a run-down outer
suburb. She still travelled to her pupils' homes. Her breathing
had become very short in the last few weeks. Inattentive and
isolated as I was, I had noticed that she was even paler than
usual.

My mother one day told me with some rancour how well the
Lapin girl was doing with the piano. 'She never had your talent
but what a worker! She's going to give a recital in the Assembly
Hall next month.' I merely shrugged. The boots of the conqueror
were no picnic. She was welcome to them. 'And while I'm about
it, I've decided to tell Miss Grunberg not to come any more. I
don't feel there's much point as you seem quite determined to do
as little with music as possible. I've done all *I* can. At least
she's on her feet now.' On her feet! Oh God! But I replied,
'That's all right with me' in as neutral a voice as I could
summon.

But that night I ground my face into the covers of my bed,
no longer a place of warmth and security but a burial trench.
At the mercy of my dreams appeared Sophie Lindauer-Grunberg,
pale as brick dust. Her face wasting, crumbling to ash, blasted
by the force of my terrible youth. And, waking in fright, I
mourned for the first time my innocent victim and our shared
fate.

ANGELINA MUNIZ-HUBERMAN

CHRISTIAN GENTLEMEN

Christian gentleman, you were greatly delayed in embarking for the New World. You had trouble proving that your veins contained no Jewish blood. Everyone said that you had only recently converted to Christianity and that your parents still lit candles on Friday nights. But you affirmed, swore over and over that you were a nobleman and a Christian of long standing. Question of honor, question of faith, question of papers.

Meanwhile, in order not to lose time or the habit, you studied. You read book after book, whether chivalric romance or pastoral or picaresque or about a certain knight, dishonored and deranged. But above all, you read the Bible. The Bible, in Castilian, translated by a remote rabbi from Guadalfahara. Occult reading, forbidden reading, solitary and satisfying reading. Profound reading too, the source of your most strongly held convictions, which years later you would have to defend, despite hell and high water, before clerics, kings and inquisitors, landholders and captains, soldiers and bishops. And the force of your convictions, which would move everyone, was like the words of a prophet, the hope of a messiah, the horizons of liberty and a longing for justice in a world born with death stuck in its throat, strangled and mute.

You had time to think a great deal while you were waiting, but you learned even more when you set foot on the first island. You had imagined paradise, a state of grace, absolute purity. And so you found it, except in reverse. Upside down. The innocent hanged and the guilty sleeping peacefully. The native dispossessed and the newcomer enriched. Families separated and women and children taken captive. Free men enslaved and enslavers free.

But what hurt you most, as if it were your own flesh and your own experience, was the disruption of the natural order, the derision of God, the torture of suffering peoples, the tears and blood of men. So you wrote and sent petitions to the earthly king, to everyone. And they put your letters aside and did not want to read them, because ignorance would serve as their excuse.

126

But you were persistent and obstinate and convinced. And you decided to sail back and go in person to relate the horrors. But they sealed their ears the more tightly, for they wanted to listen to you even less than before.

You came back again to struggle as you could, to gather new forces with which to penetrate the labyrinth and hence undo it. To this end you became a priest, Christian gentleman, clever and calculating, seeking support where there was greatest power.

As an insider, you could better manipulate things. You spoke with the prelates, troubled their consciences, shouted their own ethics at them, crushed their silence, opposed their acquiescence, created chaos and provoked uncertainty.

You wrote, among other things:

> Enough that these poor people should go to Hell because of their infidelity, little by little and alone, without those of us who are Christians and who have come to save them, in a few short days and solely out of greed, with new and exotic means of cruelty and tyranny, without our removing them from this world and accompanying them to endless darkness and lamentation, where, *non erit solatium miseris socios habere penarum,* since *non minus ardebunt qui cum multis ardebunt.* To this very different eventuality, although our Lord does not take them by the hand and in spite of the gains made by those who have labored and continue to labor every day among them, many souls bear witness, and the more from this region (the count is one hundred thousand on the entire island) that we have burned alive, roasted on iron racks, thrown to mad dogs, butchered with knives, showing no mercy toward children, old people, pregnant women or women recently delivered, sometimes even choosing the fattest ones in order to kill them and extract the fat (because it is said that it is good for curing their murderers' wounds), and other cruel means by which our Spanish nation, for no just cause, puts them to death.
>
> The outcry of so much spilled human blood is even now reaching heaven. The earth can no longer

bear to be watered by men's blood. I believe that
the angels of peace and even God Himself must be
weeping. Only Hell is glad, but I believe that
with such a rush of damned souls, those infernal
regions must be overflowing. The wars, fought
against all divine and natural right, have ended,
during which occurred the actions noted above and
a great many more and worse; this is the first
foot that Christians set upon this land; then
follows the second, of heartless cruelty and tyrannical governance, which directs its attention
primarily, you should know, toward distributing
the Indians who escaped death during the wars,
so that little by little (if only it were little
by little), in terrible servitude, mining gold
and pearls and other unjust labors, they will
finish their days.

All of these evils are great and offensive to
pious ears; and if they are horrifying and unbearable to listen to, how much more the facts to
which the descriptions of the cruelties refer. . .
Although, in the secret widsom which He alone
knows, God may permit these people to be punished,
woe unto the instruments with which they are punished. Because He wills that all should be saved
and come to know Him, because He was created,
taking on human flesh, to be called Father of
mercies . . . .

They began to label you, to write detractions, to disregard
your rights. So arrogant, so vain, so impulsive, so impious,
critic of your country and defender of pagans. But they forgot
that many men had preceded you in indicting evils and that the
idea of your country as one which "no tongue could tell its
glories" was an illusory evasion of the truth, a dream of unsatisfied desire, a bitter point of pain converted into a bright,
beautiful star.

And above all because you carried in you the seed of doubt,
a critical spirit engendered by reason, a profound and demanding
ethic of non-conformity. Because from your parents and your
grandparents, from your great-grandparents and great-great-grand-
parents, and from there on back *ad astra,* in inverse proportion
to that racial purity which they wanted you to demonstrate, you

demonstrated instead the root and origin of your being in the simple inheritance and logical deduction of a persecuted convert who
has nothing to lose and who breathes the breath of his life into
denunciations – not in the manner of the Inquisition – of all
the evils that impede the realization of a pure, utopian realm.

Of course you beat your head against not one but many walls
and you had to do and re-do, reform and transform repeatedly all
of the ideas that simmered and boiled in your soul and your
heart and your head.

One day, weary of suggesting and accusing, you began to
threaten and punish with words. It was then that you found the
formula which would cause some to repent. What else but the
threat of Hell? For believers, eternal damnation. By that means
alone, now and again, a conquistador here, a landholder there,
would return (but only on his deathbed) usurped property and
free suffering slaves.

Your outcry was echoed by some few who were convinced and
followed you. But your messianism was suspect and you attempted
to clear yourself by effacing the traces of your not-so-pure
blood. Thus you changed one letter of your name so it would
resemble a noble or established family, and when you were eighty-
five years old, you began to withdraw, perhaps in the vague fear
of being identified, and you requested that your unfinished
History not be published for forty years – Mosaic number –
asserting that it would be propitious to offer it to the glory
of God and the revelation of truth.

In doubt, agony, fear, desperation, you troubled the consciences of others, and you yourself found no peace either.

At ninety years of age, your rebellious soul escaped you,
and we do not know where it found rest.

Translator's Note: The indented passage is from a letter by the
Dominican cleric, Bartolomé de las Casas, written from Mexico to
Spain's Council of the Indies on January 30, 1531. Las Casa's
Brief Relation of the Destruction of the Indies was, from the
moment of its publication in 1552, the most effective of the
indictments of Spain's cruelties to the indigenous populations
of the New World, and it remains, along with his letters, an
essential document of the conquest of Mexico.

Translated by Lois Parkinson Zamora

BAT YE'OR

THE DHIMMI

The fundamental evil in alienation is forgetfulness
— Robert Misrahi

In this article, it is impossible to go far beyond general propositions. These will be best appreciated, however, after the reader has been provided with the basic historical framework. This is why it has seemed useful to specify briefly the socio-economic background in which the dhimmi nations evolved, while abstaining, for reasons of clarity and space, from analysing the historical context in any depth.

After the Arab conquest, the expression "dhimmi" designated the indigenous non-Arab and non-Muslim people — Jews, Christians, Zoroastrians (Persians) — whose territories came under Arab-Muslim domination. It signifies protected because these populations — in theory, if not always in practice — were protected from pillage, slavery, exile and massacre by the specific conditions of an agreed covenant between the victors and the vanquished. In return for such protection, the dhimmis were obliged to submit to a code or covenant (commonly referred to as the *Covenant of 'Umar*) a summary of which is given below. The need to control these foreign peoples naturally obliged the conquering Arab minority to adopt an oppressive political attitude which became more and more severe over the years. In order to justify their oppression, the rulers based themselves on certain religious values to the exclusion of other Koranic verses recommending charity and fraternity. Thus a common geo-political event — the conquest of foreign lands and the subjection of conquered peoples — was linked to a religious concept, the *djihad*, or holy war, which has as its inevitable consequence the oppression of the infidel. So, although the condition of the dhimmi is typical of religious intolerance — hardly exceptional in human history — only its political aspect, the spoliation and subjection of native inhabitants, will be examined here.

130

A dhimmi civilisation is characterised by a language, a history and a culture as well as specific political and juridical institutions developed in the national homeland before its annexation by the Arab conquerors. The expression "dhimmi civilisation" or "dhimmi people" refers to a nation, the ethnic origin of which is associated with a particular geographical area regardless of that nation's present dispersion. People who belong to a dhimmi civilisation are individuals who have continued to transmit to their progeny their specific heritage, without regard to their wanderings and their present domiciles which have resulted from loss of their national independence through occupation, oppression and exile. Thus, whether he is a Westerner or an Oriental, a Jew is a part of a dhimmi civilisation if he willingly perpetuates and accepts the national and cultural values of Israel. It is the same thing with the Armenians, the Assyrians and the Maronites as well as other peoples who, after the conquest of their homeland, were subjected to a legislation which either decimated them or forced them to live in exile.

Economic exploitation

A tax (the *kharadj*) was levied on the lands left to the indigenous dhimmis. This tax symbolised the Arabisation of the land of the dhimmis, i.e., its addition to the patrimony of the Arab—Islamic community. In the early period of colonisation, lands given in fief were exonerated from the kharadj.

Each male dhimmi, with the theoretical exceptions of the aged, invalids and slaves, had to pay a poll—tax (the *gizya*) which symbolized the subjection and humiliation of the vanquished.

The dhimmis also paid double the taxes of the Muslims. In addition, ransoms (*avanies*) were frequently extorted from the local Jewish and Christian communities under the threat of collective sanctions, including torture and death.

Polico—economic discriminations

It was forbidden for the dhimmi on pain of death:

— to carry or possess weapons,
— to raise a hand against a Muslim, even against an aggressor unjustly determined to kill him,
— to ally himself with the enemies of the Arabs,
— to criticize Islam, the Prophet or the Angels,

– to convert to any religion other than Islam, and having
  converted to Islam to revert to one's original religion,
– to be linked by marriage or concubinage to a Muslim woman,
– to hold a position giving him authority over a Muslim,

The dhimmis were obliged:

– to live separated from Muslims, in special quarters of a town,
  the gates of which were closed every evening; or, as in Yemen,
  outside the limits of towns inhabited by Muslims,
– to have lower houses than those of Muslims,
– to practise their religion secretly and in silence,
– to bury their dead hastily,
– to refrain from showing in public religious objects, such as
  crosses, banners or sacred texts,
– to distinguish themselves from Muslims by their exterior
  aspect,
– to wear clothes distinguished not only by shape (length, style
  of sleeves, etc.) but also by specific colours assigned to
  each group of dhimmis: i.e., for Jews, Christians and
  Samaritans,
– to have different types of tombs from those of Muslims.

It was forbidden for the dhimmis:

– to go near mosques or to enter certain venerated towns which
  would thereby be polluted,
– to have head–dresses, belts, shoes, ornate saddles or similar
  saddles to those of Muslims – all elements of their exterior
  appearance being intended to emphasize their humble or abject
  status.

They were forbidden to ride horses or camels, since these animals
were considered too noble for them. Donkeys were permitted, but
they could only ride them outside towns and they had to dismount
on sight of a Muslim. In certain periods they were forced to
wear distinctive badges in the public baths, and in certain
regions were even forbidden to enter them at all.

The dhimmis were obliged:

– to make haste in the streets, always passing to the left
  (impure) side of a Muslim, who was advised to push them to the
  wall,

- to walk humbly with lowered eyes,
- to accept insults without replying,
- to remain standing in a humble and respectful attitude in the presence of a Muslim,
- to leave Muslims the best places,
- never to speak to Muslims except to reply.

Any litigation between a dhimmi and a Muslim was brought before an Islamic tribunal where the dhimmi's testimony was unacceptable.

In North Africa and Yemen, the most repugnant duties, such as executioner, grave-digger, cleaner of the public latrines, etc., were forced on Jews; even on Saturdays and Holy days. Contempt for the dhimmi's life was expressed through inequality of punishments for the same offences. The penalty for murder was much lighter if the victim was a dhimmi. The murderer of a dhimmi was rarely punished as he could justify his act by accusing his victim of blasphemy against Islam or of having assaulted a Muslim.

Muslims were strongly advised against social intercourse with dhimmis, but if contact with them could not be avoided it was recommended that they limit relations to the strictest necessities, always showing contempt.

This brief summary provides only an outline of the rules which governed a whole system of oppression, which increased or decreased according to the specific circumstances of each region. In exchange for these obligations inflicted upon the dhimmis, their existence was tolerated on their land which was now Arabised. This tolerance was not final. It could be abrogated in two ways: the unilateral decision of the ruler to exile the dhimmis, and infraction by the dhimmis of the regulations. The latter case permitted individual or collective reprisals against the dhimmi communities, ending in pillage or massacre.

The enforcement or alleviation of the rules depended on the political circumstances and the good will of the rulers. Some orientalists have considered them "tolerant," and this was evidently the opinion of those who benefitted from them. But it is obviously not the point of view of the victims. For, how can oppression be justified or esteemed "tolerant" otherwise than by denying the humanity of those subjugated by it? Every colonising power maintains that men are not equal and considers that its yoke is benevolent and tolerant. Nor did the Arab invent this

legislation. The Byzantine clergy first elaborated it – thereby
giving an Ideological arm to the imperial power – in order to
destroy Israel in its homeland and in the diaspora. The Arabian
conquerors Islamised it, developing and using it to annihilate
in their turn both Oriental and North African Judaism and Christianity in the political, economic, religious and cultural spheres.

The situation of the Christian dhimmi was alleviated following Western European pressure to protect Oriental Christians,
pilgrimages to the Holy Land and commerce with the Orient. In
the second half of the 19th century, European Jewish organisations, aided by European consuls, were able to improve the condition of the Jewish dhimmi. It was only with European colonisation, which proclaimed *de facto* equality between Muslim, Christian and Jew, that the dhimmis, now liberated from discrimination,
could feel free and even achieve some economic progress.

After European decolonisation, Arab governments adopted a
policy of intensive Arabisation. Wiping out the sequels of
European colonisation meant, amongst other things, as far as the
indigenous national minorities were concerned, the re-establishment
of political, economic, social and cultural discrimination with
the aim of limiting those liberties which had been enjoyed
during the colonial period. This discrimination was adjusted to
new ideological formulae and was manifested in strong emphasis
on the Arab-Muslim element to the detriment of the pre-Islamic
ethnic cultures and nationalisms. The latter were either attached,
as in the case of the national movements of the Assyrians, Kurds,
Zionists and Maronites, or paralysed like the Copts of Egypt.
Thus was re-established the superiority and domination of the
Arab-Muslim community over the ethnic Oriental nationalisms, whilst
Panarabism reaffirmed its imperialist principle of universal
domination, which had been at the root of Arab colonisation of
the Near East and North Africa.

DOCUMENT

1851   No justice for the dhimmi

*"It is my duty to report to Your Excellency that the Jews
in Hebron have been greatly alarmed by threats of the Moslems
there at the commencement of Ramadan [...]*

*The Jews having complained that a freed slave named Saad
Allah was more obnoxious to them than any other person in
Hebron and that Abderrahhman had released him almost immediatel*

134

after *sentencing him to imprisonment, I applied to the Pasha to have Saad Allah brought to Jerusalem.*

His Excellency gave an order that the offender should be examined by the Council Hebron, and if convicted, be forwarded to Jerusalem for punishment.

Accordingly a Council was held there during five hours, and the result was that a report (Mazbata) was drawn up and signed by the Mufti and Kadi, declaring that none but Jewish witnesses had appeared, "and we do not receive the testimony of Jews." Saad Allah was therefore dismissed [...]"

From a letter (15.7.1851) James Finn, British Consul, Jerusalem, to Sir Stratford Canning, British Ambassador, Constantinople. (F.O. 78/874, No 10)

A.M. Hyamson, *The British Consulate in Jerusalem in relation to the Jews of Palestine,* London, 1939, Part I, pp. 171.

FROM DHIMMI TO DHIMMI STATE

Those who cannot remember the past are condemned to repeat it

                           – George Santayana

(Inscription on the gate of Dachau Museum)

Among the motivations which contributed to the elaboration of the dhimmi status, the victor-vanquished relationship in its political aspect appears as the predominant element. A distinction must be made, however, between the treatment meted out by the Arab-Muslim conquerors to non-Arab lands on the one hand, and to their inhabitants on the other. However, the lands were conquered, they were permanently annexed by the Arab-Muslim collectivity, i.e., they were Arabised. The fate of their inhabitants depended on whether they had surrendered as a result of defeat in battle or according to treaty, but in either case an indigenous inhabitant who refused conversion to Islam was tolerated only if he accepted the dhimmi status. Arabisation of the conquered lands was marked by a land-tax *(kharadj)* which was levied only on dhimmi-owned land. The tax was paid to the Islamic collectivity, since both the dhimmis and the produce of their work were considered as belonging to the conquering community of Believers.

135

Arabisation was in fact synonymous with expropriation, for it implied the dissolution of the bond between the land and its former owner. Henceforth the dhimmi was to be "tolerated" on his own land by a foreigner who had obtained possession legally – for appropriation by force was considered legal.

Exploitation of the dhimmi

Having legitimately dispossessed the conquered populations according to the law of battle, the conquerors tried to strengthen their hold by weakening the indigenous population through economic exploitation and inequitable laws. The decisive reason for the conqueror's tolerance of the dhimmi's existence was economic. They were sedentary peoples whose daily work both on the land and in the towns was productive and necessary. The empire expanded with the aid of a Bedouin army which benefitted from the spoils of war, whilst its maintenance was guaranteed by the exploitation of the dhimmis throughout the conquered territories. Henceforth the dhimmis became merely an exploitable human mass from which *corvées* were obtainable at will. At some periods they were tolerated with condescension and at others with animosity, according to the current economic and strategic needs of the empire.

Submission of the dhimmi

The victor–vanquished relationship, being one of force, compelled the master to maintain the dhimmi in a permanent state of weakness, subordination and inferiority. The dhimmi was forbidden to carry arms or keep them at home. He could be condemned to death for raising his hand against a member of the conquering race, even in defense when criminally assaulted or attacked by a child. In certain circumstances, however, the enrollment of dhimmi mercenaries was permitted; on such occasions the latter enjoyed the same rights as Muslims.

The expropriation and economic exploitation of the dhimmi peoples required a moral justification. In order to legitimise the conquerors' right over the person and property of the vanquished, the ruling power glorified the superiority of the chosen conquering race as well as the spriritual values which it upheld, contrasting them with the perversity of the vanquished dhimmis.

It was necessary for the dominating group to illustrate by its dignity, authority, and wealth the divine grace which rewarded the just cause of the conquerors in contrast with the humility, isolation and degradation of the vanquished. The conquerors endeavoured to debase the very soul of the dhimmi by imposing on him the outward signs of moral degradation. When the politico-military danger of a massive revolt on the part of the dhimmis had passed, it was this moral and social degradation of the human being, justified by the superiority of the master-race, which characterised the dhimmi condition. But even then the political implications of the victor-vanquished relationship would survive side by side with that of the dominator-dominated, oppressor-oppressed relationship.

The dominant power felt obliged to expose publicly the imputed depravity of the dhimmis, especially as their culture — as heirs to the ancient civilisations of the Orient — was imcomparably more developed than that of the conquerors. According to the renowned sheikh Damanhûrî, the dhimmis *"must not imitate the garb of the men of learning and honor, or wear luxurious garb, silk, or, say, fine cloth. They must be distinguished from ourselves in attire, as the local custom of each area may have it, but without adornment, so that it indicates their humiliation, submission, and basement. Their shoelaces must not be like ours. Where closed shoes are worn, not laced footwear, their shoes should be coarse, of unpleasant colour. The Companions* [of the Prophet] *agreed upon these points in order to demonstrate the abasement of the infidel and to protect the weak believer's faith."*[1] (Egypt, 18th century)

Debasement of the dhimmi

A code of rules (the Covenant of 'Umar) based on religious and juridical texts, enforced upon the already despoiled and subjugated dhimmi a moral debasement which reduced him to the outward appearance of complete contemptibility. He was deprived of all means of defence, either physical or legal, thus rendering him cowardly in comparison with the courage of his superior; he was obliged to grovel in a servile manner so that the victor would appear more generous; he was forced to live in fear of the morrow so that each day he was delivered from death would fill him with gratitude, stifling his will to revolt against his oppressor, who only spared him because of his productiveness. According to the Maghrebin theologian Sayh Muhammad al-Magifî, on the day set aside for collecting the poll–tax *(gizya)*, the Jews were to be asembled in a public place, such as the bazaar, at the lowest and most debasing place. The tax collectors were to stand above the Jews in a threatening position so that it should appear to everyone that the latter were to be humiliated and despoiled of their belongings. *"They will then realise what favour we bestow upon them in accepting the gizya and letting them off so easily. Then they should be dragged away, one by one... While paying, the dhimmi should be slapped in the face and pushed away so that he would consider that through this form of ransom he has escaped the sword."*[2] (Maghreb, 15th century)

Through isolation, infamy, vulnerability and poverty, the dhimmi became a social pariah. The game had been won, and from then on the plundering of this subhuman being, both his person and his possessions, was interpreted as a sign of the Divine Will rewarding the just cause of the victor. To claim that the goods and honours which certain dhimmis enjoyed were illegal and sinful was an easy next step, taken by the famous jurist, Ibn Taymiyya, who asserted that it was incumbent on rulers *"to humiliate and oppress them* [the dhimmis] by compelling them to observe the commandments of 'Umar; they have the duty to withdraw them from the important posts they occupy and generally to prohibit them from access to Muslim affairs."[3] (Egypt, 14th century)

Toleration of such a despicable creature was indeed a token of the victor's generosity, but it was not to go unpaid for. Thus, according to the same jurist, the dominant community should tighten the yoke on its *protégé* so that he may realise that to flee from this condition of infamy would be punished by reprisals: at every moment he was threatened with death or exile. He was to live in an atmosphere of permanent menace. The toleration which spared his life was not to be taken for granted, it was to be bought with gold and servility, and it would be unilaterally abolished since the punishment of the infidel was only tempor–arily held at bay. This reprieve, in order to be extended, demanded more gold and more humiliation, more work and more corruption.

Since the loyalty of the dhimmi to his religion was the corner–stone of his passive resistance to the conqueror, it was therefore necessary to debase it. The building of new religious edifices was prohibited, whereas those dating from the pre–Islamic period could be restored only under certain conditions, providing that no enlargment or embellishment should improve the original structure. In other words, any restoration merely maintained them in a constant state of disrepair. Religious objects were looked upon with scorn as symbols of contemptible practices and were frequently pillaged, burnt or profaned. Their debasement added to the degradation of the few dhimmi places of worship which had escaped destruction and confiscation.

These, then were the political, economic and moral motivations which produced both the dhimmi status and the whole system of myths which justify the infernal cycle of debasement of man by man. Indeed, the dhimmi condition was by no means an historical exception. A number of discriminatory practices already existed in Eastern Christendom, and these were transmitted by Arabised converts and assimilated into the historical, political and religious values of the Arab conquerors.

History forgotten

Nowadays, when trying to dig up the past of the dhimmi communities, the historian is overwhelmed by the silences of history which cover the deaths of nations. Standing out from the ashes of abandoned places, only ruined synagogues, churches and profaned cemeteries are to be found. Even the humiliation of the past, which symbolised the dhimmi's resistance against oppression, is forgotten, or rather denied, by his descendants – for they have been freed by the West and are eager to forget their ancestral humiliation – and by those who have deliberately falsified or concealed historical truth.

The silence which smothers the cries of past oppression and humiliation is symbolic of the dhimmi destiny. People without a past, they are also a people without rights; and in our time, when petty nationalisms spring up artificially within a decade, acquiring their national slogans at will, the rights of the dhimmis to national autonomy in their liberated homeland or equal rights with their oppressors are never mentioned. Remnants of nations – dead yet living peoples – preserved in spite of a thousand years of silence based on the principle that all criticism of the oppressor is blasphemy, they are the embodiment of silent suffering. In the victor–vanquished relationship, they are still today victims of a *totalist* policy: absolutely everything for the victor, absolutely nothing for the vanquished. The conqueror may glory in a triumphantly successful imperialism, in the lustre of pillaged civilisations, in the world's respect for strength and power. The vanquished must eke out a subordinate existence, affirming the grandeur of the masters and the contempt which history reserves for the weak, for the loser.

Israel: Dhimmi State

Is it necessary, it may be asked, to convey a message which no longer resounds in the hearts of a posterity which denies its past? For one who, herself a dhimmi, has in her quest for identity explored the abyss of oppression, the world today is full of dhimmis: for the system which produces them, not having been uncovered in our time, is still at work. The truth is that the dhimmi condition has reached the free world from the Orient, in the sense that the victims of the Arab economic boycott and of PLO-inspired international terrorism – banishing by death whomsoever blasphemes against Arabism – are also dhimmis. Worse, there is even a dhimmi state: Israel, existing yet denied. The system of values which produced the dhimmi today decrees that to harass, assassinate or mutilate the Israeli population and its sympathisers guilty of rebellion (Zionism), is legal and commendable. The same penalties were used to chastise the rebellious dhimmi, whose revolt was considered as blasphemy – contesting as it did the dogma of the victor's superiority and the inferiority of the vanquished. Racialism, imperialism, colonialism are the hateful cloth of contempt and derision thrown on the State of Israel in order to disarm and ostracise a country, whose population, largely composed of dhimmi refugees from Arab lands liberated by Zionism, struggles for survival.

But are not references to the past detrimental to any prospects of peace opening out in the Middle East, and should not such indictments be pushed into the background? These two points are important. The first implies that the teaching of history must submit to the political expediencies of the present, a policy which would result not only in historical falsification, but also in the denial of history. If this is so, world peace will demand the destruction of all the history books of humanity which henceforth, deprived of its memory, experience, culture and intelligence, will revert to barbarism. Once the utility of human history has been admitted, to deny this principle to the dhimmi nations exclusively, on the pretext that their past is merely a denunciation of oppression, would raise a moral problem for history itself. Are persecuted and humiliated peoples to be rejected on the grounds that history is destined to become the narcissistic reflection of supermen and victors who boast unremorsefully of their glory, who are steeped in the blood and misery of the vanquished?

It is my belief that an objective knowledge of the past, though not itself the fundamental condition in bringing about brotherly understanding among mankind, is nevertheless a necessary stepping-stone. To deny the objective data of history reflects the same mentality which once taught, in defiance of all evidence, that the sun orbits the earth.

And then . . . there is peace . . . and peace.

There is the *pax arabica* imposed by Khaled of Arabia in order to halt Communist progress in the Orient and to create the requisite conditions for the destruction of Israel: to isolate the Hebrew State, whilst arming its neighbours to the teeth during a "cold war" aimed at weakening it by the return to its territory of Palestinised Arabs. That kind of peace is no more than a tactical peace in a strategy of war.

There could be another kind of peace, however, the only real peace which makes sense in the geo-political history of the Orient. And this peace can only come about after a revolutionary recasting of the values of Arabism which will, for the first time, bring about a renunciation of totalist concepts and the acceptance of equal rights and national autonomy for dhimmi nations. But, one might object, is Israel — a part of whose population is of European extraction — really a dhimmi nation? If the Hebrew people can resurrect on their ancestral soil the language, the institutions, the historical geography, the culture and the pre-Islamic national traditions characteristic of this land, then Israel is truly a dhimmi nation which has achieved its decolonisation. The dispersion of the Hebrew nation following an imperialist annexation of territory cannot be advanced as a justification for this annexation. In other words, the defects which the victim develops as a result of oppression cannot be used by the oppressor as a pretext for his oppression (dominator-dhimmi relationship). But it is in fact this dispersion, resulting from the expropriation of the land of the Jewish dhimmi, which is invoked in order to legitimise the Arabisation of the conquered territory.

Article 20 of the PLO's National Covenant claims that Jews do not form a real people and are no more than citizens of the states to which they belong. Article 1 explains the reasoning behind this attitude: *Palestine is the homeland of the Arab Palestinian people; it is an indivisible part of the Arab homeland, and the Palestinian people are an integral part of the Arab nation.*"[4] – which in modern terminology is the Arab empire.

The rebirth of a pre–Islamic Hebrew language and culture, in a land conquered and Arabised by force, constitutes a revolutionary defiance of the totalist mentality that has so long conditioned the dominator–dhimmi relationship. In Israel, the Hebrew language – the pre–Arabic national vernacular – enjoys equality with Arabic and is not considered an inferior or non–existent language, as is Kurdish, which is today struggling to survive, or Syriac, which has long since disappeared in Iraq and Syria. And Judaisation or re–Hebraisation of Arabised lands re–instates a dhimmi culture – exterminated in some parts, held in contempt in others, particularly in the Land of Israel in order to affirm and maintain its Arabisation – on an equal footing with the conqueror's culture.

Thus it can be seen that the recognition of Israel must be not merely a tactical toleration for a limited period. A true recognition would demand from Arabism – as a necessary pre-requisite for peaceful coexistence between Arabs and dhimmi nations including respect for each other's rights – a total revision of the values which assured its expansion and domination. Such a critical revision of Panarabism as an ideological movement would bring to an end the historical perspective in which the dhimmi nations have been dehumanised for so long and would open the first breach in the totalist mentality.

Against the background of these historical and political motive forces, the territorial aspect of the Israelo–Arab conflict seems of secondary importance and will finally depend on the evolution of the mental attitudes elaborated in the Orient during centuries of Arabisation. In order that a process towards peace may last and bear fruit between Arabs and liberated dhimmi nations, it must take into account the sociological and cultural human substratum fashioned by history. To succeed in making peace – to work for a peace which is not a temporary expedient – one must know the dhimmi history.

THE LIBERATION OF THE DHIMMI

The day on which crime adorns itself with the effects of innocence, by a strange reversal . . . innocence is summoned to provide its own justification – Albert Camus

During the sessions of the colloquium on Zionism which took place at the College de France (Paris, October 1976) the ideological attitudes of European Zionism were discussed by noted specialists. With the exception of Madame Bensimon–Donath, no one appeared to remark the absence of that forgotten representative, Oriental Jewry, still waiting for the doors of history to open. It is important, not perhaps numerically (it forms only a small part of the Jewish people) but by virtue of the lessons to be learned from its history. Leaving aside the political context and the misrepresentation of Zionism as Western imperialism, it serves the interests of scientific research as well as of the Jewish people to discover this other Zionism – the Zionism of fervour, backbone Zionism, which motivated the transplantation to Israel of entire Oriental communities. It is a Zionism of the humble which was never spoken about because it was as natural and as necessary to the Oriental masses as the air they breathed. And if Oriental Jews produced neither great theoretical debates nor organisational structures, the reason, is, judging by their massive Return to Israel, that Zionist teaching would have been superfluous; and also because, in Arab lands, Zionism was often forced to operate clandestinely. Moreover, if the emigration of Oriental Jewry was not set in motion until 1948, it was because its leaders understood that the saving of European Jewry was a vital priority. Besides, Arab pressure reduced the possibilities of emigration.

Certainly, it would be as well for European Jewish intellectuals – particularly for the new generation overflowing with political generosity – to turn towards this venerable ancestor of Western Jewry in order to discover the greatness and nobility of its destiny. For Western Jewry, even though it represents the majority does not constitute the totality of the Jewish people, and its history, although interesting, does not cover that of all the people of Israel. Oriental Jewry, whose past is torn down and used unscrupulously by political opportunists, can and must make an indispensable moral and historical contribution to the history of Israel.

The history of Oriental Jewry is interesting from many points of view. First it gives us an insight into the significance and specific evolution of Arab–Jewish relations. Second, it explains the later development of the dhimmi nations, since the fate of the Jews of Arabia foreshadowed the fate of the dhimmis and was accepted as standard procedure throughout the period of Arab conquest. The Jewish condition in traditional Islam – similar

143

to that of the Christian — was determined by the manner in which the Arabs in their expansion refused to recognize the national autonomy of the pre—Islamic cultures and civilisations whose lands they had usurped. But like all national histories, that of the dhimmis is not confined to a framework of cause and effect, i.e., a chain of facts and political and economical phases. It spills over into a specific spiritual universe, the moral dimensions of which, forged in the course of thirteen centuries, are still noticeable in the reaction of peoples when confronted with history. And the cardinal historical event that changed Jewish life in the Orient was the massive Return to Israel in a period of less than two decades. So the traditional attitudes of the Jewish dhimmis show themselves in their return to Zion.

In the first place, this "Gathering in of the Exiles to Israel" is in keeping with the Messianic current which traversed and invigorated the history of dhimmi Jewry — and only this current can explain the collective determination to remain Jewish in the face of the persecution stemming from this determination. This hope of Return is expressed in a dual attitude, apparently contradictory: a collective faithfulness to a national past, paradoxically related to a futurist vision of a better society, for every Messianic expectation necessarily implies faith in the future. The massive transfer of Oriental Jews to Israel is in accordance with historic continuity; it is the fulfillment of their Messianic—national aspirations, cherished throughout their Exile.

In respect of their relations with the Arab world, Oriental Jews also perpetuate the traditional attitudes of the dhimmi towards the Muslim. Indeed in Islam the dhimmi has a very precise economic function which the builders of the Muslim Empire con-ferred upon him and which was subsequently confirmed in all the legislative texts which governed his status. The Caliph 'Umar, who is considered the founder of the Muslim Empire, had already commanded, during the conquest of Syria, that the indigenous peoples should not be shared out among the Arabs, but should be subjected to taxation so that the following generations of Muslims might benefit from their labour: *"Our children will live off them indefinitely for as long as they survive and these people will remain slaves to the adherents of Islam for as long as the latter endure. Therefore, strike them with the poll-tax. . ."*[5] The taxes imposed on dhimmis, writes the famous jurist al—Mâwardî (ob. 1058) *"are two burdens imposed on the polytheists by Allah for the benefit of the Faithful."* The dhimmis were thus a human mass which was to be tolerated as long as it could be exploited.

144

When the interests of Islam required it, the community of
the Faithful were duty-bound to execute dhimmi males and reduce
their women and children to slavery while taking possession of
their belongings; or, as an alternative, they could be expelled
and their property confiscated. Both measures were legal, and
they were left to the whim of the ruler holding the religious
and political authority. In modern times the second alternative
was applied to Jews in many Arab countries.

It is true that Oriental Jews had *chosen* to return to Israel,
but nonetheless they did not *depart* from Arab countries, in most
cases, they were *expelled* under the most painful circumstances,
forced to leave behind them all their belongings whilst suffering brutality and humiliation — for, it should be added, the
humiliation and degradation of the dhimmi is also the legal
prerogative of the community of the Faithful.

Hence, in the 20th century, Jews were treated as dhimmis —
in conformity with tradition — by some Arab states which had
just obtained their independence. And, curiously enough, the
Jews reacted in exactly the traditional manner of dhimmis. As
in the past, they resigned themselves to suffer massacre, rape
and pillage, being disarmed in the face of violence and the law
by the prohibition to carry arms and the lack of the right of
appeal to the courts. Thus in modern times they silently accepted
confiscation of the fruit of generations of dhimmi labour. For
thirteen centuries, men's justice had relegated them to a condition which was in reality permanent injustice. Could justice
imply for them anything else but nothingness or derision? Such
ideas as vindicating their rights or even imagining that they
had any rights were so revolutionary that they were inconceivable
to the dhimmi mentality. Thus the dhimmis never even dreamed of
complaining to international organisations. Neither did they
organise themselves into terrorist gangs to kill innocent Arab
civilians in order to take revenge on the governments which had
exploited and robbed them. They never required the international
community to provide for their needs. They never exploited the
compassion of public opinion for destructive political aims.
Conditioned to submissiveness, to humility and to silence by the
moral after-effects of a prolonged condition of fear, injustice
and oppression, heroically endured during thirteen centuries,
the Jewish refugees from Arab countries were able to find within
themselves the moral force necessary to overcome these ordeals.
Because of this, the psychological and physical problems of
social and economic integration affecting about two million

Oriental Jews, including children, are today practically unknown to the world at large or even to Western Jewry.

How then did the modern dhimmis manage? Exactly as their forefathers when driven out, exiled and pillaged; they had to face adversity with nothing but their own resources. They returned to their economic function as dhimmis: that of tireless creative workers. But there was one difference: they had now broken the pact of servitude and were henceforth masters of their own destiny.

The Oriental Jews returned to Israel, cultivated the desert, built up border towns, elaborated the country's industrial infra-structure and participated in the war of national defence. And when the Arab nations, who had exploited, oppressed and robbed them, hired terrorists to kill their children and dynamite their new homes, they replied yet again as would dhimmis, with a peace offer – in other words, with a Messianic vision of the redemptions of peoples, a Messianism which, as has been seen, was engendered by the determination to remain dhimmis in the hope that one day their servitude would come to an end.

The Oriental Jewish refugees who emigrated to Europe and America had to confront difficulties which were in no way less arduous. Without any help whatever they had to integrate themselves into a highly technical society and provide for their families and the education of their children. Today, when the Arab economic boycott again threatens the efforts of these refugees, the Jews of the Orient respond once more with a call for peace.

The study of the dhimmi condition is a rich source of instruc-tion. It invites us to ponder on the destiny of the exploited and oppressed human being, not because of any fatality of his (race, colour, social clan) but as a result of *his* deliberate choice, renewed throughout the ages, to remain on a spiritual plane higher than that of his oppressors whatever the brand of infamy imposed upon him. In the oppressor–oppressed dialectic which ensured, one can see the typical profile of the dhimmi: a courage manifesting itself in silence rather than in words, a tragedy forever overcome because chosen, the humble nobility of daily heroism re-enacted time and again.

This is also the meaning of the extraordinary lesson in bravery given to the world by a handful of men ready to die, misunderstood, despised and forsaken: the Maronites of Lebanon.

DOCUMENT

Jewish dhimmis of Jerusalem

"Agreeably to Your Lordship's commands, I have the honour to report on the state of the Jews in Palestine, so far as I am able in the present state of the country, when owing to the Quarantines, our means of communication are very limited. [...]

The spirit of toleration towards the Jew, is not yet known here to the same extent it is in Europe – though their being permitted to live in the Musulman Quarter, is some evidence that the fierce spirit of oppression is somewhat abated. It should however be named that they pay more than others do for the rent of their Houses, thus they may be considered in some measure to purchase toleration.

The Pacha* has shewn much more consideration for the Jews than His people have. I have heard several acknowledge that they enjoy more peace and tranquility under his Government, than ever they have enjoyed here before. Still, the Jew in Jerusalem is not estimated in value much above a dog – and scarcely a day passes that I do not hear of some act of Tyranny and oppression against a Jew – chiefly by the soldiers, who enter their Houses and borrow whatever they require without asking any permission – sometimes they return the article, but more frequently not. In two instances, I have succeeded in obtaining justice for Jews against Turks. But it is quite a new thing in the eyes of these people to claim justice for a Jew – and I have good reason to think that my endeavours to protect the Jews, have been – and may be for some little time to come, detrimental to my influence with other classes – Christians as well as Turks. [i.e., Muslims]

[...] another Despatch to Her Majesty's Agent, on the subject of a new Proclamation which has been issued here, forbidding the Jews from praying in their own Houses – and reporting a most barbarous punishment of a Jew and Jewess that took place in Jerusalem this week. [...]

What the Jew has to endure, at all hands, is not to be told.

Like the miserable dog without an owner he is kicked by one because he crosses his path, and cuffed by another because he cries out – to seek redress he is afraid, lest it bring worse upon him; he thinks it better to endure than to

live in the expectation of his complaint being revenged upon
him. Brought up from infancy to look upon his civil dis-
abilities everywhere as a mark of degradation, his heart
becomes the cradle of fear and *suspicion – he finds he is
trusted by none – and therefore he lives himself without
confidence in any. [...]*

*Ibrahim Pacha, son of Muhammed Ali, ruler of Egypt. He
conquered and controlled Syria and Palestine from 1832-
1840. From a report (23.5.1839) W. T. Young, British
Vice-Consul, Jerusalem to Viscount Palmerston, Foreign
Minister, London (F.O. 78/368 No 13)
A.M. Hyamson, *The British Consulate in Jerusalem in
relation to the Jews of Palestine,* London, 1939, Part I,
pp. 4-7.

RETROSPECTIVE ON DHIMMI LAND

Judaea and Samaria

July. the light blazes in the silence. On every side:
Judaea. There's a hillock . . . hardly a hill, a tear-drop on
the Judaean land. It is Bethar, where once stood the fortress of
the courageous Bar Kochba, the last stronghold of ancient Hebrew
resistance. The stones testify in silence, for the earth cannot
lie. It confides its message to whomsoever listens, without even
the need to turn over the soil with a trowel. All is there,
laid bare as in an open book, despite the ravages of conquerors.
A square tower and a wall joining two bastions bear witness to
the beauty and solidity of the typical Hebrew architecture of
the First Temple period. Over there a wall and tower built by
Herod more than half a millenium later. And crowning it all,
Bar Kochba's fortification: a square tower faced with stones,
semi-circular watch-towers and gates. Further away the traces of
the Roman encampment can still be seen. Here, on the 9th of Ab
in the year 135, the Hebrew resistance was annihilated by the
Roman army.
Silence. We have taken cover in the shade of an olive tree.
Instantly the children have nestled in the branches, listening
solemnly to our guide. Somewhere a fig-tree perfumes the air
. . . or is it merely the breeze of the Judaean hills? Circular
gesture by Ya'acov Meshoreer, chief curator of archaeology at
the Israel Musem, renowned numismatist and former supervisor of
excavations in Jadaea-Samaria.

148

"Excavations in Judaea have brought to light flourishing towns possessing numerous synagogues. The architecture as well as the ornemental patterns are typical of the attractive pre-Islamic Hebrew civilisation, represented in Galilee by the synagogues of Capernaum, Beth Shearim, Chorazim, Kefar Baram, Meron and other places. Between the years 70 A.D. and the Arab invasion and occupation in 640, these hills were dotted with Hebrew towns and villages where an intense national, religious and cultural life prospered. Deprived of its independence, the nation concentrated its genius by reflecting upon the richness of its national past. This is the period in which Mishnah was elaborated and completed in the second century, shortly to be followed by the Talmud – monumental religious, legal and social compendia. Completed in about 400, this work was continued for another two centuries, keeping alive an intense Messianic fervour whose force was to be felt as far as Arabia.

The Arab occuption scarcely modifed the Hebrew place-names, and the Jewish inhabitants, now considered as dhimmis, remained on their lands. It was only later that the relentless mechanism typical of every colonisation gradually wiped out the indigenous populaton, thereby encouraging a progressive Arabisation of the soil."

In the former Jewish town of Bethar, there are now 1500 Arabs. They call the place where the Jewish vestiges stand Khirbet al-Yahud, the ruins of the Jews. Nevertheless, were the Israelis to return, the Arabs would not hesitate to chase them away with indignation, referring to them as foreign intruders. Mystery of the Oriental mind or logic of the occupant? These Arabs, hardly interested in a past which is not theirs, ignore totally the history of the places where they live. Of course they know that the spot was inhabited formerly by Jews, as the name indicates, but these ruins, relating to a people dispos-sessed and driven out, are only of interest as a quarry conven-iently providing stones which others have hewn. But the excited comments from the olive tree taught me that any Jewish child knows more about the history of this place than its Arab inhab-itants.

In Eshtemoa, a biblical name Arabised by the occupants into Es-Samoa, the Arab inhabitants still live in houses built prac-tically fifteen centuries earlier. The architectural elements and decorative designs, including the menorah, are all typical of pre-Islamic Hebrew art. It is common to find Arab villagers cooking on ancient mosaic floors. In the centre of the village was once a three-storied synagogue, of which only two ruined floors remain. The size of the synagogue suggests that there flourished here an important community. Like many other indigenous monuments, the synagogue was destroyed at the beginning of the Arab occupation. Its stones, particularly those decorated with bas-reliefs, were used by the Arabs and today adorn their door-posts.

At Yata, the biblical name of a Hebrew village, beautifully decorated Jewish ossuaries typical of the 1st and 2nd centuries are scattered around Arab houses and used as drinking-troughs for their cattle. Many troves of coins dating from the 2nd Temple and Hasmonean periods have been found in this area.

The discrepancy between history and population in Judaea and Samaria troubles the traveller constantly. It is true that the Hebrew place-names have been Arabised, that Jewish religious shrines have been Islamised – as in Hebron and elsewhere – and that Arabisation has succeeded in effacing all traces of Hebrew nationalism. It is also true that from afar the Arab villages seem picturesque. This is only a superficial impression, however, for if the traveller, endeavouring to account for his troubled spirit, were to look more closely he would often discover a mere heap of ruins. The neglect of the surrounding vegetation is so general that one is reminded not of a biblical landscape of wooded hillsides, but of the sandy wastes of Arabia. One is struck with pity, for people do not generally live in ruins, however poor they are. Ruins are seen everywhere, so much so that they are no longer noticed.

In 1864, Arthur Penrhyn Stanley, the Dean of Westminster, remarked that Palestine, more than any other country, was a land of ruins. *"In Judaea it is hardly an exaggeration to say that whilst for miles and miles there is no appearance of present life or habitation, except the occasional goat-herd on the hillside, or gathering of women at the wells, there is yet hardly a hill-top of the many within sight which is not covered by the vestiges of some fortress or city of former ages. Sometimes they are fragments of ancient walls, sometimes mere foundations and piles of stone, but always enough to indicate signs of human habitation and civilisation."*[6]

The hillside terraces which in ancient times were planted with vineyards and olive trees are not the only aspect of destruction. What could be more distressing than these poor settlements without streets, houses – or rather dilapidated cubes – devoid of architecture, haphasardly propped up with sculptured blocks, broken columns and capitals ransacked from the monuments of previous civilisations. Banished or massacred, the indigenous dhimmis have completely disappeared. The nomads became sedentary, the colonists came. They camped in the houses of others, patching them up when necessary by destroying monuments which they had not built. Its past hardly interested them, strangers on this land taken from others: it was not theirs. And when the relentless torment of the Exile brought the indigenous inhabitants back to their land, the fear of this continual return and prospect of having to share the land with the despoiled victims resulted in animosity and bloodshed. Historical evidence is not wanting, but it will suffice to quote one or two testimonies from the last century. In a report to Palmerston in 1836, Colonel Campbell, the British Consul-General in Egypt describes how *"their Mahomedan fellow-countrymen of Saffet took advantage of the disorderly state of the country, and fell, on the 16th of June, on the innocent Jews of that town, robbed their property, violated their women, assassinated those who attempted resistance, and continued their lawless proceedings for thirty-three days."*[7] At about the same time in 1834, the American traveller John Lloyd Stephens, describes similar scenes perpetrated against the Jews of Hebron, who witnessed with their own eyes the rape of their wives and daughters.[8]

In 1872, the English traveller, Thomas Jenner, was deeply moved during a visit to Nablus by the distress of two Jews, *"the government having chased them from their homes and thrown them into the street with their belongings because they had need of their abode in order to quarter soldiers."*[9] Nothing exceptional about such a measure, for the lodging and maintenance of Muslim troops was often an obligation imposed by the conqueror on the native dhimmis. At times of rampant anarchy the invaders were encouraged by such a law to dispossess their predecessors "legally" – especially if it is remembered that the latter were completely unarmed and their sworn testimony refused. This is only an insignificant element alongside so many others in the long chain of events which transformed the dhimmi peoples from majorities to "tolerated" minorities in their own land.

But nowhere else is the tragedy of history so poignant as in Shomron-Sebastia in Samaria. Nowhere else is the devastation so sinister as in the ruins of this ancient capital of the northern Kingdom of Israel, founded about 880 B.C. Here, more than anywhere else perhaps, the contrast is striking between the present desolation and the magnificent vestiges of a flourishing and active population. There are the fortifications and palaces of Omri, Ahab and Jezebel, the granaries of Jeroboam II (787–749). Herod built here an avenue bordered with columns. A theatre, a stadium, a city wall with gates and towers testify to the solid, elegant, Hebrew architecture of this period.

Today, Shomron–Sebastia is nothing more than a miserable village where 1300 Arabs camp among the ruins. The church built by the Crusaders, in which lie ancient tombs attributed to the Hebrew prophets Elisha and Obadiah, has become their mosque. Despite the rubble on the floor – due to an accumulation of centuries of neglect – the building remains impressive. Foreigners to this past, the present inhabitants ignore it and cover their misery in the ruins. These columns, these sculptured stones are merely used as material for repairing their poor hovels. Human distress and the cataclysms of history are brought together here to make of Shomron–Sebastia the symbol of the greatness and extermination of a people.

This people, victim of the world's longest–lasting genocide, is represented today by a remnant. 250 Samaritans, no more, "tolerated" by 44,000 Arabs in their former capital of Shechem–Neapolis, Arabised to Nablus. This is not the place to describe the massacres, confiscations and persecutions of all kinds which reduced this numerous population of farmers and skilled artisans to the size of a pathetic remnant. The interested reader can consult the article *Samaritan* in the Encyclopaedia Judaica (1971), where mention is made of the threat of total extermination which, in 1842, would certainly have overcome this inoffensive and dying community of 142 souls had not another dhimmi community – the Jews of Jerusalem – come to their rescue at the last moment. Benyamin Tsedaka, a 125th generation descendant of Manessah (son of the patriarch Joseph), explains that the reason for the numerical difference today between Jews and Samaritans is that his people refused to go into exile. *"Our principle was not to leave* [the Land of] *Israel."* (International Herald Tribune, 8 March 1977.) This is the simple explanation of the historical anomaly of a Samaria without Samaritans and a Judaea without Jews. Today, the magnificent ruins of Shomron–Sebastia are among the most moving monuments in Israel. Because they were a Jewish sect attached to the soil, the Samaritans suffered their "final solution" in obscure and humble silence in which history has buried the dhimmis.

Today the dhimmi's spectre, shrouded in hatred, despoiled and despairing of all human justice since he has been rejected by it

– so often described for those who know where to look – haunts the deserted hills of Judaea and Samaria where his destiny was embodied.

Today the populations of these regions are Muslims, with the exception of a few pockets of Arabised Christians, remnants of the Byzantine occupation or of Crusader times, who have survived thanks to the protection of European Christendom. The Samaritans have been reduced in their homeland to 470 survivors, of whom 250 still live in Nablus. Up until 1948, Jewish inhabitants of the region were massacred or expelled and the right to reside was prohibited them until 1967. The Arabisation of the region resulted in a *judenrein* Arab province, i.e., "cleaned" of all trace of its pre–Arab culture.

The indigenous peoples were replaced by Greeks, Arab–Beduins, Persians, Druzes, Circassians, Turks and Slavs, who were thus able to benefit from the Arabised land of the dhimmis. Yet since 1967, these peaceful villagers, with unperturbed consciences, who justified their Arab rights established by the martyrdom of the banished or annihilated native peoples, are now experiencing a nightmare. The Hebrew, exiled in the wake of successive waves of occupation and its sequels, or tolerated in his own homeland but in a state of subjection – this Hebrew now returns. And he comes back, no longer as a dhimmi – the sole status acceptable for a native – but as a citizen enjoying all the rights of a free man. It is true that however scandalous it may seem, such an occurrence is not unique. Several dhimmi peoples have recovered their independence: Sicilians, Spaniards, Greeks and Maronites, but not without leaving open wounds in the Panarabic consciousness. "We intend to fight in order that our Palestinian homeland will not become a new Andalusia", declared Abu Iyad, one of the principal leaders of the P.L.O. (Le Monde, 20–21 January 1974). Should one be surprised that certain Arab circles deplore the Hispanisation of Spain, the Lebanisation of Lebanon and Hebraisation of Israel?

Thus the Hebrew returns. . . With care he searches among the ruins and brings to light thousand–year–old documents bearing Hebrew inscriptions, meaningless to the villagers. The monuments and coins which he discovers confirm his history. The Hebrew, treated as a foreigner, reaches out to the soil which yields up its history. A perfectly harmonious dialogue in time and space is established between them.

The nightmare postponed for all these centuries by inhuman laws suddenly becomes a reality. There is no doubt about it, the native has returned. And what if he were to take back his land, restore the destroyed hill-terraces, rebuild his innumerable ruined synagogues? What if it were possible to evaluate the suffering of thirteen centuries of forced exile? If there was exile, then there must have been occupation – the two concepts are inseparable – and each knows his respective history. So a resistance is prepared against the gathering-in of the Exiles in an Arabised land.

But the Israeli is not interested in quibbling over the past, all he wants is to build a new future. Without chasing anyone away, all he wants is to return home. These Arabs born and bred on this soil are in no way responsible for a thousand-year-old imperialism, even if they are its heirs and benefactors. No one is to be a foreigner, thus the Israeli proposes a peaceful coexistence on the land of his history in the towns and villages which bear Hebrew names. He is ready to share with his Arab cousin, whose language is so similar to his own. It is all very simple: a discriminatory legislation, like that to which the dhimmi was submitted, does not exist in either the history or jurisdiction of Israel. Thus, from the Israeli point of view, there is nothing to impede a normal relationship of equality being established between the two parties.

The present Arab populations are faced with a choice: acceptance of peaceful coexistence and a relationship of equality between Arabs and Hebrews instead of the traditional dominator-dhimmi relationship; or a continuance of the traditional *Jihad* in massacring, exiling or dominating the legitimate heir in a renewed effort of total Arabisation. *"The civil war in Lebanon is not over and blood will continue to flow! Our war in Lebanon will save the Arabisation of the Lebanon. I declare in the name of the Palestinian movement, and for the national leftwing Lebanese forces, that Lebanon will remain Arab,"* Arafat declared on 30 November 1975 in Damascus. This choice also concerns other Oriental peoples other than Israel. It opposes a tradition of Arab domination to a revolutionary liberation movement striving for *the rights of other non-Arab Oriental peoples.*

With these thoughts in my mind, I strolled through an Arab quarter on the outskirts of Jerusalem, hardly a hundred yards from Mount Zion. Suddenly a hail of stones welcomed me. A group of Arab adolescents shielding behind oil drums were hurling projectiles and curses at me whilst they screamed their loyalty to the P.L.O. The movement I made in order to protect myself took me back twenty years to the Jewish cemetery in Cairo

154

where I had accompanied some elderly relatives, widows who were taking leave of their departed, for, as Jewesses, they were effectively being banished from Egypt. They were startled by a hail of stones strown by a group of Arabs. Chased off by jeers, they fled as fast as they could, as vulnerable in their old age as the mortal remains which they were abandoning to probable depredations. And the gesture which we then made, they to protect themselves and I to shield them, was the same as I was now making under Arab projectiles in Jerusalem, city of David, King of Israel. A gesture repeated for a thousand years by the dhimmi burying his dead in secret and in haste or attached and humiliated in the streets. Traditional gesture of the Arab, passed on from father to son with the same contemptuous hatred of the oppressor towards his victims.

In that same month of July 1977, the waves of bomb-attacks in Israel and the attempts to wipe out the Maronites in southern Lebanon reminded me that the spilling of dhimmi blood was still lawful. . . .

NOTES

1) Ed. & tr. Moshe Perlmann, *Shaykh Damanhuri On the Churches of Cairo* (1739), University of California 1975, p. 56.

2) Georges Vajda, *Un traité Maghrébin: "Adversus Judaeos" Akham Ahl Al-Dimma, du Sayh Muhammad b.'Abd Al-Karim Al-Magili,* in Etudes d'Orientalisme dédiées à la mémoire de Lévy-Provencal, Tome II, Paris 1962, p. 811.

3) Martin Schreiner, *Contributions à l'Histoire des Juifs en Egypte,* in Revue des Etudes Jives, Tome XXXI, Paris 1895, p. 11.

4) Palestine National Covenant of the PLO, in Y. Harkabi, *Palestinians and Israel*, Keter, Jerusalem, 1974, pp. 51-69.

5) Abou Yousof Ya'koub, *Le livre de l'Impôt Foncier (Kitâb el-Kharadj)*, tr. E. Fagnan, Paris 1921, pp. 217-218.

6) Arthur Penrhyn Stanley, *Sinai and Palestine,* London 1866, p. 117.

7) John Bowring, *Report on the Commercial Statistics of Syria, (addressed to Lord Palmerston and presented to both Houses of Parliament)*, London 1840, p. 129 (Reprinted Edition 1973 by Arno Press Inc.).

8) John Lloyd Stephens, *Incidents of Travel in Egypt, Arabia Petraea, and the Holy Land*, New York 1837 (New edition, University of Oklahoma Press 1970, p. 32).

9) Thomas Jenner, *Palestine et Liban*, Paris et Neuchâtel 1883, p. 142.

ESTHER CAMERON

.c

or

The Autoanalysis of a Golem

> No one's
> root——0
> ours.
> Paul Celan

Places where I have been: in Seattle Nadine's room, in the attic of the commune house where we both lived in the summer of 1970. The room was low, you could stand up only in the middle, but it was neatly painted white and made homey by details: a South American blanket on the bed, a machine—lace tablecloth from Good Will, only slightly torn. At one end of the room was a window in the shape of a half—moon, whose frame Nadine had painted a pale blue, and under this window was a table with sawed—off legs, which held her typewriter. I came up there for some purpose once when the rays of the setting sun were just glancing through the half—moon window. She was not there. I walked in anyway, sat down tailor—fashion at the typewriter, and put in a sheet of the yellow newsprint paper that was lying there.

at evening
shadows link arms, dance
away from the sun:

goodbye my straight treetrunks
my broad housefronts
my polished windows glinting in answer

goodbye my
children I have never
seen

It was the summer after c's death, the beginning of a long
year when I walked around stunned, searching not so much for
ways to express my grief as for the feeling itself. It was not
inside me, it was too big for that; it had gone flying in all
directions and I could only find pieces of it now and then in
the world. The setting, the typewriter under the window, the
room itself, so makeshift and at the same time so homelike . . .
The poem was in Nadine's style. I never really had a style,
though I could imitate almost anyone when the mood hit. The
poem was really Nadine's, is still.

* * *

The dreams about c: they return, at longer and longer intervals, it is true. The other night: he had come to my home town,
I saw him sitting in a room somewhere, perhaps also in the airplane. He was looking straight ahead, sitting motionless. The
colors of the dream are muted and nothing extraordinary occurs
in it except that the walls of the — I cannot say rooms — are at
odd angles and levels, as in a cubist painting: c and I are not
exactly in the same room, I perceive him through a general dis-
organization of space. But this is by no means emphasized. Nine
years ago I had violent apocalyptic dreams, dreams in which
symbolism was a palpable dimension, dreams in unnaturally vivid
colors. Finished. Each day takes me farther from the center of
my life — the outbound half of a hyperbolic orbit. Soon the light
of the sun will no longer reach and illuminate me. Then I shall
travel on in the faint general starlight, unseen.

* * *

"Someone who has no choice, for instance if he got up
early to go on the road in a place where there are packs
of wild animals or robbers, so that he cannot stay to
recite even the first paragraph, even up to the words
"Upon thy heart," or else if the people in his caravan
are traveling fast and will not wait for him at all,
may recite (the Shm'a) with its accompanying blessings
as soon as the morning star has risen. . . ."

I found this in a book called the Mishnah Brurah, and for one
moment Judaism stood before me as a person, a person for whom I
felt a mild but unqualified affection. I could see that man in

158

the wilderness, worrying about wild dogs or robbers, or unable
to persuade the others to stop long enough for him to pray. It
was like a moment in Berkeley once, when a man I was not sure I
loved began describing some incident from his past. He described
exactly where he had been in his room relative to the other
person, what had happened and how he had reacted. He seemed to
be describing it not to me (another person) but to himself. What
it was was not important; just that I saw completely how it was
for him, so that an incident in his life became an incident in
mine.

What comes of such occurrences, I wonder? Do they, like the
performance of a commandment, create angels? Or would it be
more correct to say that a room is added onto a certain house, a
large rambling house with no outside and no locations, and no
architecture, as far as anybody knows.

I am at an Orthodox yeshiva for women. – Myself of nine years
ago looks up, astonished. – We learn Judaism here, I explain. I
converted to Judaism, you know. – She did not know, neither does
she understand. Explaining it to her is not going to be easy.

* * *

It was not a good life we led then; more and more I have to
admit it. We spoke many words in vain; we were promiscuous,
mostly unhappily, but seeking happiness as the one goal and
justification of our existence; and we tried innumerable ways to
assert our power over one another without admitting our need for
one another or making promises. Never were we whole; just when
we had managed to retrieve some part of us that had been torn
off and stick it back again, something else would be torn off
and we would have to go looking for it.

For me, beneath all the memories of those years there draws,
like an undertow, like the unceasing, unvarying sound of a drone
instrument, a certain anguish. It is in the background when I
see again the clear colors of a December morning in Berkeley,
with the fog lifting and the roses and the fuchsias still in
bloom; I have to imagine its accompaniment in remembering the
walks through the eucalyptus groves in the hills, the visits
with Ismene and Thomas and Gabriel to the beach, the drives down
to Big Sur. Writing poetry relieved it, or even taking pictures;
also marijuana, because it made everything, colors, sounds
music, words, seem more beautiful and significant, and gave my
thoughts an unaccustomed mobility which distracted me from the

fear they might otherwise have caused. Or rather, like poetry, it taught me to take a certain delight in the fear. As though through the fear something was calling to me, as though within it were safety.

Perhaps that is also why the others turned talkative, around a candle, against a background of Mozart, or Dylan or Joan Baez or the Beatles. It was not that we trusted each other. Rather, trust seemed unnecessary: in the world of words and colors, images and melodies, there wasn't much we could do to each other. The way in which c's poems showed me the world — forgive the comparison — was a little like that. It was a world in which everything had already happened, there remained only the knowing. Because of this I remember those years, despite everything, as a time of freedom.

The marijuana was not the essential ingredient; years later, after my mother had made me swear off it forever, I was able to achieve the same effects with a couple of semi-friends, by means of appropriate lighting, camomile tea, halva, and a record of the songs of the humpback whale. And words. Words were after all the real psychedelic. And what was truly at stake in those years: no one foregathered in its name or demonstrated on its behalf. Perhaps I should say: what was at stake then for me. It did not hold together, I have no mandate now to speak for others.

*   *   *

Tentative bridges, here:

Last week I went with Rachel, who studies in Geulah, to learn with Rabbi S. It was dark, we walked downhill with buildings on one side and rubble on the other, till we came to a house built on so steep a slope that we had to cross from the street to the street-level on a walkway, as if the place were surrounded by a moat. Rabbi S. greeted us, a thin man in a black sweater, with a thin grey-and-black beard and a smile of perpetual delight. Four boys were in the entrance with him; he instructed the two youngest to "give Shalom" to Rachel and me, and they came up, grinning and squirming, to offer us their little hands. These were the first male hands which had been extended to me in Israel, except that of c's friend in Tel Aviv who is not religious. Later of course they would not be able to. Then we went into the main room — it was a very plain apartment, repeating the statement of religious homes all over Geulah and Mea Shearim that material things do not count for much — and sat around the table. Rabbi S. was in no hurry to open the Chumashim, he wanted to find out who the new person was. A poet? Did I have any poems with me? Rachel and I each had a poem, and he read them aloud, explaining them as he went, looking over at us for confirmation. Rachel's poem was a hymn of praise to Jerusalem; mine tried to evoke a gathering of kindred minds in counsel. Although Rabbi S. claimed not to know much about poetry, he grasped Rachel's images, and the thoughts my poem struggled to express, very well. What he said was almost exactly what I had meant, except in one place where he added something. And it seemed that he was pleased, that he wanted what I wanted.

After the lessons he walked us back to the main road. In response to Rachel's saying that she was no longer worrying about whether she could become a *tsadeket*, he said, "Long ago I gave up trying to become a *tsaddik*. Now I just try to enjoy life. And it turns out that I don't really get enjoyment from anything except Torah. Well — hardly anything."

Afterwards, back in Bayit ve–Gan, I thought of him and of Rachel and it was as though I was really in the city for the first time. Perhaps I should trust that he will be able to perceive my design, passing the few doors which must always remain locked with forgiveness and reverence ("We should stand before each other as reverently as before the gates of Hell," wrote Kafka); that he will even comprehend my continuing to look back on a past which, for all the acts which I would neither repeat nor counsel to others, still has for me a certain radiance.

* * *

On the campus at Tel Aviv, waiting to meet c's friend, I thought: I am at an age where it is no longer easy to learn a new language. Is it that my mind has no more room for paradigms and vocabulary? Have my facial muscles grown too stiff to form the new sounds? Perhaps; but the worst is that the zest for new words and idioms is gone, and also a certain delight in masquerade, which vanishes when one has finally come to know oneself.

And those others with whom I spoke, the poets and the friends, in foreign languages and in my own: because I did not possess the secret of my own being I had to assme that they held it. And so they did: one by one they handed me pieces of something, I did not know what it was, until the encounter with c and the one flash which assembled it all. And then I had it.

It is a configuration which life since then has only repeated to me, in transparent variations. To recognize its recurrence is a form of fidelity, unavoidable no doubt. But in learning languages and in making friends it is a handicap. I lack the deepest sense of potential discovery; and the others too are deprived of a certain pleasure of creation.

* * *

The friends: I had been in Berkeley for some time before I met them, solitary amid a decor of incredible emptiness. Above the town rose the hills like something painted on a Chinese screen; below was Telegraph Avenue, a jumble of gauds and poses. The stark plains of Sproul Plaza, when not filled with shouting students, reminded me of De Chirico.

I arrived there shortly after my twenty-third birthday. In the apartment which I rented with a roommate who turned out to be slightly hostile and usually absent I read Claudel's *L'Annonce faite a Marie* and a recent pornographic novel which had been erroneously reviewed as witty. The moral of the first-mentioned work seemed to be that if you were beautiful and good the only thing left for you to do was to contract leprosy out of charity and then let yourself get pushed into a sand-pit; it depressed me even more than the pornographic novel, which I read because, like its humorously naive heroine, I wanted to keep up with things. I had been unable to write poetry for almost three years. In seminars and at parties, words were exchanged which I could not make sense of. I wrote competent papers for the German depart-ment, and no one suspected that when I got home in the evening I would torture the cat.

I would like to believe there is a reason why I have to remember this: if for instance we could learn from it that people do these things out of isolation and entrapment in mean-inglessness. Like the Ugandan terrorist on the eve of a massacre who is quoted as saying: "Tonight there will be world." Perhaps there can be another way of giving people a world. A way out.

In the middle of the year a little boy ran into me on this tricycle, perhaps on purpose, and I grasped the handlebars and very deliberately overturned the tricycle. He was not injured, but the shocked expression on his face brought me to my senses and I went in for therapy. Only the psychologist did not know a way out. I took to cutting myself — not deeply, it was to get

attention — and was hospitalized for a month with "mild depression." During the day I still went to classes, the plastic
hospital band around my wrist. In my second year I happened on
a "behavior therapist" who suggested, among other wild ideas,
that I might try writing poetry since I was always talking about
it. The other therapists had treated poetry as a neurotic symptom I should give up if I wanted a normal life. The lifting of
this ban was half of what helped me; the friends were the other.

* * *

I had seen Isadora before, around the German department: a
definitely Jewish-looking girl with long black hair, heavy bosom,
and expression half serious, half distantly humorous. She carried
a dark green book bag and wore black stockings, and I automatically classified her with the girls from New York whose way of
dressing I had imitated in Madison, but who had seldom found
time to speak to me. I was surprised, then, when Isadora
invited me to visit her. She was from Los Angeles and not at
ease in Berkeley society. You had to see her house in order to
know her.

She lived about five blocks off campus with three other girls
in a small, not especially well-constructed house surrounded by
a few square yards of neglected garden. You stepped from the
outside directly into the living-room, which occupied all the
ground floor except for the kitchen and the stairs. This room
had dark wainscoting and a fireplace. Its furniture was old:
almost-shapeless overstuffed chairs and sofa, a rug whose
original color or pattern were no longer to be discerned. To
the left of the door, as you came in, stood an ancient square
piano, which belonged to Isadora. The room did not get much sun,
and a pleasant gloom lingered there during the daytime.

Isadora and her housemates had not known each other before
renting the house together, and they were all different from
each other. Lynne, composed, reserved, with a quiet wit, was
from England; that year she was listening to Aretha Franklin and
going with a sophisticated, problematic Black man twenty years
her senior. Marcy — "lark-like Marcy" as Isadora used to call
her — came from Massachusetts. She had a relationship with a
boy named Evan which no one doubted would be permanent; they and
their friends used to go up to the Berkeley hills at dawn and
take LSD, and she would come down and tell what everyone had

said and how beautiful things had looked. It didn't seem to be
doing her harm. The house cat, with her periodic batches of
kittens, belonged to Marcy. The fourth girl, Serena, left not
long after I started to frequent the house. She had a quiet,
womanly presence. I think she was in African studies; she was
mothering a beautiful, golden-skinned young man who was caught
up in Sufism and put himself through all kinds of mortification
trying to reach enlightenment.

It was Isadora who made these people into a family, so that
they ate their meals together and entertained their friends
together and took delight in their improvised community. She
did this by being there, a matronly and vestal presence. She
had an antique robe of dark-blue velvet – slightly tattered,
that was Berkeley – which she used to put on at home, and one
day I took pictures of her in it, bending over the fireplace, at
the piano, on the sofa.

Isadora's great love, besides literature, was classical music;
she was a fine pianist. She had only taken marijuana once and
had not liked it. But she would listen with interest to the
music of Dylan and the Beatles and Aretha Franklin which was
part of her friends' lives, and to the stories of their adventures
on marijuana and LSD. She did not have a boyfriend, though the
house was frequented by a small group of young men, her friends
from Los Angeles. Isadora was lonely, but not enough to shake
her tranquility; if anything, it added to the grace with which
she presided over the house. Once she showed me a sonnet written
in anticipation of a future encounter. It was lovely; I still
have it, among my things in Madison.

Isadora was the only Jew living in the house; at that time
it was rather fashionable to be Jewish, though of course not to
practice. At Passover a very informal seder was held in the
house, for Jews and non-Jews alike. One day it was decided that
I should be an "honorary Jew" because I had curly hair and was
bright and had a lot of problems. I treasured the compliment.

It was a house where people played – with words, with images
and ideas. Every now and then they would spend an evening
reading Shakespeare, together. They remembered each other's *bons
mots* and repeated them to those who had been absent. Isadora
had a talent for constructing rebus pictures, which I was
invariably the last to figure out; the games and repartee always
made me feel untalented. They also dabbled in psychic matters,
again half as a game; all of them, especially Lynne, used the I
Ching, while Isadora's specialty was the Tarot. She would lay

out the cards with a mischievous smile which allowed no certainty
as to whether or not she believed in them. Sometimes the messages
seemed apposite, sometimes not.

I spent a lot of time there during my third year in Berkeley,
when I had a one-room apartment two blocks away. It was after
the breakup with Thomas, I was depressed and pessimistic, and
Lynne and Marcy often found my presence irksome. One night Marcy
said, "Bea is like *this*" (shrinking into herself) "when she
should be like *this*" (flinging her arms wide in her characteristic
gesture of welcome to life). I was tolerated mainly for the sake
of Isadora, who needed a companion in loneliness and poetry.
Nevertheless, their society warmed me.

In the daytime, when the sun shone in dustily on the dark
floors, walls, and furniture, recollections of my grandmother's
house in Ridgewood sometimes stirred in my mind. But of course
the next year Isadora went to study in Freiburg, and the household disbanded; I believe the house was razed soon after. The
piano ended up in my care, in an apartment which I had through
the kindness of Jason and Marsha, whom I had gotten to know just
as Isadora was leaving.

*   *   *

Jason was a Utopian. I had met him through a group therapy
organization, some of whose members lived together in an economic
community; it was this aspect that interested Jason.

He was the son of Orthodox Jews; his father ran a small
business in the Bronx. He and his wife had broken with Orthodoxy
a few years previously. His marriage had not lasted, and he had
come to Berkeley as a graduate student alone. He considered himself a Marxist but did not apply Marxist categories to everything
he saw or read. He was attracted to writers like Konrad Lorenz
who explained human behavior according to a biological determinism
which most Marxists repudiate. Once he explained to me that the
difficulties of communication between the sexes are found at the
primate level: female primates are attracted by behavioral
traits, whereas male primates react mainly to physical stimuli. He
summed it up by quoting Verdi's *Rigoletto* "Povero cuor di donna
(poor heart of woman)." This theory assured Jason of his attract-
iveness to women despite a physique which was not the American
male ideal: small, dark, shoulders slightly hunched with tension,
nervous gestures, features which contorted with the effort and
pleasure of expressing his thoughts. Perhaps, I now think, the

165

theory represented an ancestral memory of another kind: he was only two generations away from the world of Polish Jewry, where he would have been a son–in–law prized for his learning. The memory of that ancestry hovered around him and gave him a certain princely dignity amid a present which involved him in much absurdity.

He was magnanimous: in the group meeting where he and I were often attacked because neither of us conformed to the others' ideas of what men and women were, I would react by being as wounding as I could toward everyone, including him; but he would never take revenge. He would only get upset over being misunderstood.

His objectivity allowed him to see that, regardless of Marx, he was not going to begin by organizing the working class. He would have to begin with people whose reasons for wanting change were psychological and spiritual, if not intellectual. That is why, despite his *mitnaged* background, he thought he could work with the "hippie" movement: he believed they shared a protest against "anomie," the state of meaninglessness produced by socio-economic alienation. He believed that "anomie" could be counter-acted if people would live in small groups of ten or twelve adults, all engaged in some small business enterprise. These groups would be connected by a network of exchange and some higher council. His association would begin with one or two such groups; gradually others would be added, until perhaps someday the whole of society would be transformed.

Jason thought that a certain amount of emotional as well as economic reorganization would have to take place in order for this scheme to be realized. He felt that the root of economic and social alienation was to be found in the "dyadic" nature of marriage – the turning–in of the couple upon itself in alliance against the rest of society. It was necessary to form other bonds that would hold in a crisis. But the exact nature of these was not clear. His own nature was too refined for the promiscuity associated with the communes of that period; but he had a fantasy of himself surrounded by several women. Perhaps the experience of his marriage had made it hard for him to imagine trusting again in one. He had one very close friend from high school, Richard, who had participated in the planning of the association and who was his partner in those aspects of it that did material-ize. Richard and his wife, Ellen, lived in Seattle.

Jason's and my friendship was complex, as was inevitable given our respective confusions. Neither of us was in love with the other, but each was a little put out with the other for not being so, until the appearance of Marsha, Jason's obviously pre-destined mate, put an end to the embarrassment. He was not wholly pleased with my alacrity in accepting the clarification and making friends with Marsha; but his pique was minor and the impartial sympathy that he gave me was large. He denied there was anything wrong with me; it was just that there was no function for me in society. In the society he was constructing, people wouldn't go to therapists; they would go to people who would direct them to the place and the activities where they would be most useful and accepted.

Despite the pleasures of our long conversations, we were never able to collaborate intellectually. We tried once; he was trying to write a leaflet describing the aims and structure of his organization, and he asked me, or perhaps I offered, to help with the expression. I responded by putting what I thought were his ideas into a rather simple statement. It did not please him; he read every sentence over with a fussy impatience and proceeded to do the job alone. I never comprehended what it was exactly that I had missed. Then at meetings, when he would debate the theoretical foundations of his association with Michael and the others, I would often lose the thread and begin to wonder whether the debate was not being conducted for its own sake, rather than for the sake of the enterprise. Jason was similarly restive with the poems I showed him, though he liked my folksinging. He told me that he himself wrote poetry but would never show it to anyone, and I could never make out whether his guarded reaction was aesthetic disdain, or another kind of disapproval.

Or perhaps a fear which I glimpsed in him only once: at the commune house in Seattle I had found a novel, the title now escapes me, about a man who discovers, in the African jungle that the world is beginning to "crystallize." The people caught up in the crystallization are at peace in their eerily perfected state, and at the end, the narrator knows he will join them. When I began telling this story to Jason, he stopped with a gesture that was half shrug, half shudder. He had already read it; he thought about such things too much as it was. I don't remember whether I had shown him a poem recording some first impressions of c's poetry, that talked about a "crystallization" of the world. I was not at all afraid then; perhaps, indeed, he knew better than I.

. . . .

For the "conventional" interpretation of my past there had, of course, been ample material. Our family was middle class, and had been for generations, on both sides. My parents voted Republican, believed in American democracy and the free enterprise system, and sent us to Sunday school at the Congregational Church even though, as I learned on reaching adolescence, my father did not believe and my mother was never sure. Although both had begun college with an interest in literature, neither read much while I was growing up. They attended faculty gatherings, went to the homes of colleagues for dinner and invited them in return, but there was seldom much ease on those occasions. Both my parents' relatives lived far away, in the East, so there was no middle ground between the confines of the immediate family and the larger world to which one had to present a facade.

The moral standards by which we were raised were quite strict. We were taught to respect rules and property, not to lie, not to swear or use profanity. Sexual immorality was treated as unthinkable. My parents did not give many sermons, but they knew how to communicate moral aversion. Work, especially intellectual work, was understood to be the main thing in life. My father had worked his way through college during the Depression almost at the price of his health. He worked not only by day but also in the evenings, at home, and in summer he would go away on field trips; on weekends he would fix things around the house. He was known in his profession as a man of integrity. He was a utilitarian; although he liked occasionally to listen to classical music and would sometimes quote a line of poetry, he considered such thing impractical. He once said to me, "You must simply recognize that some people can be hail–fellow–well–met with everyone, while others have to gain people's respect through their work – and you are one of those." He could bear physical pain; Mother said he was a Spartan.

In my mother's case, it was difficult to tell where scruple became anxiety and concern turned into possessiveness. It was impossible to lie to her, because she knew immediately, and for this reason she could permit me, as a child, to leaf through the *Saturday Evening Post* – the only magazine they subscribed to – on condition that I would not read the love stories, which were "too old" for me. From the age of five I was aware of a shrinking horror of the body, which could only have come to me from her. This might have come from her Catholic upbringing; yet she never spoke of sin or evil in that connection. Rather it seemed related to the way she prepared for guests, as for an invasion or the way she once clutched my arm, while engaged in apparently casual conversation with an acquaintance, so that the nails dug in. Perhaps I was a child of anxiety. I was born in New York in 1941; my mother's obstetrician, the doctor who delivered me, and the pediatrician were all Jews. The pediatrician, a woman, warned my mother to feed me only every four hours regardless, and my mother followed those instructions to the letter, although I screamed like a banshee. This fashion in child-rearing passed, leaving my mother with a sense of guilt. "I wanted to do every-thing *just right*," she would tell me. During my second year of college, when Selma and I started rooming together, my mother became afraid we were having an affair. It took me a while to understand her, and then my astonishment and outrage did not immediately set her fears to rest. "You'll be *ostracized!*" she warned me, again and again. I felt violated, and it was a long time before I could forgive my mother, let alone admit to myself that − if there was any meaning to the dream of the lady and the bronze boy, if what happened between me and c really happened − she had perhaps, in that most unpleasant moment of our lives, given me something necessary. For the time being my reaction was to adopt a view of my parents as cold and repressive, guilty of a denial of nature which was the cause of my solitude. The remedy was to try to overcome the inhibitions they had inflicted on me. I was assisted in forming this interpretation by the therapists I saw − mostly at my parents' expense − but even more by friends who held certain ideas about human psychology as part of the wisdom of the times.

When I first related my past to Irene, it was in this light, and she shared enough of the time's hostility toward the genteel, the righteous, the inhibited, to encourage me in it with the rest. But now and then she would drop a remark that was at odd angles to the standard interpretation. Once she said that with such an intellectual father and such an emotional mother, it must be hard for me to strike a balance. Another time, when I spoke of my fear of men, she said there was some reason to be afraid of men. When I said I had accomplished nothing, she said I should be glad I had not done great harm: I should see that as a positive accomplishment. She said she did not understand how I could bear to live alone, but there was a note of admiration in her voice. And once she said to me that she felt guilty at times for having brought someone into this world. There was a still darkness in her words that checked my desperation, so that I too stood still and looked at my past without the distortions imposed by a wish to change things, seeking not the origin of the curse of solitude that dogged me, but my parents' being – what they were in themselves.

As I think about it now, my mother had some things in common with Irene, one being a feeling of exile. My mother had been born in America, but her father was Lebanese, her mother the daughter of French immigrant parents. In the home they had spoken French; my mother did not learn English until she went to school. She had married a man of Anglo–Scotch descent and had ended up living in Madison, a thousand miles away from her relations, among Germans and Scandinavians. She felt that she was seen as a foreigner, she felt like a foreigner, she did not want to be one and did her best to imitate the manners of those around her, the manners of strangers. Her life acquired a strained surface, and she could not teach me how to join the world.

What I had long forgotten was that, somewhere between the dual hostilities of body and society, she had managed to create a small world, a miniature tradition with history, proverbs, half-formed prophecies, which she handed on to me as the eldest child and only daughter. She scarcely meant to do this; she did it with an absentminded concentration, like a child playing with her doll.

When I was five, the Sunday school teacher told us, "G–d made you." I can still hear myself answering, "My mommy made *me*" and see the smile exchanged by my mother and the teacher after class, and it seems to me that I was referring not only to the confused biological knowledge I had recently acquired, but from the way she dressed me, sang to me, admonished me, made my clothes, entered into my childish projects: with the attention to detail, the hidden sense of overall design, said to characterize the artist. I had the feeling then of *being created,* which until the encounter with c I could not dream of recapturing, and there-fore forgot. That exchange in Sunday school happened near the end of a long winter which we had spent in the Great Smoky Moun-tains of North Carolina, a mile from the nearest neighbor, while Father did surveying work. At night he would come home and color in green the area on a map that he had surveyed that day, while Jim, my brother, and I watched in fascination. But we spent the day with Mother, walking beside the rushing river some hundred yards from the back door, under the walnut trees quiet with winter, picking up walnuts, or sticks for the wood stove. Hers was the only voice that spoke to us, in a wilderness imbued with her presence.

She would tell us stories about her childhood. They always began with the formula "When I was a little girl" and were more magical than fairy tales, although she invented nothing and recounted nothing extraordinary. They were stories of the every-day doings of her mother and brothers and sisters, whom I knew vaguely in their present-day disguises, and of her father who had died before I was born; of the house in Ridgewood which must have seemed different with all those people moving around in it and the summer house in Milford which I was to see only once, years later. For us it was enough magic that things which had happened once somewhere else and were no more should return to happen again through her. Or rather that she could let us look, as through a window, into the time and place where these things were still happening, always would be. And for her it must have been an act of mastery, to recreate a world in which she had been one of the smallest actors and give it to us, with her small self still in it.

Once, many years later, in Madison, while we were driving between her house and my apartment, she described an associate at work whose funeral she had recently attended. She spoke of this woman's black hair and blue eyes, of her bright manner, of the way she had arranged her life, of the little mannerisms and reactions my mother had observed in her over the five years they had worked together. At the end of her description this woman stood before me, and I almost wished I had written it down. "So long lives this, and this gives life to thee."

She was not a literary artist; her powers would take refuge in secrecy at the slightest suggestion that someone might look at what she was doing as a performance. Once, in adolescence, I was criticized by her for striking a pose at the piano in which she detected affectation. She insisted on my practicing piano, but would not let me take voice lessons, because she thought it vulgar and immodest to sing in public. She claimed to have no singing voice and did not sing around the house; yet she was proud of all the songs I had learned as a small child, and I could only have learned them from her. Her speaking voice was very beautiful, in the carefulness of its intonations and pro-nunciations; you sensed her desire to say things exactly the right way. She treated each word, instinctively, as a thing she had heard from her mother, but most were English proverbs which she must have collected later in life, and passed on to us as if they were an ancestral heritage. When we asked her what they meant she would improvise a story to illustrate them.

The stories which she read to us did not remain mere stories; like Irene, she glimpsed their counterparts in life. I can remember her saying to me, "You're just like the Princess and the Pea!" or "You're just like a little Fisherman's Wife!" She had no concept of aesthetic distance; although she would sometimes remind me that a story I had taken "too much to heart" was "only a story," it never sounded convincing. One day, after we moved to Madison, she told me the plot of *Hamlet,* which she had read the night before in a playreading group. "So they all died!" she concluded, looking at me and trying to smile, but not con- vincingly. There were a number of real-life stories which she told in a similar manner – the end was something bad, but she would give her voice a forced upward intonation, as if to re- assure herself, or ask the listener for reassurance, that she had indeed succeeded in exorcising the story by telling it. The endings were not actually that terrible: someone had gotten cheated by a contractor, a friendship had been broken by a careless word, someone had received a doll for a present and had taken off the elaborate handmade doll clothes and put them on the cat, and the cat had run away. It was because of her way of telling them that they haunted me, more painfully than real tragedies.

It might have been because of something in her past which did not enter into her repertoire. Mother had always said that there were seven children in her family, but one day I realized that I knew the names of only six. It was father whom I first asked about this; he told me only, "Your Aunt Lolly is sick." It was several more years before I learned the story.

Aunt Lolly – her real name was Nazleh – was the second sister, and for the first nine years of her life she was the prettiest and brightest. Then one day she fell and hit her head on the sidewalk, and developed a form of epilepsy, which grew worse and worse. Her parents collected the money together for an operation by a great brain surgeon. In the middle of the operation the surgeon went out to talk to the parents. He said that there was a mass of scar tissue in the brain which he could remove, and the convulsions would stop, but she would be crippled for life. If he did not remove the scar tissue, there was still a chance she would outgrow the convulsions. My grandparents could not bring themselves to make their daughter a cripple; they chose to

hope. But it was the wrong choice. The convulsions not only
worsened, but Aunt Lolly's personality changed; she became violent.
My mother, the youngest of five sisters, was the most frequent
victim. Then my mother could not bring her friends home from
school, because of her strange sister. I wonder now whether that
memory might have been behind her fear of visitors to our house,
years after she had grown up and gone away, and Aunt Lolly had
been placed in an institution. Aunt Lolly died in the institution
at the age of fifty, and my mother went back East for the funeral.
I was fifteen at the time. When my mother returned she told me,
"There was no peace on her face; only deep suffering."

I remember the tone of voice in which she pronounced those
words; it was the same tone with which she told me, when I was
five in Bryson City, "Old Mrs. Delaney died." We had sung carols
at her bedside, I remember the closed eyes, the white hair, the
open sunken mouth, and then I see the fresh grave in the cemetery
with the rough stones, the stiff artificial tulips stuck in the
earth. It was the tone of voice of a person unable to withhold
the truth, but wanting to offer her love with it, for what
consolation it might bring. Years later, the reading of certain
passages by Simone Weil on the nature of affliction brought it
again to mind.

My mother was beautiful, with the kind of beauty which is
difficult to describe because it is not conformity to a predeter-
mined type, but a unique and unrepeatable harmony. I used to
study her face, trying to discover the secret of its loveliness;
perhaps it was the way the unhurried angle between the vertical
forehead and the rather long, straight nose was repeated between
lower lip and chin. She had brown eyes, and her hair was a rich
dark brown, framing her face in orderly natural waves. Her mouth
was thin, but agreeably shaped, and when she smiled, pressing
her lips together a little as if enjoining silence, this thinness
lent a spiritual quality to the warmth diffused. Her figure was
not striking, and she used to look with distress at her hand
which she considered coarse; but she dressed with great care and
with an exquisite, though reticent taste, and the touch of her
hand on a child's hand, or even on the head of a dog or cat, was
almost weightless. She was never wholly free from tension. The
calm which she willed to surround her, for us to take refuge in,
had a slightly fictitious quality. This impression of a bravely
sustained fragility was part of her grace.

After the move to Madison — I was six then — she might have
liked to find an old house to make her own. But my father could

not live in an old house, just as he was not ordinarily fond of
telling stories about his childhood. "You can't live in the
past," he would always say. But she and I continued to look
back to her mother's house in Ridgewood, New Jersey. Together
with my brother Jim we went back there for several summers,
while my father was on his field trips.

. . . .

Even after my first, Conservative conversion, when I was
already a daughter of Abraham, they found something to say to
me. My mother told me one evening, a few months after the event,
that she had been looking my father's family Bible and had
discovered that the Hebrew name I had chosen because it had been
favored by Sylvia Plath and by c, and because of a mystical work
that had made a deep impression on me, had been the name of my
father's maternal grandmother, the mother of the woman who had
suggested that other name which was to have such far-reaching
consequences for me. It was almost the first time I had heard
of Esther Jane Bennett, the doctor's wife in Toronto. My mother
had culled only one anecdote about her: that when the family
went out driving in the country she would keep her eye out for a
rotted stump, and when she saw one she would get out and dig up
some of the earth around it to spread on her plants at home.
But my father, when we questioned him, remembered her. She was
a religious woman, who read her Bible regularly and did a lot of
charitable works. After her husband's death she lived with my
father's parents. My father remembered her as very strict, but
strict with herself first of all; she taught by example: "We
children adored her." She always ate alone, and there were
certain foods which she carefully avoided. After her death the
family doctor was puzzled by something and asked permission to
perform an autopsy. He discovered that she had been living for
several years without kidneys. They thought that her strict,
instinctive control of diet must have had something to do with
it. My parents had one picture of her taken in her last years.
It shows a face, slightly smiling, but deeply lined as if from
an effort of long endurance.
    I felt now that I understood better the root of my father's
moral character; I marveled at the Providence which had brought
me through such vicissitudes, through the adoption of a faith
none of my ancestors had acknowledged, so that I might revive

174

the name and memory of this woman. The light of endurance on the deeply-cleft face said: this is what you must be.

* * *

The rav's house had no number; it stood in the middle of a large courtyard; as one stepped through the archway carved with the Star of David the light from the kitchen shone as though far away. The room in which we spoke was square; the window niche revealed walls four feet thick. The walls were painted with a faded design like wallpaper, and the paint was peeling in spots. Along the walls were bookcases with glass fronts, three lumpy day-beds covered with identical reddish-brown spreads, a playpen with an infant sleeping in it; on one of the bookcases stood a clock in a plain wooden case, which struck with a metallic sound every quarter-hour. The light in the room was what my mother would have considered bad for reading. In the middle of the room was a long table, which must have served for the Shabbos meal as well as study. I thought by contrast of the little garden house Nadine had rented in Berkeley, a house in which there was no wealth, but a luxuriance of matter. Here it was like a threadbare spot in the fabric of the world, where another world had begun to show through. The rav's voice was balanced, quiet; he spoke in Hebrew, but slowly and with carefully chosen words, so that I understood. "You must not think about the 'tragedy.' If he despaired, it was because his senses were stopped up, he could not perceive the truth. The whole world is one great song; there is no tragedy. It is good that you under- stood enough to come in under the wings of the Shekhina; that is the main thing. The six million who went to their deaths in the Holocaust, they knew that G-d is ruler of this world. There is no despair." The quiet, which had stood at his shoulder while he spoke, went about its business, clearing away whatever I might have found to answer. No, it was impossible to sit in this room and not believe in G-d, and there was no despair anywhere in the world. Except in my heart.

and

on

waves

of

revolution

if I can't dance, I don't want to be part of your revolution
- emma

EMMA GOLDMAN

from *THE ROLE OF WOMEN IN THE SPANISH REVOLUTION*

† *For several years Goldman exchanged letters with anarchist Max Nettlau on the issue of women's liberation. In this passage from her 2/8/35 letter, Goldman places her impression of Spanish women (from her earlier visit and from her U.S. experience) within the broader framework of this discussion. At both levels, this provides a solid introduction to her subsequent comments in the late 1930's.*

I have your letter of January 12th. I am terribly sorry to have hurt you. Believe me, I had no intention to do it. I understood perfectly that in referring to the "innermost wish" of the Spanish woman to have broods of children you were teasing me and that you meant it as a joke. Those who know me more intimately than you, dear comrade, know perfectly well that I appreciate humor because I have a considerably developed sense of it myself. How do you suppose I would have survived my struggle, if I lacked that sense? But there are certain things which somehow don't lend themselves to joking. And one of them is the male contention that woman loves to have broods of children. Please don't feel hurt again when I tell you that, like the rest of your sex, you really know nothing about woman. You take too much for granted. I would have to talk with Spanish women myself to get beneath the age-long tradition which has put her into the sexual straight-jacket. I am sure that I would get quite a different picture than you have painted of her.

You charge me with having a hasty and superficial opinion about the Spanish mother from my short visit in Spain. You forget, dear comrade, that I had been thrown together with Spanish men and women in America for over a period of thirty-five years. We had quite a Spanish movement when [Pedro] Esteve[1] was alive. Not only did I know all the comrades merely in a public way from meetings and gatherings, but I knew their private lives. I nursed

1. Editor of *Cultura Obrera* (N.Y.), Esteve died in 1925.

their wives in childbirth and I was with them and the male comrades in a special way. Long before I went to Spain I knew the
relation between Spanish men and women. As I knew the relation
between the Italian men and women. My visit in Spain merely
verified all that I had learned from them over many years. And
what is it that I have learned? It is that all Latin men still
treat their wives, or their daughters, as inferiors and consider
them as mere breeding machines as the caveman did. And not only
the Latin men. My connection with the German movement gave the
same definite impression. In other words, with the exception of
the Scandinavians and the Anglo-Saxons, the most modern is the
Old Adam in his inhibitions to woman. He is something like most
Gentiles are to the Jew: when you scratch deep down to their
inner being you will find an anti-Semitic streak lurking somewhere in the makeup. Now, of course, dear comrade, you call
that "terrible Russian rigorousness and severity." Aside of the
fact that you are the only one of my friends who has discovered
this trait in me, I wish to say it is nothing of the kind. When
one feels deeply, one's expression sounds "rigorous and severe."
And I do feel the position of woman very intensely. I have seen
too many tragedies in the relation between the sexes; I have
seen too many broken bodies and maimed spirits from the sex
slavery of woman not to feel the matter deeply or to express my
indignation against the attitude of most of you gentlemen.

All your assurance not withstanding, I wish to say that I
have yet to meet the woman who wants to have many children. That
doesn't mean that I ever for a moment denied the fact that most
women want to have a *child*, although that, too, has been exaggerated by the male. I have known quite a number of women, feminine
to the last degree, who nevertheless lack that supposed-to-be
inborn trait of motherhood or longing for the child. There is no
doubt the exception. But, as you know, the exception proves the
rule. Well, granted that every woman wants to become a mother.
But unless she is densely ignorant with an exaggerated trait of
passivity, she wants only as many children as she can decide to
have and, I am sure, the Spanish woman makes no exception. Certainly habits and traditions play a tremendous part in creating
artificial desires that may become a second nature. The church,
especially the Catholic Church, as you know yourself, has done
its utmost to impress upon woman that she must live up to the
dicta of God to multiply. But would it interest you to know that
among the women who apply to birth control clinics the Catholics,

regardless of the hold the priest has over them, represent a very large percentage? You may suggest that in America they have already become "infected with the horror of horrors" of limiting the number of offspring. Well, I would be willing to put it to a test, if it were possible to reach the women in Spain with lectures on birth control and birth control methods. Just how many would demonstrate your romantic conception of what they want or my suggestion of "artificial" limitation of offspring? I am afraid, dear comrade, you would lose the bet.

Your interpretation of matriarchy as meaning that the mother must keep her sons tied to her apron strings, accept his earnings, and act the generous godmother in giving him pocket money, was to say the very least amusing to me. To me this merely indicates the unconscious revenge of the enslaved female on the male. But it doesn't indicate the least freedom of either the man or the woman. Besides, matriarchy means more to me than this cleavage which exists between mother and son or father and daughter. Where such conditions exist no one is free. . . .

Aside from these considerations, it is the continuation of the conservatism of woman which has undoubtedly been a great contributory force to the reaction in Spain, the complete collapse of everything worthwhile in Germany, and the continued existence of Mussolini. Or will you deny the fact that the first thing after the Spanish women were given the vote was to vote back black reaction?[2] Or will you deny the fact that the German women have been driven back to the Kirche and Kinder[3] without as much as a protest? Or that the Italian women have been hurled back at least fifty years into their old position as mere sex objects? Heaven knows, I hold no brief for the American woman. I know the majority is still as conservative and as much in the clutches of the church as the women of the countries I have mentioned.

2. The parliamentary elections of November 1933 were the first under the new Second Republic consitution which granted equal suffrage to women. Apparently there was a significant loss of strength for Republican candidates due to middle-class women following the directions of their priests rather than the preference of their husbands (Brenan, *The Spanish Labyrinth,* p. 266).

3. "Church, Children and Kitchen was one of the basic themes of the Nazis to guide German women back to the supposed strength (and docility) of traditional culture.

But I do insist that there is in America a large minority of
women, advanced women, if you please, who will fight to the last
drop of their blood for the gains which they have made, physical
and intellectual, and for their rights to equality with the man.
Anyway, dear comrade, it seems futile to argue this matter
between us. We will never agree. It is a commentary, however,
on how little theories fight inhibitions. Here you are an
anarchist, firmly believing in the utmost freedom of the individual,
and yet you persist in glorifying woman as the cook and breeder
of large families. Do you not see the inconsistency of your
claims? But the inhibitions and traditions of the male are too
deep set. I am afraid they will continue long after anarchism
has been established. . . .

I know you are too generous to harbor a grievance too long.
You must not be angry with me for having called you antidiluvian.
I meant no hurt, but I will fight you to the last stitch on the
question of woman and her great desire to have broods of children.

† In this 4/24/36 letter to a comrade, Goldman announces her
first contact with the "Mujeres Libres" group in Spain.

Yesterday I had a letter from Mercedes Comaposada[4] of Madrid
asking for an article to a magazine called *Free Women [Mujeres
Libres]*. I was not able to write an article now but I wrote her
a letter [stating] how very glad I was that such a paper is
being issued to emancipate the Spanish women from bondage. Do
you know anything about this comrade?

4. Mercedes Comaposada was one of the founding members of the
Madrid women's group of the same name, "Mujeres Libres,"
before 1936.

† *In the midst of her first visit to revolutionary Spain, Goldman informs her niece Stella Ballantine (11/18/36) of the work that needs to be done among women and the difficulty of doing it in the midst of a civil war.*

I find my energies instead of declining are growing stronger. Especially since I came here and saw all that needs to be done among women and children for instance. You have no idea how primitive everything in this direction is. Enlightenment among women is desperately needed. But our comrades are too engrossed in winning the anti-Fascist war to devote much time to this kind of necessary labor. A beginning has been made of course. But one cannot sweep away the ignorance, prejudice and superstition of a people in four months. However, I could do much, I know, and my efforts would be welcomed. But it is again the language, in Catalonia not only Spanish but Catalan. You see then how paralyzed I feel. There is no way out, I will have to leave.

† *To comrade Harry Kelly on 12/5/36 she speaks again of important tasks for Spanish women's emancipation and their relative neglect in the past.*

You must remember that the anti-Fascist war and the revolutionary reconstruction our Spanish comrades have before them are not all of their colossal task. There is the education and emancipation of woman, the new approach to the child, to common ordinary questions of health. All that has been sadly neglected by our comrades. Perhaps they had to concentrate all their energies on the economic struggle [so] they could not reach out into many directions. But that does not alter the low status of woman and the child. This field alone is large enough to keep one busy. And there are others. Yes, I will go back to Spain.

† *A few days later, the* Mujeres Libres *periodical published this important Goldman appeal to Spanish women.*

Human progress is very slow. In fact it has been said that for every step upward the human race has made, it retreated two steps into the bondage it has striven to escape. It has taken centuries for man to rise from his prostrate position — his blind belief in the superstition of the church, the divine right of kings and the power of a master class. True, this vicious trinity still holds sway over many millions in every part of our planet. Still it can no longer rule with an iron rod or exact obedience at the point of torture or death, though this is still the case in Fascist lands. However, Fascism is, historically speaking, only of the hour. And even under the black pest the rumbling of the approaching storm is coming nearer and growing ever louder. In Spain Fascism is meeting its Waterloo, all along the line. On the other hand it is the ever increasing volume of active protest in the world at large against the evil institutions of capitalism. Strangely enough, the average male, so ready to fight heroically for his own emancipation, is far from believing in the same for the opposite sex.

To be sure, the women of many countries have brought about a veritable Revolution in their own social, political and ethical status. They have done so through years of bitter struggle — after heartbreaking defeat and discouragement, but also final triumph.

Unfortunately this cannot be said for the women of all countries. In Spain, for instance, woman seems still be considered very much inferior to man, a mere sex—object for his gratification and child—bearing. This attitude would not be so surprising were it only to be found among the bourgeoisie. But to find the same antideluvian conception among the workers, even among our comrades, is a very great shock indeed.

Nowhere in the world has Libertarianism so entered the very life of the workers as it has the life of the Spanish masses. The glorious victory of the Revolution, born in the pangs of the July battle, testifies to the superior revolutionary stamina of the Catalan and Spanish working men. One would assume that their passionate love of liberty also includes that of women. Far from this being the case, most men in Spain either do not seem to understand the meaning of true emancipation, or they know, yet prefer to keep their women in ignorance of its meaning. The fact is, many men make themselves believe that women enjoy being kept in an inferior position. It was said that the Negro also enjoyed being owned by his plantation master. In point of truth, there can be no real emancipation so long as any form of mastery of one individual over another exists, or any group over another. Much less has emancipation of the human race any meaning so long as one sex dominates another.

After all, the human family presupposes both sexes. Of the two, woman is the more important because she is the bearer of the race. And the more perfect her development, the more perfect the race will be. If for no other reason, this alone should prove the importance of woman's place in society and the social struggle. There are other reasons. Foremost among them is woman's awakening to the fact that she is a personality in her own right. And that her needs and aspirations are as vital and important as those of the male.

Those who still imagine they can keep woman in a strait-jacket will no doubt say, "yes, but woman's needs and aspirations are different, because she is inferior." This only goes to prove the limitation of the male and also his arrogance. Else he would know that her very differentiation enriches life individually as well as socially.

Besides, the extraordinary achievements of woman in every walk of life have silenced forever the loose talk of woman's inferiority. Those who still cling to this fetish do so because they hate nothing so much as to see their authority challenged. This is the characteristic of all authority, whether the master over his economic slaves or man over woman. However, woman is everywhere escaping her cage, everywhere she is going ahead with free, large strides. Everywhere she is bravely taking her place in the battle for economic, social and ethical transformations. It is not likely that the Spanish women will escape much longer the trend of emancipation.

It is true of woman, as it is of the workers. Those who would be free must themselves strike the first blow. The workers of Catalonia, of all of Spain, have struck the first blow. They have freed themselves, they are shedding their blood to safeguard their freedom

Now it is your turn, Catalan and Spanish women, to strike the blow to break your fetters. It is your turn to rise in your dignity, your self-respect, to stand proudly and firmly on your rights as women, as free individualities, as equal members of society, as comrades in battle against Fascism and for the Social

Revolution. Only when you have freed yourself from the super-
stitions of religion – the prejudice of the double standard of
morality, the degrading and enslaving obedience to a dead past,
will you become a great force in the anti–Fascist battle – in
the defense of the Revolution. Only then will you be able and
worthy to help build the new free society where every man, woman
and child will be truly free.

† *In a published interview (1/8/37) upon her return from
Spain, Goldman assesses the progress, yet long distance
ahead in the effort for women's emancipation.*

So far the women in Spain have hardly been given a chance to
contribute much [to the Revolution]. They are not sufficiently
awakened and advanced. Nevertheless I did find a difference in
women as compared with 1929 when I visited Spain. They are much
more alert and are beginning to show interest in the social
struggle.

Yes, most certainly [woman will find her place in the new
society], but it means an enormous amount of work yet to be done
for the emancipation of woman. Once that is achieved, the
Spanish woman will take equal place in the constructive work.

NANCY KEESING

LADIES ONLY

Only a woman rushes off 'to put on my face' before going out,
though some feminine usages and colloquialisms are used by male
transvestites who borrow them along with women's clothes, acces-
sories and make-up. First she may apply 'spackle filler' (foundation make-up), then 'lippie' and powder from her 'flapjack'
(powder compact).* She 'runs a comb' through her 'hairdo' and
reflects that it's about time she had a fresh 'perm' as she frantically looks for a 'grip' or 'bobbie pin' to restrain a cowlick.
If she's the enviable kind of woman whose hair 'behaves itself,'
rather than the more usual female 'who can't do a thing with it,'
she may, these days, own a blowdrier and give herself a 'blow-
wave' each morning; this invention has superseded the rollers and
'butterfly' grips (metal hairwavers) which used to sprout from
suburban heads and look like surrealist sculpture albeit they
were often partly hidden under a scarf.

Only women enter the 'Ladies' or 'Powder Room' to 'spend a
penny' (urinals for men are free) or to 'wash my hands' or 'powder
my nose.'

Both sexes may endure that mysterious affliction known to
Australians as 'nerves of the stomach' and, after a heavy night
at pub or club, men and women equally might feel as if their
eyes were 'like two holes burned in a blanket' or their mouths
like 'the bottom of a bird cage.' But women only 'get caught,'
or 'let down' or 'fall,' and endure the 'tube trouble' or 'womb
collapse.'

Among 'the girls' (girls being women friends of any age up
to senility) gynaecological and surgical gossip remains popular.
Often meanings are conveyed as much by facial expression or
nuances of speech as by words. One woman mentioned in a letter

* Dr. Margaret Diesendorf, who was born and educated in Austria,
says that in 1928–30 Viennese teenage girls used the work
'flapjack' for *Puderdoes* (powder box). She adds that 'interestingly *Flappe* is a wry face referring mainly to the shape
of the mouth.'

184

that during her childhood the overhead phrase 'She's had her tonsils out' invariably referred to any major operation. A woman might have 'dropped a few pegs,' 'had a re-bore' or need treatment 'in the pipes.' 'Mummy's going in [to hospital] for a little op,' might indicate a simple curettage or be a euphemism for abortion; men more often spoke of women 'having the boilers scraped down.' Other synonyms include 'slip a joey,' 'crack an egg,' 'need a scrape' (which can be a curette recommended for other reasons), or 'have appendicitis,' This last example is equivocal Sheilaspeak; with the co-operation of a sympathetic 'medico' it can be used to excuse absence from work or unaccountable illness.

Lactating mothers can make the unique choice to keep the baby's feed 'where the cat can't get at it.' It is only women (and those, perhaps, of Cornish descent, for they are invariably miners' wives) who describe a baby that is not truly ill, but not thriving, as 'teasy.'

'Boddies' or bodices, 'chimmies,' 'pettis,' 'slips,' 'scanties,' 'drawers' and 'pinnies' are worn only by females, though children of both sexes may have 'a pain in the pinny,' and both sexes wear 'long Johns,' 'coms' or 'combies' (combinations). 'Leos' (leotards or long tights) are also popular winter wear for women; like 'nylons,' whether stockings or panty-hose, they are prone to 'snags' that lead to ladders and to 'pilling.' (Pills, which also form on woolen fabrics, are little balls of fibre that form on surfaces, especially after prolonged or careless washing.)

Nothing is cosier on a cold night than a nice knitted or crocheted 'hugmetight' around the shoulders of your 'nightie' though, at a pinch, a 'cardie' will serve. Nowadays panty-hose have largely superseded 'roll-ons' or 'step-ins' (suspender belts), but 'control briefs' are often worn to restrain fleshy bulges, and some panty-hose have 'control tops.' The 'merry widow,' a corselet or belt designed to pinch in the waist, came in with Dior's 'new-look' fashions of the 1940s and remained to torture all but the slimmest of girls until the early 1960s.

It is not easy to decide whether certain fashion terms are slang or, rather, descriptive terms for kinds of clothes and decoration that come and go with fashion itself. A peplum is a peplum, a stole a stole, a puffed sleeve a puffed sleeve. But other terms, sometimes deriving from brand names, 'catch on' and are used for garments that could easily be described in another way, or called something different. 'Witches' britches' are a case in point.

'Witches' britches' were winter garments of the mini–skirt era. Made of brightly coloured warm–knit nylon and trimmed with lace, these tight–fitting pants peeped under short skirts. Bolder spirits had hearts, monograms or other devices, embroidered on one leg of the britches just above the lace. One woman school-teacher of that time intercepted a note that read, 'Let's go to C–'s (a chain store) after school and snitch some witches' britches.' To shoplift is to get 'a five finger discount.'

An outmoded feminine slang word was reported by a New South Wales woman whose grandmother, a strict Methodist lady, died aged ninety–four in the 1920s.

Until she died my grandmother would not wear ordinary 'bloom-ers' (as they were called by the 1920s) so her daughters still had to make her traditional pants which (vulgarly) were known as 'free traders.' They comprised knee–length calico pants trimmed with lace but, instead of a front and back seam, were open from the front waist to the back waist, and fastened *around* the waist by long tapes. It meant you could use the toilet without pulling your pants down.

The woman who has to stop scrubbing the floor or weeding the garden when unexpected visitors arrive and 'turns around' to 'run up' a batch of scones and 'throw them' in the oven seems to be using exclusively Australian terms. As for talented girls who can 'run up a dress'. . . .

It is astonishing that the 'duchess' has been overlooked in compilations of Australian slang. If every duchess set that has been embroidered with lazy daisies or crocheted in lacy patterns were laid end to end, the arrangement would cross and re–cross the Nullarbor or, perhaps more appropriately, outline the coast of the Gulf of Carpentaria, for it is chiefly in Queensland that a dressing–table is called a duchess, though nationwide a runner and two flanking small mats is known as a duchess set. Once, in a Queensland pub with flimsy walls between bedrooms, a mystified southerner heard a loud crash from the adjoining room that was shared by two seasonal workers, followed by some furious swearing and then, 'Wake up and help, Blue. Me duchess is losing her drawers.'*

* I mentioned the 'duchess' as a peculiarly Queensland usage to a group of Rockhampton girls, one of whom asked, in a very puzzled way. 'Well what else *would* you call it?'

Women have a particular emphasis in their voices when they say, of some man or other who has infuriated them, 'He's thick!' Men who behave insensitively or badly are accused of having their minds only 'on their bellies and what's hanging off them,' and of dreary marriages it is said that 'women put up with sex to get marriage and men put up with marriage to get sex.'

A widely used Australian term for the sexual act is 'to have a naught,' but one religious lady, circa 1930s, referred to intercourse as 'a naught.' This irony was probably unintended since she was the contented wife of an affectionate husband. A story is told of one clergyman's wife whose daughter invited a young man home for dinner. The mother wanted to indicate her broadmindedness to this guest whom she considered rather worldly, and, as she cleared the meat dishes from the table, and substituted pudding plates, she set an ashtray beside his place and invited him to enjoy 'an inter-course cigarette.'

Veneral disease makes no gender distinctions but only women exhibit a symptom known as 'the whites' (which may have non-specific causes). But while pubescent boys welcome the appearance of body hair few girls desire 'a forest' or 'mohair stockings,' and will assiduously 'mow the lawn' to control them. Feminine pubic hair is 'a thicket.'

Who but a woman would complain that a man is a 'linen lifter,' or is 'trying to pirate me' or 'put on the hard word' or 'get me into the bushes/scrub/mulga?'

One country family spoke of anyone taking a big risk as 'doing what the girl did,' it being understood that the girl 'fell in.' In this same family, someone voicing mock displeasure would say, 'Ahrrr, give me my hat and pants!' The phrase derived from a story often told by one of their aunts in warning tones – aunty plainly missed the point of the joke. A girl who was displeased by her boyfriend's importunate behaviour in a park at night exclaimed, 'Give me my hat and pants, I'm going home.'

A similar story from the same period, circa 1940s, concerned a young man who, with the help of his girlfirend, was polishing his car. He needed a soft cloth to complete the job and asked, 'What do you do with your pants when you wear them out?' 'I wear them home if I can find them.'

During World War II Australian girls who wore long, elaborately dressed 'pompadour' hair styles were said by some of their disapproving sisters to be 'dangling Yank bait.'

The slang for prostitutes (prostitution is 'cracking it') alters constantly. But even in such a group, in Australia, a few old English low-life words seem to remain current perpetually although with subtle alterations to definition and emphasis. One example is 'moll.' To some Australians 'moll' has an affectionate connotation very puzzling to non-Australians or to locals who do not understand the conventions of certain unconventional speakers. (This usage is akin to the way Australian males intend words like 'bastard' and 'bugger' to be terms of friendship and acceptance.) At present a 'charity moll' is the equivalent of a World War II 'EA' or 'enthusiastic amateur': a promiscuous woman whose sexual favours are theoretically not available for sale, or not for honest sale for an agreed cash payment. A charity moll barters herself, instead, for presents, dinners, theatre and show tickets. 'Working women' or women 'in the trade' (prostitutes) have a deep scorn for charity molls not so much because they represent a threat to business, but because they delude them-selves and are not prepared to admit that they are just as 'bad' as a harlot, or conversely that any harlot is as good as they are. The dividing line is cold cash. Prostitutes, rightly or wrongly, accuse charity molls of being responsible for spreading venereal disease because they *are* amateurs. Interestingly, venereal disease retains its very old generic term, 'the pox.'

Prostitutes, too, have other strong feelings that are mir-rored by language. At present to work in a 'massage parlor' is regarded as professional; to work the streets is not. To work in or conduct a parlor carries connotations of professionalism and self respect that the word 'brothel' is denied by the women themselves.

In degree at least, women are distinguished from charity molls if they provide 'an after dinner mint' to men who expect, and ask for, this sweet conclusion to an expensive night out. The impli-cation is that 'minters' are less promiscuous, and more often are 'going steady' with their men.

HALF ENGLISH, HALF SOMETHING ELSE

Since white settlement, Australian general slang has con-tained words and phrases from languages other than English. Some of these words were acquired from, or shared with, English and American colloquial speech. For instance 'shiker'* or 'shickered'

* Yiddish spellings and definitions in this section are from *The Joys of Yiddish,* Leo Rosten, Penguin, 1971.

for drunk is a direct borrowing from the Yiddish *shikker,* as is 'mozzle' for luck which comes from the Yiddish *mazel* (pronounced to rhyme with nozzle). Thus, an Australian usage noted by Baker, 'Kronk mozzle' for bad luck, comes from the Yiddish *krenk,* an illness, or *kronk,* to have an illness (Baker's spelling).

One woman who wrote to me grew up in Kings Cross during the 1930s and has remembered three colourful phrases used by one of the neighbours, a Jewish woman. In my correspondent's spelling and interpretation these were: a *schmozzle* (a mess); a real *Shemile* or *Chemile* (a very naive person); a *missamushia* (my correspondent was not sure of the meaning).

These are my explanations of the three examples. *Shemozzl* or *shlemozzl* (pronounced sheh–mozzle or shleh–mozzle – rhyming with den–nozzle): Leo Rosten, who is an American expert on the Yiddish language, says 'these words are not Yiddish, and not Yinglish, but slang used by our cousins in England and Ireland . . . they are often spelled and pronounced like the Yiddish *sclimazl* to which they bear not the slightest resemblance.'

A *shemozzle* is an uproar, a fight, and can also mean to decamp or abscond. (It is notably used by race–course touts says Rosten.) A *shlimazl,* however, is a born loser. According to Rosten 'when a *shlimazl* winds a clock, it stops; when he kills a chicken, it walks; when he sells umbrellas, the sun comes out; when he manufactures shrouds, people stop dying.'

Schlemiel (pronounced *schle*–meal – to rhyme with reveal): indeed a naive person. A simpleton might be said to 'have the brains of a schlemiel – when he falls on his back he breaks his nose.'

Missamushia: such a gorgeous word that one is not surprised it has lived in a memory for some fifty years. Its meaning is a bit less certain than the other two words, but I imagine the woman who used it had in mind one or other of the following three Yiddish phrases.

Mishegoss literally means insanity but is more often used to describe tomfoolery, absurd belief, nonsense. It derives from *meshuga* which is the Hebrew word meaning insane; meshuga, too, is more widely used in Yiddish to mean wildly and extravagantly bonkers – 'rats in the attic bang! bang!' as Australian speakers might say. A crazy man is a *meshuggener.* A crazy woman is a *meshuggeneh.*

It is just possible, however, that the word remembered as *Missamushia* was 'mish–mash' (as the *Oxford English Dictionary* spells it), or *mish–mosh* as Yiddish usage and custom prefers. A *mish–mosh* is a state of utter confusion.

Another widely used Yiddish expression – also present–day German – is *gesundheit* (pronounced ge–zund–hite). This means, literally, 'health' and is said, in the same way that English–speakers say 'bless you,' to someone who sneezes.

There is a fair degree of *mish–mosh* in a lot of speech used in Australia. Aborigines, for instance, have incorporated some non–Aboriginal words into the *patois* they speak, and these ways of speech reflect wide regional differences in languages and dialects across the country. They have incorporated Aboriginal words in the forms of English they use, also. In the 1950s a Thursday Island grandmother of Sri Lankan/Anglo–Saxon descent, who was born at about the turn of the century, had some unusual expressions. To someone 'flapping around' or over–reacting: 'Stop ginning around!' 'You're like a gin in bloomers!'; 'You're carrying on like a gin at a christening!' To someone offering the excuse, 'but I thought. . .' – who had been thought-less: 'You know what thought did – he thought he'd shat himself but he hadn't.' People or things that would not mix were 'like shit to an oily rag.'

Germans, Greeks, Italians and, no doubt, other migrant groups have altered their speech very much as the Aborigines have done. Because German and Italian speaking people have been established in some parts of Australia over many generations, their usages tend to have been studied more closely. But even recent migrants who have come from areas where fenced, individual yards and gar-dens are unknown, speak of *to backyardou* (Greek) and *la fensa (Italian). Italians working on the Snowy River scheme called the kookaburra, or 'laughing jackass,' 'Ha–ha Pigeon.'*

Anne Lloyd, a linguist working in Rockhampton, has provided most of the German and Italian examples that follow. Over several generations, some German speakers have incorporated such words as 'beach,' 'surf,' 'gum–tree,' 'drover,' 'council,' 'township' and 'tractor.' Often, gender is assigned to this kind of usage: *die fire, der creek, die road.* Assigned gender is an indication of integration in the adopting language. Verbs are transferred also: *trainen, relieven, joinen, driven, cutten.* Instead of the normal German tag question *'Nicht wahr?'* Australian German has invented *'Ist es?'* ('Is it?') and *'Tut er?'* ('Does he?'). Aus-tralian German has also 'invented' some phrases that are literal translations from English and serve to fill gaps where no equi-valent German phrase exists: 'For better or for worse' become *Für Schlecter oder besser.*

Australian Italian uses some words that have a different meaning in Italian:

Australian Italian		*Italian*	
lodare	to load (in preference to Italian *caricare*)	*lodare*	to praise
fattoria	factory	*fattoria*	farm
parenti	parents	*parenti*	relatives in general
relativi	relatives (coined because of the restricted meaning of *parenti*)		

Australian Italian also contains some words that have no literal meaning in Italian.

Australian Italian		*Italian*	
arvesto	harvest	*raccolito*	harvest
landa	land	*terra*	land
nido	I need	*ho bisogno*	I need

The first two Australian Italian words have no meaning in Italian, but *nido* in the original language means 'birds' nest.' *Vegetabili* has been invented instead of *verdura* for vegetables, and *russiano* instead of *russo* for Russian. The kind of words that have been coined for uniquely Australian concepts include *billicàno* (billycan); *tièbi* (TAB); and *milchibar* (milkbar).

I borrowed the title of this chapter from the poet Les Murray. Les and his wife, Valerie, contributed phrases that their family uses and which derive from Valerie's background both as a teacher of English as a second language and because of her mixed-language family background: her mother was Swiss, her father Hungarian. With Les Murray's permission I substantially quote his words:

Schmückedein: in the Murray household 'kitschy' objects are *Schmückedein*, deriving from *Schmücke dein Heim* (Decorate your Home), which is the common sign over shooting galleries and similar sideshows at fairgrounds in Switzerland.

Trouser: in the singular, i.e., 'he was wearing a trouser' not a pair of trousers, or 'wearing trousers.'

es laat: Swiss German, literally 'it gives way.' Used humorously when demonstrating that something you meant to discard anyway really has had it. Ripping a worn—out but beloved shirt straight up the back, a cheerfully merciless wife will say *'Sehsch, es laat!'* ('See, it tears; no more wear in that!')

bicyclist: a high and mighty crawler, a toady. "One who bows to that which is above while treading on that which is below.' From the Hungarian *biciklista* (pronounced bitz—ik—lish—to), this is old Budapest slang.

Once: translation of the ubiquitous German adverb *mal, einmal.* einmal. For example, 'I'll have to go up to Newcastle once and see him.' Also heard in the Barossa Valley, South Australia.

To dress: to dress a bed is to make a bed; *to open* a bed means to pull back the covers.

Schön: something more intimate, warmer, and even more beautiful than beautiful, which is its exact English translation; the youngest child of a loving family might be not only beautiful but also *schön.*

Gigampfe: a Swiss verg, pronounced *gi—gampfa.* It is a splen-did example of a useful word existing in one language and having no exact equivalent in another. One example might be the French *en rapport* which means so much more than 'to be in sympathy with.' *Gigampfe* is 'to lean back on a chair and rock on the rear legs to the great detriment of the chair and peril to the rocking party.' It can also mean to 'see—saw.'

Ohrfeige: as in 'simple as an Ohrfeige,' 'simple as a box on the ears.' This is an ordinary German idiom, and the word is pronounced *or*—faiga.

Faxen: faces, in the sense of grimaces: 'Don't make faxen!'

Szegen: pronounced *sag—ehn* to rhyme with nag—pain. This is the Hungarian word for 'poor' in the sense of something or some-one worthy of pity. In the Australian household of the Murray family it is used of things which have sagged or lost their crispness. For example: 'Poor candle. It's melted. *Szegen* candle.'

Prost, prosit: 'Your health.' This German toast is used a good deal in the family. Similarly, many Jewish people use the toast, *'L'haim'* ('To life'), and Scandinavians in Australia perpetuate *skol.*

Les Murray goes on to say that lots of other non-English words, usually from standard German, make ephemeral guest-appearances in the speech of his family. Foreign usages do not carry over to or affect his writing because they belong to a completely different sphere of life.

VIRILITY

You are too young to remember Edmund Gate, but I knew him when he was Elia Gatoff in knickers, just off the boat from Liverpool. Now to remember Edmund Gate at all, one must be a compatriot of mine, which is to say a centagenerian. A man of one hundred and six is always sequestered on a metaphysical Elba, but on an Elba without even the metaphor of a Napoleon — where in fact, it has been so long forgotten that Napoleon ever lived that it is impossible to credit his influence, let alone his fame. It is harsh and lonely in this country of exile — the inhabitants (or, as we in our eleventh decade ought more accurately to be called, the survivors) are so sparse, and so maimed, and so unreliable as to recent chronology, and so at odds with your ideas of greatness, that we do indeed veer toward a separate mentality, and ought in logic to have a flag of our own. It is not that we seclude ourselves from you, but rather that you have seceded from us — you with your moon pilots, and mohole fishermen, and algae cookies, and anti–etymological reformed spelling — in the face of all of which I can scarcely expect you to believe in a time when a plain and rather ignorant man could attain the sort of celebrity you people accord only to vile geniuses who export baby–germs in plastic envelopes. That, I suppose is the worst of it for me and my countrymen in the land of the very old — your isolation from our great. Our great and especially our merely famous have slipped from your encyclopaedias, and will vanish finally and absolutely when we are at length powdered into reconstituted genetic ore — mixed with fish flour, and to be taken as an antidote immediately after radiation–saturation: a detail and a tangent, but I am subject to these broodings at my heavy age, and occasionally catch myself in egotistical yearnings for an ordinary headstone engraved with my name. As if, in a population of a billion and a quarter, there could be space for that entirely obsolete indulgence! — and yet, only last week, in the old Preserved Cemetery, I visited Edmund Gate's grave, and viewed his monument, and came away persuaded of the beauty of that ancient, though wasteful, decorum. We have no room for physical memorials nowadays; and nobody pays any attention to the pitiful poets.

Just *here* is my huge difficulty. How am I to convince you of that, during an interval in my own vast lifetime, there was a moment when a poet – was noticed, and noticed abundantly, and noticed magnificently and even stupendously? You will of course not have heard of Byron, and no one is more eclipsed than dear Dylan; nor will I claim that Edmund Gate ever rose to *that* standard. But he was recited, admired, worshiped, translated, pursued, even paid; and the press would not let him go for an instant. I have spoken of influence and of fame; Edmund Gate, it is true, had little influence, even on his own generation – I mean by this that he was not much imitated – but as for fame! Fame was what we gave him plenty of. We could give him fame – in those days fame was ours to give. Whereas you measure meanly by the cosmos. The first man to the moon is now a shriveling little statistician in a Bureau somewhere, superseded by the first to Venus, who, we are told, lies all day in a sour room drinking vodka and spitting envy on the first to try for Pluto. Now it is the stars which dictate fame, but with us it was *we* who made fame, and we who dictated our stars.

He died (like Keats, of whom you will also not have heard) at twenty–six. I have this note not from Microwafer Tabulation, but from the invincible headstone itself. I had forgotten it and was touched. I almost thought he lived to be middle–aged: I base this on my last sight of him, or perhaps my last memory, in which I observe him in his underwear, with a big hairy paunch, cracked and browning teeth, and a scabby scalp laid over with a bunch of thin light–colored weeds. He looked something like a failed pugilist. I see him standing in the middle of a floor without a carpet, puzzled, drunk, a newspaper in one hand and the other tenderly reaching through the slot in his shorts to enclose his testicles. The last words he spoke to me were the words I chose (it fell to me) for his monument: "I am a man."

He was, however, a boy in corduroys when he first came to me. He smelled of salami and his knickers were raveled at the pockets and gave off a saltiness. He explained that he had walked all the way from England, back and forth on the deck. I later gathered that he was a stowaway. He had been sent ahead to Liverpool on a forged passport (these were Czarist times), from a place full of wooden shacks and no sidewalks called Glusk, with instructions to search out an old aunt of his mother's on Mersey Street and stay with her until his parents and sisters

could scrape up the papers for their own border—crossing. He
miraculously found the Liverpudlian aunt, was received with joy,
fed bread and butter, and shown a letter from Glusk in which his
father stated that the precious sheets were finally all in order
and properly stamped with seals almost identical to real govern—
ment seals: they would all soon be reunited in the beckoning
poverty of Golden Liverpool. He settled in with the aunt, who
lived tidily in a gray slum and worked all day in the back of a
millinery shop sewing on veils. She had all the habits of a
cool and intellectual spinster. She had come to England six
years before – she was herself an emigrant from Glusk, and had
left it legally and respectably under a pile of straw in the
last of three carts in a gypsy caravan headed westward for
Poland. Once inside Poland (humanely governed by Franz Josef),
she took a train to Warsaw, and liked the book stores there so
much she nearly stayed forever, but instead thoughtfully lifted
her skirts onto another train – how she hated the soot! – to
Hamburg, where she boarded a neat little boat pointed right at
Liverpool. It never occurred to her to go a little further, to
America: she had fixed on English as the best tongue for a
foreigner to adopt, and she was suspicious of the kind of English
Americans imagine they spoke. With superior diligence she began
to teach her great—nephew the beautiful and clever new language;
she even wanted him to go to school, but he was too much absorbed
in the notion of waiting, and instead ran errands for the green—
grocer at three shillings a week. He put pennies into a little
tin box to buy a red scarf for his mother when she came. He
waited and waited, and looked dull when his aunt talked to him
in English at night, and waited immensely, with his whole body.
But his mother and father and his sister Feige and his sister
Gittel never arrived. On a rainy day in the very month he burst
into manhood (in the course of which black rods of hair appeared
in the trench of his upper lip), his aunt told him, not in English,
that it was no use waiting any longer: a pogrom had murdered
them all. She put the letter, from a cousin in Glusk, on exhibit
before him – his mother, raped and slaughtered; Feige, raped and
slaughtered; Gittel, escaped but caught in the forest and raped
twelve times before a passing friendly soldier saved her from
the thirteenth by shooting her through the left eye; his father,
tied to the tail of a Cossack horse and sent to have his head
broken on cobblestones.

　　All this he gave me quickly, briefly, without excitement,
and with a shocking economy. What he had come to America for,

he said, was a job. I asked him what his experience was. He reiterated the fact of the greengrocer in Liverpool. He had the queerest accent; a regular salad of an accent.

"That's hardly the type of preparation we can use on a news-paper," I said.

"Well, it's the only kind I've got."

"What does your aunt think of your leaving her all alone like that?"

"She's an independent sort. She'll be all right. She says she'll send me money when she can."

"Look here, don't you think the money ought to be going in the opposite direction?"

"Oh, I'll never have any money," he said.

I was irritated by his pronunciation – "mawney" – and I had theories about would-be Americans, none of them complimentary, one of which he was unwittingly confirming. "There's ambition for you!"

But he startled me with a contradictory smile both iron and earnest. "I'm very ambitious. You wait and see," as though we were already colleagues, confidents, and deep comrades. "Only what *I* want to be," he said, "they don't ever make much money."

"What's that?"

"A poet. I've always wanted to be a poet."

I could not help laughing at him. "In English?" You want to do English poetry?"

"English, righto. I don't *have* any other language. Not any more."

"Are you positive you have English?" I asked him. "You've only been taught by your aunt, and no one ever taught *her*."

But he was listening to only half, and would not bother with any talk about his relative. "That' why I want to work on a paper. For contact with written material."

I said strictly, "You could read books, you know."

"I've read *some*." He looked down in shame. "I'm too lazy. My mind is lazy but my legs are good. If I could get to be a reporter or something like that I could use my legs a lot. I'm a good runner."

"And when," I put it to him in the voice of a sardonic archangel, "will you compose your poems?"

"While I'm running," he said.

I took him on as office boy and teased him considerably. When-ever I handed him a bit of copy to carry from one cubbyhole to another I reminded him that he was at last in contact with

written material, and hoped he was finding it useful for his
verse. He had no humor but his legs were as fleet as he had
promised. He was always ready, always at attention, always on
the alert to run. He was always *there*, waiting. He stood like
a hare at rest watching the typewriters beat, his hands and his
feet nervous for the snatch of the sheet from the platen, as
impatient as though the production of a column of feature items
were a wholly automatic act governed by the width of the paper
and the speed of the machine. He would rip the page from the
grasp of its author and streak for the copy desk, where he would
lean belligerently over the poor editor in question to study the
strokes of this cringing chap's blue pencil. "Is that what
cutting is?" he asked. "Is that what you call proofreading?
Doesn't 'judgment' have an 'e' in it? Why not? There's an 'e'
in judge,' isn't there? How come you don't take the 'e' out of
'knowledgeable' too? How do you count the type for a headline?"
He was insufferably efficient and a killing nuisance. In less
than a month he swtiched from those ribbed and reeky knickers to
a pair of grimy trousers out of a pawnshop, and from the ample
back pocket of these there protruded an equally ample dictionary
with its boards missing, purchased from the identical source:
but this was an affectation, since I never saw him consult it.
All the same we promoted him to proofreader. This buried him.
We set him down at a dark desk in a dungeon and entombed him
under mile-long strips of galleys and left him there to dig himself out. The printshop helped by providing innumerable shrdlus
and inventing further typographical curiosities of such a nature
that a psychologist would have been severely interested. The
city editor was abetted by the whole reporting staff in the
revelation of news stories rivaling the Bible in luridness, sex-
uality, and imaginative abomination. Meanwhile he never blinked,
but went on devotedly taking the "e" out of "judgment" and
putting it back for "knowledgeable," and making little loops for
"omit" whenever someone's syntactical fancy had gone too raptur-
ously far.

When I looked up and spotted him apparently about to mount my
typewriter I was certain he had risen from his cellar to beg to
be fired. Instead he offered me a double information: he was
going to call himself Gate, and what did I think of that? – and
in the second place he had just written his first poem.

"First?" I said. "I thought you've been at it all the while."

"Oh no," he assured me. "I wasn't ready. I didn't have a
name."

"Gatoff's a name, isn't it?"

He ignored my tone, almost like a gentleman. "I mean a name suitable for the language. It has to match somehow, doesn't it? Or people would get the idea I'm an imposter." I recognized this word from a recent fabrication he had encountered on a proof — my own, in fact: a two-paragraph item about a man who had successfully posed as a firewarden through pretending to have a sound acquaintance with the problems of water-pressure systems, but who let the firehouse burn down because he could not get the tap open. It was admittedly a very inferior story, but the best I could do; the others had soared beyond my meager gleam, though I made up for my barrenness by a generosity of double negatives. Still, I marveled at his quickness at self-enrichment — the aunt in Liverpool, I was certain, had never talked to him, in English, of imposters.

"Listen," he said thickly, "I really feel you're the one who started me off. I'm very grateful to you. You understood my weakness in the language and you allowed me every opportunity."

"Then you like your job down there?"

"I just wish I could have a light on my desk. A small bulb maybe, that's all. Otherwise it's great down there, sure, it gives me a chance to think about poems."

"Don't you pay any attention to what you're reading?" I asked admiringly.

"Sure I do. I always do. That's where I get my ideas. Poems deal with Truth, right? One thing I've learned lately from contact with written material is that Truth is Stranger than Fiction." He uttered this as if fresh from the mouths of the gods. It gave him a particular advantage over the rest of us: admonish him that some phrase was as old as the hills, and he would pull up his head like a delighted turtle and exclaim, "Now that's perfect. What a perfect way to express antiquity. That's true, the hills have been there since the earth was just new. Very good! I congratulate you" — showing extensive emotional reverberation, which I acknowledged after a time as his most serious literary symptom.

The terrible symptom was just now vividly tremulous. "What I want to ask you," he said, "is what you would think of Edmund for a poet's name. In front of Gate, for instance."

"*My* name is Edmund," I said.

"I know, I know. Where would I get the idea if not from you? A marvelous name. Could I borrow it? Just for use on poems. Otherwise it's all right, don't be embarrassed, call me Elia like always."

199

He reached for his behind, produced the dictionary, and cautiously shook it open to the Fs. Then he tore out a single page with meticulous orderliness and passed it to me. It covered Fenugreek to Fylfot, and the margins were foxed with an astonishing calligraphy, very tiny and very ornate, like miniature crystal cubes containing little bells.

"You want me to read this?" I said.

"Please," he commanded.

"Why don't you use regular paper?"

"I like words," he said. "Fenugreek, an herb of the pea family. Felo-de-se, a suicide. I wouldn't get that just from a blank sheet. If a see a good word in the vicinity I put it right in."

"You're a great borrower," I observed.

"Be brutal," he begged. "Tell me if I have talent."

It was a poem about dawn. It had four rhymed stanzas and coupled "lingered" with "rosy-fingered." The word Fuzee was strangely prominent.

"In concept it's a little on the hackneyed side," I told him.

"I'll work on it," he said fervently. "You think I have a chance? Be brutal."

"I don't suppose you'll ever be an original, you know," I said.

"You wait and see," he threatened me. "I can be brutal too."

He headed back for his cellar and I happened to notice his walk. His thick round calves described forceful rings in his trousers, but he had a curiously modest gait, like a preoccupied steer. His dictionary jogged on his buttock, and his shoulders suggested the spectral flutes of a spectral cloak, with a spec-tral retinue following murmurously after.

"Elia," I called to him.

He kept going.

I was willing to experiment. "Edmund!" I yelled.

He turned, very elegantly.

"Edmund," I said. "Now listen. I mean this. Don't show me any more of your stuff. The whole thing is hopeless. Waste your own time but don't waste mine."

He took this in with a pleasant lift of his large thumbs. "I never waste anything. I'm very provident."

"Provident, are you?" I made myself a fool for him: "Aha, evidently you've been inditing something in and around the Ps – "

"Puce, red. Prothorax, the front part of an insect. Plectrum, an ivory pick."

"You're an opportunist," I said. "A hoarder. A rag-dealer. Don't fancy yourself anything better than that. Keep out of my way, Edmund," I told him.

After that I got rid of him. I exerted — if that is not too
gross a word for the politic and the canny — a quiet urgency here
and there, until finally we tendered him the title of reporter
and sent him out to the police station to call in burglaries off
the blotter. His hours were midnight to morning. In two weeks
he turned up at my desk at ten o'clock, squinting through an
early sunbeam.

"Don't you go home to sleep now?" I asked.

"Criticism before slumber. I've got more work to show you.
Beautiful new work."

I swallowed a groan. "How do you like it down at headquarters?"

"It's fine. A lovely place. The cops are fine people. It's
a wonderful atmosphere to think up poems in. I've been extremely
fecund. I've been pullulating down there. This is the best of
the lot."

He ripped out Mimir to Minion. Along the white perimeter of
the page his incredible handwriting peregrinated: it was a poem
about a rose. The poet's beloved was compared to the flower.
They blushed alike. The rose minced in the breeze; so did the
lady.

"I've given up rhyme," he announced, and hooked his eyes in
mine. "I've improved. You admit I've improved, don't you?"

"No," I said. "You've retrogressed. You're nothing but
hash. You haven't advanced an inch. You'll never advance. You
haven't got the equipment."

"I have all these new words," he protested. "Menhir. Eximious.
Suffruticose. Congee. Anastrophe. Dandiprat. Trichiasis. Nid-
ificate."

"Words aren't the only equipment. You're hopeless. You
haven't got the brain for it."

"All my lines scan perfectly."

"You're not a poet."

He refused to be disappointed; he could not be undermined.
"You don't see any difference?"

"Not in the least. — Hold on. A difference indeed. You've
bought yourself a suit," I said.

"Matching coat and pants. Thanks to you. You raised me up
from an errand boy."

"That's America for you," I said. "And what about Liverpool?
I suppose you send your aunt something out of your salary?"

"Not particularly."

"Poor old lady."

"She's all right as she is."

"Aren't you all she's got? Only joy, apple of the eye and
so forth?"

"She gets along. She writes me now and then."

"I suppose you don't answer much."

"I've got my own life to live," he objected, with all the
ardor of a man in the press of inventing not just a maxim but a
principle. "I've got a career to make. Pretty soon I have to
start getting my things into print. I bet you know some magazine
editors who publish poems."

It struck me that he had somehow discovered a means to check
my acquaintance. "That just the point. They publish *poems*. You
wouldn't do for them."

"You could start me off in print if you wanted to."

"I don't want to. You're no good."

"I'll get better. I'm still on my way. Wait and see," he said.

"All right," I agreed, "I'm willing to wait but I don't want
to see. Don't show me any more. Keep your stuff to yourself.
Please don't come back."

"Sure," he said: this was his chief American acquisition.
"You come to me instead."

During the next month there was a run on robberies and other
nonmatutinal felonies, and pleasurably and with relief I imagined
him bunched up in a telephone booth in the basement of the station
house, reciting clot after clot of criminal boredoms into the
talking-piece. I hoped he would be hoarse enough and weary
enough to seek his bed instead of his fortune, especially if he
conceived of his fortune as conspicuously involving me. The mornings passed, and, after a time, so did my dread – he never
appeared. I speculated that he had given me up. I even ventured
a little remorse at the relentlessness of my dealings with him,
and then a courier from the mail room loped in and left me an
enormous envelope from an eminent literary journal. It was filled
with dozens and dozens of fastidiously torn-out dictionary
pages, accompanied by a letter to me from the editor-in-chief,
whom – after a fashion – I knew (he had been a friend of my late
and distinguished father): "Dear Edmund, I put it to you that
your tastes in gall are not mine. I will not say that you
presumed on my indulgence when you sent this fellow up here with
his sheaf of horrors, but I will ask you in the future to
restrict your recommendations to *simple* fools – who, presumably,
turn to ordinary foolscap in their hour of folly. P.S. In any
case I never have, and never hope to, print anything containing
the word 'ogdoad.'"

One of the sheets was headed Ogam to Oliphant.

It seemed to savage a hardship to rage all day without release: nevertheless I thought I would wait it out until midnight and pursue him where I could find him, at his duties with the underworld, and then, for direct gratification, knock him down. But it occurred to me that a police station is an inconvenient situation for an assault upon a citizen (although it did not escape me that he was still unnaturalized), so I looked up his address and went to his room.

He opened the door in his underwear. "Edmund!" he cried. "Excuse me, after all I'm a night worker – but it's all right, come in, come in! I don't need a lot of sleep anyhow. If I slept I'd never get any poems written, so don't feel bad."

Conscientiously I elevated my fists and consicentiously I knocked him down.

"What's the idea?" he asked from the floor.

"What's the idea is right," I said. "Who told you you could go around visiting important people and saying I sicked you on them?"

He rubbed his sore chin in a rapture. "You heard! I bet you heard straight from the editor–in–chief himself. You would. You've got the connections, I knew it. I told him to report right to you. I knew you'd be anxious."

"I'm anxious and embarrased and ashamed," I said. "You've made me look like an idiot. My father's oldest friend. He thinks I'm a sap."

He got up, poking himself for bruises. "Don't feel bad for me. He didn't accept any at all? Is that a fact? Not a single one?" I threw the envelope at him and he caught it with a surprisingly expert arc of the wrist. Then he spilled out the contents and read the letter. "Well, that's too bad," he said. "It's amazing how certain persons can be so unsympathetic. It's in their nature, they can't help it. But I don't mind. I mean it's all compensated for. Here *you* are. I thought it would be too nervy to invite you – it's a very cheap place I live in, you can see that – but I knew you'd come on your own. An aristocrat like yourself."

"Elia," I said, "I came to knock you down. I *have* knocked you down."

"Don't feel bad about it," he repeated, consoling me. He reached for my ear and gave it a friendly pull. "It's only natural. You had a shock. In your place I would have done exactly the same thing. I'm very strong. I'm probably much stronger than you are. You're pretty strong too, if you could knock me down. But to tell the truth, I sort of *let* you. I like to show manners when I'm a host."

He scraped forward an old wooden chair, the only one in the room, for me to sit down on. I refused, so he sat down himself, with his thights apart and his arms laced, ready for a civilized conversation. "You've read my new work yourself, I presume."

"No," I said. "When are you going to stop this? Why don't you concentrate on something sensible? You want to be a petty police reporter for the rest of your life?"

"I hope not," he said, and rasped his voice to show his sincerity. "I'd like to be able to leave this place. I'd like to have enough money to live in a nice American atmosphere. Like you, the way you live all alone in that whole big house."

He almost made me think I had to apologize. "My father left it to me. Anyway, didn't you tell me you never expected to get rich on poetry?"

"I've looked around since then, I've noticed things. Of America expect everything. America has room for anything, even poets. Edmund," he said warmly, "I know how you feel. R.I.P. I don't have a father either. You would have admired my father — a strapping man. It's amazing that they could kill him. Strong. Big. No offense, but he restrained himself, he never knocked anyone down. Here," he pleaded, "you just take my new things and look them over and see if that editor-in-chief was right. You tell me if in his shoes you wouldn't publish me, that's all I want."

He handed me Gharri to Gila Monster: another vapid excrescence in the margins. Schuit to Scolecite: the same. But it was plain that he was appealing to me out of the pathos of his orphaned condition, and from pity and guilt (I had the sense that he would regard it as a pogrom if I did not comply) I examined the rest, and discovered, among his daisies and sunsets, a fresh theme. He had begun to write about girls: not the abstract Beloved, but real girls, with names like Shirley, Ethel, and Bella.

"Love poems," he said conceitedly. "I find them very moving."

"About as moving as the lovelorn column," I said, "if less gripping. When do you get the time for girls?"

"Leonardo da Vinci also had only twenty-four hours in his day. Ditto Michelangelo. Besides, I don't go looking for them. I attract them."

This drew my stare. "You attract them?"

"Sure. I attract them right here. I hardly ever have to go out. Of course that sort of arrangement's not too good with some of the better types. They don't go for a poet's room."

"There's not a book in the place," I said in disgust.

"Books don't make a poet's room," he contradicted. "It depends on the poet — the build of man he is." And, with the full power of his odious resiliency, he winked at me.

The effect on me of this conversation was unprecedented: I suddenly began to see him as he saw himself, through the lens of his own self-esteem. He almost looked handsome. He had changed; he seemed larger and bolder. The truth was merely that he was not yet twenty and that he had very recently grown physically. He remained unkempt, and his belly had a habit of swelling under his shirt; but there was something huge starting in him.

About that time I was asked to cover a minor war in the Caribbean — it was no more than a series of swamp skirmishes — and when I returned after eight weeks I found him living in my house. I had, as usual, left the key with my married sister (it had been one of my father's crotchets — he had several — to anticipate all possible contingencies, and I carried on the custom of the house), and he had magically wheedled it from her: it turned out he had somehow persuaded her that she would earn the gratitude of his posterity by allowing him to attain the kind of shelter commensurate with his qualities.

"Commensurate with your qualities," I sing-songed at him. "When I heard that, I knew she had it verbatim. All right, Elia, you've sucked the place dry. That's all. Out." Every teacup was dirty and he had emptied the whiskey. "You've had parties," I concluded.

"I couldn't help it, Edmund. I've developed so many friendships recently."

"Get out."

"Ah, don't be harsh. You know the little rooms upstairs? The ones that have the skylight? I bet those were maids' rooms once. You wouldn't know I was there, I promise you. Where can I go where there's so much good light? Over at the precinct house it's even worse than the cellar was, they use only forty-watt bulbs. The municipality is prodigiously parsimonious. What have I got if I haven't got my eyesight?

Take my pen and still
I sing. But deny
My eye
And Will
Departs the quill."

"My reply remains Nil," I said. "Just go."

He obliged me with a patronizing laugh. "That's very good. Deny, Reply. Quill, Nil."

"No, I mean it. You can't stay. Besides," I said sourly, "I thought you gave up rhymes long ago."

"You think I'm making it up about my eyes," he said. "Well, look." He darted a thick fist into a pocket and whipped out a pair of glasses and put them on. "While you were gone I had to get these. They're pretty strong for a person of my age. I'm not supposed to abuse my irises. These peepers cost me equal to nearly a month's rent at my old place."

The gesture forced me to study him. He had spoken of his qualities, but they were all quantities: he had grown some more, not upward exactly, and not particularly outward, but in some textural way, as though his bigness required one to assure oneself of it by testing it with the nerve in the fingertip. He was walking around in his underwear. For the first time I took it in how extraordinarily hairy a man he was. His shoulders and his chest were a forest, and the muscles in his arms were globes darkened by brush. I observed that he was thoroughly aware of himself; he held his torso like a bit of classical rubble, but he captured the warrior lines of it with a certain prideful agility.

"Go ahead, put on your clothes," I yelled at him.

"It's not cold in the house, Edmund."

"It is in the street. Go on, get out. With or without your clothes. Go."

He lowered his head, and I noted in surprise the gross stems of his ears. "It would be mean."

"I can take it. Stop worrying about my feelings."

"I'm not referring just to you. I left Sylvia alone upstairs when you came in."

"Are you telling me you've got a *girl* in this house right now?"

"Sure," he said meekly. "But you don't mind, Edmund. I know you don't. I't only what you do yourself, isn't it?"

I went to the foot of the staircase and shouted: "That's enough! Come down! Get out!"

Nothing stirred.

"You've scared her," he said.

"Get rid of her, Elia, or I'll call the police."

"That would be nice," he said wistfully. "*They* like my poems. I always read them aloud down at the station house. Look, if

you really want me to go I'll go, and you can get rid of Sylvia
yourself. You certainly have a beautiful spacious house here.
Nice furniture. I certainly did enjoy it. Your sister told me
a few things about it — it was very interesting. Your sister's
a rather religious person, isn't she? Moral, like your father.
What a funny man your father was, to put a thing like that in
his will. Fornication on premises."

"What's this all about?" But I knew, and felt the heat of
my wariness.

"What your sister mentioned. She just mentioned that your
father left you this house only on condition you'd never do
anything to defame or defile it, and if you did do anything like
that the house would go straight to her. Not that she really
needs it for herself, but it would be convenient, with all those
children of hers — naturally I'm only quoting. I guess you
wouldn't want me to let on to her about Regina last Easter, would
you? — You see, Edmund, you're even sweating a little bit your—
self, look at your collar, so why be unfair and ask me to put on
my clothes?"

I said hoarsely, "How do you know about Regina?"

"Well, I don't really, do I? It's just that I found this
bunch of notes from somebody by that name — Regina — and in one
or two of them she says how she stayed here with you over Easter
and all about the two of you. Actually, your sister might be a
little strait-laced, but she's pretty nice, I mean she wouldn't
think the family mansion was being desecrated and so on if *I*
stayed here, would she? So in view of all that don't you want
to give your consent to my moving in for a little while, Edmund?"

Bitterly I gave it, though consent was academic: he had
already installed all his belongings — his dictionary (what was
left of it: a poor skeleton, gluey spine and a few of the more
infrequent vocabularies, such as K, X, and Z), his suit, and a
cigar box filled with thin letters from Liverpool, mostly unopened.
I wormed from him a promise that he would keep to the upper part
of the house; in return I let him take my typewriter up with
him.

What amazed me was that he kept it tapping almost every even—
ing. I had really believed him to be indolent; instead it
emerged that he was glib. But I was astonished when I occasionally
saw him turn away visitors — it was more usual for him to grab,
squeeze, tease and kiss them. They came often, girls with hats
brimmed and plumed, and fur muffs, and brave quick little boots;
they followed him up the stairs with crowds of poems stuffed in

their muffs – their own, or his, or both – throwing past me jagged hillocks and troughs of laughter, their chins hidden in stanzas. Then, though the space of a floor was between us, I heard him declaim: then received a zephyr of shrieks; then further laughter, ebbing; then a scuffle like a herd of zoo antelope, until, in the pure zeal of fury, I floundered into the drawing room and violently clapped the doors to. I sat with my book of maps in my father's heavy creaking chair near a stagnant grate and wondered how I could get him out. I thought of carrying the whole rude tale of his licentiousness to my sister – but anything I might say against a person who was plainly my own guest would undoubtedly tell doubly against myself (so wholesome was my father's whim, and so completely had he disliked me), and since all the money had gone to my sister, and only this gigantic curio of a house to me, I had the warmest desire to hold onto it. Room for room I hated the place; it smelled of the wizened scrupulousness of my burdensome childhood, and my dream was to put it on the market at precisely the right time and make off with a fortune. Luckily I had cozy advice from real-estate friends: the right hour was certainly not yet. But for this house and these hopes I owned nothing, not counting my salary, which was, as my sister liked to affirm, beggar's pay in the light of what she called our "background" Her appearances were now unhappily common. She arrived with five or six of her children, and always without her husband, so that she puffed out the effect of having plucked her offspring out of a cloud. She was a small, exact woman, with large, exact views, made in the exact image of a pious bird, with a cautious jewel of an eye, an excessively arched and fussy breast, and two very tiny and exact nostril-points. She admired Elia and used to ascend to his rooms, trailing progeny, at his bedtime, which is to say at nine o'clock in the morning, when I would be just departing the house for my office; whereas the poetesses, to their credit, did not become visible until romantic dusk. Sometimes she would telephone me and recommend that I move such-and-such a desk – or this ottoman or that highboy – into his attic to supply him with the comforts due his gifts.

"Margaret," I answered her, "have you seen his stuff? It's all pointless. It's all trash."

"He's very young," she declared – "you wait and see," which she reproduced in his idiom so mimetically that she nearly sounded like a Glusker herself. "At your age he'll be a man of the world, not a house-hugging eunuch."

I could not protest at this abusive epithet, vibrantly meant for me; to disclaim my celibacy would have been to disclaim my house. Elia, it appeared, was teaching her subtlety as well as ornamental scurrility – "eunuch" had never before alighted on Margaret's austere tongue. But it was true that since I no longer dared to see poor Regina under our old terms – I was too perilously subject to my guest's surveillance – she dropped me in pique, and though I was not yet in love, I had been fonder of Regina than of almost anyone. "All right," I cried, "then let him be what he can."

"Why that's *everything*," said Margaret; "You don't realize what a find you've got in that young man."

"He's told you his designs on fame."

"Dear, he doesn't have to tell me. I can *see* it. He's unbelievable. He's an artist."

"A cheap little immigrant," I said. "Uncultivated. He never reads anything."

"Well, that's perfectly true, he's *not* effete. And about being a foreigner, do you know that terrible story, what they did to his whole family over there? When you survive a thing like that it turns you into a man. A fighter. Heroic," she ended. Then, with the solemnity of a codicil: "Don't call him little. He's big. He's enormous. His blood hasn't been thinned."

"He didn't *survive* it," I said wearily. "He wasn't even there when it happened. He was safe in England, he was in Liver- pool, for God's sake, living with his aunt."

"Dear, please don't exaggerate and *please* don't swear. I see in him what I'm afraid I'll never see in you: because it isn't there. Genuine manliness. You have no tenderness for the children, Edmund, you walk right by them. Your own nieces and nephews. Elia is remarkable with them. That's just a single example."

I recited, "Gentleness Is the True Soul of Virility."

"That's in very bad taste, Edmund, that's a very journalistic way to express it," she said sadly, as though I had shamed her with an indelicacy: so I assumed Elia had not yet educated her to the enunciation of this potent word.

"You don't like it? Neither do I. It's just that it happens to be the title of the manly artist's latest ode," which was a fact. He had imposed it on me only the night before, whereupon I ritually informed him that it was his worst banality yet.

But Margaret was unvanquishable; she had her own point to bring up. "Look here, Edmund, can't you do something about getting him a better job? What he's doing now doesn't come near to being worthy of him. After all, a police station. And the hours! — "

"I take it you don't think the police force an influence suitable to genuine manliness," I said, and reflected that he had, after all, managed to prove his virility at the cost of my demonstrating mine. I had lost Regina; but he still had all his poetesses.

Yet he did, as I have already noted, now and then send them away, and these times, when he was alone in his rooms, I would listen most particularly for the unrelenting clack of the type-writer. He was keeping at it; he was engrossed; he was serious. it seemed to me the most paralyzing sign of all that this hollow chattering of his machine was so consistent, so reliable, so intelligible, so without stutter or modern hesitation — it made me sigh. He was deeply deadly purposeful. The tapping went on and on, and since he never stopped, it was clear that he never thought. He never daydreamed, meandered, imagined, meditated, sucked, picked, smoked, scratched or loafed. He simply tapped, forefinger over forefinger, as though these sole active digits of his were the legs of a conscientious and dogged errand boy. His investment in self-belief was absolute in its ambition, and I nearly pitied him for it. What he struck off the page was spew and offal, and he called it his career. He mailed three dozen poems a week to this and that magazine, and when the known periodicals turned him down he dredged up the unknown ones, shadowy quarterlies and gazettes printed on hand-presses in dub-ious basements and devoted to matters anatomic, astrohomic, gastronomic, political, or atheist. To the publication of the Vegetarian Party he offered a pastoral verse in earthy trochees, and he tried the organ of a ladies' tonic manufacturing firm with fragile dactyls on the subject of corsets. He submitted everywhere, and I suppose there was finally no editor alive who did not clutch his head at the sight of his name. He clattered out barrage after barrage; he was a scourge to every idealist who had ever hoped to promote the dim cause of numbers. And leaf by leaf, travel journals shoulder to shoulder wtih Marxist tracts, paramilitarists alongside Seventh-Day Adventists, suffra-gettes hand in hand with nudists — to a man and to a woman they turned him down, they denied him print, they begged him at least to cease and desist, they folded their pamphlets like Arab tents and fled when they saw him brandishing so much as an iamb.

Meanwhile the feet of his fingers ran; he never gave up. My fright for him began almost to match my contempt. I was pitying him now in earnest, though his confidence remained as unmoved and oafish as ever. "Wait and see," he said, sounding like a copy of my sister copying him. The two of them put their heads together over me, but I had done all I could for him. He had no prospects. It even horribly developed that I was looked upon by my colleagues as his special protector, because when I left for the trenches my absence was immediately seized on and he was fired. This, of course, did not reach me until I returned after a year, missing an earlobe and with a dark and ugly declivity slashed across the back of my neck. My house guest had been excused from the draft by virtue of his bad eyesight, or perhaps more accurately by virtue of the ponderous thickness of his lenses; eight or ten of his poetesses tendered him a party in celebration of both his exemption and his myopia, at which he unflinchingly threw a dart into the bull's-eye of a target-shaped cake. But I was myself no soldier, and went only as a correspondent to that ancient and so primitive war, naïvely pretending to encompass the world, but Neanderthal according to our later and more expansive appetites for annihilation. Someone had merely shot a prince (a nobody – I myself cannot recall his name), and then, in illogical consequence, various patches of territory had sprung up to occupy and individualize a former empire. In the same way, I discovered, had Elia sprung up – or, as I must now consistently call him (lest I seem to stand apart from the miraculous change in his history), Edmund Gate. What I mean by this is that he stepped out of his attic and with democratic hugeness took over the house. His great form had by now entirely flattened my father's august chair, and, like a vast male Goldilocks, he was sleeping in my mother's bed – that shrine which my father had long ago consecrated to disuse and awe: a piety my sister and I had soberly perpetuated. I came home and found him in the drawing room, barefoot and in his underwear, dirty socks strewn over the floor, and my sister in attendance mending the holes he had worn through the heels, invigilated by a knot of her children. It presently emerged that she had all along been providing him with an allowance to suit his tastes, but in that first unwitting moment when he leaped up to embrace me, at the same time dragging on his shirt (because he knew how I disliked to see him undressed), I was stunned to catch the flash of his initials – "E.G." – embroidered in scarlet silk on a pair of magnificent cuffs.

"Edmund!" he howled. "Not one, not two — two *dozen*! Two dozen in the past two months alone!"

"Two dozen what?" I said, blinking at what had become of him. He was now twenty-one, and taller, larger, and hairier than ever. He wore new glasses (far less formidable than the awful eights his little nose had carried to the draft board), and these, predictably, had matured his expression, especially in the area of the cheekbones: their elderly silver frames very cleverly contradicted that inevitable boyishness which a big face is wont to radiate when it is committed to surrounding the nose of a cherub. I saw plainly, and saw it for myself, without the mesmerizing influence of his preening (for he was standing before me very simply, diligently buttoning up his shirt), that he had been increased and transformed; his fantastic body had made a simile out of him. The element in him that partook of the heathen colussus had swelled to drive out everything callow — with his blunt and balding skull he looked (I am willing to dare the vulgar godliness inherent in the term) like a giant lingam: one of those curious phallic monuments one may suddenly encounter, wreathed with bright chains of leaves, on a dusty wayside in India. His broad hands wheeled, his shirttail flicked; it was clear that his scalp was not going to be friends for long with his follicles — stars of dandruff fluttered from him. He had apparently taken up smoking, because his teeth were already a brown ruin. And with all that, he was somehow a ceremonial and touching spectacle. He was massive and dramatic; he had turned majestic.

"Poems, man, poems!" he roared. "Two dozen poems sold, and to all the best magazines!" He would have pulled my ear like a comrade had I had a lobe to pull by, but instead he struck me down into a chair (all the while my sister went on peacefully darning), and heaped into my arms a jumble of the most important periodicals of the hour.

"Ah, there's more to it than just that," my sister said.

"How did you manage all this?" I said. "My God, here's one in *The Centennial!* You mean Fielding accepted? Fielding actually?"

"The sheaf of horrors man, that's right. He's really a very nice old fellow, you know that, Edmund? I've lunched with him three times now. He can't stop apologizing for the way he embarrassed himself — remember, the time he wrote you that terrible letter about me? He's always saying how ashamed he is over it."

"Fielding?" I said. "I can't imagine Fielding — "

"Tell the rest," Margaret said complacently.

"Well, tomorrow we're having lunch again — Fielding and Margaret and me, and he's going to introduce me to this book publisher who's very interested in my things and wants to put them between, how did he say it, Margaret? — between something."

"Boards. A collection, all the poems of Edmund Gate. You see?" said Margaret.

"I *don't* see," I burst out.

"You never did. You haven't the vigor. I doubt whether you've ever really *penetrated* Edmund." This confused me, until I understood that she now habitually addressed him by the name he had pinched from me. "Edmund," she challenged — which of us was this? from her scowl I took it as a finger at myself — "you don't realize his level. It's his *level* you don't realize."

"I realize it," I said darkly, and let go a landslide of magazines: but *The Centennial* I retained. "I suppose poor Fielding's gone senile by now. Wasn't he at least ten years older than Father even? I suppose he's off his head and they just don't have the heart to ship him out."

"That won't do," Margaret said. "This boy is getting his recognition at last, that's all there is to it."

"I know what he means, though," Edmund said. "I tell them the same thing, I tell them exactly that — all those editors, I tell them they're crazy to carry on the way they do. You ought to hear — "

"Praise," Margaret intervened with a snap: "praise and more praise," as if this would spite me.

"I never thought myself those poems were *that* good," he said. "it's funny, they were just an experiment at first, but then I got the hang of it."

"An experiment?" I asked him. His diffidence was novel, it was even radical; he seemed almost abashed. I had to marvel: he was as bemused over his good luck as I was.

Not so Margaret, who let it appear that she had read the cosmic will. "Edmund is working in a new vein," she explained.

"Hasn't he always worked in vain?" I said, and dived into *The Centennial* to see.

Edmund slapped his shins at this, but "He who laughs last," said Margaret, and beat her thimble on the head of the nearest child: "What a callous man your uncle is. Read!" She commanded me.

"He has a hole in the back of his neck and only a little piece of ear left," said the child in a voice of astute assent.

"Ssh," said Margaret. "We don't speak of deformities."

"Unless they turn up as poems," I corrected; and read; and was startled by a dilation of the lungs, like a horse lashed out of the blue and made to race behond its impulse. Was it his, this clean stupendous stuff? But there was his name, manifest in print: it was his, according to *The Centennial*, and Fielding had not gone senile.

"Well?"

"I don't know," I said, feeling muddled.

"He doesn't know! Edmund" – this was to Edmund – "he doesn't know!"

"I can't believe it."

"He can't believe it, Edmund!"

"Well, neither could I at first," he admitted.

But my sister jumped up and pointed her needle in my face. "Say it's good."

"Oh, it's good. I can see it's good," I said. "He's hit it for once."

"They're *all* like that," she expanded. "Look for yourself."

I looked, I looked insatiably, I looked fanatically, I looked frenetically, I looked incredulously – I went from magazine to magazine, riffling and rifling, looking and looting and shuffling, until I had plundered them all of his work. My booty dumb-founded me: there was nothing to discard. I was trans-fixed; I was exhausted; in the end it was an exorcism of my stupe-faction. I was converted, I believed; he had hit it every time. And not with ease – I could trace the wonderful risks he took. It *was* a new vein; more, it was an artery, it had a pump and a kick; it was a robust ineluctable fountain. And when his book came out half a year later, my proselytization was sealed. Here were all the poems of the periodicals, already as familiar as solid old columns, uniquely graven; and layered over them like dazzling slabs of dappled marble, immovable because of the per-fection of their weight and the inexorability of their balance, was the aftermath of that early work, those more recent produc-tions to which I soon became a reverential witness. Or, if not witness, then auditor: for out of habit he still liked to compose in the attic, and I would hear him type a poem straight out, without so much as stopping to breathe. And right after-wards he came down and presented it to me. It seemed, then, that nothing had changed: only his gift and a single feature of his manner. Unerringly it was a work of – yet who or what was I to declare him genius? – accept instead the modest judgment of

merit. It was a work of merit he gave me unerringly, but he
gave it to me – this was strangest of all – with a quiescence, a
passivity. All his old arrogance had vanished. So had his vanity.
A kind of tranquillity kept him taut and still, like a man leashed;
and he went up the stairs, on those days when he was seized by
the need for a poem, with a languidness unlike anything I had
ever noticed in him before; he typed, from start to finish, with
no falterings or emendations; then he thumped on the stairs
again, loomed like a thug, and handed the glorious sheet over to
my exulting grasp. I supposed it was a sort of trance he had to
endure – in those dim times we were only just beginning to know
Freud, but even then it was clear that, with the bursting forth
of the latent thing, he had fallen into a relief as deep and
curative as the sleep of ether. If he lacked – or skipped –
what enthusiastic people call the creative exaltation, it was
because he had compressed it all, without the exhibitionism of
prelude, into that singular moment of power – six minutes, or
eight minutes, however long it took him, forefinger over forefinger,
to turn vision into alphabet.

He had become, by the way, a notably fast typist.

I asked him once – this was after he had surrendered a new-
hatched sheet not a quarter of an hour from the typewriter – how
he could account for what had happened to him.

"You used to be awful," I reminded him. "You used to be
unspeakable. My God, you were vile."

"Oh, I don't know," he said in that ennui, or blandness, that
he always displayed after one of his remarkable trips to the
attic, "I don't know if I was *that* bad."

"Well, even if you weren't" I said – in view of what I had
in my hand I could no longer rely on my idea of what he had been
– "this! This!" and fanned the wondrous page like a triumphant
flag. "How do you explain *this*, coming after what you were?"

He grinned a row of brown incisors at me and gave me a hearty
smack on the ankle. "Plagiarism."

"No, tell me really."

"The plangent plagiarism," he said accommodatingly, "of the
plantigrade persona. – Admit it, Edmund, you don't like the Ps,
you never did and you never will."

"For instance," I said, "you don't do *that* any more."

"Do what?" He rubbed the end of a cigarette across his
teeth and yawned. "I still do persiflage, don't I? I do it out
of my pate, without periwig, pugree, or peril."

"That. Cram grotesque words in every line."

"No, I don't do that any more. A pity, my dictionary's practically all gone."

"Why?" I persisted.

"I used it up, that's why. I *finished* it."

"Be serious. What I'm getting at is why you're different. Your stuff *is* different. I've never seen such a difference."

He sat up suddenly and with inspiration, and it came to me that I was observing the revival of passion. "Margaret's given that a lot of thought, Edmund. *She* attributes it to maturity."

"That's not very perspicacious," I said — for the sake of the Ps, and to show him I no longer minded anything.

But he said shortly, "She means virility."

This made me scoff. "She can't even get herself to say the word."

"Well, maybe there's a difference in Margaret too," he said.

"She's the same silly woman she ever was, and her husband's the same silly stockbroker, the two of them a pair of fertile prudes — she wouldn't recognize so-called virility if she tripped over it. She hates the whole concept — "

"She likes it," he said.

"What she likes is euphemisms for it. She can't face it, so she covers it up. Tenderness! Manliness! Maturity! Heroics! She hasn't got a brain in her head," I said, "and she's never gotten anything done in the world but those silly babies, I've lost count of how many she's done of *those* — "

"The next one's mine," he said.

"That's an imbecile joke."

"Not a joke."

"Look here, joke about plagiarism all you want but don't waste your breath on fairy tales."

"Nursery tales," he amended. "I never waste anything, I told you. That's just it, I've gone and plagiarized Margaret. I've purloined her, if you want to stick to the Ps." — Here he enumerated several other Ps impossible to print, which I am obliged to leave to my reader's experience, though not of the parlor. "And you're plenty wrong about your sister's brains, Edmund. She's a very capable businesswoman — she's simply never had the opportunity. You know since my book's out I have to admit I'm a bit in demand, and what she's done is she's booked me solid for six months' worth of recitations. And the fees! She's getting me more than Edna St. Vincent Millay, if you want the whole truth," he said proudly. "And why not? The only time that dame ever writes a good poem is when she signs her name."

All at once, and against his laughter and its storm of smoke, I understood who was behind the title of his collected poems. I was confounded. It was Margaret. His book was called *Virility.*

A week after this conversation he left with my sister for Chicago, for the inauguration of his reading series.

I went up to his attic and searched it. I was in a boil of distrust; I was outraged. I had lost Regina to Margaret's principles, and now Margaret had lost her principles, and in both cases Edmund Gate had stood to profit. He gained from her morality and he gained from her immorality. I began to hate him again. It would have rejoiced me to believe his quip: nothing could have made me merrier than to think him a thief of words, if only for the revenge of catching him at it — but he could not even be relied on for something so plausible as plagiarism. The place revealed nothing. There was not so much as an anthology of poetry, say, which might account for his extraordinary bur- geoning; there was not a single book of any kind — that sparse and pitiful wreck of his dictionary, thrown into a corner together with a cigar box, hardly signified. For the rest, there were only an old desk with his — no, my — typewriter on it, an ottoman, a chair or two, an empty chest, a hot bare floor (the heat pounded upward), and his primordial suit slowly revolving in the sluggish airs on a hanger suspended from the skylight, moths nesting openly on the lapels. It brought to mind Mohammed and the Koran; Joseph Smith and the golden plates. Some mysterious dictation recurred in this rooms: his gift came to him out of the light and out of the dark. I sat myself down at his desk and piecemeal typed out an agonized letter to Regina. I offered to change the terms of our relationship. I said I hoped we could take up again, not as before (my house was in use). I said I would marry her.

She answered immediately, enclosing a wedding announcement six months old.

On that same day Margaret returned. "I left him, of *course* I left him. I had to, not that he can take care of himself under the circumstances, but I sent him on to Detroit anyhow. If I'm going to be his manager, after all, I have to *manage* things. I can't do all that from the provinces, you know — I have to *be* here, I have to see people . . . ah, you can't imagine it, Edmund, they want him everywhere! I have to set up a regular office, just a *little* switchboard to start with — "

"It's going well?"

"Going well! What a way to put it! Edmund, he's a phenomenon. It's supernatural. He has *charisma*, in Chicago they had to arrest three girls, they made a human chain and lowered themselves from a chandelier right over the lectern, and the lowest-hanging one reached down for a hair of his head and nearly tore the poor boy's scalp off – "

"What a pity," I said.

"What do you *mean* what a pity, you don't follow, Edmund, he's a celebrity!"

"But he has so few hairs and he thinks so much of them," I said, and wondered bitterly whether Regina had married a bald man.

"You have no right to take that tone," Margaret said. "You have no idea how modest he is. I suppose that's part of his appeal – he simply has no ego at all. He takes it as innocently as a baby. In Chicago he practically looked over his shoulder to see if they really meant *him.* And they *do* mean him, you can't imagine the screaming and the shoving for autographs, and people calling bravo and fainting if they happen to meet his eyes – "

"Fainting?" I said doubtfully.

"Fainting! My goodness, Edmund, don't you read the headlines in your own paper? His audiences are three times as big as Caruso's. Oh, you're hard, Edmund, you admit he's good but I say there's a terrible wall in you if you don't see the power in this boy – "

"I see it over you," I said.

"Over me! Over the world, Edmund, it's the world he's got now – I've already booked him for London and Manchester, and here's this cable from Johannesburg pleading for him – oh, he's through with the backwoods, believe you me. And look here, I've just settled up this fine generous contract for his next book, with the reviews still piling in from the first one!" She crackled open her briefcase, and flung out a mass of files, lists, letterheads, schedules, torn envelopes with exotic stamps on them, fat legal-looking portfolios, documents in tiny type – she danced them all noisily upon her pouting lap.

"His second book?" I asked. "Is it ready?"

"Of course it's ready. He's remarkably productive, you know. Fecund."

"He pullulates," I suggested.

"His own word exactly, how did you hit it? He can come up with a poem practically at will. Sometimes, right after a reading, when he's exhausted – you know it's his shyness that exhausts him that way – anyhow, there he is all fussed and worried about whether the next performance will be as good, and he'll suddenly get this – well, *fit*, and hide out in the remotest part of the hotel and fumble in his wallet for bits of paper – he's always carrying bits of folded paper, with notes or ideas in them I suppose, and shoo everyone away, even me, and *type* (he's awfully fond of his new typewriter, by the way) – he just types the glory right out of his soul!" she crowed. "It's the energy of genius. He's *authentic*, Edmund, a profoundly energetic man is profoundly energetic in all directions at once. I hope at least you've been following the reviews?"

It was an assault, and I shut myself against it. "What will he call the new book?"

"Oh, he leaves little things like the title to me, and I'm all for simplicity – *Virility II*," she announced in her shocking business-magnate voice. "And the one after that will be *Virility III*. And the one after that – "

"Ah, fecund," I said.

"Fecund," she gleamed.

"A bottomless well?"

She marveled at this. "How is it you always hit on Edmund's words exactly?"

"I know how he talks," I said.

"A bottomless well, he said it himself. "Wait and see!" she warned me.

She was not mistaken. After *Virility* came *Virility II*, and after that *Virility III*, and after that an infant boy. Margaret named him Edmund – she said it was after me – and her husband the stockbroker, though somewhat puzzled at this human production in the midst of so much literary fertility, was all the same a little cheered. Of late it had seemed to him, now that Margaret's first simple switchboard had expanded to accommodate three secretaries, that he saw her less than ever, or at least that she was noticing him less than ever. This youngest Edmund struck him as proof (though it embarrassed him to think about it even for a minute) that perhaps she had noticed him more than he happened to remember. Margaret, meanwhile, was gay and busy – she slipped the new little Edmund ("Let's call *him* III," she laughed) into her packed nursery and went on about her business, which had grown formidable. Besides the three secretaries, she had two assistants: poets, poetasters, tenors, altos, mystics, rationalists, rightists, leftists, memoirists, fortune-tellers, peddlers, everyone with an *idée fixe* and therefore suitable to the lecture

circuit clamored to be bundled into her clientele. Edmund she
ran ragged. She ran him to Paris, to Lisbon, to Stockholm, to
Moscow; nobody understood him in any of these places, but the
title of his books translated impressively into all languages.
He developed a sort of growl — it was from always being hoarse;
he smoked day and night — and she made him cultivate it. Together
with his accent it caused an international shudder among the
best of women. She got rid of his initialed cuff and dressed
him like a prize fighter, in high laced black brogans and tight
shining T-shirts, out of which his hairness coiled. A long
bladder of smoke was always trailing out of his mouth. In Paris
they purused him into the Place de la Concorde yelling *"Virilité!
Virilité!" "Die Manneskraft!"* they howled in Munich. The reviews
were an avalanche, a cataslysm. In the rotogravure sections his
picture vied with the beribboned bosoms of duchesses. In New
Delhi glossy versions of his torso were hawked like an avatar in
the streets. He had long since been catapulted out of the hands
of the serious literary critics — but it was the serious critics
who had begun it. "The Masculine Principle personified, verified,
and illuminated." "The bite of Pope, the sensuality of Keats."
"The quality, in little, of the very greatest novels. Tolstoyan."
"Seminal and hard." "Robust, lusty, male," "Erotic."

Margaret was ecstatic, and slipped a new infant into her
bursting nursery. This time the stockbroker helped her choose
its name: they decided on Gate, and hired another nanny to take
care of the overflow.

After *Virility IV* came *Virility V*. The quality of his work
had not diminished, yet it was extraordinary that he could continue to produce at all. Occasionally he came to see me between
trips, and then he always went upstairs and took a turn around
the sighing floors of his old rooms. He descended haggard and
slouching; his pockets looked puffy, but it seemed to be only
his huge fists he kept there. Somehow his fame had intensified
that curious self-effacement. He had divined that I was privately
soured by his success, and he tried bashfully to remind me of
the days when he had written badly.

"That only makes it worse," I told him. "It shows what a
poor prophet I was."

"No," he said, "you weren't such a bad prophet, Edmund."

"I said you'd never get anywhere with your stuff."

"I haven't."

I hated him for that — Margaret had not long before shown me
his bank statement. He was one of the richest men in the country;

my paper was always printing human—interest stories about him —
"Prosperous Poet Visits Fabulous Patagonia." I said, "What do
you mean you haven't gotten anywhere? What more do you want
from the world? What else do you think it can give you?"

"Oh, I don't know," he said. He was gloomy and sullen. "I
just feel I'm running short on things."

"On triumphs? They're all the time comparing you to Keats.
Your pal Fielding wrote in *The Centennial* just the other day
that you're practically as great as the Early Milton."

"Fielding's senile. They should have put him away a long
time ago."

"And in sales you're next to the Bible."

"I was brought up on the Bible," he said suddenly.

"Aha. It's a fit of conscience? Then look, Elia, why don't
you take Margaret and get her divorced and get those babies of
yours legitimized, if that's what worrying you."

"They're legitimate enough. The old man's not a bad father.
Besides, they're all mixed up in there, I can't tell one from
the other."

"Yours are the ones named after you. You were right about
Margaret, she's an efficient woman."

"I don't worry about that," he insisted.

"*Some*thing's worrying you." This satisfied me considerably.

"As a matter of fact — " He trundled himself down into my
father's decaying chair. He had just returned from a tour of
Italy; he had gone with a wardrobe of thirty—seven satin T—shirts
and not one of them had survived intact. His torn—off sleeves
sold for twenty lira each. They had stolen his glasses right off
his celebrated nose. "I like it here, Edmund," he said. "I like
your house. I like the way you've never bothered about my old
things up there. A man likes to hang on to his past."

It always bewidlered me that the style of his talk had not
changed. He was still devoted to the insufferably hackneyed. He
still came upon his clichés like Columbus. Yet his poems . . .
but how odd, how remiss! I observe that I have not even attempted
to describe them. That is because they ought certainly to be
presented — read aloud, as Edmund was doing all over the world.
Short of that, I might of course reproduce them here; but I must
not let my narrative falter in order to make room for any of them,
even though, it is true, they would not require a good deal of
space. They were notably small and spare, in conventional stanza—
form. They were, besides, amazingly simple. Unlike the productions
of Edmund's early phase, their language was pristine. There were

no unusual words. His poems had the ordinary vocabulary of ordinary men. At the same time they were immensely vigorous. It was astonishingly easy to memorize them — they literally could not be forgotten. Some told stories, like ballads, and they were exhilarating yet shocking stories. Others were strangely explicit love lyrics, of a kind that no Western poet had ever yet dared — but the effect was one of health and purity rather than scandal. It was remarked by everyone who read or heard Edmund Gate's work that only a person who had had great and large experience of the world could have written it. People speculated about his life. If the Borgias, privy to all forms of foulness, had been poets, someone said, they would have written poems like that. If Teddy Roosevelt's Rough Riders had been poets, they would have written poems like that. If Genghis Khan and Napoleon had been poets, they would have written poems like that. They were masculine poems. They were political and personal, public and private. They were full of both passion and ennui, they were youthful and elderly, they were green and wise. But they were not beautiful and they were not dull, the way a well-used, faintly gnarled, but superbly controlled muscle is neither beautiful or dull.

They were, in fact, very much like Margaret's vision of Edmund Gate himself. The poet and the poems were indistinguishable.

She sent her vision to Yugoslavia, she sent it to Egypt, she sent it to Japan. In Warsaw girls ran after him in the street to pick his pockets for souvenirs — they came near to picking his teeth. In Copenhagen they formed an orgiastic club named "The Forbidden Gate" and gathered around a gatepost to read him. In Hong Kong they tore off his underwear and stared giggling at his nakedness. He was now twenty-five; it began to wear him out.

When he returned from Brazil he came to see me. He seemed more morose than ever. He slammed up the stairs, kicked heavily over the floors, and slammed down again. He had brought down with him his old cigar box.

"My aunt's dead," he said.

As usual he took my father's chair. His burly baby's-head lolled.

"The one in Liverpool?"

"Yeah."

"I'm sorry to hear that. Though she must have gotten to be a pretty old lady by now."

"She was seventy-four."

He appeared to be taking it hard. An unmistakable misery creased his giant neck.

"Still," I said, "you must have been providing for her nicely these last few years. At least before she went she had her little comforts."

"No. I never did a thing. I never sent her a penny."

I looked at him. He seemed to be nearly sick. His lips were black. "You always meant to, I suppose. You just never got around to it," I ventured; I thought it was remorse that had darkened him.

"No," he said. "I couldn't. I didn't have it then. I couldn't afford to. Besides, she was always very self-reliant."

He was a worse scoundrel than I had imagined. "Damn you, Elia," I said. "She took you in, if not for her you'd be murdered with your whole family back there — "

"Well, I never had as much as you used to think. That police station job wasn't much."

"Police station!" I yelled.

He gave me an eye full of hurt. "You don't follow, Edmund. My aunt died before all this fuss. She died three years ago."

"Three years ago?"

"Three and a half maybe."

I tried to adjust. "You just got the news, you mean? You just heard?"

"Oh, no. I found out about it right after it happened."

Confusion roiled in me. "You never mentioned it."

"There wasn't any point. It's not as though you *knew* her. Nobody knew her. I hardly knew her myself. She wasn't anybody. She was just this old woman."

"Ah," I said meanly, "so the grief is only just catching up with you, is that it? You've been too busy to find the time to mourn?"

"I never liked her," he admitted. "She was an old nuisance. She talked and talked at me. Then when I got away from her and came here she wrote me and wrote me. After a while I just stopped opening her letters. I figured she must have written me about two hundred leters. I saved them. I save everything, even junk. When you start out poor, you always save everything. You never know whan you might need it. I never waste anything." He said portentiously, "Waste Not, Want Not."

"If you never answered her how is it she kept on writing?"

"She didn't have anybody else to write to. I guess she had to write and she didn't have anybody. All I've got left are the ones in here. This is the last bunch of letters of hers I've got." He showed me his big scratched cigar box.

"But you say you saved them – "

"Sure, but I used them up. Listen," he said. "I've got to go now, Edmund, I've got to meet Margaret. It's going to be one hell of a fight, I tell you."

"What?" I said.

"I'm not going anywhere else, I don't care how much she squawks. I've had my last trip. I've got to stay home from now on and do poems. I'm going to get a room somewhere, maybe my old room across town, *you* remember – where you came to see me that time?"

"Where I knocked you down. You can stay here," I said.

"Nah," he said. "Nowhere your sister can get at me. I've got to work."

"But you've *been* working," I said. "You've been turning out new poems all along! That's been the amazing thing."

He hefted all his flesh and stood up, clutching the cigar box to his dinosaurish ribs.

"I haven't," he said.

"You've done those five collections – "

"All I've done are those two babies. Edmund and Gate. and they're not even my real names. That's all I've done. The reviews did the rest. Margaret did the rest."

He was suddenly weeping.

"I can't tell it to Margaret – "

"Tell what?"

"There's only one bundle left. No more. After this no more. It's finished."

"Elia, what in God's name *is* this?"

"I'm afraid to tell. I don't know what else to do. I've *tried* to write new stuff. I've tried. It's terrible. It's not the same. It's not the same, Edmund. I can't do it. I've told Margaret that. I've told her I can't write any more. She says it's a block, it happens to all writers. She says don't worry, it'll come back. It always come back to genius."

He was sobbing wildly; I could scarcely seize his words. He had thrown himself back into my father's chair, and the tears were making brooks of its old leather cracks.

"I'm afraid to tell," he said.

"Elia, for God's sake. Straighten up like a man. Afraid of what?"

"Well, I told you once. I told you because I knew you wouldn't believe me, but I *did* tell you, you can't deny it. You could've stopped me. It's your fault too." He kept his face hidden.

He had made me impatient. "What's my fault?"

"I'm a plagiarist."

"If you mean Margaret again – "

He answered with a whimper: "No, no, don't be a fool, I'm through with Margaret."

"Aren't those collections yours? They're not yours?"

"They're mine," he said. "They came in the mail, so if you mean are they mine *that* way – "

I caught his agitation. "Elia, you're out of your mind – "

"She wrote every last one," he said. "In Liverpool. Every last line of every last one. Tante Rivka. There's only enough left for one more book. Margaret's going to call it *Virility VI*," he bawled.

"Your aunt?" I said. "She wrote them all?:

He moaned.

"Even the one – not the one about the – "

"All," he broke in; his voice was nearly gone.

He stayed with me for three weeks. To fend her off I telephoned Margaret and said that Edmund had come down with the mumps. "But I've just had a cable from Southern Rhodesia!" she wailed. "They need him like mad down there!"

"You'd better keep away, Margaret," I warned. "You don't want to carry the fever back to the nursery. All those babies in there – "

"Why should he get an infant's disease?" she wondered; I heard her fidget.

"It's just the sort of disease that corresponds to his mentality."

"Now stop that. You know that's a terrible sickness for a grown man to get. You know what it does. It's awful."

I had no idea what she could be thinking of; I had chosen this fabrication for its innocence. "Why?" I said. "Children recover beautifully – "

"Don't be an imbecile, Edmund," she rebuked me in my father's familiar tone – my father had often called me a scientific idiot. "He might come out of it as sterile as a stone. Stop it, Edmund, it's nothing to laugh at, you're a brute."

"Then you'll have to call his next book *Sterility*, I said.

He hid out with me, as I have already noted, for nearly a month, and much of the time he cried.

"It's all up with me."

I said coldly, "You knew it was coming."

"I've dreaded it and dreaded it. After this last batch I'm finished. I don't know what to do. I don't know what's going to happen."

"You ought to confess," I advised finally.

"To Margaret?"

"To everyone. To the world."

He gave me a teary smirk. "Sure. The Collected Works of Edmund Gate, by Tante Rivka."

"Vice versa's the case," I said, struck again by a shadow of my first shock. "And since it's true, you ought to make it up to her."

"You can't make anything up to the dead." He was wiping the river that fell from his nose. "My reputation. My poor about-to-be-mutilated reputation. No, I'll just go ahead and get myself a little place to live in and produce new things. What comes now will be *really* mine. Integrity," he whined. "I'll save myself that way."

"You'll ruin yourself. You'll be the man of the century who fizzled before he made it to thirty. There's nothing more foolish-looking than a poet who loses his gift. Pitiful. They'll laugh at you. Look how people laugh at the Later Wordsworth. The Later Gate will be a fiasco at twenty-six. You'd better confess, Elia."

Moodily he considered it. "What would it get me?"

"Wonder and awe. Admiration. You'll be a great sacrificial figure. You can say your aunt was reticent but a tyrant, she made you stand in her place. Gate the Lamb. You can say anything."

This seemed to attract him. "It *was* a sacrifice," he said. "Believe me it was hell going through all of that. I kept getting diarrhea from the water in all those different places. I never could stand the screaming anywhere. Half the time my life was in danger. In Hong Kong when they stole my shorts I practically got pneumonia." He popped his cigarette out of his mouth and began to cough. "You really think I ought to do that, Edmund? Margaret wouldn't like it. She's always hated sterile men. It'll be an admission of my own poetic sterility, that's how she'll look at it."

"I thought you were through with her anyhow."

Courage suddenly puffed him out. "You bet I am. I don't think much of people who exploit other people. She built that business up right out of my flesh and blood. Right out of my marrow."

He sat at his typewriter in the attic, at which I had ham-
mered out my futile proposal to Regina, and wrote a letter to
his publisher. It was a complete confession. I went with him
to the drugstore to get it notarized. I felt the ease of the
perfect confidence, the perfect counsel, the perfect avenger.
He had spilled me the cup of humiliation, he had lost me Regina;
I would lose him the world.

Meanwhile I assured him he would regain it. "You'll go down,"
I said, "as the impressario of the nearly-lost. You'll go down
as the man who bestowed a hidden genius. You'll go down as the
savior who restored to perpetual light what might have wandered
a mute inglorious ghost in the eternal dark."

On my paper they had fired better men than I for that sort of
prose.

"I'd rather have been the real thing myself," he said. The
remark seemed to leap from his heart; it almost touched me.

"Caesar is born, not made," I said. "But who notices Caesar's
nephew? Unless he performs a vast deep act. To be Edmund Gate
was nothing. But to shed the power of Edmund Gate before the
whole watching world, to become little in oneself in order to
give away one's potency to another – *that* is an act of profound
reverberation."

He said wistfully, "I guess you've got a point there," and
emerged to tell Margaret.

She was wrathful. She was furious. She was vicious. "A
lady wrote 'em?" she cried. "An old Jewish immigrant lady who
never even made it to America?"

"My Tante Rivka," he said bravely.

"Now Margaret," I said. "Don't be obtuse. The next book
will be every bit as good as the ones that preceded it. The
quality is exactly the same. He picked those poems at random
out of a box and one's as good as another. They're all good.
They're brilliant, you know that. The book won't be different
so its reception won't be different. The profits will be the
same."

She screwed up a doubtful scowl. "It'll be the last one.
He says *he* can't write. There won't be any more after this."

"The canon closes," I agreed, "when the poet dies."

"This poet's dead all right," she said, and threw him a
spiteful laugh. Edmund Gate rubbed his glasses, sucked his
cigarette, rented a room, and disappeared.

Margaret grappled in vain with the publisher. "Why not
Virility again? It was good enough for the other five. It's a
selling title."

227

"This one's by a woman," he said. "Call it *Muliebrity,* no one'll understand you." The publisher was a wit who was proud of his Latin, but he had an abstract and wholesome belief in the stupidity of his readers.

The book appeared under the name *Flowers from Liverpool.* It had a pretty cover, the color of a daisy's petal, with a picture of Tante Rivka on it. The picture was a daguerrotype that Edmund had kept flat at the bottom of the cigar box. It showed his aunt as a young woman in Russia, not very handsome, with large lips, a circular nose, and minuscule light eyes – the handle of what looked strangely like a pistol stuck out of her undistinguished bosom.

The collection itself was sublime. By some accident of the unplanned gesture the last poems left in Edmund Gate's cracked cigar box had turned out to be the crest of the poet's vitality. They were as clear and hard as all the others, but somehow rougher and thicker, perhaps more intellectual. I read and marveled myself into shame – if I had believed I would dash his career by inducing him to drop his connection with it, I had been worse than misled. I had been criminal. Nothing could damage the career of these poems. They would soar and soar beyond petty revenges. If Shakespeare was really Bacon, what difference? If Edmund Gate was really Tante Rivka of Liverpool, what difference? Since nothing can betray a good poem, it is pointless to betray a bad poet.

With a prepublication copy in my hand I knocked at his door. He opened it in his underwear: a stink came out of him. One lens was gone from his glasses.

"Well, here it is," I said. "The last one."

He hiccuped with a mournful drunken spasm.

"The last shall be first," I said with a grin of disgust; the smell of his room made me want to run.

"The first shall be last," he contradicted, flagging me down with an old newspaper. "You want to come in here, Edmund? Come in, sure."

But there was no chair. I sat on the bed. The floor was splintered and his toenails scraped on it. They were long filthy crescents. I put the book down. "I brought this for you to have first thing."

He looked at the cover. "What a mug on her."

"What a mind," I said. "You were lucky to have known her."

"An old nuisance. If not for her I'd still be what I was. If she didn't run out on me."

"Elia," I began; I had come to tell him a horror. "The publisher did a little biographical investigation. They found where your aunt was living when she died. It seems," I said, "she was just what you've always described. Self-sufficient."

"Always blah blah at me. Old nuisance. I ran out on her, couldn't stand it."

"She got too feeble to work and never let on to a soul. They found her body, all washed clean for burial, in her bed. She'd put on clean linens herself and she'd washed herself. Then she climbed into the bed and starved to death. She just waited it out that way. There wasn't a crumb in the place."

"She never asked me for anything," he said.

"How about the one called 'Hunger'? The one everybody thought was a battle poem?"

"It was only a poem. Besides, she was already dead when I got to it."

"If you'd sent her something," I said, "you might have kept Edmund Gate going a few years more. A hardy old bird like that could live to be a hundred. All she needed was bread."

"Who cares? The stuff would've petered out sooner or later anyhow, wouldn't it? The death of Edmund Gate was unavoidable. I wish you'd go away, Edmund. I'm not used to feeling this drunk. I'm trying to get proficient at it. It's killing my stomach. My bladder's giving out. Go away."

"All right."

"Take that damn book with you."

"It's yours."

"Take it away. It's your fault they've turned me into a woman. I'm a man," he said; he gripped himself between the legs; he was really very drunk.

All the same I left it there, tangled in his dirty quilt.

Margaret was in Mexico with a young client of hers, a baritone. She was arranging bookings for him in hotels. She sent back a photograph of him in a swimming pool. I sat in the clamorous nursery with the stockbroker and together we rattled through the journals, looking for reviews.

"Here's one. 'Thin feminine art,' it says."

"Here's another. 'A lovely girlish voice reflecting a fragile girlish soul: a lace valentine.'"

"'Limited, as all domestic verse must be. A spinster's one-dimensional vision.'"

"'Choked with female inwardness. Flat. The typical unimaginativeness of her sex.'"

229

"'Distaff talent, secondary by nature. Lacks masculine energy.'"

"'The fine womanly intuition of a competent poetess.'"

The two youngest children began to yowl. "Now, now Gatey boy," said the stockbroker, "now, now, Edmund. Why can't you be good? Your brothers and sisters are good, *they* don't cry." He turned to me with a shy beam. "Do you know we're having another?

"No," I said. "I didn't know that. Congratulations."

"She's the New Woman," the stockbroker said. "Runs a business all by herself, just like a man."

"Has babies just like a woman."

He laughed proudly. "Well, she doesn't do that one by herself, I'll tell you that."

"Read some more."

"Not much use to it. They all say the same thing, don't they? By the way, Edmund, Did you happen to notice they've already got a new man in *The Centennial*? Poor Fielding, but the funeral was worthy of him. Your father would have wept if he'd been there."

"Read the one in *The Centennial*," I said.

""There is something in the feminine mind which resists largeness and depth. Perhaps it is that a woman does not get the chance to sleep under bridges. Even if she got the chance, she would start polishing the poles. Experience is the stuff of art, but experience is not something God made woman for . . .' It's just the same as the others," he said.

"So is the book."

"The title's different," he said wisely. "This one's by a woman, they all point that out. All the rest of 'em were called *Virility*. What happened to that fellow, by the way? He doesn't come around."

The babies howled down the ghost of my reply.

I explained at the outset that only last week I visited the grave of Edmund Gate, but I neglected to describe a curious incident that occurred on that spot.

I also explained the kind of cameraderie elderly people in our modern society feel for one another. We know we are declining together, but we also recognize that our memories are a kind of national treasury, being living repositories for such long-extinct customs as burial and intra—uterine embryo—development.

At Edmund Gate's grave stood an extraordinary person – a frazzled old woman, I thought at first. Then I saw it was a very aged man. His teeth had not been trans–rooted and his vision seemed faint. I was amazed that he did not salute me – like myself, he certainly appeared to be a centagenerian – but I attributed this to the incompetence of his eyes, which wore their lids like bunched capes.

"Not many folks around here nowadays," I said. "People keep away from the old Preserved Cemeteries. My view is these young-sters are morbid. Afraid of the waste. They have to use every-thing. We weren't morbid in our time, hah?"

He did not answer. I suspected it was deliberate.

"Take this one," I said, in my most cordial manner, inviting his friendship. "This thing right here." I gave the little stone a good knock, taking the risk of arrest by the Outdoor Museum Force. Apparently no one saw. I knocked it again with the side of my knuckle. "I actually knew this fellow. He was famous in his day. A big celebrity. That young Chinese fellow, the one who just came back from flying around the edge of the Milky Way, well, the fuss they made over *him*, that's how it was with this fellow. This one was literary, though."

He did not answer; he spat on the part of the stone I had touched, as if to wash it.

"You knew him too?" I said.

He gave me his back – it was shaking horribly – and minced away. He looked shriveled but of a good size still; he was uncommonly ragged. His clothing dragged behind him as though the covering over the legs hobbled him; yet here was a hint of threadbare flare at his ankle. It almost gave me the sense that he was wearing an ancient woman's garment, of the kind in fashion seventy years ago. He had on queer old–fashioned woman's shoes with long thin heels like poles. I took off after him – I am not slow, considering my years – and slid my gaze all over his face. It was a kettle of decay. He was carrying a red stick – it seemed to be a denuded lady's umbrella (an apparatus no longer known among us) – and he held it up to strike.

"Listen here," I said hotly, "what's the matter with you? Can't you pass a companionable word? I'll just yell for the Museum Force, you and that stick, if you don't watch it – "

"I watch it," he said. His voice burst up and broke like boiling water – it sounded vaguely foreign. "I watch it all the time. That's my monument, and believe you me I watch it. I won't have anyone else watch it either. See what it says there? 'I am a man.' You keep away from it."

"I'll watch what I please. You're no more qualified than I am." I said.

"To be a man? I'll show you," he retorted, full of malice, his stick still high. "Name's Gate, same as that on that stone. That's my stone. They don't make 'em any more. *You'll* do without."

Now this was a sight: madness has not appeared in our society for over two generations. All forms of such illness have vanished these days, and if any pops up through some genetic mishap it is soon eliminated by Electromed Procedure. I had not met a madman since I was sixty years old.

"Who do you say you are?" I asked him.

"Gate, born Gatoff. Edmund, born Elia."

This startled me: it was a refinement of information not on the monument.

"Edmund Gate's dead," I said. "You must be a literary historian to know a point like that. I knew him personally myself. Nobody's heard of him now, but he was a celebrated man in my day. A poet."

"Don't tell *me*," the madman said.

"He jumped off a bridge dead drunk."

"That's what you think. That so, where's the body? I ask you."

"Under that stone. Pile of bones by now."

"I thought it was in the river. Did anybody ever pull it out of the river, hah? You've got a rotten memory, and you look roughly my age, boy. My memory is perfect: I can remember perfectly and I can forget perfectly. That's my stone, boy. I survived to see it. That stone's all there's left of Edmund Gate." He peered at me as though it pained him. "He's dead, y'know."

"Then you can't be him," I told the madman; genuine madmen always contradict themselves.

"Oh yes I can! I'm no dead poet, believe you me. I'm what survived him. He was succeeded by a woman, y'know. Crazy old woman. Don't tell *me*."

He raised his bright stick and cracked it down on my shoulder. Then he slipped off, trembling and wobbling in his funny shoes, among the other monuments of the Preserved Cemetery.

He had never once recognized me. If it had really been Elia, he would certainly have known my face. That is why I am sure I have actually met a genuine madman for the first time in over forty years. The Museum Force at my request has made an indefatigable search of the Cemetery area, but up to this writing not so much as his pointed heel-print has been discovered. They do not doubt my word, however, despite my heavy age; senility has been eliminated from our modern society.

232

ROBERTA KALECHOFSKY

MEDITATION ON AN ANIMAL

"In the circumstances, death may come, but it is superfluous."

The Savage God, Alvarez

"self—mutilation has run riot."

"I have many times witnessed some of the most fantastic
incidences of self—mutilation. I have seen convicts swallow huge
numbers of nails and quantities of barbed wire; I have seen them
swallow mercury thermometers, pewter tureens (after first breaking them up into edible portions), chess pieces, dominoes,
needles, ground glass, spoons, knives and many other similar
objects; I have seen convicts sew up their mouths and eyes with
thread or wire; sew ropes of buttons to their bodies; or nail
their testicles to a bed, swallow a nail bent like a hook, and
then attach this hook to the door by way of a thread so that the
door cannot be opened without pulling the 'fish' inside out. I
have seen convicts cut open the skin on their arms and legs and
peel it off as if it were a stocking; or cut out lumps of flesh
(from their stomach or their legs), roast them and eat them; or
let the blood drip from a slit vein into a tureen, crumble bread
crumbs into it, and then gulp it down like a bowl of soup; or
cover themselves with paper and set fire to themselves or cut
off their fingers, or their nose, or ears, or penis. . . .
Having tried all other forms of protest against the lawlessness
and caprice of the prison and all other authorities, they have
finally resorted to self—mutilation."

Edward Kuznetsov, *Prison Diaries*

The subject is unpleasant. Suicide can be romantic, but not
self—mutilation, except for those occasions of the few who set

fire to themselves to attract attention, to be reckoned with, to change the world.

For the others there is no such dissimulation. The goal of self dismemberment has no other purpose, and the methods are wretched, but what would we poor prisoners do if we could not destroy ourselves, and we were left utterly in the hands of the enemy. It is this self awareness that makes self destruction possible. It is because of awareness of the all that self destruction is necessary.

> At Columbia University as many as a thousand blows on each leg of dogs were administered by a rawhide mallet to induce shock. Nervous depression, gasping, thirst and vomiting——— not to mention the agonizing pain of crushed muscles, nerves and bones———were some of the effects of the beatings. The researcher who performed this experiment stated that three dogs who survived shock resulting from the beating suddenly expired the following day when they were again placed on the animal board.
>
> John Vyvyan, *The Dark Face of Science*

How is this possible without memory, without foreknowledge and without judgment on the all. Is it not like the slave who swallows his tongue because he knows the present and sees the future? All flesh is equal in pain.

So, my sister, I contemplate an identity with you, trapped as we both are in this messy secret. Formerly we knew God, but now we know the adversary. Formerly we were distracted by Job's refutation, whose wounds were imposed upon him, but now we have absorbed the adversary's position and do his work for him. For this reason, I love your soul and prefer your cage to chambers of learning and heady reflections on civilization. I prefer your cage to a museum, to a clergyman's office, to the Pope's study. Everything that is holy in this century is in this cage, and it is holy without God. He has kept His promise not to destroy the world again, but we could not imagine, as in the myth about human desire where we get everything we wish for, that that would be our undoing. We could not imagine that. So consumed we were in our circumstances of belief and unbelief, our denials, our refutations, our proofs, our progress, we could not imagine that the thread of sufferance by which we held our lives would snap, and leave us in this cage.

Thus, Stanley Kaliban, technican at Ana-Human Laboratories, found his chimpanzee, B-306A, one morning with her front paw gnawed to the bone and blood scattered on the floor of the cage where she had paced through the night. Not back and forth in her usual way, but in a new patternless fashion.

There was nothing in her cage that could cut a thread, there was not even a bowl of water because it had been policy for some time to leave nothing with B-306A, dubbed Wanda the Witch, and when Stanley arrived this morning Wanda was sitting in a back corner of her cage, still as a stone. The cessation of her pacing was the first thing he noticed that alerted him that something was different today, perhaps hopefully better, for his days began and rotated around the disagreeable orientation of her pacing. The methodical monotony of her paws erected a rhythmic prison around his days and set the pace of his pulse and nerves. Pat, pat, pat, pat. Every morning, as soon as the elevator door opened on the basement level where his laboratory was, and he stepped out, the padded fall of her paws seeped into his nerves and dispirited him. She had not ceased pacing for six months, not even to eat or sleep, except if they sedated her or when she was taken upstairs. The monotonous sound had been with him eight and ten hours a day for six months, as punctual as a drop of water falling on a stone, undercoating all the other noises in the laboratory until it came to dominate them: the telephones and typewriters, the computer printers, the elevator buzzers and monitoring bleeps. It had worn through his brain making him feel more grim than usual, as if he were clinging to the edges of a machine travelling on a rail that had nothing to do with him. It was not his job to question where the machine was going. It was his job to take care of the animals. Pat, pat, pat, pat. Her pacing penetrated everything. Her eyes gleamed at him constantly, except when her gaze was directed towards the ringing of the telephone or the buzz of the intercom or the elevator, because she knew what these sounds meant, and when it suited her she fabricated or arranged her responses accordingly. Otherwise she looked at him with an intent he tried to ignore. He trained himself not to look back at her except when he had to, but he could not prevent himself from hearing her incessant step.

In some countries, he knew, prisoners were tortured with the mechanical repetition of a sound, until it produced hypnosis, amnesia, and finally meaninglessness. The world decomposed into a flailing of nerves. It was forgotten, everything about the self was forgotten, why it was there, what the cause of its captivity was, whether it had existed at all. The self became absorbed into the sound. Like a sponge the sonorous tedium sucked everything out from the world, so that when he left his laboratory down in the basement at the end of the day, with its isolated sounds of monitoring boards and bleepers recording messages, the padded step of her paws, the scurrying noises of the mice and the whining of the other animals, and he went upstairs into the world of crashing noises, honking cars and buses, he felt like a miner coming up to the surface of the earth, with its own rules of life and death which he must not forget.

Something was wrong this morning, or perhaps it was finally right, because he had never found a way to stop her from pacing unless they sedated her. The cessation was neither pleasant nor unpleasant, but it aroused suspicion as if a predictable mechanism had failed, a natural phenomenon such as wind. Who could say whether this would be good or bad? The generation that comes after the wind stops will not miss it.

She was still this morning, though there had been no orders to sedate her. He surmised that she was awake. She always was unless they sedated her, and there was a limit to how often they could do that, which Wanda knew. She had learned the rhythms of their coming and going, their clocks, their buzzers, their voices, their footsteps, and what each sound meant. Formerly, she paid attention to the sounds and calculated her safety by them. She had learned when to pretend to be asleep to avoid being sedated. She had learned how to pretend to be sick to avoid being sent upstairs, how to appear listless and unalert, comatose, but he knew these things about her and only rarely did she surprise him. Sometimes he even let her get away with a pretense and ran a risk on her behalf, a small risk that would not be picked up by the monitor. She did not know it and could not develop a strategy to take advantage of this, nothing to bribe him with. He knew that she viewed him as her jailor. That was unjust. Things could be worse for her. She did not know this, but he did. She was his special animal because he had taken care of her from the beginning and had become expert in handling her. No one else had wanted the job. She was perceived as troublesome from the moment they got her, more than a year ago. He had not wanted this job either, but he got sucked down into this quicksand of compliments. "Ataboy," Lew had said, "I know you can do it," and he found himself unable to say when he had had enough.

Lew had already arrived, Stanley noted, hanging his coat
next to his in the closet. He glanced at the clock above the
elevator door, a habit when he arrived and pursued periodically
throughout the day. Five, six, eight glances a day, mostly unconscious, not noting the time. The clock itself was large,
round, white, and faceless, stolidly unpretentious, shatteringly
bereft of character, except for a bar of sunlight from the space
above the window shade on the opposite wall which was reflected
on its glass, blotting out the 6, the 8, the 10, depending on
the hour, and making it more useful as a sundial. Otherwise it
had no pretensions of belonging to an era, not even to modernity.

There was already a set of instructions on his desk, pinned
beneath the company's paperweight, Ana-Human Laboratories: Knowledge Is Power and Profits. The note was written in Lew's breezy
style which contrasted with the grain of his tight handwriting,
painfully legible like a buzzer: "Bascher due at ten. Need guillotine and three disposal units, get lead lined baggies, a dozen
brain probes and microprobes, a chill table – get a good sized
one this time! and a large incinerator. Also need a new set of
alarms, and whole bunch of stuff to clean the place with – back
cages leaking all night – half the mice boiled. Big day ahead.
Wanda has found a new trick. Better get a strait jacket."

He crumpled the note and threw it in the waste basket. Except
for the reference to Wanda, he knew all the rest, had it down on
his own notepad. It was the last thing he had written the day
before: "Basher at ten," anticipating an unpleasant morning. Like
Lew, the salesman brought out an unaccountable streak in him. He
only saw him four times a year, but the encounters had come to
punctuate his life like that of a stranger on a bus whose path
we cross rhythmically and whom we unwillingly dislike, and will
never know whether the stranger is innocent or sinister, whether
it is we or the stranger who is at fault. The salesman, an old
type, though his business card credited him with a modern posture:
M.S. Apparatus in Bioscience Applications, mobilized a moral itch
in Stanley. He made him buy things he wasn't sure he wanted, made
him feel he had been taken in. His strategy was to let the salesman have his shpiel and then tell him to send a provisional bill
of sales. It always needed Lew's O.K. anyway. Stanley did not
have the final say in these matters, something about which he
felt both good and bad, a conflict between status and conscience.
Commenting about Bascher to Lew, after his last visit, Stanley
said, "Wonder what it's like to sell electric chairs. How do
you figure the salesman does the pitch?"

Lew said it was a bad analogy, but added, "Reckon he can't get too many testimonials."

Stanley accepted the fact that Lew was witty by what others said about him, but in his own territory he was not conciliatory. Once when his mother had commented about Lew, after she had met him and as she was entitled to say, "That it must be wonderful to work with such an agreeable person," he said, "Shut up."

Something amiss she sensed, and wishing to make the claim that she was not to blame for it, she responded with motherly pique, "You're not the son I raised."

"So what," he said, "I'm not the me I was planning on being. Guess we both have something to get used to."

Her remark about Lew was innocent and resplendent of goodwill and optimism, though most civilizations, as she should know, have a lot of dirty work that needs to be done. His father had been a garbage collector, his uncle cleaned sewers, a great uncle did the housekeeping in a prison, which he described as "not a bad job, feed the inmates, keep the cells clean, empty the slop pails, fill up the water bowls, disinfect the area, keep the noise level down and don't let anything develop that will cause a scandal." On his mother's side, a cousin cleaned the animals' cages in a circus. An ancestor had had the job of collecting the bones from the auto da fes and sweeping away the ashes. Their lineage was an old one, and all the family were close knit. All lived in the same neighborhood, beyond the city limits, where the graveyards and the dumps are kept. They were their own community, living on a bypath like circus people or gypsies, with their own gossip and their own perspective on "the world out there." It was difficult for them to cross over to that world. Too much was demanded of them: They had to disembowel the past and replace it with other states of significance, philosophical ventures that allowed them to walk upon the earth without thinking of what was beneath it.

Stanley only partly succeeded, which accounted for his lack of humor and lapses. It is a difficult fate to undergo a partially successful operation of plastic surgery so that one does not have the face one expected to have and has lost the face one had, to stand in two different places simultaneously, possessing and dispossessing, like owning a grand sand castle. One part of him lived on the frontier of history where trails into the future seemed marked out. This part of him demanded ascetic restraints and extraordinary acrobatics of mind and will. It bred a philosophy of triage, the sense of desperate choices over what and what and who and whom, for the sake of the future. But it was a place of undoubted preference to the what had been and to the what is. The other part of him lived at home, in a small two bedroom house with a den, a lawn and a cat, the only son of parents who alternated between being proud and loving, and viewing him quizzically as if he had turned into something foreign to their species. They looked at him through two sets of eyes, alternately worshipful and suspicious, as parents usually view successful sons who have become what they wanted them to be and what they themselves are not, and then do not recognize them for what they are.

He, in turn, looked at the world through two sets of eyes. One set of eyes saw himself as his parents saw him, saw the building he worked in, the industrial park it was set in, the manicured lawns that surrounded it, the azalea bushes in the spring that made him glad. It read the morning newspapers and the professional journals left in the magazine rack next to the elevator door under the faceless clock, it read his mail from across the world delivered to his desk, and it read the superfluous notes in Lew's incised script.

His other set of eyes was equipped with olfactory bulbs and smelled foul odors in cages and pipes and dumpsites, and the rot beneath the city streets, which was his native air, the smell from the crater-like pit where the city's refuse was thrown. He used to go there with his father to the city dump and explore the garbage heap with him. He always found something he wanted, like a scooter, surprised that someone else had thrown it away. There was a mountain of stuff to explore: old rockers, phonographs, car parts, fish tanks, hiking boots, fishing gear, sleds, skis, broken equipment of all kinds, couches torn apart, old mattresses. The incinerator burned night and day. He could see it from his bedroom window, the tail of flame spouting like a comet from the chimney throughout the night. It burned garbage lasciviously and industriously, its red tongue licking the black sky until a spent trail of smoke was left in the dawn. But when he came down the next day the mountain was as high as the day before: medicine cabinets, pipes, porcelain sinks, toilet bowls, pictures, discarded animals, cats partly ground up, flung among the used up tires and bicycle tubes, all manner of dislocated household equipment, vacuum cleaners, dishwashers without motors, twisted garbage disposal units, empty television sets, gas ranges with their wires exposed, refrigerators without motors.

In the summer, when he went to the beach with his uncle his uncle would show him the place where the sewerage emptied into the ocean, a small round hole in a pipe in the breakwall, so small no one would know it was there, except someone who worked for the sewer department. It looked like a secret part of the body he was not to name. In fact, it had no existence. Except for his uncle, everyone else walked past it, but his uncle was proud of the little hole and told him that if it wasn't for people like himself, civilization would come to a halt in a week. He laughed curiously, as if he had a conspiracy in mind, and each time they came down to the beach he plugged the hole up with small rocks with the air of a whimsical anarchist. But whenever Stanley came down to the beach again the rocks had been pushed out and the sludge was flowing freely from the hole.

He poured himself a cup of coffee. It was fresh, one of the benefits of Lew's early arrival. Stanley almost never had breakfast in the morning before he left for work, and he cherished this cup of coffee which he sipped meditatively every morning as he glanced through the day's memos, instructing his mind about the day's work. "What've you been up to?" he called to Wanda from his desk across the room. He did not expect a response, because Wanda could not give one. He spoke randomly as he went through his notes, not as he would have spoken had she not been there because that would have been madness, but neither as if she was there. The question was directed indeterminedly to magical forces that make things go right or wrong, make the morning coffee good or bad, bring friendly or unfriendly messengers to the door. He spoke with jauntiness to help start the day right with the right combination of mood and fact, because fetching her from her cage each morning was a bad way to start anybody's day. He had a history of her trickiness to consider and could not rule out a sly move on her part to avoid going upstairs to the rack. Once she had played dead and when he had thoughtlessly put his unprotected hand inside the cage to reach for her, she bit him.

She used to throw her water at him, her regurgitated food, her feces, or anything else that was in the cage. So they left her with nothing at night, no water, no food, not a bar to swing from, nothing she could take apart, swallow or do anything with. That's when she started to screech. She screeched right around the clock, right through the day and the night and through the week end. She screeched at everything. Evert time a light went on or off. Every time the elevator came down or went up. Every

240

time he came near her, even when he brought her her food, which she would not eat. They sedated her and fed her intravenously and when she awoke, she shrieked again, without stop, except when they came to take her upstairs for her shocks, and then her shrieks became harsher. He could hear her all the way up the elevator shaft, and again when she came down later in the day. Her screeching was contagious. The other animals caught it like a disease. When she returned, pandemonium broke out, chittering mice and squealing guinea pigs, cats fretting, snarling, whimpering, wizened baboons shook the bars of their cages, sick dogs struggled against unconsciousness. They were forced to cut her vocal cords, but she found other ways to make trouble. She banged her head against the bars until she provoked the animals again, and again they whined and scratched, they snarled and shrieked until the room sounded like a dislocated jungle. They were forced, finally, to remove her from the room altogether. They put her in a mobile cage and moved her into his office where she could not disturb anyone, except him. Back and forth, back and forth, all day and all night, pat, pat, pat, pat so that he hated the sound of his own cat at home. His office smelled from her cage. It was wheeled away each weekend for a cleaning, but the cleaning was not always efficient and by week's end his office smelled of excrement, bloody fur and bandaged wounds.

"Lew!" he called out, standing in front of the cage and surveying the scene.

"Yeah?" The response was bedraggled with the feeling of an unpleasant task ahead of them, like that of a beleaguered housewife whose washing machine has overflowed.

"What the hell's going on around here?" Stanley said. His voice registered defensiveness against forces that might implicate his integrity: barbarism of the night shift, the irresponsibility of cheap help, though he felt a variety of other things, chiefly puzzle as he tried to assemble what he saw into the trials of the day and the questions they would not be able to answer.

There was a pause, long enough for Stanley to hope that Lew would have an explanation, but Lew responded in a voice a shade declaratory as if his conscience was off limits: "How the hell should I know! Just clean it up," he added in a conciliatory tone, as befits the partner in an enterprise who shirks the dirty part of the business but wants to avoid a grudge. He kept the door open a crack with his toe, feeling justified in not allowing the mishap to interfere with his morning ritual.

"For God's sake, keep your crap to yourself," Stanley said, but the familiarity of the remark, usually said semi–jocularly, softened the insult. It was a remark he made often, and not necessarily meant to wound. Even if he had meant to wound, Lew would not have been wounded. He had an attitude that repelled insult. Where others found Lew agreeable, Stanley found him dense, and unless he were willing to resort to violent assault – something he felt that was alien to his character – his words blew away like feathers. The speech that flowed between them was often this way, never meant as seriously as it was said, or meant more seriously than it was said, but not accepted seriously. Calling down the corridor to Lew in the lavatory, he made the same speech every morning: "For God's sake, keep your crap to yourself." It was Stanley's way of saying that he had standards of his own, things Lew did that he wouldn't do, a position they both accepted, that Stanley had the right not to do anything he found really objectionable if he could give adequate reasons and justify his position, prove that an atrocity that was required to save the world was repugnant to him; if he could establish it as a fact that moral inflammation threatened him, his objection would be considered. But Stanley wanted to know how to get Lew to cooperate with him since Lew cooperated with everyone else, and was agreeably industrious with others, as a public servant should be.

Taking further stock of the situation in the cage, Stanley felt beleaguered, also like Lew, like a housewife whose equipment has broken down: no way to bridge the distance between himself and a dirty task that has to be done, vomit to be mopped up, the dog's mess to be cleaned from the rug. No way to clean the toilet bowl but to stick your hand into it. Wanda was wedged into a corner beyond his reach. Her paw looked infected, the bone was chewed badly, but her body was stone still. She looked obstinate and he braced himself for her. Her eyes did not focus on him, or on anything else. She could be really sick, but she was so clever at pretending. He had no choice but to go in after her, and past experience in doing this was unpleasant – poking her out with a pole – not hard enough to cause damage but hard enough to make her want to avoid his thrusts and come out. If he could reach her by hand, a pinch on her windpipe brought her to her senses. He could protect himself against her scratches and bites, but not against her making him feel unpleasantly deadly.

He poured himself another cup of coffee and thought about
this strategy and whether he should bother until after the salesman's visit. Most likely she would struggle and he'd have to
knock her about a bit, though she might really be sick this morning and compliant. Probably not. Most likely she would struggle.
"Why do you want to make things difficult?" he asked her. His
speech was for no practical purpose. He did not expect an answer.
He wanted her, or the universe, to know that this was not his
fault: it was an assignment from outer space. He called out to
Lew, "I just remembered she's not needed today until later. Lucky
us. I'm going to let her go until after Bascher."

"O.K. with me," Lew called back buoyantly, as if a successful
resolution had been reached.

It was the right decision. The light above the elevator door
indicated that someone had buzzed for it upstairs and that someone was coming down to the basement. Undoubtedly Bascher. He
always came on time, like a servant for his task, never earlier
or later. Where goods come from and how they come to be where
they are no one knows. One day a salesman shows up with snake
oil for skin rashes or a trunkful of stilettoes, and everyone
needs some.

Bascher gave Stanley his business card – gestures set a tone
– he was not a circus barker, but the gesture rubbed Stanley's
moral itch the wrong way. It was not that he didn't appreciate
professionalism, and there was no other formula in his head for
how to go about this business: Bascher was not a stranger in
town, like the door to door peddlar, exhausted and dusty with
ten miles of unpaved road, startling a housewife in her yard.
He came by appointment, well dressed and shaven, invited to have
coffee. Stanley's dislike was insoluble, and like most disaffec-
tions that are not felt to be serious, he explained it in a
usual way: It was something about the way Bascher dressed or
spoke or moved his hands, or always came on time with suave inevitability. But Basher was dressed no differently than he was,
in a business suit, summery weave, open shirt collar, casual,
democratic, accessible, friendly sober but light. He made the
usual polite inquiries of any civilized human, reviving a detail
from his last visit: "I'm glad to see the mobile cage is working
out. It's quite an advance over the stationary kind, gives you
freedom and even provides some stimulation for the animal if you
wheel her to another part of the room." He glanced into Wanda's
cage like a neighbor into the carriage of a newborn baby, praise
on his lips, though he registered the disagreeable sight and
tucked his comment about it into his mental filing cabinet.

Bascher was accustomed to public speaking. He lectured at conferences and demonstrated technical equipment at science fairs, suits and boots and bouffant caps to be worn in radioactive rooms, how to operate shield barriers or use biodegradable bags to dispose of diseases, spinal probes and brain tissue separators, never splicers and electric implants, decapitators and incinerators. In deference to this material, his voice had become unctuous — the occupational hazard of undertakers. Reality sucked at his vocal cords and left him a bell-like tone, reverently concerned, but never enthusiastic, a voice like a set of chimes where one inflection rang subliminally against the other.

The customers came and looked and listened and streamed through the conference corridors in comfortable couples and triplets, glancing at the equipment like healthy people ordering their coffins for an unlikely event. If death comes, it will not be their doing.

As he perceived it, there was small difference between himself and them. Perhaps his lineage was not as old as Stanley's, having come along at a further stage in civilization when trade routes and paths had been opened, but old enough to earn respect. In his heart of hearts, in the gut of his soul where judgments on civilizations are made and swallowed like poison, he would like to know what the difference was between the seller and the buyer. The difference he ascribed to an accidental pathology in the social fabric, but it rearranged matters between them and constrained him into the deferential posture of the seducer. They could afford to leave the mean decisions to him, they let him advise them on how to dispose of unused diseases, how to eliminate bodies and the smell of ammonia buildup, they left the housekeeping details to him or to magic, air ducts and vacuum cleaners that suck out death, animal incinerators that leave only ashes to be swept out. They were raped by methodology: no one chooses his civilization. Consequently, he did not arrive with a trunkful of notions — today's salesman does not carry the guillotine on his back — but with a trim briefcase which he rested on Stanley's desk, and a half dozen catalogues which he spread out with the theatrical gesture of a footman opening the door to a gilded carriage.

"Is that Bascher?" Lew called from the bathroom. "Give him my list."

Stanley unpinned Lew's note from under the Ana-Human Laboratories paperweight and gave it to Bascher who read it with modest

244

signs of his knowledge. The list, as usual, was inadequate. Bas-
scher opened catalogues and discussed improved models over those
Lew had indicated. There always were newer models. There was
nothing that could not be improved upon. Strait jackets were
passé. Tethering swivel harnesses were more practical, and also
more humane, and also came equipped with as many as ten electrical circuits. "A normally active animal can be restrained for
months at a time and monitored both for fluids and electrical
currents." But he did not give Stanley time to consider this at
all, as if it had been a blunder to show him a picture of equipment which became outdated as he spoke. Confessionally, he referred to other improvements and took out another catalogue
which dexterously fell open to the proper page which displayed a
picture, in autumnal colors of gold and brown, of his company's
latest achievement, the Universal Do–All Stereotaxic Device,
"developed for multiple types of research on multiple size
animals for multiple types of experiments to replace the multiple
reduplication of other devices and instruments."

"The Universal Do–All" he said in an autumnal voice the color
of his catalogue, "revolves and turns an animal in any position
or direction, upside down, inside out, for genitalia or head
research, for stimulation or sedation, it can be immersed in a
tank of water with a drowning animal strapped to it and prevent
it from struggling, it can adjust to the size of a rabbit or a
baboon, it automatically feeds the animal and automatically
monitors its metabolism, it automatically disposes of its waste
and automatically eliminates odor, it can prevent the animal
from sleeping, swallowing or breathing, it can interfere with
any bodily function, it can halt any bodily function and restore
it according to a timer, it can exhale fumes, tobacco smoke,
noxious gases, and dyes. Equipped with leg straps and headholder,
penal elevator and vaginal spreader, skull drilling equipment
and bone crusher, it allows for genitalia, brain or spinal pene-
tration, and contains a humane cervical vertebrae decapitator.
If the animal dies naturally, it flushes away the remains. It
can strip Leviathan of skin and bones in thirty seconds and
emulsify his parts.

He spread the literature across Stanley's desk like a croupier
with a deck of cards. Stanley looked at it with polished pretensions. He just wanted things to work. He knew he should be
more interested than that. He should want them to work very
well, but his ambitions remained suspended, like Macbeth's,
wanting success holily. He needed the prophecy of witches.

Bascher sipped the coffee Stanley had offered him, and waited. Stanley's eyes glanced about on the golden polished pages of the catalogues, arrested by a smiling face, a woman who looked domestic in a large bouffant cap, like his mother when she was going for a shower, coyly holding a rat on her open palm.

Parentally, Bascher turned the pages for him, back to the picture of the Universal Do-All. "You won't have to own any other equipment," he said insinuatingly, as if Stanley's daydream's were sinful. "The Universal makes everything else look like a Model-T Ford. It will do for your laboratory what the computer is doing for the office." He glanced in Wanda's direction. "Nasty business," he said feelingly. "But this is not the only laboratory with this kind of problem and I can tell you now there isn't any other solution. The Universal Do-All may seem like a big investment, but it's a pittance compared to what it would cost you to replace expensive animals like her. Think about that."

He did not wait for Stanley to do that. The issue would not be forced to conclusion the first time around. He put his half-finished cup of coffee in the waste paper basket and collected his catalogues together, sweeping them from Stanley's desk. "Think about it," he said again, and zipped the catalogues closed into his briefcase. He rang for the elevator, aristocratically indifferent. "The equipment speaks for itself, like a Rolls Royce." Nothing further to be said after that, except, "Let me just leave you this." The Universal Do-All Catalogue appeared in his hand like rabbit in a magician's hat. He slipped it into the magazine rack. "Dont make your mind up in a hurry," he warned, "you can let me know the next time I come by." The elevator door opened. Stanley braced himself for his departure, the final priestly gesture: Basher said generously, "If you want to discuss the matter a little earlier, give me a ring. You have my number. It's on the inside cover of the catalogue." The door opened and he stepped inside the elevator like a mannequin inside a box. "But I wouldn't wait if I were you," he said urgently. "Things may just be too late." The door closed and the voice was gone, and the elevator button registered the lobby floor a few seconds later. Stanley glanced at the clock on the wall. A shaft of light, sharp as a stiletto, devoured the numbers, but he surmised that it was close to eleven.

Lew called from the john, "Did you give him my list?"

"Why don't you keep your crap to yourself," Stanley said, "and why don't you keep that goddamned door closed?"

"You know I have claustrophobia."

"Are you going to get out of there and help me with Wanda?"

"I also have constipation."

It was hopeless to expect anything from Lew. Lew would out-sit the problem. "It doesn't take two of us to get her out of there," Lew called down the corridor.

"Then why the hell don't you get down here and do it your-self?" Stanley called back.

"For God's sake, you've been handling her from the day she got here! Who do you think is likely to have an easier time of it?"

"Fuck off!" Stanley said ruefully because the argument was convincing. He'd prefer to let Lew do it, but he'd hate to see him do it. There are big bang evils like bombs and war and fall-ing stock markets, and there are evils which go unheard, no-bang evils that one cannot hear, cannot see, cannot know about unless you walk out of the your life pattern and look into sewers and beneath the grassy quadrangles with its students scattered like daisies across the lawns.

Stanley put on a see-through acrylic mask that covered his head, face and throat, a steel mesh cape over his shoulders and elbow-length gloves made of leather encased in steel mesh links, and opened the door to the cage.

Wanda's eyes did not move. Of course, she was used to his coming into her cage like this, and his appearance did not startle her as it might startle us. He waited for an attack, but she made none. He tried to coax her out with words, and a little light probing with the pole, but he knew it would be futile. She was playing dead. There was no light in her eyes, not a speck of life, not a hint, not a clue to her whereabouts. He poked her a little harder, but her eyes did not shift their focus. She had discovered the trapdoor to indifference, and sat stone still like a taxidermist's creation. Her obstinacy enraged him. He poked at her harder, furious with restraint and the necessity to get the job done, but she was indifferent to her fate. The last shudder to be felt had left her body, the last electrical spasm had run its course along her vaginal tract, the last elec-trical shock had died in her braincells.

But her paw betrayed her. It trembled involuntarily, and he saw that the wound had life in it. "You know I'm going to get you," he said grimly, and whacked at the paw as if it were evi-dence of her trickiness. "I know you know what I'm doing. Why don't you just come out and make things easier for both of us." He smelled her damp fur and sour blood, the foul diseases inside

her body. The smells victimized him. They claimed half his brain.
They reminded him of everything about himself, of dark holes
unknown to sun and air, of slime and the swelling furies of his
body. "I'm going to get you," he said with grim conviction.
The certainty goaded him even further. His was one of the oldest
jobs in the world. Maybe not as old as the age of cave dwellers,
but soon after when houses were built above the caves and civilization became a two-story affair or multi-leveled, with living
and working quarters above the basements. Excrement slipped
loose from her body as if an organ had disintegrated and turned
into sludge. But she did not attempt to move away from it. The
dissolution of her body was certain.

Behold, death was good. Death is wise.

BARBARA MUJICA

DON BERNARDO'S SECOND DEATH

Excerpt from the novel, *The Deaths of Don Bernardo*

Tadea was afraid of what would happen when Don Bernardo
found out the gun was missing, but Julio told her not to worry,
by tomorrow morning Don Bernardo would be dead. The *patrón*,
the Indian girl insisted, got mad when things were out of place.
Julio repeated that there was no need to worry. Expressionless,
Tadea handed over an object wrapped in a coarsely woven cloth,
once an interplay of reds, magentas, yellows, greens, and browns,
but was now a hodgepodge of grimy fibers.

"*Gracias, linda*," Julio murmured.

The Indian girl did not respond.

The gun was an Allen pepperbox, a .31-caliber percussion
pistol with revolving barrels. It had lain in Don Bernardo's study
between a Remington Army revolver and a Colt Walker .44. All
three guns had been used in the American Civil War. Don Bernardo
was a Yankophile as well as a gun collector. He had a book in
English called *The War Between the States: A Reevaluation,* and
he had read most of it. Tadea had chosen the Allen out of the
hundreds of weapons in Don Bernardo's collection because, with
its curved design and decorative engraving, it was prettier than
the other models. Don Bernardo had bullets for most of his guns
and Tadea had taken some of those as well.

"Don't worry," Julio said softly. He spoke in Quechua this
time.

The girl shrugged. She would rather have stolen a kilo of rice
or even a bottle of whiskey. Don Bernardo was liberal with food-
stuffs. The servants plundered the larder with an easy mind. Corn,
flour, the ubiquitous red pepers called *ají,* sometimes cigarettes
– these staples regularly disappeared. Don Bernardo looked the
other way. On the other hand, Doña Enriqueta, his eagle-eyed,
tight-fisted wife, had been known to swoop down on a maid off to
visit an aunt, mother, or boyfriend and snatch a five-gram package of chocolate or a dead chicken out from under the girl's
skirt. But Don Bernardo never made a fuss over what he considered petty pilfering. It was to be expected, he said, of Indians.

A gun was different. Guns were among the *patrón*'s treasures. A servant had only to touch an antique pistol to set off a rage worse than a storm in the Sierra. Tadea cringed. She was a light-framed, copper-colored girl of perhaps twelve, with a broad forehead and sculpted cheeks, an aquiline nose and elongated black-brown eyes. She reminded Julio of a twig. In a storm, she would snap.

In the opinion of Tadea and most of the older women servants, the *patrón* suffered from *paca*, a combination of a damaged soul and bad blood producing excessive irritability. The servants' quarters were an enclave of superstition and folk wisdom where maids explained the actions and whims of Don Bernardo and his insensate clan the same way as they might those of an unhinged Indian in their native villages. When the *patrón* struck a bewildered stable hand for brushing the imported palomino insufficiently, María Domitila, cook and curer, would lament: "Poor Don Bernardo. The devil got into him, most probably through the feet. He was out in the rain yesterday." The other women would nod sadly and continue shucking corn.

When the rotund, quick-tempered Doña Enriqueta hurled a brush at Teófila, her chambermaid, for mislaying an ornament, María Domitila concluded, "The *patrona*, she has eaten too much *kalor*. It makes her disposition hot."

"You think that she had a devil living in her soul?" María Azucena, the thirteen-year-old apprentice cook, once asked.

"She has a *viento,* child, a hot hell-wind. I could draw it out for her if she would let me. But for now, it is impossible. She is too hot. No one can touch her."

"Ah!"

"Lettuce, child, lettuce and oca. And most important, plenty of cold water. The best thing for *viento*."

Tadea did not know how Don Bernardo's soul had been damaged – it had been that way since she had come to work for him – but she thought that perhaps on one of his trips, he had been in an *akce,* a dangerous, demon-infested ruin. The hills were full of Inca ruins, and Tadea knew that if a man went into one of them when he was upset, he was especially susceptible to spirits. It seemed likely to Tadea that Don Bernardo, who had a lot on his mind and a lot to be angry about – judging from the fact that he was often angry – could have a mutilated soul. Or maybe he had fallen into or bathed in water that was too cold. This could give a person an *aire*, the cold version of *viento*.

There could be no doubt that Don Bernardo and Doña Enriqueta
and their brood were sickly. And what made it worse, as far as
Tadea was concerned, was that the *patrones* and their family ate
wrong. They consumed too much beef and chicken — meats that
were "hot." It was true that they also ate boiled potatoes,
which were *fresku*, "cool," but with sauces of pepper, garlic,
and salt, which were *kalor.* Tadea did not know the classification
of as many foods as María Domitila, but she knew that all foods
were either "hot" or "cool." Tadea knew that when a person ate
too much of one or the other, he became ill, both in the head
and in the body. It was necessary to eat a balanced combination,
but whites never did. They didn't know about the right kinds of
food, so they stuffed themselves with *kalor*, and it ruined their
blood. No wonder Don Bernardo was sick.

To the Quechua-speaking domestics, he was clearly a man possessed. At the slightest provocation he ranted like a bull.
María Domitila had once prepared a plaster of medicinal herbs in
order to draw the evil out of Don Bernardo. But the *patrón*
would have none of it. María Domitila was offended. She was
an expert curer who took care of nearly all the servants when
they were ill. She knew countless incantations and prayers, and
she would cure anything from skin lesions to dirty stomach, a
state resulting from eating wrong.

When she wasn't in a fury, Doña Enriqueta often came to María
Domitila for help. Menstrual cramps, minor depressions, diarrhea,
or pimples, María Domitila could remedy them all with a proper
diet. Doña Enriqueta pooh-poohed the servant woman's miraculous
successes in the presence of her husband, but on days when her
head throbbed or her back tormented her in protest over the
excessive weight it had to support, Doña Enriqueta curled up
under woolen blankets and called for María Domitila. The Indian
woman would come, often accompanied by her apprentice, María
Azucena.

"*Por favor*, Tila, see what you can do."

"Of course, *señora.*"

"It's my right side again. Such pain, Tilita. You cannot
imagine."

"It is the mutton stew you ate last night, *señora.* You know
it does not agree with you. Again, too "hot," *señora.* And the
potatoes with the sauce and the eggs. You insist on eggs, *señora*,
but eggs are not a proper food for people to eat. I will prepare
a brew."

"Thank you, Tilita."

"Of course."

María Domitila would give María Azucena instructions in Quechua and the little maid would run off to prepare a lemon balm.

"And while you're at it, say a prayer for me, Tilita. You know . . ."

"The same one?"

"Yes, so that I don't . . ."

"But *señora*, children are a gift from God."

"Seventeen pregnancies, Tila. It is too much to go through again."

"But only twelve children, *señora*. It is not excessive."

"Please, Tilita."

"All right, *señora*. I will pray to Saint Ursula, the patron saint of my village. And I will prepare a brew, another one, a strong one that only I know. If you conceive again, you will not carry it to term."

"Thank you, Tilita."

"My wish is to serve you, *señora*."

If only Don Bernardo were as cooperative as his wife, thought María Domitila. But since he would not consent to be treated, the best thing was to keep him satisfied and calm.

Like all the servants, Tadea feared Don Bernardo's temper. When the *patrón* discovered that the gun was missing, the demons would take over.

Julio understood her thinking.

"He won't find out." Again he spoke Quechua with a soothing, velvety voice. But, he thought, it might have been easier to deal with Azucena. The apprentice cook was far more quick-witted. Then again, Azucena would not have consented to steal the gun. She had other plans for Don Bernardo.

"The *patrón* knows everything," Tadea responded.

"No," said Julio. "There are many things the *patrón* does not know."

Tadea looked down.

"Anyway, if he does find out, he won't blame you."

"I am the one who cleans the study. He will blame me. He will say I took it, or that I was stupid and left the door unlocked, so that somebody else got in and took it. He trusts me with the key. I am the only one. I am one of his favorites."

"I know," said Julio, glancing at the girl's belly. It did not appear to be swollen, but her time would come, he thought. And then Don Bernardo would send her back to her village to have the bastard and raise it on her own.

She was simple, thought Julio. Like all woman, she attributed evil to demons. She had come to the city with her father a year before. It was unusual for a woman, especially such a young one, to leave her village, but Tadea's father had had a contract with a mestizo hacienda owner to help with the construction of his Lima residence. The worker had brought his daughter with him and, through his employer, had placed her as a servant in Don Bernardo's home.

Like Tadea, Julio was from a village in the Hualcan, but he had lived among whites and mestizos since the war with Chile. A long time. More than thirty years. He was assimilated.

Tadea had disappeared. Julio gripped the weapon concealed under his poncho. He had never shot a man before, not even in the army.

The day, like most days, was grey. The sky was an enormous dirty sheet that backdropped the distant mountains. The parapet that protected Clairvaux, Don Bernardo's majestic summer residence, was made of drab stones that Indian workmen had carried in from distant quarries centuries before. Only a political epithet condemning the current president, José Pardo, and his Civilista party, provided color. The words – "Down with Pardo!" and "Death to the Civilistas!" – had been painted in bright red by an anarchist worker earlier in the year and Don Bernardo had not yet bothered to have them removed. It was a blessing that the anarchists had been giving Don Bernardo so much trouble lately, thought Julio. They, not he, would be blamed for the murder.

Nearly three meters high and a meter thick, the wall extended around several acres of land on which horses grazed. The Alvarez summer house, identifiable as a relic of the early post–colonial period by its sprawling stucco hacienda style and its wrought–iron window grating, was invisible from the road. But Julio knew the layout perfectly. He had spent every summer there for years.

A prune–faced old woman with a whitish pigtail limped by. Her eyes were stony from coca. On her back she carried a bundle wrapped in rags. She grunted at Julio by way of salutation, and the man grunted back. Julio was not afraid of being recognized. When the time came to investigate the murder, no one would think to question the Indian whose job had been to fill Don Bernardo's wine glass during dinner. The *patrón* had too many other enemies.

Julio tucked the Allen pepperbox under his poncho and crouched by the wall. He was glad that the family was at the summer estate instead of Lima. It would be safer, he thought, to murder Don Bernardo in the country.

Dusk shrouded the parapet. Julio got up and crossed the road that led to the entrance gate, then crouched behind a shrub. He was ready.

Attempts had been made on Don Bernardo's life before. In the turbulent climate that dominated Peru in the years preceding the outbreak of World War I, Don Bernardo had been the anarchists' bull's eye. Rumor had it that the fabulous Alvarez holdings in the North were so immense that they bordered on Ecuador and Colombia, and extended into Brazil. Actually, the property in question was two different ranches, and, in Don Bernardo's estimation, not very valuable. Don Bernardo believed the entire Amazon territory to be unexploitable, but he had more productive lands elsewhere. Also in the north, but closer to the coast, he owned an impressive sugar plantation and, in the same area, although not adjacent to the cane fields, he had a cotton operation. Don Bernardo employed thousands of Indian workers. In 1916, when the government supported a law establishing a minimum cash wage of the equivalent of approximately ten cents a day for farm hands, Don Bernardo opposed it. The law was passed anyway, but Don Bernardo ignored it. The Indians, he thought, wouldn't know the difference.

Don Bernardo was right. The vast majority of his workers did not even know that there existed a central government claiming to look out for them. Don Bernardo's labor problems originated not from his rural enterprises, but from his other commercial pursuits.

The Alvarez family owned several textile factories. With the outbreak of World War I, a large domestic market for cotton goods emerged. The industrialized nations were at war, so their economies were tied up with military production. Materials normally exported to South America were no longer available. Besides, traditional shipping lanes were obstructed. Don Bernardo had no patience with the old-style aristocrats who disdained commerce and devoted their lives to squandering their inherited fortunes. He was one of a new breed, a consummate businessman who recognized opportunity when he saw it. He pounced on the textile market like a mountain lion on a baby condor. He ingested it and made it his, squeezing out of it every life-giving ounce of blood.

Which is not to say that Don Bernardo had no headaches. Factory wages were fixed, but the cost of living was spiraling and factory workers were not complacent the way farm workers were. The industrial proletariat was testing its muscle. Men like Don Bernardo were sure quarry for anarchist leaders on the hunt. Once the labor agitators began scrutinizing Alvarez's factory practices, they became aware of the plantation that supplied the raw cotton with thousands of Indian workers bound in virtual serfdom. During the period from 1914 to 1919, Don Bernardo de Alvarez y Oviedo increased his security staff from eight to forty-three.

In spite of threats and bombs, Don Alvarez's businesses thrived. By the day in 1919 when Julio slipped the pepperbox that Tadea had stolen for him under his poncho in anticipation of Don Bernardo's nightly outing, the factory owner had quadrupled his original fortune.

It was good that the anarchists had been so active lately, thought Julio. The authorities would think that this was just another anarchist assassination. There would be an investigation, of course. Don Bernardo was an important man. But it would be easy for Julio to fade into the mountains. He would go back to Luz Divina. If the authorities came looking for him, the family would cover up. He couldn't count on the neighbors. They were a rancorous lot and would be resentful because he had been gone for so long, had done so well, had worked in a grand house and knew Spanish. The government agents would have a hard time tracing him up the steep paths to the lost little village in the Andes. To them, one native community looked like another. One Indian looked like another. He would put on a homespun shirt and simple homespun pants. He would put on a black poncho and he would work the family parcel side by side with his brothers. It was not the future he had hoped for, but there was no alternative. He had to kill Don Bernardo.

Julio reassured himself. He probably wouldn't have to stay in the village for long. The investigators would be looking for an anarchist with a beard and a political cause, not a hoe-bearing Indian.

Julio stretched and yawned. It would be hours before Don Bernardo left for the city to visit his mistress, Flor.

The Alvarez summer estate had sixty-four bedrooms, but the bedrooms that Don Bernardo preferred as a youth were in the servant's quarters. Flor was a hunchback who had been born at

Clairvaux. Her mother was an ordinary maid – not a cook or a laundress or a nanny – and her father was believed to be a former soldier whom the older Don Bernardo employed as a guard. Bernardo Junior and little Flor had been playmates, but when they began to play for real, Bernardo Senior sent the girl – then about eleven – off to the Sierra to have her baby. After his father died, the new head–of–household sent for her and set her up with her little daughter in an apartment on an inconspicuous side street near the Plaza Dos de Mayo.

Flor asked for nothing more. In the village, she had been one more half–breed concubine, abandoned by a light–skinned aristocrat. But in her niche in the capital, she was something else. She was the powerful Don Bernardo's preferred mistress. True, she was allowed neither to go out nor to invite anyone in. But Don Bernardo filled her cupboards and her closet. Periodically he also filled her belly, which kept her content and at home. Don Bernardo was not one for sharing.

Not that he had competition. Hunched and minuscule, Flor resembled a turtle whose dazed green face reaches out from under a deformed shell. She still wore pigtails and sandals most of the time, althought sometimes she tied her hair back into a bun for Don Bernardo's visits. Don Bernardo didn't care how she did her hair. She was the same with it up or down. She was the way he wanted her. Don Bernardo thought that every man should have one mistress like Flor.

Flor had been a part of his life for as long as he could remember. The two of them had romped in the maids' patio while Flor's mother scrubbed the bathroom floors. They had picked walnuts in the garden at Clairvaux. They had confided all kinds of secrets to one another and had giggled over the furor of old Don Bernardo when he caught his eldest son and namesake peeing on the chickens behind the eucalyptuses. With Flor, the master of countless acres could kick off his shoes. He could stop being Don Bernardo and be the Bernardito he had been. He could laugh and remember – remember, for example, that fitful afternoon when an angry hen had mistaken the source of her torment as a worm, and had attacked with such determination that she had damn near plucked it off. It was Flor who had treated the swollen member amid gales of laughter and had wiped Bernardito's tears.

Theirs was a special relationship and Flor was grateful. With her looks and without Don Bernardo's affection, she would have wound up as a scrubwoman or as a whore in Callao, working at the kind of brothel that is frequented by sailors who have been gone

so long that they'll settle for anything. Flor knew she was lucky.
She took care of Don Bernardo's needs and catered to his whims.
She overlooked his moods and his tantrums. When he wanted to
talk, she talked. If he wanted his back rubbed, she rubbed it.
If he wanted his feet kissed, she kissed them, toe by toe, ankle
and heel. She made love any time, day or night, any way he wanted.
She was ugly, thought Don Bernardo, but she was perfect.

Flor spent her days caring for her brood and watching the
comings and goings on the tiny street, barely wide enough for a
man to pass on horseback. All day long Indian women trudged up
and down with bundles of vegetables, cheese, meat or wool slung
over their backs. Flor thanked the dark, squint-eyed saints
whose pictures hung on her walls that she wasn't one of them.

Don Bernardo kept another mistress named Milagritos. She was
a more recent acquisition. He had seen her at the home of his
friend Don Hugo, where she was placing *hors d'oeuvres* on a silver
tray for the waiter to serve in the parlor. Disinclined to mince
words, Don Bernardo told his host that he liked her. Don Hugo,
who liked her himself, was hoping that his guest wouldn't pursue
the matter because if Don Bernardo asked for Milagritos, it would
be impolite to refuse. But Don Bernardo was the kind of man who
went after what he wanted. He suggested that his host trade the
girl for another who worked in the Alvarez nursery. She was a
very clean woman and very competent with newborns, he said. Don
Hugo said he would think about it, although he had no intention
of doing so. Don Bernardo got the message, but pressed on anyway.
Don Hugo wavered. He was having financial problems and Don
Bernardo was in a position to help. Besides, he prided himself
on his respect for social decorum. Very well, he said, he would
send her over in a few days. Don Bernardo smiled and his host
smiled, but by the time the waiter had come around with refills
of *pisco* sour, Don Hugo had forgotten his promise. Don Bernardo
waited three days, and then sent Julio over to his friend's house
to bring back Milagritos.

Don Bernardo set the new girl up in a place on the edge of
town. It was true that her house was larger and more comfortable
than Flor's apartment, but Milagritos was a prettier woman. In
fact, she was as beautiful as Flor was homely. She had delicate
features, thin Caucasian-like lips, a bronze color, a tiny, graceful torso and buttocks like almond halves. Furthermore, she was
unencumbered by children and was versed in refinements that Flor
couldn't even imagine. No wonder, thought Don Bernardo, that
Hugo had been reluctant to give her up.

257

In the winter, when the family was in Lima, Don Bernardo visited either Flor or Milagros nearly every night. Dinner at the Alvarez home was at ten. Afterwards, with the predictability of sunset, Don Bernardo told Doña Enriqueta that he was going to the Club to read the newspapers, Doña Enriqueta, who knew where he was going, said yes, fine. Julio had witnessed the scene countless times. Don Bernardo sat at one end of the huge table and Doña Enriqueta sat at the other. To the right of the head were Don Bernardo's sister Damiana, his half-brother Víctor, Víctor's mother Clara, then Víctor, another half-brother named Eusebio, and an assortment of Alvarez children. Across the table were Riqui and Bernardito – the oldest Alvarez children – Don Bernardo's brother-in-law Enisberto, Eusebio's wife Chabuca, a half-brother named Mario, Mario's wife María Elena, and the rest of the older children. Guests were always expected and inevitably appeared, and these were seated near the family member who had made the invitation. Julio, until the day he left the Alvarezes, stood behind Doña Enriqueta, white-jacketed and with a beige linen towel with the family crest folded over his left arm. His brother Gabriel, identically outfitted, stood behind Don Bernardo. The youngest children were not present. They ate earlier, in the kitchen.

"I'm going to the Club to read the newspapers," Don Bernardo would say.

"All right."

Chabuca and María Elena would exchange knowing glances and Doña Enriqueta would busy herself correcting one of the children's manners or giving instructions to the waiters. Sometimes Chabuca and María Elena and their husbands weren't present – either they were eating at their own homes or had invitations for dinner – and then Doña Enriqueta would give her husband an understanding and, yes, grateful look and bid him good night. Better he should expend his energy elsewhere, she thought. There would be less chance of another baby.

Don Bernardo's extra-marital activities caused him no shame. On the contrary, his exploits were a source of pride. Few maids escaped his lightning-quick fingers. The girls who scrubbed, cleaned, and cooked for the Alvarezes considered succumbing to Don Bernardo part of their regular household duties, and Don Bernardo shared that view. As for his after dinner engagements, he considered a busy social life to be a male prerogative. Not just the teas and dinners and theater parties planned by his sister-in-law, Chabuca. Don Bernardo needed a social life more ample than that. He needed the staples of his diet, Flor and Milagros, and he needed side dishes, too.

In the summer, Don Bernardo visited his favorites less frequently. He kept them in the city – although he was contemplating a summer residence for Milagritos in a nearby village – and it was inconvenient to cover the eighty kilometers between Clairvaux and Lima more than once or twice a month, unless he had to go to town anyway on business. Besides, there were side dishes enough in the country. Tender, young, and succulent, the fruits of the rural areas abounded in the towns and neighboring estates. Julio knew Don Bernardo's schedule, and he knew that tonight belonged to Flor. But even if Don Bernardo were not going back to the city to visit Flor or Milagritos, Julio was certain that he could count on the magnate's taking off after dinner either in his elegant leather-upholstered carriage or in his flashy new motorcar.

It didn't matter much to Julio where Don Bernardo intended to spend the evening. What did matter was whether he planned to take the carriage or the car. The carriage would be easier to assault. The motorcar, a black 1912 Cadillac, with an electric self-starter and beige interiors, was less open and moved faster. In the case that Don Bernardo took the motorcar, it would be necessary to aim from a distance and target him as the vehicle rolled out onto the street. There would be at least one bodyguard, maybe more. Julio would have to move quickly in order to fire, turn, and flee during the initial instants of confusion. Julio knew the kind of guard that Don Bernardo employed: brawny, but not too bright. He knew, too, the value of split-second timing.

Julio crouched. The heavy gate would open soon. It was past dusk now. Perhaps more than an hour past dusk. Julio's eyes were accustomed to the dark. There had been other times in his life when his survival had depended on his night hunting skills.

Julio preferred the carriage scenario: The driver would yank on the reins and swerve. The horses, terrified, would take off at a frantic gallop. The first reaction of the guards would be to grab Don Bernardo and to push him down, out of danger. In the meantime, Julio, still as fleet-footed as a mountain cat, would disappear.

Julio tensed. The minutes crept like snails. A blurred pastel image of Azucena gathering herbs came to mind. Herbs for a potion. Azucena with her braids resting on her back, her feet bare. Then there was a sharper image – an image of Gabriel in blues and blacks and reds.

From the other side of the bulky gate came a sound: the unsteady rrrr of the Cadillac. The first disappointment. There was no scenario for the Cadillac. Julio waited unflinching. He would just have to be that much quicker, he thought. That much more accurate. He had learned long before that it was useless to lament the unchangeable. But it would have been wise to invent a scenario for the Cadillac.

Julio bared his weapon. His hand was steady, his breathing slow and regular. The gate inched open and the lights of the car became visible. Julio felt Gabriel's presence near him, on him. He was, he knew, a split second from vengeance. He cocked the gun.

The car began to turn onto the road. The driver did not stop to check for traffic. There were never any vehicles in the vicinity but Don Bernardo's.

The headlights illuminated the gravel. The outlines of the passengers were more difficult to make out than Julio had anticipated. He leapt forward, as silent as a snowflake on a rugged mountain bluf. Don Bernardo was oblivious to his presence. The magnate's mind was on the evening's escapades.

Don Bernardo opened a gold case and removed a pre-rolled cigarette. Then he lit it. For an instant, the flame flickered near his jaw. Julio watched the lips suck on the paper. Fabulous fortune. This was the moment. The finger on the trigger was firm. Julio raised his arms. He took aim. He fired.

There was a shatter and a groan.

LUISA FUTORANSKY

from *SON CUENTOS CHINOS . . .*

In the beginning a blustery wind, bright sun, and me indoors.
My free time and I'm not going to spend it trudging the dirt lane
left to Jaitien or right toward the People's Cooperative. Various
places intersect my thoughts to take me away from where I am now,
suggested by a snapshot and a postcard I stuck under the glass
top of my writing desk – a flowering branch on one of the cherry
trees at the house where I spent four years in Sakuradai, Tokyo,
and the Lion Gate, in Jerusalem.

I crack my knuckles – my right hand louder than my left, and
every crack a lie: I've got more lies in my right hand than my
left. I agree: the left is closer to the heart.

I can hear the tonjis, the girls, comrades–in–Chinese, screech–
ing in the hall outside my room, or maybe that's just what the
four tones of their language sound like to me and instead of
squabbling they're discussing their favorite topics – the weather,
prices, the quality and scarcity of vegetables.

I cancel my homesickness with a stroke of the pen and won't
speak of the last time I saw the Southern Cross, only in Bali.
What, then? I feel ill because I don't know what isn't worth tell–
ing and what it is I have to go on telling. Excuses, temptations
that I will not give in to: to crawl into bed for a little while
and masturbate . . . go visit my neighbor and ask about her hus–
band's multiple fractures after the accident – the latest scandal
on the part of the South Americans at the Friendship Hostel –
when after endless scheming to get hold of one through diplomatic
channels, the only Latin with his own car out of all of us who
work for the Chinese government in Peking, takes it out for a
maiden spin with his friend, and that same day cracks it up blind
drunk at 3 A.M. trying to pick up girls in Beihai park . . . or
go kill time talking with Ana, presuming that time is willing.
Then I yield to nature's calls: take a pee and wash out my hankies
– I'm horribly stuffed up – holding off my nausea until I've got
all the crusted snot out, and laid the hankies to dry on the
bathroom tiles to iron themselves out. Here too, obviously, I
set myself a text, a guide, a signal.

I can't begin this by saying, "I was born in 1632, in the
city of York," like Robinson, since I was born in Buenos Aires
on the fifth of January, 1939. My parents always said that I
had two little veins at the base of my neck that formed a perfect
V, the V for Victory, they said.

Practically no memory of the war, though if I try hard I can
vaguely recall in the room we used as both dining room and bedroom, very high ceilinged with whitewashed bricks between the
beams, a conversation between papa and my uncles: "I'll bet you
anything the Allies win it." And another, more hushed: "They say
they're building concentration camps in Entre Rios." And a
third in which mama is trying to calm him down and he pounds the
table and turns red in the face, like when he's angry at me:
"When the rest of you were saying London would never hold out, I
was the only one who called it right, as usual" . . . note the
as usual. But much more than any of this I remember my celebrated
resemblance to Shirley Temple; on account of which a woman even
tried to hand me money in the subway: "The child is a beauty,
God keep her; here, sweetheart, take it, buy something you like."
And papa, naturally, stopping me with his eyes: "I'm sorry, ma'am,
but say thank you anyway." And her: "But sir . . ." The episode
left me feeling guilty, ashamed, afraid, because papa was angry
and I didn't know what I'd done wrong . . . Another woman with
papa and me in the Plaza de Santos Lugares, and this time papa,
who never lets me go off alone — how strange! — sent me to play
by myself; later they call me and the woman, who was always
laughing, gives me some big Uruguayan five-cent pieces, very
heavy. "Pichita, say thank you," and I do but not meaning it
since they aren't really for me, since it's papa who's always
getting coins from people. From that day on I lost all taste for
my favorite game, climbing up on the big double bed with papa
and spreading out his coin collection, because of "these" I
mustn't breathe a word of, or the woman either. I remember my
grandmother ordering me to answer anyone who told me I was
pleasingly plump: "Do I eat your bread?" and at the same time to
make the sign of the fig where they couldn't see it to ward off
the evil eye. I remember the chicken coop, the medlars and the
quince over by a spot they wouldn't let me go near that they
called a plugged blind well . . . I remember my grandfather always
coughing and sewing ties, his hand the fairest of all those that
held my hand in the street, his mouth the most truthful, and the

"gypsy" stories he told me . . . I remember the powdery dust that
rose from the lining as he sewed and coughed because I always
tried to be standing right beside him at the machine, and then
one day my grandfather dead and papa leading me into the next
room to look at him and though he looked very strange and yellow,
half white and half green, and I didn't want to, I still had to
kiss him. I remember the pump way at the back of the house, the
freezing cold water in the morning . . . better to die like grandfather and grandfather's canaries and grandfather's dog than
have to wash for school — "in the capital, because though it's a
great sacrifice for my husband to take the girl and pick her up
every day at school, the teaching is much better than in the
provinces."

* * *

derelict shacks, tumble-down huts, clouds of rising dust
(wind, not some foot-stamping folk dance) . . . from home to
work and from work to home (and I don't mean that old knee-jerk
Peronist slogan) . . . almost unintentionally, from train to
train, plane to plane, I wound up here, the end of the road.
the scenography is rudimentary, primitive. trucks dump animals
and vegetables destined for consumption on the ground and there
they remain for hours on end. now that the free market is in
official favor, the peasants sometimes bring plucked pigeons and
chickens in their baskets and sell them on the main street.
nothing is packaged like in Japan. everything is precarious.

* * *

I've lived under bureaucrats all around the world and always
they seem to wear gray on top.

* * *

I know the censor inside of us, the gossip, the egoist, the
coward and the braggard inside us in many, many languages.

* * *

also fleeting love. lightning love, flashing love, idle
love, love like sand the wind blows away.

* * *

263

doing exactly what I never wanted to do. sitting on my butt
in an office every day, day after day, Saturdays included. thread-
ing through Kafkaesque labyrinths, dark, squalid, stinking of
urine. an acrid, spectacular, and clinging smell of urine. you
can find any bathroom in Peking for miles around without asking.
piles of busted-up furniture, mountains of filthy papers stacked
in the halls and coated with thick layers of dust. nothing's
thrown out, just in case, and nothing is dusted, out of habit;
the used color film rolls are recycled with black-and-white Chinese film, disposable lighters are collected and various ingenious
methods are applied to them in hopes of restoring them, banished
leaders are kept – God knows where – with all their belongings,
whatever will fit, in case they get rehabilitated some day and
have to come back with all their junk; everyone, I mean everyone,
drinks hot water or tea out of empty marmalade jars and wraps
their ball-point refills in little strips of paper. in Japan
the emptying of space, here the filling. they fill their dead
hours not making photocopies but rather writing with pen and
ink, not using carbons but typing page for page – giving rise to
an endless chain of errors, corrections and proofreaders – ,
copying and recopying in files or notebooks the most outlandish
definitions in Maria Miliner's dictionary (considered throughout
China as the bible of the Spanish language) or reading or pretending to read a couple of Spanish-language newspapers that
come to the section six months late, at the very least.

* * *

the smells of Peking penetrate even my stuffy nose. skin
exudes garlic. they start eating garlic first thing in the
morning. but time will pass and then when they press close to
hand me my work the blasts of garlic will fade into scenery and
I'll never smell them again.

* * *

what dark obstinacy, what stubbornness landed me here? what
vanity to come out here on my own two legs where others never
make it on canes and crutches? what am I trying to prove, what
answer don't I want to hear and what am I trying to run away from?
for the last couple of years, first in Tokyo and now in Peking,
I haven't understood a word of what's said around me. here,
even when they speak some language you understand, if you're

264

not absolutely alone with someone, they ask you a question, you
answer and then they launch into a big discussion with the other
interlocutors in Chinese while you stand by steaming, pissed off.

* * *

I've got to discover in the habitual gestures and the daily
paraphernalia some common meeting ground. in the hot water
thermos, for example. to accept that for some reason you don't
drink water cold or from the tap. only hot water and from a
thermos; the ubiquitious artefact of hotel room, dining tables
and office desk. children drink cold water − they tell me −
grownups never; it's not good for your health. I'm all confused
by the mystery of these new symbologies. peach = long life; for
us, soft skin, adolescent skins, now long gone . . .

* * *

they've got products here − my neighbors at the hotel are
constantly telling me − to curb the sex drive. paranoia inquires:
are they putting it in our soup, our aspirin, the tea they give
us at the office or our beauty creams, and is that why we walk
around like zombies? aren't I poisoning myself every day on the
news items I read and edit, the foul medicines, my obsessions
over how much they're controlling us and spying on us, and above
all, my queen, these eight hours on my ass in the Spanish department of Radio Peking, China?

* * *

bicycling from the radio station back to the hotel with Franz,
my German colleague, Pol Pot fanatic, just back from visiting
the Kampuchean front. we're pedaling along and I ask him so hey,
what's with the genocide; there wasn't any of that, he answers,
half offended . . . well a zero more or a zero less, you can't
explain three million dead with 300,000 . . . Franz ignores me
to pontificate instead that looking back it could be objected
that the revolution was in too big of a hurry and committed a few
technical errors admittedly like for example proceeding too
quickly with the collectivization of kitchen utensils; aha says
I, and I can see some guy all serious, invulnerable and business-
like like Franz putting the number on my arm to take me off to
the final delousing station this way gentlemen then he tells me

265

that his biggest fear when riding his bike is getting a gob of
spit in the face from the guy in front of him and that once he'd
barely managed to dodge out of the way but with the wind and
everything he'd practically got one in the mouth and complaining
"They never look where they're spitting!" So here I am, combining
pleasure with good advice, exercise with information, politics
with culture.

* * *

How, when to get out of here? And where to?

* * *

The body doesn't want to write (but it writes because I tell
it it has to). It doesn't want to work, doesn't want to tidy
up. It doesn't want to see anyone. It doesn't want to go to
the Latin American cookout, nor to the beauty parlor for a scalp
massage nor to the Frenchman's party. Nor read, nor lay out the
cards, nor throw the I Ching. The body doesn't feel just now
like going to the program of Chinese songs and dances that it
already bought tickets for. Everything the body doesn't want.
The body — what would it like? To be naked on the warm beach at
Kuta at Naxos at Mikonos, especially at Juta with Juan Daniel.
Let it be Kuta, with juandaniel. To eat mushroom omelette eight
hallucinatory hours at a stretch with Daniel. A long kiss with
Daniel's saliva. The body would like to be tanned put on a
stylish summer sun dress walk along the beach at dusk listen to
gamelan music and watch the dances of La Baron while the Bali-
nese or Jananese flutter dizzying hands and eyes and when one
lifts up one's own there it is, looking down on you, smiling
down at you once again as it did when you were born: the Southern
Cross. The body says it's forgotten how it feels to have Juanda
inside. The body is lonelier than ever.

* * *

The Silk Road, a three-hour modern ballet that feels more
like six . . . All striving is in vain, I nod off the minute the
curtain goes up, my wayward eyelids plummeting like lead weights
cast from the upper balcony. The dancers' acrobatics and quad-
ruple tones, the ingenuousness of the clashing colors, the shiny
chiffons, all those scarves and plastic flowers and my inter-

266

preter detailing the plot, emphasizing that the ultimate message
is friendship between peoples of the earth, leave me as zonked-
out at 7:30 in the evening as at any yoga—meditation session
back in Paris. Come to think of it, they're pretty much the
same thing.

I can't figure out how people could choose such godforsaken
cities to live in. A short time in Peking and you're thinking
please, anything for a spot of green. The only plot of grass
they cultivate with absolute tenacity, wall off, rake, fence in,
water perpetually and still it grows all straggly and yellow, is
a strip around the official Residence for Guests of the State.
Everywhere else the ground is so bare you have to keep telling
yourself that someday winter, too, will pass.

* * *

I smoke Chinese cigarettes they call "Double Happiness." Just
as well, because after all this time I doubt if one happiness
would do it for me. Oh baby!

* * *

The usual thing is to take your interpreter along to the
hospital, which is sort of like being back in kindergarten since
one is utterly powerless on account of the language and the
bureaucratic rigamarole to do the slightest thing without somebody else's help. Naturally this means extending their watchful
eye even to our most intimate and embarrassing weaknesses – our
private aches and pains – which will soon be the talk of the
local office and embassy staffs, since our interpreters are
always upstanding Party members whose duty, habit, and pleasure
it is to inform on everything that concerns us. Thus, partly
out of exaggerated curiosity over these weird foreigners, how
they live, what they're like, partly because the right to even
the strictest, most basic privacy is quite unknown, and to a
certain degree out of obligation, our grumblings and periods are
the subject of the most detailed, disembodied, and malevolent
commentaries of all the Chinese who have anything to do with us:
monkeys in the zoo; those devilishly clever but so unpredictable
dolphins at the aquarium.

As my interpreter usually manages to irritate and humiliate
me to the point that I lose my taste even for the hours I spend
at the office, I sometimes play dumb and go to the hospital by

267

myself. The tender ritual I act out with the lady doctor of
traditional medicine is always the same: she has me stick out
the tip of my tongue, which she peers at from a distance, top
and bottom . . . she takes my pulse through a threadbare cotton
pad . . . she smiles a jao, jao, – good, good – and proceeds to
write out long prescriptions in duplicate: five days of assorted
herbal treatments for taking off weight, for moodiness, for
appendicitis and whatever else I mime to her is bothering me;
sometimes all these things at the same time. At the clinic in
my hotel they boil up the packets for me, strain them and bottle
them in little glass vials which are to be heated in the bain
marie and taken twice a day – dark brown, vile-tasting stuff,
but it makes us feel like we're doing something constructive for
our health.

Upon buying a slab of pinkish quince jelly from a street
vendor as I stroll down Wan–Fu–Jing, the main drag downtown, en
route to the inevitable Hotel Peking, I ponder the question the
doctor always puts to me when I go with my interpreter: What
color is your menstruation? How should I answer next time? The
color of Argentine quince jelly, which is much redder than the
Chinese? or less scatalogically (shhh . . . one doesn't write
these things, girl) – less nostalgically, I suppose I'll answer,
in modesty, "Dark, just plain old dark."

Translated by David Pritchard

SHIRLEY ESKAPA

from *BLOOD FUGUE*

And then, one morning, Johannesburg experienced snow.

For Ceza that morning was moist with perpetuity, and so prominent in her consciousness that it permitted infinite surprise.
The snow had seduced professors into cancelling lectures, and
alone with Indra, Ceza had watched the snow drop in forgiving
flakes against his skylight, until the grimed glass became a
white wall. Then, discloistered, and lying with him on his pseudo-
slum bed, when even the sustained weeping from the room next door
was no more than another lulling sound, she knew that it was not
just that she had begun another affair which so overwhelmed her,
nor even that Indra was not white – the strange thing was that
he was not a Jew. *That* seemed to be the point, the whole point;
and in the kind of panic which burst safes, she had turned to
him, and in her wild drive to expel her water–tight blooded
legacy, she'd shocked them both.

They'd transcended the bounds of ordinary secrecy, of ordinary conspiracy; they'd become lawless. Ceza was not sure when
it was that she began watching for Indra's immaculate university
blazer. She half believed that it was some time before she'd
let herself in for that protest march. She longed to ask when
he'd noticed her, but knew instinctively that she must not. In
any case, he was asleep, though restlessly, almost uncomfortably.
His head moved, rather sprang, about the pillow, as if it would
never be palliated, still less, settled. She ached to soothe
him, and to calm, and knew – resoundingly – that there was nothing she would not do and that because he'd left her senseless
(as he would always?) she would never have enough to give him.
His nostrils twitched. As if to apply a compress she would have
touched his forehead yet forced herself not to; an uninvited
touch now seemed unchaste, over–familiar. His clothes spilled
over the chair and on to his desk – she observed them minutely
and was certain that she was as aware of their arrangement as of
a jigsaw puzzle many times completed. But her own clothes, sent
skidding across the room by him, would not easily tolerate her
gaze. The skirt and cashmere pullover embarrassed her; she

wondered whether she would ever be able to place her clothes alongside his, but the question slipped from her mind and gave way to the real problem of how and when they would be able to meet again. Would it be as easy the next time? Would there be a next time?

It had begun so simply.

She'd been standing on those university steps watching the students fooling with the miraculous snow when he'd asked her to come to his place.

'Where?' she heard herself say matter-of-factly.

'Cross Street.'

He took her books. 'I have a car,' he said.

'I know. I've seen it.'

'Uh huh –'

But they were walking towards the parking lot. She wondered how her legs could move. Then they drove silently. He said once, 'To think the populace are concerned over whether or not to have a state lottery. Ludicrous, isn't it?'

She said mechanically, 'Of course.' A little later, she repeated too fervently, as if she were learning a new word, 'Ludicrous. Quite ludicrous.'

Ceza knew Cross Street well. Once, it had been a Sunday outing for the family – the buying of fresh fruit and vegetables on Sunday mornings had been something of a ritual that had only been abandoned when the Indian 'Sammy' brought his green vegetable truck to Villa Evermor. The street, even then, had excited her, if only because the always-crying children always cried differently. The unexpected memory of those sounds (wailing, not crying, she now realized) was dizzying, and she almost tumbled from the car when he opened the door for her. All her concentration was invested in walking; much in the way she had once pushed out her tongue, she tiptoed.

'There's no need to walk like that,' he said irritably. 'There's a very fashionable Hindu dressmaker here. You can always say that's where you went if anyone sees you!'

'Yes.' She wanted to tell him that she hadn't even thought of being seen until he mentioned it, that she felt dizzy with disbelief. The earlier memory that had crowded her ears was forgotten. She thought she saw someone who looked like Sarah, but put that down to suggestion. She tendered a laugh, 'You've made me nervous,' she said.

He walked more briskly.

His keys jangled.

Locking the door he said mildly, 'Well, this is it. It may not be grand. But it's mine. And private.'

He would tell Ceza later – much later – that his father owned the building. The room had once been a small chapel, Ceza decided; with skylights set into the small dome, it was something like an artist's studio.

Somewhat defensively Ceza said, 'It's a beautiful room.'

'You think so?' he said.

She perceived that things like rooms didn't matter to him.

'There's something I've always wanted to ask you –'

'What?'

'Don't be so impatient. How did you get your name?'

Stung, she said, 'Ceza or Steele?'

'Ceza, of course.'

'Caesarean section. It was my father's idea. That's how I was born.'

'Well, I'm glad you were,' he said. And took off his jacket.

She laughed and knew she'd been listening with her entire body.

'Another question. D'you mind?' he asked, with conspicuous tact.

'Certainly not.'

'Are you initiated?'

'A little.'

So it had happened easily – unspoilt – without virtue and without shamelessness.

And now she watched him and watched him as though she might never see him again, like this, with the small scar on his right cheek resting helplessly in that restless face, looked at his beard-stubble and wished she had a magnifying glass the better to examine. She memorized the arrangement of his bones as she had his clothes. She needed to be aware of every bump, every impurity; and scarcely realized that she was mapping his moles and one or two blemishes on her own face. It was then his un-whiteness struck her again, and without pain. A non-Jew and a non-white . . . Incredible . . . Incredible . . . Well, there was nothing she could do about *that.* He'd turned her into a woman, and there was nothing she could do about *that,* either. Now now . . . Not now . . . Her wrist was stiff with the watching weight of her head. And now he settled into his own sleep and held his head in a scaffold of both his hands; slim fingers laced his forehead and trussed the back of his skull.

She saw she'd been no more than curious about Paul – she could not now assemble his features in her mind. It was capricious of him to have faded so thoroughly, she thought, and indecent of her to have allowed it.

But Indra stirred.

Which wasn't enough to eclipse all of Paul.

Then he came awake. Quickly, and without the merest hint of having been asleep.

'My goodness, what time is it? I must have been asleep for ages. Now I'm late. We'd better hurry.' He patted her thigh companionably, 'You'd better get dressed.'

She did as she was told without the least resentment, indeed, in a glitter of gratitude.

'I had an appointment with Mr Crowley about my thesis. I think I'll make it, though. With just a little bit of luck. A little. Like you. You're more than a *little* initiated now, aren't you? Come on, tell me. Tell me.'

"I'm almost a graduate.'

'You'll have your doctorate before we're through.' He patted her thigh again. 'You must be starving. Next time I'll give you some food. I'll even let you see my kitchen.'

Her honesty took her unawares: she said, 'I can hardly wait.'

Before they left he checked himself in the mirror. Ceza knew she would watch him do this many more times.

When they came together the next day he indicated where she should put her clothes, but only after he had shown her the kitchen. It was a small room, fragrant with a cinnamon–like spice instead of the curry she'd expected. She supposed she thought of cinnamon because that was how she saw his colour, as a confederacy of gold and cinnamon genes that had been collected from more than a thousand life–times for her. It was not yet the time for them to discuss the illegality of what they were doing and for the moment Ceza put aside all thoughts of prison. They would get to the mechanics of how the thing was to be arranged soon enough – he was probably expert at this, too: she was not – she was convinced – his first white girl, no, not by a long shot! At the moment, she was the subject of his excellence. It didn't matter that no end was or could be in sight: the beginning, rather, *the* beginning was enough – and he had severed the last edge of improbability.

They had almost the whole afternoon together. He gave her some granidilla juice, then invited her to take a shower with him.

'But my hair —?' she said.

He laughed and the unpolished sound excused them both, though she felt foolish. 'My goodness,' he said. 'You can't be serious?'

'Well — it will show. It'll look odd. My mother will notice —'

'Oh, well — join me anyway —'

And so Ceza — who had become the servant of her surrender — went under the shower. Where desire mounted again.

Presently she said seriously, as if she were making a vow, 'I'm going to invest in a shower cap.'

'I think you should,' Indra said.

She felt she'd been hugged.

Driving back to the univeristy he said, 'D'you think you could get to my place on your own tomorrow?'

'Yes.'

He went on as if she'd said nothing. 'You see, it won't do us any good if you're seen with me too often. You know that, don't you?'

'Yes.'

'Discretion, as Molière has said, is always in season . . .' He added bitterly, 'Why should we make it easier for them than It Is already? The public library is two minutes away from my place. You can always go there. You ought to anyway. That's where the reference library is. *I* can't use it, of course. Did you know that?'

'No.'

'I thought not.' He laughed briefly; the sound neither rose nor excused. 'I take it you are not aware that one of the provinces in this country is like another country for me. I have to get something like a visa to get there —'

She sighed.

'Of course you're not culpable. It's not even your fault that your hair can't take an ordinary soaking. With respect, we'll change all that.'

Ceza bought a shower cap anyway. And found an obscure hairdresser to put matters right. Of course she telephoned to ask her mother to send the driver a little later. She would handle discretion with nothing but respect and compunction.

Dinner that night was as usual. Surprisingly, nothing at Villa Evermor had changed.

The silver bell, having sounded now as always, waited along with the scarlet-sashed waiter, Johannes, with the blue-black Jessica, purified grey evening apron, and Jacob, ready with his freshly picked vegetables, to chop the mint for the sauce. On one of the everyday, and therefore lesser, Madeira cloths, would be fruit in its inevitable Sèvres bowl. Philip Steele really believed that he had 'no time for formality' because he would come to the table in summer wearing shorts and no shoes – and sometimes no shirt either.

Philip said, 'You'll never guess who called on me today.'

'Well, what could you do?' said Irene, indicating that she had already been told.

A sudden fear nagged at Ceza. Silence, measured by her rapid heartbeat, elongated. Had someone reported having seen her with Indra?

'Don't you want to know who it was?' Philip asked.

'Sorry, my mind was far away,' Ceza said carefully.

'Sarah Goodman.'

'Sarah Goodman?'

'She's a woman going sour,' Philip said dismissively. 'She's started collecting for some charity or other. Can't remember which. Anyway, she wanted a donation, wanted the firm to take an advertisement.'

'Did you give her anything?' Ceza asked.

'What else could I do? It cost me a small fortune. I took an expensive back page – some nonsensical programme –'

'How did she look?' Irene wondered.

'She looked as sour as ever,' Philip said. 'Paul's changed his mind, she said. He's now going to England to study paediatric neurology. She asked after you, Ceza. Said she was surprised you'd never contacted her. Hoped you'd nothing against *her* – That sort of thing.'

'I should have phoned her – at least –' Ceza said miserably.

'You still can –' meditated Irene. 'It's not too late. Perhaps?'

'But what could I say to her?' said Ceza, suddenly pessimistic.

'You could always tell her that you thought you didn't have what it takes to be a doctor's wife,' Irene said over-earnestly. Her deep frown let Ceza know that this had been often and deeply considered. Irene had, as usual, chosen her moment. 'You know, she probably felt worse than Paul. It's a terrible thing for a mother to have her son rejected. If I had a son I'd hate that, I know – she must resent *you*, too –'

In his most ominous tone Philip said, 'Your mother's right.'

Irene brought her hands in an attitude of prayer to her chin. She said, 'It's silly and too easy to make enemies.'

That settled things. Why invite the evil eye? Which was almost as dangerous as talking about *luck* . . . Ceza opted for the simplest. She said, 'I'll phone her soon.'

But was not altogether taken aback by the prospect of telephoning. It would be evaded, that was all. There might never have been a time when the Goodman family had crowded and stifled her mind. And yet Paul was, in some way, a remnant of the fraudulent past that Indra had made visible.

Paul's sluggishness could not now be refuted. For all that, she could not help knowing that she and Sarah had had something other (but what?) than Paul in common . . .

No, she would not telephone.

A certain insistence brought Ceza and Indra together every day. Ceza felt herself unravelling, then unravelled. Love had not been mentioned. She wondered at this, and understood how much of her energy had been consecrated to its avoidance; in spite of that underbelly so miraculously nerved, she'd let herself in for the kind of nervelessness that put her out of touch with the whole notion of consequence.

There were mechanics, even so, to be worked out.

These, somehow, abridged time and encapsulated trust: a certain type of legality settled upon them. For another had to be told.

'D'you mind if I tell Neville Levin?' Indra said one day. The question surprised Ceza, but then everything he said, or left unsaid, astonished. Still she asked, 'Why –?'

'I'd like to see you at night. He could fetch you –'

'You trust him so much?'

'There are moments when one must –'

'Of course.'

'Besides, who could be more suitable? You've said your parents wonder why you stay at home at night so much these days, haven't you? Neville's a qualified engineer as well as a final year medical student – perfection.' He laughed briefly. 'What do you think? Go on, tell me. Tell me!'

She said helplessly, 'Has Neville done this sort of thing for you before?'

'Only when the girl was married.'

Stricken, she said, 'You can't mean it –'

He laughed again and she warmed to its sound the way she warmed to his voice, to the lilting accent which reached, she sometimes thought, the perfection of a lullaby. She outlasted her need to take his hand — his laugh, his laugh was enough. She said, 'But won't it be an awful bother for him?'

'What — to fetch a pretty girl like you?' He added seriously, 'No, Neville and I have been good friends for a long time. His mind is excellent. You must ask him, one day, what he has to say about medical school —'

'Ah, Indra, *you* tell me.'

'Some other time —' He leaned over and, in a movement she had come to know so well and want so much, tugged her hair. 'Come next to me,' he said. 'Next to me. Next to me.'

'You know what?' she murmured into his throat, 'My mother will like Neveille Levin very much.'

She held tight to his laugh and was not in the least let down.

So Neville Levin became a frequent visitor at Villa Evermor. In his mild grey eyes there lurked a faintly amused grin, a dark forelock spilled touchingly onto this forehead; his hearty weather-proof youthfulness was authenticated by excellent manners. Philip's notions of informality were not in the least disturbed by the way in which Neville addressed him as 'sir.' Neville had done very well academically, and insisted that it was all due to very hard work and 'the reading of next year's text books this year.' The Steele family delighted in his modesty. Ceza was never able to pinpoint how, or even when, Neville and Indra had become friends. And then, of course, there was Neville's altogether changed atti-tude — less a weakening than a rearrangement of his personality — whenever he was with Indra. Under the spell, as it were, of blatant admiration his animation was inexhaustible; he never seemed quite at ease. And when he listened to Indra it was as if he longed to see as much as hear each word. His eyes took in Indra's every movement and Ceza felt herself disappear from his sight. Because Neville's adoration was in line with — and as mysterious — as her own.

Soon after Neville had seeped into her family, she'd begun to anticipate his asking her how she could have let herself in for such an affair, how she could have even thought of doing such a thing to her family. Later, when it became apparent that the question would never be asked, she knew it was because Neville saw her as the honoured one: any other way would have been as illogical as punishing innocence . . .

The first night Neville had fetched her had passed easily enough.

She said awkwardly, 'It's very nice of you –'

'I have to go to the library anyway. Couldn't be more convenient.'

'Isn't it terrible that *he* can't use it?' she said.

'He has a photographic memory, you know,' Neville said, appeasingly.

'I know, Indra's fantastic. I've even tested him – would you believe it?' she said making it clear that she wanted to talk about him.

'But how could you dare?'

'I don't know how I had the nerve. I simply asked him to tell me what he'd read while I checked. He even put the commas in.'

The night that Neville first fetched her was the night that Indra gave her the sari. It lay on his bed in a shimmer of gold and emerald, and was the first thing she saw when, with even more than her usual nervousness, she entered. For a moment, because Indra was nowhere to be seen, she'd thought the sari belonged to an unexpected visitor and she'd known the unreasonableness of body–toothache.

'D'you like it?' he called out from the bathroom. 'D'you like? Tell me – Tell me –'

'I've never seen anything so beautiful.'

'Well, it's for you, and I'm going to teach you how to wear it myself!'

Wrapped in a towel, but still dripping, he came towards her, and Ceza, taken aback by his shape, said, 'Oh, but the sari is not nearly as beautiful as you.'

'Take your things off and we'll get you into this –'

But her hands fumbled.

He helped her and she was overcome with the gratitude she could not understand.

He tied a cord about her waist. Then she saw him make rapid pleating movements with the spread of gold and green silk. He let it fall back. He said, 'An Indian woman is judged by the pleats of her sari. You didn't know that did you? You should have a petticoat, but this cord will do just as well. You see, you have to tuck it in –' He stood back to look at his handiwork. 'My word, I've neglected the choli. Can't have bare breasts, can we? No matter how comely.'

When at last he was done, he said, rather commanded, 'Walk. Let me see how you walk. Walk to that mirror.'

277

And she felt her walk change — touched by the skin—silk her legs seemed to take on the flexiblity of arms while her back straightened. She said tentatively, 'I feel graceful —'

He, meanwhile studied her with an expression that leaned somewhere between astonishment and greed. 'It's a very old sari,' he said. 'It belongs to my sister. Told her I needed it for a demonstration at university. So, of course, she gave me her best one. It was actually bought in India. My mother takes regular pilgrimages, a silk pilgrim. Anyway, this one is special because it comes from Benares. It was woven there, but with yarn that comes from Lyons.'

Dazzled, she stared into the glittering mirror and saw the end of her transformations. She said shyly, 'What a wonderful idea you had.'

'Come here,' he said. 'And I'll show you a more radical idea.' He thrust his fine—wristed hand into her skirt, untied the knotted cords, and unwrapped her. 'We like unwrapping our women, you see.'

Later he told her that he'd get hold of another sari which he would give to Neville. It would be kept in Neville's car, and she was to slip it over whatever she was wearing and cover her head with it so that she'd be less conspicuous at night. 'You see,' he ended grimly, 'once we are breaking the law we might as well be professional about it. After all, don't forget — the penalty is usually six months' imprisonment without the option of a fine! So we mustn't be caught, must we? What d'you say?'

It was good that he could trust Neville, Ceza thought, if only because it was good that someone else *knew* . . . Her sense of privacy was in no way diluted — it had merely extended into a conspiracy of responsible silence. Besides, Neville's unquest-ioning acceptance added to a certain dimension of legality in opposing the law. When Neville did not come to fetch her it was because Indra could not see her. The Steele family understood Neville's absences very well — a final year medical student has to study. Neville had proved to be skillful at deception. He took Ceza to a family wedding where she was introduced to his mother.

Things would have to take their natural course, Irene decided, there was no point in rushing anything. Of that, at least, there was no doubt. Besides that, all was uncertain. True, Neville was too often at Villa Evermor to be only a casual friend of

Ceza's. Besides, Ceza's excitement *before* she was to see Neville was definite — yet, when she was with him, there was about her a vagueness that perhaps discipline tagged to patience; it was the form of their open understanding that troubled Irene. Certainly Ceza spoke of Neville as often as she could have been expected to — her admiration, though nimble, seemed less than ultimate. Irene might have rushed things if she had not felt that avoidance of touch that cut the young couple into the kind of halves that are resoundingly complete. It was all as disconcerting as Ceza's overwhelming conscientiousness. Ceza was, after all, a student . . . Which did not mean that she should become a professor! All those books on politics and economics had kindled more than a flicker of panic that even those harmless, if rather stupid, books on child psychology could not placate. Those *political* books — weren't some of them banned —? She would not ask. Nor think. Unformulated notions are more easily rejected: it was as if this instinct had been shaped by a thorough understanding of the value of ignorance.

Even in summer, when the grass was green you could still feel the bristly residue of the shortest winter. It pricked through Ceza's light blouse as she lay flat under the fruit trees. A pile of plums and figs, just picked, lay beside her. It was the end of the afternoon, when indolence is not only forgiven but expected. From under the trees even the sweet smell of rotting fruit seemed stationary, reminding Ceza of the fruity mist that penetrated Indra's room from the street of green-grocers below. Her head lay flat and seemed lower than the rest of her. She wished she had no clothes on, and of course that Indra . . . She was aware of grass in her hair, of small ants or other insects dawdling over her legs, of the pressing of the thick rooted arteries that sent up the strong blades of grass. Yes, she thought, Indra had taught her to see, and the more she noticed, the more there was. Perhaps it was Indra's lightly sing-song accent which made her listen as carefully to tone as to content. Ceza was reading Bob de Jong's *Johannesburg Diary* in the early edition of *The Star*.

EUGENIA GINZBURG

from *WITHIN THE WHIRLWIND*

1

. Here lived children

The children's home was also part of the camp compound. It had its own guardhouse, its own gates, its own huts, and its own barbed wire. But on the doors of what were otherwise standard camp hutments there were unusual inscriptions: "Infants' Group," "Toddlers' Group," and "Senior Group."

After a day or two I found myself with the senior group. The very fact of being there restored to me the long-lost faculty of weeping. For more than three years my eyes had smarted from tear-less despair. But now, in July 1940, I sat on a low bench in a corner of this strange building and cried. I cried without stop-ping, sobbing like our old nurse Fima, sniffing and snuffling like a country girl. I was in a state of shock. The shock jerked me out of a paralysis that had lasted for some months. Yes, this undoubt-edly was a penal camp hut. But it smelled of warm semolina and wet pants. Someone's bizarre imagination had combined the trap-pings of the prison world with simple, human, and touchingly familiar things now so far out of reach that they seemed no more than a dream.

Some thirty children, about the age my Vasya was when we were separated, were tumbling and toddling about the hut, squealing, gurgling with laughter, bursting into tears. Each of them was upholding his right to a place under the Kolyma sun in a perpe-tual struggle with his fellows. They bashed each other's heads unmercifully, pulled each other's hair, bit each other . . . .

They aroused my atavistic instincts. I wanted to gather them all together and hug them tight so that nothing could hurt them. I wanted to croon over them, like my old nurse, "My sweet little darlings, my poor little dears."

I was rescued from my trance by Anya Sholokhova, my new work-mate. Anya was the embodiment of common sense and efficiency. Her married name was Sholokhova, but she was a German, a Mennon-ite, taught as a child that there was a right way to everything. In the camps they called people like her "sticklers."

"Listen, Genia," she said, placing on the table a pan that gave off a heavenly aroma of something meaty, "if one of the bigwigs finds you behaving like that you'll be packed off to the tree-felling site tomorrow. They'll say you're high-strung, and in this place you need nerves like steel hawsers. Pull yourself together. Anyway, it's time to feed the children. I can't do it all by myself."

It would be wrong to say that the children were kept on a starvation diet. They were given as much to eat as they could manage, and by my standards at the time the food seemed quite appetizing. For some reason, though, they all ate like little convicts: hastily, with no thought for anything else, carefully wiping their tin bowls with a piece of bread, or licking them clean. I was struck by the fact that their movements were unusually well coordinated for children of their age. But when I mentioned this to Anya she made a bitter gesture of dismissal.

"Don't you believe it! That's only at mealtime, that's their struggle for existence. But hardly anyone asks for the potty – they haven't been trained to it. Their general level of development . . . well, you'll see for yourself."

I saw what she meant the following day. Yes, outwardly they did remind me painfully of Vasya. But only outwardly. Vasya at four could reel off vast chunks of Marshak and Chukovsky,* could tell one make of car from another, could draw superb battleships and the Kremlin bell tower with its stars. But these poor things! "Anya, haven't they even learned to talk yet?" Only certain of the four-year-olds could produce a few odd, unconnected words. Inarticulate howls, mimicry, and blows were the main means of communication.

"How can they be expected to speak? Who was there to teach them? Whom did they ever hear speaking?" explained Anya dispassionately. "In the infants' group they spend their whole time just lying on their cots. Nobody will pick them up, even if they cry their lungs out. It's not allowed, except to change wet diapers – when there are any dry ones available, of course. In the toddlers' group they crawl around in their playpens, all in a heap. It's all right as long as they don't kill each other

---

* Samuel Marshak (1887–1964): writer of children's verse, satirist, and translator. Kornei Chukovsky (1882–1969): popular and influential writer, critic, translator, and author of children's verse.

or scratch each other's eyes out. Well, now you can see how it is. We're lucky if we can just get them all fed and put on the potty."

"But we ought to try and teach them something. Some songs . . . some poems . . . tell them stories."

"You can always try! By the end of the day I have barely enough strength left to climb into bed. I don't feel like telling stories."

It was true. There was so much work to do that you did not know which way to turn. Four times a day we had to lug water from the kitchen — which was at the far end of the compound — and haul back heavy pans full of food. Then, of course, there was the business of feeding the children, sitting them on their pots, changing their pants, rescuing them from the enormous whitish mosquitoes . . . . But the main preoccupation was the floors. Camp bosses everywhere had a mania for clean floors. The whiteness of the floor was the one criterion of hygiene. The fumes and stench in the huts might be suffocating, and our rags might be stiff with dirt; but all this would pass unnoticed by the guardians of cleanliness and hygiene. Heaven help us, though, if the floors did not shine brightly enough. The same unblinking watch was kept on the "floor situation" in the children's home; the boards there were not stained, so they had to be scraped with a knife until they shone.

For all that, I did one day try to put into effect my plan for giving lessons to improve the children's speech. I unearthed a pencil stub and a scrap of paper, and I drew for them the conventional picture of a house with two little windows and a chimney with smoke coming out of it.

The first to react to my initiative were Anastas and Vera, four-year-old twins, more like normal mainland children than any of the rest. Anya told me that their mother, Sonya, was doing time as a petty offender and not as a "professional." She was some sort of cashier who had made a mistake with her books — a quiet, decent, middle-aged woman now working in the camp laundry, in other words, in one of the most privileged jobs in the camp. Two or three times a month she used to slip into the children's home, profiting from her contacts with the guards: she had an "arrangement" to launder their clothes. Once inside, sobbing quietly, she would comb Anastas's and Vera's hair for them with the remains of a comb and pop villainously red fruit drops into their mouth straight from her pocket. Outside, in the "free" world, Sonya had been childless, but here she had acquired from a casual encounter two of them at once.

"She adores her children, but just before you got here the poor girl was caught with one of the free employees. So now she's on detachment, as far away as you can get, haymaking. They've separated her from the children," Anya explained in her calm Mennonite voice.

It suddenly came to me that Anastas and Vera were the only ones in the entire group who knew the mysterious word "Mamma." Now that their mother had been sent elsewhere, they sometimes repeated the word with a sad, puzzled intonation, looking around uncomprehendingly. "Look," I said to Anastas, showing him the little house I had drawn, "what's this?"

"Hut," the little boy replied quite distinctly.

With a few pencil strokes I put a cat alongside the house. But no one recognized it, not even Anastas. They had never seen this rare animal. Then I drew a traditional rustic fence round the house.

"And what's this?"

"Compound!" Vera cried out delightedly, clapping her hands with glee.

One day I noticed the man on duty in the guardhouse playing with two small puppies. They were gamboling around on a sort of bed he had made for them on the guardhouse desk, by the telephone. Our guard was tickling the puppies around their ears and under their neck. There was such a sentimental, good-natured look on his peasant face that I plucked up my courage.

"Citizen Duty Officer! Let me have them for the children! They've never seen anything like them. Never in their lives . . . We'll feed them. Sometimes the group has leftovers . . . ."

Startled by the unexpectedness of the request, he had no time to erase the look of humanity from his face and reassume his customary mask of vigilance. I had taken him by surprise. And so, opening the door of the guardhouse a fraction, he reached out and handed me the puppies and their bedding.

"Just for a week or two . . . till they get a bit bigger. And then you must return them. Working dogs, they are."

On the porch at the entrance to the senior group's hut we created our "pets' corner." The children quivered with delight. The worst punishment imaginable now was the threat: "You are to stay away from the puppies!" And the greatest possible incentive was: "You can help me feed the puppies!" The most aggressive and greediest of the children gladly broke off a bit of their white-bread ration for "Pail" and "Ladle." These were the names the children gave the puppies – familiar with words that they heard regularly in their daily life. They understood the comic quality of the these nicknames and giggled over them.

It all came to an end some five days later, amid great unpleasantness. The head doctor of the children's home, a free employee, Eudokia Ivanovna, discovered our pets' corner and was terribly upset.

A source of infection! They'd warned her that the new "fifty-eighter" was capable of anything, and how right they were!

On her orders the puppies were immediately returned to the guards, and for several days we went around with our hearts in our boots, awaiting reprisals — removal from this cushy job and assignment to haymaking or tree felling.

But just then there occurred an epidemic of diarrhea among the infants group. The head doctor had so much on her mind that she forgot all about us.

"Well," said Anya Sholokhova, "that's over. It's no good grieving. Especially as the little dogs really are working dogs. They're the Alsatians who'll be taking us on parade when they grow up. And if necessary they'll seize any prisoner by the throat . . . ."

Yes, but that would be when they grew up. Till then . . . I remembered how our children had smiled at them just like mainland children. How they had put their food aside for them, saying "that's for Pail" and "this is for Ladle." They had realized for the first time that it was possible to think of someone other than themselves.

The diarrhea outbreak proved very persistent. The infants died off in droves, although they received intensive care from both free and prisoner doctors. The conditions in which the mothers had lived during pregnancy, the high acidity of their milk, and the climate of Elgen had all taken their toll. The main trouble was that there was so little even of this milk — acidulous from their grief — and less of it with each day that passed. A few lucky infants were breast-fed for two to three months. The rest were all artificially fed. But if they were to hold out against toxic dyspepsia, nothing would help as much as even a few drops of mother's milk.

I had to take leave of my senior group. Petukhov, the prisoner-doctor who had been called in for consultation, recommended that as a "nurse with a bit of education," I should be transferred to look after the sick infants. He undertook to instruct me himself. For several days I attended the prisoners' hospital, where Petukhov worked, and he hurriedly taught me all I needed to know. I conscientiously worked through *The Medical Assistant's Handbook*, I learned to apply cupping glasses and to give injections, even intravenous solutions. I returned to the children's home a full-fledged "member of the medical staff," much encouraged by Dr. Petukhov's kind words about me.

Dr. Petukhov was rewarded for his goodness, his intelligence, and his decency with a great happiness, a unique event in those days: he was suddenly rehabilitated in that very same year, 1940, and left for Leningrad. People said that the famous flier Molokov, his brother-in-law, had personally interceded with Stalin on his relative's behalf.

The infants' little cots were pushed close together. There were so many children that to change every single diaper in quick succession would have taken an hour and a half. They all had bedsores, they were getting thinner, and they were wearing themselves out with crying. Some of them gave out a thin, plaintive wail, no longer expecting anyone to take notice. Others set up a desperate, defiant howling, vigorously fighting back. And there were those who no longer cried at all. They simply groaned as adults do.

We performed like clockwork. We fed them bottles, administered medicines, gave injections, and – our main activity – changed diapers. We endlessly folded and refolded the still-damp calico diapers. We grew giddy from contant to-ing and fro-ing for fourteen hours at a stretch and from the powerful stench given off by the enormous pile of soiled diapers. We even lost all desire to eat, we who were always hungry. We gulped down with revulsion the watery semolina left over from the children's meal, just to keep body and soul together.

But the most appalling thing of all was the arrival every three hours, with every change of shift, of the nursing mothers to "feed" their infants. Among them there were some of us – political prisoners – who had taken the risk of bringing an Elgen child into the world. They peered in through the door with an anxious question on their miserable faces, and it was hard to tell what they feared more: that the infant born in Elgen would survive or that it would die. But the vast majority of the nursing mothers were professionals. Every three hours they staged a persecution campaign against the medical personnel. Maternal feelings are a splendid rationale for misbehavior. They hurled themselves on our group with unrepeatable language, cursing us and threatening to kill or maim us the very day that little Alfred or little Eleanor (they always gave their children exotic foreign names) died.

When I was transferred to the isolation ward, at first I was even glad. There were, after all, fewer children there; only the complicated and acutely infectious cases. There it would be physically possible to attend to each individual case. But the very first night shift I was there I felt an unbearable spiritual nausea.

There they lay, little martyrs born to know nothing but suffering. The one-year-old over there, with the pleasant oval face, already had a spot on his lung. He wheezed and made convulsive movements with his hands, which exhibited bright blue nails. What should I say to his mother? She was Marya Ushakova from our hut.

Or take this one, on whom the sins of his father were visited. The progeny of that cursed criminal underworld: a case of congenital syphilis.

Those two little girls at the end would probably die today, while I was there. It was only the camphor that kept them alive at all. The prisoner-doctor, Polina Lvovna, before she went out into the compound, begged me not to forget the injections.

"If they can only hold out until nine in the morning, so that their death throes don't come while we are on duty."

Polina Lvovna was from Poland. She had only been in Russia two years when she was arrested. It may have been from unfamiliarity with our ways, or simply because it was in her nature, but she was scared of her own shadow, poor thing. Scared and absentminded. She was capable of holding a stethoscope to the chest of a two-month-old baby and instructing it in a matter of fact way: "Patient, breathe in. Now hold your breath!" She was a neuropathologist, and not used to treating children.

I particularly recall one night in the isolation ward. Not just an ordinary night but one of those "white nights" you get in the far north. It was almost the last of the year. But it was not at all like the ones in Leningrad: no gold-colored skies and, of course, no huge buildings asleep beneath them. Indeed, there was something primeval about it, a feeling of something deeply hostile to man in that icy white flush in which normal outlines were held in quivering suspense: the bare sugar-loaf hills, the vegetation, and the buildings. And the night was infested with the buzzing of mosquitoes. This buzzing drilled its way not only into our ears but into our hearts. No mosquito net could save you from the poisonous bites of this winged pestilence, which resembled the normal mosquitoes of our mainland about as much as a rabid tiger resembles a tabby cat.

The light suddenly went out, as so often happened, and all that remained was a small night light, dimly winking on the table. By the flickering glow of that night light I administered hourly injections to a dying baby. She was the five-month-old daughter of a twenty-year-old inside for some petty crime. The baby had been in the isolation ward for some time; whoever was on duty would say as she was relieved, "Well, that one will probably go today."

But there was still a spark of life in her. She was a skeleton clad with aged, wrinkled skin. But the face! The baby's face was such that we called her the Queen of Spades. The face of an octogenarian, wise, sardonic, full of irony. As if she knew it all — she who had stopped in our compound, in that little world of hatred and death, for a brief moment of time.

I was using the large needle for her injection, but she didn't cry. She only grunted feebly and looked straight at me with the eyes of an infinitely wise old lady. She died just before dawn, on the very borderline, when the first faint patches of pink are seen against the lifeless backcloth of Elgen's white night.

The dead body became once more that of an infant. The wrinkles smoothed themselves away. The eyes, prematurely initiated into all the mysteries, closed. There lay the emaciated body of a dead child.

"Little Sveta has passed away!" I said to the woman who was taking over from me.

"Sveta? Oh, the Queen . . . ."

She broke off and glanced down at the rigidly extended little body.

"No, she doesn't look like the Queen of Spades any more. And her mother's away . . . . She's been drafted to Mylga."

They are never to be forgotten, those Elgen children. I'm not saying that there is any comparison between them and, say, the Jewish children in Hitler's empire. Not only were the Elgen children spared extermination in gas chambers, they were even given medical attention. They received all they needed by way of food. It is my duty to emphasize this so as not to depart from the truth by one jot or tittle.

And yet when one calls to mind Elgen's gray, featureless landscape, shrouded in the melancholy of nonexistence, the most fantastic, the most satanic invention of all seems to be those huts with signs saying "Infants' Group," "Toddlers' Group," and "Senior Group."

. *"A breeze amid the sweetbrier"*

Where had all these children come from? Why were there so many of them? Was it possible in this world of barbed wire, watchtowers, parades, inspections, curfews, solitary confinement cells, and work parties that anyone could still experience love or even primitive sexual attraction?

I remember how excited I had been in my youth – which fortunately was over before the epoch of the sexual revolution – by Hamsun's[1] definition of love: "What is love? A breeze rustling amid the sweetbrier, or a squall that snaps the masts of boats at sea? . . . It is a golden glow in the blood." By way of contrast, there was this cynical aphorism from one of Ehrenburg's[2] early characters: "Love is when people sleep together."

For Kolyma in the forties, even the second definition would have been too idealistic. When people sleep together . . . But this implies that they have a roof over their heads, the same roof; and that they have some sort of couch where they can sleep; and that they belong, in their sleep, only to themselves and to each other.

In the Kolyma camps love meant hasty, perilous meetings in some sketchy shelter at your place of work in the taiga or behind a soiled curtain in some "free" hut. There was always the fear of being caught, exposed to public shame, and assigned to a penal labor brigade, i.e., posted to some lethal spot; you might end up paying for your date with nothing less than your life.

Many of our comrades solved the problem not just for themselves but for everyone else in a ruling the ruthless logic of which showed them to be genuine descendants of Rakhmetov.[3] "Love is impossible in Kolyma," they said, "because here it expresses itself in forms offensive to human dignity. There must be no personal relationships in Kolyma since it is so easy to slip into prostitution pure and simple."

1. Knut Hamsun (1859–1952): Norwegian novelist, awarded Nobel prize in 1920.
2. Ilya Ehrenburg (1891–1967): Russian novelist and journalist.
3. Principal male character in Chernyshevsky's novel *What Is to Be Done?* (1863); he represents the embodiment of positive, revolutionary virtue.

There would appear to be no room here for argument on principle. Nothing, indeed, is to be done except to illustrate the theme with scenes showing the traffic in living human bodies in Kolyma. Here, then, are some such scenes. (I should add that I am writing only of cases concerning women from the intelligentsia, imprisoned on political charges. The professional criminals are beyond the bounds of humanity. I have no desire to describe their orgies, although I had much to put up with as an involuntary witness.)

A tree-felling site at Kilometer 7 from Elgen. Our brigadier, "Crafty Kostya," was doing the rounds, not on his own, but with two of his cronies. They looked us women over as we set to with our saws and axes.

"Goners!" commented one of the cronies, with a dismissive gesture.

"They need fattening up. Where there are bones, there's bound to be some meat," philosophized Kostya.

"What about that young one over there, the small one?"

Seizing their opportunity while the guards were warming themselves at the campfire, they approached two of the youngest girls from our brigade.

"Hey, sweetie! My pal here would like to compare notes with you."

"Compare notes" was a euphemism, a concession to the proprieties. Without it not even the most case-hardened professional would open negotiations. But the fancy talk stopped there. The high contracting parties now descended to a form of speech stripped of all euphemisms.

"I'm the forwarding agent at Burkhala" (one of the most terrible of the gold mines), "so I can put you in the way of sugar, butter, and white bread. I'll give you shoes, felt boots, and a really good padded jacket. I know you're a prison detainee. It doesn't matter — we can come to an arrangement with the guards. We'll have to fork out, of course! There's a shack available. About three kilometers from here . . . It's not too bad; you can toddle that far . . . ."

More often than not merchants such as these went away empty-handed. But occasionally they did get themselves a deal. However sad it may seem, it went like this. From stage to stage: at first tears, terror, indignation; then apathy; then the stomach protested more loudly, and not only the stomach but the whole body, every muscle — for trophic starvation leads to the breakdown of proteins in the body. And sometimes there was the voice of sex too, which made itself heard from time to time despite everything. And above all there was the example of one's neighbor in the bunks who had recovered her health, had acquired some sort of clothing, and had been able to exchange her sodden, tattered sandals for high felt boots.

It is hard to describe the way in which someone ground down by inhuman forms of life loses bit by bit all hold on normal notions of good and evil, of what is permissible and what is not. Otherwise how else could there have been in the children's home infants whose mother might have a diploma in philosophy, and whose father might be a well-known burglar from Rostov?

Some of the women who had short sentences or who had managed to get out of the camps before the outbreak of war but without the right to return to the mainland (often former Communists sentenced for CRTA — counter-revolutionary Trotskyist activity — which in 1935 had meant a mere five-year sentence) rushed head-long into Kolyma marriages as soon as they were through the camp gates, totally disregarding the possibility of mésalliances. I remember one such woman, Nadya, who the day before her release defiantly challenged those of her hutmates who sought to scare her off: "You will all end up as withered old maids, you pinched virgins! I'm damn well going to marry him, whatever you say! I know he spends his time playing cards. I know that he's a yokel and that I am a university graduate in Scandinavian languages. But who need my Scandinavian languages? I'm tired out. I want my own quarters and my own fireside. And children of my own . . . New ones. . . Those back on the mainland we shall never see again. So the thing is to have some more while I can."

Sometimes the result was not heartbreak but a real comic turn. For example, there was the story of Sonya Bolts's "instantaneous" marriage.

Sonya, a quiet, unassuming textile worker from a little town in Byelorussia, had somehow managed to collect a stiff sentence for CRTA — a fact at which she herself never ceased to marvel. She had already served five of her eight years when all of a sud-den a paper arrived from Moscow regrading her offense from CRTA to "negligence," and her sentence was correspondingly reduced to three years.

Sonya was beside herself with joy and so overlooked the fact that the document had been two years in transit. The main thing was that she had to proceed immediately to Yagodnoye, which was where people were released. It was there that the sacred rite of "regularizing" one's Form A, which redesignated convicts as "former prisoners," i.e., discharged prisoners, was solemnized.

At the headquarters of the Area Administration for Camps in Yagodnoye a little window like that of a ticket office opened up on certain days of the week. It was from this window that the ex—zek (ex from that very moment) received the hallowed Form A, her hands trembling with happiness. The workers at the gold mines in the vicinity always knew when the release of a contingent of women from Elgen was due to take place, and the suitors would gather there to await the event.

After folding her Form A once and once again, Sonya Bolts reverently tied it up in her kerchief. At that point a large individual in a shaggy fur hat came up to her and said in a hoarse voice: "Beg your pardon, citizen . . . You've been released? Well, that's grand. . . . I'm from Dzhelgala. My own master, as anyone will tell you. I'd like to compare notes with you."

Sonya scrutinized her suitor critically and put to him a somewhat unexpected question.

"Tell me, you are not a Jew, are you?"

"No, citizen, I can't say I am. . . . Mustn't tell a lie. . . . I'm from Siberia myself, from near Kansk."

"Why do I even ask?" sighed Sonya. "Who'd ever expect to find a Polish Jew in this benighted corner of the earth! I suppose it's lucky you're not one of those . . . Karakalpaks. . . . How should I know?" And after a short pause Sonya said, "I'm willing."

The funniest thing of all was that this couple subsequently lived for many a long year in total harmony, and in 1956, after their rehabilitation, husband and wife left together for Kansk.

There was everything — from comedy to tragedy — to be encountered in our strange, primordial existence.

Love too? Love, as seen by Hamsun, that "golden glow in the blood?" I would maintain that it did sometimes put in an appearance among us. However heatedly our rigorists (and they were particularly numerous among the Mensheviks and the Social Revolutionaries) denied the possibility of pure love in Kolyma, love there was. It sometimes visited our huts unrecognized by the bystanders, humiliated, abashed, and defiled; but for all that it was love, true love — that very same "breeze amid the sweetbrier."

One of its mysterious visitations took the following form. After roll call one day the list of punishments ordered by Camp Commandant Zimmerman was read out. Zimmerman herself was an educated person, but she merely signed the orders drafted by the chief disciplinary officer. The form of the words varied: "Five days solitary, escort to work" . . . "Five days solitary, not to go to work."

Finally we heard one extract from the orders of the day which aroused laughter even from our ranks, from those who had been listening despondently with a sinking heart, wondering for which of us that night would mean not the blessed luxury of collective bunks and huts but the stinking frozen planks of the solitary confinement cell.

". . . relations between a male and a female convict," the duty guard read out, "involving a horse standing idle for two hours. . . . Five days solitary, not to be taken to work." Later on the phrase "relations between male and female convicts involving a horse standing idle for two hours" would become a popular joke in the camp. But at the time our laughter quickly died out and gave way to horror. Those two were done for. . . .

He was a former actor, who had worked with Meyerhold.* She was a ballerina. For a time their previous professions had given them a privileged position in the camp. At Magadan they had both been with the "cultural brigade." This was a serf theater that staged shows for the camp officials who were bored in those provincial backwaters. It fed its actor-prisoners on a comparatively generous scale, and under one pretext or another left them more or less free to go around without escort. The two of them managed to meet from time to time outside the camp. What happiness! It was all the more acutely felt, perhaps, for its fragility, its precariousness from one minute to the next. It was to endure for exactly five months. And then she was discovered to be pregnant. There was one well-trodden path for pregnant women in the camp; it led to Elgen, to the ranks of the nursing mothers recruited from the criminal riff-raff, to the children's home.

They were separated. The convict-nursing mother was now issued with rough boots and a third-hand quilted jacket instead of tutu and ballet slippers. Her little son died in the children's home before he was six months old.

In order to get to see her he pretended to have lost his voice. He was "unable" to act on stage any more, and so the work assigner, whom he knew, after calling him a blockhead, agreed to "fix him up" as one of a prison draft assigned to Burkhala, a gold mine located in the vicinity of Elgen.

* Vsevolod Meyerhold (1874–1940): director and drama theorist; from 1923 director of the Meyerhold Theater in Moscow. Arrested and deported in 1937; died in camp.

And now in place of the happy-go-lucky life of an actor in
the serf theater he endured by his own choice all the horrors of
the hell on earth that was Burkhala. He worked his insides out
at the mine face: he fell ill, he became a goner. After a certain time he succeeded in getting taken into the Northern Camps
(Sevlag) Cultural Brigade, which from time came to visit us in
Elgen to relieve the tedium by entertaining the camp officials
with a variety show. A number of prisoners selected from the
trusties and shock workers were allowed into the back rows.

They met! They actually met! Speechless with joy and anguish,
she stood there beside him in the wings of the Elgen camp club
hall. Old beyond her twenty-six years, all skin and bones, no
longer beautiful, his heart's desire was restored to him.

Finding it hard to put the words together, she could only
repeat over and over again how their little son had been him to
the life, how even the tiny fingernails had been his daddy's all
over again, how within three days the baby had succumbed to toxic
dyspepsia because she had had no milk to give him and the little
mite had to be fed on artificial milk. She couldn't stop talking
and he kissed her hands with their broken, hopelessly grimy nails
and implored her to be calm for they would have other children.
And he slipped into the pocket of her jacket a crust of bread he
had saved up and some sugar lumps with shreds of plug tobacco
adhering to them.

He had good contacts in influential trusty circles and he
arranged to have her assigned to what by Elgen standards was a
plum job – carter at the stables. It was the nearest thing to
happiness. Going around without a guard, after all! She started
to get well, recovered her looks, and received notes from him
regularly. But what had they to look forward to? Each of them
had a ten-year sentence plus five years' deprivation of civil
rights. But was it so imperative to look forward? She read his
notes a hundred times over and beamed with happiness.

So why all of a sudden "five days solitary, not to be taken
to work?" It emerged that he, with the help of some people he
knew in the camp administration who were patrons of the arts,
had contrived to obtain a fictitious work assignment to Elgen
and had lain in wait for her and her horse near Volchok, a spot
some five kilometers from the camp compound. And then of course
the two of them had tethered the knock-kneed, stunted apology
for a yakut horse to a tree. But some wretched creature had
spotted them and denounced them to the authorities. Hence the
incident, punishable with solitary confinement, "relations

between a male and a female convict involving a horse standing idle for two hours."

Roll call was over, and it was time for the guard to arrive to take the culprits off to the punishment cells. "As long as they don't take him," she said, pulling her rags around her more tightly in anticipation of the penetrating dampness of the cell. "As long as they don't take him. He's had chronic pleurisy ever since he was in the gold mines."

"Where is she? I have a note for her," said a voice.

The voice belonged to Katya Rumyantseva, who was allowed around without an escort. She had the job of bringing in the water supply on her ox. What a splendid girl! She had managed to get a note past the guards.

"Thank God! It's all right!" she exclaimed with joy, scanning the letter. "Tomorrow and the day after they're putting on per- formances for the camp officers at Yagodnoye. So they're not sending him to the punishment cell after all, merely giving him a reprimand. . . . They need him! And as for me . . . I can stick it out. . . ."

She was the first of all those sentenced to the cells to arrive at the punishment block, making her way with her gaceful ballerina's walk to spend five days in hell.

Who would not envy them!

. . . .

17

. Mea culpa

Is the need for repentance and confession an integral part of the human soul? This was something that Anton and I had discussed at length in our endless, whispered conversations during those nights in Taskan. We were surrounded by a world that seemed to refute any notion that not by bread alone . . . Here the quick, the half-dead, and even the all-but-dead lived by bread, by bread alone, by the goddess of the bread ration. perhaps we ourselves, though we talked about such things because we were intellectuals and couldn't break the habit, were in fact as morally dead as the rest. I used to parade before Anton a whole string of arguments to prove that our society had reverted to barbarism. True, the new barbarians were divided into the active and the passive, that is, into butchers and victims; but this division did not invest the victims with moral superiority, for slavery had corrupted their souls.

Anton was horrified to hear these ideas from me, and was passionately concerned to refute them. I was glad when he succeeded in demolishing my arguments. My only purpose in flinging these hard sayings at him, sayings that I myself loathed, was to get him to prove me wrong. I hoped that a gleam of the astonishing serenity with which every particle of his being was infused might also illumine my soul.

There in Belichye I found myself brought up against facts that tended to confirm Anton's ideas. As a result of certain painful, but at the same time comforting encounters, I saw for myself how from the depths of moral savagery there suddenly arose the cry *"mea maxima culpa,"* and how with this cry the patient recovered the right to call himself a human being.

The first encounter was with Dr. Liek. One evening, in the icy January twilight, two people who were not patients knocked at the door of the tuberculosis ward. One of them I recognized; Anton had introduced us at Taskan. He was also a doctor but a free man, having been released on expiry of his sentence. He was now employed at one of the gold mines and looked as though he was doing very well. In his mainland overcoat with its astrakhan collar and with his curly black beard (also reminiscent of lambswool) his whole appearance served, as it were, to underline the pitiful status of his companion. The latter resembled an ostrich, with his height, his small head, and the frayed camp sandals on his long feet. He had reached that stage of emaciation at which even the most conscientious of Medical Section heads write: "Light work only."

This was Dr. Liek, through whose help Anton had five years previously, in the first year of the war, lost the sight of his right eye. At that time all Germans, including doctors, were employed exclusively at hard manual labor. There were not enough protective glasses to go around, so the unrelenting ultraviolet rays of the Far East, reflected in the whiteness of the primeval snows, had burned Anton's eye. There was no question of anyone ever being released from work. A corneal cyst developed. Vision in the affected eye grew worse and worse. Anton went for the second time to visit the dispensary attached to the gold–mining camp. The doctor in the dispensary was a prisoner, Dr. Liek. It is difficult to say why he had been allowed to remain in his medical job despite being a full–blooded German. Was it an oversight, or did Liek have special services to his credit? No matter; the fact was that, at a time when a mass witch hunt against German doctors was in progress, Liek continued in charge of the prisoners' hospital at this mine.

"Yes," he said to Anton, "it's a cyst on the cornea." But he couldn't put him in the hospital, because Anton Walter was a German and a doctor. Liek could then be accused – almost certainly would be accused – of seeking to save his fellow countrymen.

Anton said nothing for a moment and then asked discreetly whether his colleague realized that parasympathetic infection of the second eye was possible, and as a result, total blindness. Yes, Liek did realize this. In a frenzied whisper he replied in German that if he had to choose between Liek's life and Walter's sight, he would choose the former.

I had long known about this from Anton; now my unexpected guest repeated it all exactly as I had heard it and in virtually the same words. He spoke almost without emotion, in the slow way that is characteristic of dystrophics. Sometimes he repeated the same sentence, as if afraid of leaving out something important. His unshaven face, covered with a reddish stubble, retained an unnatural composure.

"Why did you decide to tell me all this?"

"Because I can't sleep. I'm not yet forty and I have incurable insomnia. Of course I should go and speak to Walter himself. But I'm under escort, so I've no way of getting there. They brought me here under guard to attend a doctors' conference. And here I met this colleague of mine who's now being released, and he told me of you. I want you to tell Walter . . ."

"But we've been separated. I'm also under guard. I don't know whether I shall ever see him again."

"You have only a little more than a year left to serve. You'll see him. But I have a twenty–five–year sentence; I still have sixteen and a half years left to do. So I beg you to tell him . . ."

Then Liek's deceptively calm face twitched desperately with a nervous tic. But I called to mind the thick cataract on the pupil of Anton's right eye, and I asked him relentlessly:

"Tell him what, exactly?"

And then he shrieked out loud:

"Tell him that I am a shit! That I am a greater shit than

even the butchers themselves. At least they are honest murderers . . . . Tell him I ought to be stripped of my doctor's diploma. . . . And tell him too that I can't sleep. And that I have night-mares even when I am awake."

He had a very unpleasant, squeaky falsetto. And the grimace that distorted his face was quite revolting. But there was so much suffering and self-accusation in his cry that I suddenly touched his sleeve and said:

"The diameter of the cataract has grown smaller over the past year. He is treating it by homeopathic means. He can now see a little with that eye."

Another of the Belichye encounters, similar to this one, was still more painful for me. This time the person in question was someone who had helped me in '39, but who two years later had become a witness in the new case against Walter.

I have already written about him. It was Krivitsky, who used to work as a doctor on board the convoy ship *S. S. Dzhurma*, the same man who had saved my life by putting me in the isolation ward in the *Dzhurma's* hold and hospitalized me on arrival in Magadan. But by '41, at the Dzhelgala gold mine, he had become an informer, and at the dictation of the local MGB representative, Fyodorov, had signed the deposition giving "particulars of the anti-Soviet agitation by Walter in the prisoners' hut." This served as the basis for a new trial and a new sentence – his third! In court Krivitsky brazenly repeated all his incriminating fabrications to Anton's face and made it much easier for the court to hand down a further ten-year sentence. In fact, this unhappy man must have slid much farther down his appalling path; in Moscow during the sixties I was to come across the name Krivitsky when I read the camp memoirs of Varlam Shalamov. In them he figures in the same despicable role.

I don't know whether he's alive now. It's hardly likely. Even then, in the winter of '46, he had been brought into Belichye after a stroke, suffering paralysis of the leg and arm, and partial aphasia. When he learned I was there, he sent me a note through the orderly. In atrocious squiggles, evidently writing with his left hand, he asked me to visit him. He didn't know, of course, that I had anything to do with Anton Walker. He cannot, evidently, have supposed that I knew abut his feats of treachery.

For more than a week I put off visiting him, merely sending him my sugar ration, care of Gritsko. Then Dr. Barkan, who had been called over to look at him, said to me with a wry grin:

"Why do you want to speed up Krivitsky's death? He's going out of his mind because of your not visiting him. And after a stroke of that sort, the least upset . . ."

I went to see him. The power of speech had returned to him a few days before. It was confused and difficult to follow, but nevertheless speech. He was in a state of acute excitability. He talked without stopping . . . in denunciation of me! For my shameful, black ingratitude. If it hadn't been for him, what chance would I have had of surviving aboard the *Dzhurma*? And now when he was in trouble, I didn't want to visit him! I'd waited three weeks before putting in an appearance. . . .

What was I to reply? To explain the reason for my black ingratitude would have meant causing a deterioration in his physical condition. To say nothing? That would have been unbearable. His present appearance, as much as my knowledge of his past, made me shrink from him as from something slimy. His lackluster eyes, already on the point of glazing over, even now conveyed cunning and deceit. His mouth was contorted, not merely with paralysis but also with profound malice. I put the food package down on his bedside table and left without saying a word.

A few days went by and I learned that Krivitsky had had a second stroke. He was once more unable to speak and almost unable to move. Only his left hand was still capable of movement, with it he had written me another note. As he handed it over, our senior orderly said to me:

"Some new patients have let the cat out of the bag – he knows you know who gave Dr. Walter his third sentence."

Among the three of us we tried to decipher the note. It was a pretty lengthy one, but it was almost impossible to make sense of his hieroglyphics – the only words we could read were "forgive" and "I shall die tomorrow."

His left hand was still mobile. It plucked feverishly at the hem of my gown. It clawed at the blanket. It had an extraordinary expressiveness about it. It was his hand that told me he was asking forgiveness; his eyes were shut. I sat down on the stool, leaned toward him, and whispered:

"You did me a good turn. I remember that. As to the rest . . . I am glad you are asking for forgiveness. I am sure Walter will forgive you when I tell him how you suffered. I curse those who took advantage of your weakness. . . ."

One of his eyes opened. Tears poured from it, and it was alive, not spiteful or unhappy.

On yet another occasion at Belichye I saw how a man can be racked by the pangs of conscience, and how prison, starvation, and even, perhaps, death are nothing in comparison with this torment.

A patient named Fichtenholz had been brought to us with the last contingent from Burkhala. About thirty years old, he was ethereally handsome, with a pale, soft-skinned beauty. From his documents it appeared that Fichtenholz was a special contingent detainee who had been sentenced to resettlement until further orders; and he was identified as an Estonian from Tartu. But the odd thing was that he had great difficulty making himself under-stood in Estonian.

"What sort of Estonian is he?" our old Estonian patients mut-tered, with hostility. "He can't even ask for bread in Estonian!"

He knew hardly a word of Russian, either. It soon came out that Joseph Fichtenholz was Estonian only on his father's side, and he had lost his father early in his childhood. On his mother's side he was German, and his native language was German.

He was very ill indeed. His temperature refused to drop. At nights he would gasp for breath, fall into a delirium, and toss about frantically on his bunk.

The Baltic eyes of our Dr. Barkan looked more and more dis-tantly on the world immediately around him as the date of his release approached. He didn't bother too much about diagnostic differentiation. All our patients were considered to be tuber-cular before they came to us and they were all given the same treatment – calcium chloride injections. But one day, on Barkan's day off, the rounds were made by Dr. Kalambet, the spit and image of Taras Bulba;* even here in camp the doctor had contrived to retain his portly figure. When he arrived in our antechamber to the morgue, life itself seemed to enter with him. Kalambet, who always filled out his diagnoses with jingles, funny faces, and Ukrainian proverbs, thus cheered up many of his patients, had only this to say about Joseph Fichtenholz:

"He's not your patient, he's mine. He's got bronchial pneu-monia. Tell Barkan to transfer him to us in the main block."

But this caused Barkan to mount his high horse. His diagnosis could not be wrong. He continued to prescribe the same pointless treatment for Joseph.

* Jolly, fat, mustachioed Cossack, hero of novella (1842), by Gogol.

One night Gritsko woke me up.

"you'd better come and see the cherub. . . . It looks as if he's on his way. . . ."

Fichtenholz was completely doubled up, barely able to breathe. His light blue eyes were bulging from their sockets; cold sweat was streaming down his face.

"Ich kann nicht mehr. . . . Bitte . . . Luftembolie . . . Machen Sie Luftembolie um Gotteswillen. . . ."

I didn't at first realize what was meant by *Luftembolie*. When I did, I shuddered. I had heard that this particular form of murder was practiced by doctors in Hitler's Germany: when a syringe that is filled with air is introduced into the vein it causes an air bubble and death. And he wanted me to do just that!

"You're mad! We're not fascists. We don't murder our patients, we treat them."

Yes, but he was beyond treatment by now. So the nurse should-n't prolong his agony; he was at the end of his tether.

What was to be done? It was quite useless to run for Barkan. Kalambet wouldn't come either – he wouldn't want to get on the wrong side of Barkan. Then I put to myself the question that had more than once come to my aid here in Belichye. What would Anton have done in similar circumstances?

The sick man had an emphysema. He must be bled. Under camp conditions, the old methods of letting blood had more than once saved people in the Taskan hospital.

There was nothing to lose by it. . . . I put the bowl in position and introduced a large needle into the vein. The blood started to trickle into the bowl in large, slow drops like red currants and spread out over its white base in rivulets. My heart beat frantically. Was I doing something wrong? How many grams of blood had Anton taken using this method?

The sick man stopped groaning, and even seemed to have fallen asleep. With trembling hands I gave him a camphor injection. What else was there? Ah yes, hot, sweet tea, the stronger the better. . . .

In short, I managed to save him. And on our rounds of inspec-tion the following morning, Barkan said to me sarcastically:

"Now do you see? You and Kalambet doubted my diagnosis. See how the patient's condition has improved on calcium chloride."

I don't know whether Fichtenholz understood this remark, but in any case it had been decided between us – without any form of words, simply by an exchange of glances – not to say anything to Barkan about the previous night's bloodletting or about my not giving him the calcium chloride injection.

He became dear to me, as the fruits of our efforts always are dear to us. When he was put on the convalescent list and his temperature returned to normal (37 degrees), I deliberately wrote down 38 degrees on his chart. I wanted to give him a chance to get stronger and keep him away from Burkhala as long as possible. I used to slip him half my ration. It wasn't all that difficult, because what with the exhausting work and the stuffy atmosphere I had almost entirely lost my appetite. But he ate with the keen appetite of a condemned man restored to the land of the living. He was visibly recovering his health.

He repaid my attentions with silent adoration. He was generally taciturn, and would not talk about himself, even when I put questions to him in German. But one evening our senior orderly, Nikolai Aleksandrovich, after collecting the supper from the canteen – the place where all the Belichye news circulated from mouth to mouth – brought back some distressing information about Joseph Fichtenholz.

"He's a Nazi officer! Just think of it! And he's been here on the same footing as our boys who fought honorably and were guilty only of having been taken prisoner. . . ."

It was a blow for me. It would seem that I had saved a murderer, perhaps a member of the SS!

"How did you learn of it?"

"They all say so. . . ."

The source was far from reliable. It was well know how camp rumors get distorted out of all proportion in the telling. I said nothing to Fichtenholz, but began to keep a critical eye on his behavior. It was impeccable. He tried his level best to be useful to the block. "Neat and tidy" were the approving comments of Gritsko, whom he helped with the cleaning. He worked particularly hard on the floor in my little room, scrubbing the pine planks until they were pristine. In addition, he used to present me with little wooden figures he had made himself. By some miracle he had retained a small penknife; with it he used to carve amazing objects from chunks of wood – gawkily graceful little figures, full of thought and talent. Once he brought me two small cherubs, similar to those at the foot of the Sistine Madonna.

"They're for you," he said, giving me a look of utter devotion, "because you are an angel."

We were alone together. I found myself saying some terrible things which would probably have been better left unsaid:

"I, an angel? What do you mean? I'm just an ordinary person. But if you had met me three years ago and in different circumstances, you would have burned me alive, poisoned me in a gas chamber, or hanged me on the gallows. . . ."

"I? You?" His handsome face broke out in dark red blotches. "But why?"

"Because I'm a Jew. And you are a Nazi officer, aren't you?"

He went ashen white and fell to his knees. I had the impression that he was afraid of being denounced, and I struck again.

"Don't be afraid. If they don't know about you, I won't be the one to denounce you. . . ."

He cried out as if a bullet had hit him. And I realized my mistake. It was not fear, but pangs of conscience that were tormenting him. Those excruciating pangs that will break a man down far more effectively than any form of physical pain. To this day I still don't know whether he had been in the service of the Nazis and in what precise capacity. But it was evident that he had something to repent of.

Poleaxed by the unexpectedness of the blow, he forgot his normal restraint and caution. Kneeling before me, he burst into loud sobs like a child, grabbed my hands, and tried to kiss them, endlessly repeating one and the same thing: "I'm a Christian. . . . It wasn't as if I wanted to! It wasn't as if I wanted to!"

There was such profound anguish in all this that for a fraction of a second I was sorry I had struggled so hard to save his life. Perhaps it would have been better for him to die than to live with such a burden on his soul. I don't know — perhaps he was a fascist monster, perhaps merely a blind executant of inhuman orders. In any event, as of that moment, in that supreme anguish of his, he had become a man.

People may reply that it is more common to come across cases of those who loudly protest their innocence while seeking to put the blame on the era they live in, on their neighbors, or on their own youthfulness and inexperience. . . . And that is so. Yet, I am all but convinced that the very loudness of these protestations is meant to drown the quiet and inexorable voice that keeps reminding a man of his guilt.

Today, as I near the end of my allotted span, I know for certain that Anton Walter was right. *Mea culpa* knocks at everyone's heart and the only question is when that person will hear these words resounding deep within him.

These two words are easy to hear during sleepless periods when you look back on your life with loathing, when you tremble and curse. When you can't sleep, the knowledge that you did not directly take part in the murders and betrayals is no consolation.

After all, the assassin is not only he who struck the blow, but
whoever supported evil, no matter how: by thoughtless repetition
of dangerous political theories; by silently raising his right
hand, by faint-heartedly writing half-truths. *Mea culpa* . . .
and it occurs to me more and more frequently that even eighteen
years of hell on earth is insufficient expiation for the guilt.

Translated by Ian Boland

LILIANE ATLAN

Excerpt from the play:

THE CARRIAGE OF FLAMES AND VOICES

"The Carriage of Flames and Voices" is not a poem, but the adventure, the voyage, the combat of a woman suddenly cut in two, thrown into a world governed by laws other than those which rule our own, a world that is always complete and, in a word, simple.

What counts is to go forward, to not get lost, to come out of it whole and matured by a forced march into the interior, into a self remodeled by flames and voices.

Louise and Louli are frequently funny.

THE CHARACTERS:

LOUISE	Louise Polomian, married, mother of three
LOULI	Literally, Louise's other half
LOUIS	Louise's husband
THE VOICES	They torment Louise and Louli

There are also numerous, at times miniature, Louises and Loulis who overrun the set.

THE DOOR OF TEARS

"The earth is blue as an orange."

LOUISE   *Starting off on the Sixth Path*
I knew it
I knew it
I've returned too late
to this Path
whose key I never lost
I've come crawling
half dead
condemned
         a beat
The harm I've done is done

LOUIS   You have the Key
to an Earth
we can ascend
what is twisted you can straighten

LOUISE   I saw everthing in shadow
as though worlds deciphered themselves
in a language I was gradually
forgetting

LOUIS   Let's consult the Sages
they will make
legible
that which is sacred in us
       Flashes of Louise clutching enormous stone
       Tables of The Law. They look like head-
       stones.

THE VOICES It's the End
Lightning
I run among flames clutching the Book
it will not burn it is sacred
I'm looking for a safe place in the earth to bury it
suddenly I see myself running
every Evening I run to bury it someplace In the earth
chapters are being lost

my mind is going
I don't know any more whom I'm protecting
from world's end
to world's end
a Know—ledge that end less ly es capes me
> *The set is overrun with Louises – blind,*
> *bent under their Tables of The Law. Every*
> *Table carries an ideological symbol*
> *(crosses, sickles, etc.), some ancient.*
> *Gradually, stone triumphs over human matter.*

LOULIS   *flocking*
what a waste
these young people
drugged
deluded
blinded by the light they contemplated too long
> *guiding the Louises away from Louli-in-the-*
> *Swamp*

SWAMP   above all don't return to the mentors
they practice their religions
in Swamps
gorged on wine
caressing mad women
spouting nonsense about messiahs whose tongues
were cut out
> *giving the Tables of The Law to Louise*
Evening Universal you can't do a thing there's no
 more truth
> *triumphant*
Everything that is has become evil
> *A beat. Louise, helped by Louis, breaks*
> *the Tables of The Law*

THE LOULIS   *piercing*
Louis!

LOUISE   I no longer
want to walk
on these
Paths

THE LOULIS   You must
             go
             to the
             end
             of the
             Sixth
             or
             we're
             walled in

LOUISE   *overturning, breaking the carriages*
             I read the books
             and was not enlightened
             I've known caresses
             and was not consoled
             I spilled blood so that peace would reign
             blood washes back over hands that have spilled it
             I don't know which of my infirmities
             caused all this pain
             Your remedies
             lost me

THE LOULIS   *Charging, like the police, armed with*
                      bits of the Tables. Louise barricades
                      herself with the carriage.

             Ingrate
             I should never had had you enter the Garden of the
                Wise
             the Little Bibles for Bad Times that I invent for
                you
             not one ever works
             because you're an ass
             you rebel too late when you're too far gone
             you should have observed your laws when you were
                alive
             but you you build your ramparts after you're done
                for
             the fruits of Knowledge are useless when eaten out
                of their time
             they only help the living to live for you there's
                nothing left but Massacre
                     softly
             go
             forward
             forward
             since it's inevitable

307

LOUISE   It's
your
fault
it's years
since I've smile
but I'm going
to rip off
this face
you foisted on me
with your madness
> *She tries to remove the wax head,*
> *unsuccessfully.*

LOUISE   How can you not say
monsters created the world
and rule
but
at bottom
I know
only joy is true
> *She has removed the wax head, she has*
> *real real hair, a real face.*

ONE LOULI   Her heart is beating again

THE OTHER LOULIS *listening*
She won't escape
unless she borrows the Carriage of Flames and
  Voices
the one that gives peace to the soul
the one that cannot be caught
> *Other Louises, in waves, have removed*
> *their wax heads. They are young, with*
> *well—defined features. They look at*
> *one another. Beat. Heartbeats grow*
> *louder. Louise rocks Louli, the*
> *rocking spreads, in waves.*

LOUISE   *to Louli*
Louli, speak, speak, speak, only you will make of
  yourself a miracle.
> *The Louises, free of their wax heads,*
> *sway, in ecstasy, shoulder to shoulder,*
> *a living raft beneath the stars. Some*

of the Loulis imitate, or join them,
their red hands searing. A beat. Louli
is deeply shaken by The Voices. They
are hoarse and breathless. Their rhythm
gives the impression of an
uncontainable, sharp sea. At first, we
cannot understand a word.

THE VOICES . . . out of a long dream long fallen from memory
swayed a soldered human mass
pushed onto
pushed off
a Bridge
increasingly shaken
disagregate
stubbornly singing
celebrating anything just to stay soldered
despite the shifting crazy feline earth
and I heard the echo of an enormous laugh
gods passing gold clouds already fading to thin air
   were laughing
ceaselessly smearing human Wax on the depths of
   their despair

> *The Voices cease. Louli cries hoarsely,*
> *as though in warning. Gradually,*
> *everything contracts into the meat pile*
> *of the Second Path. Hands teem, red,*
> *obscene.*

LOUISE *becoming gradually twisted, breathless,*
   as before.
Calm down, what you need is a law, or something
   like that,
to prevent ruin (*She gathers The Tables of the Law*)
   they're
all crumbling, desperately senile but
that's not   a reason
to starve One day I saw the Light
my soul is large and even larger the Hand
that makes it turn
a bit of that is within me within you a spark I
   feel too keenly confusedly to know where to walk
again
my head
is locked

309

as there are
rooms in a palace one doesn't enter
ever
I would like to see my children again
    clarify my life
I don't understand why it's all barred to me

THE LOULIS   *very softly*
One morning the world began
then it was ruined
Massacre will be
Red Night as is written will triumph
        Red Night

LOUISE   *lost among the Hands*
This Red Night
must have
begun the day I assassinated
the little girl named Celeste that I was at the start
I don't know any more why or how I finished with
    holiness
all I see is a luminous child in mourning for her
    clarity
            A little three year–old Louise appears.
            She is very beautiful, wears a black
            schoolgirl's smock. Light, on a Louise,
            who is burned, riddled with knives,
            rocking the broken Tables of the Law.

ONE LOULI   *sewing Louise's lips closed*
This dead woman
burned
hilarious
never ceases to bore me
with her complaints and mutterings
as though it weren't unhealthy
to stick to the same old story

ANOTHER LOULI   *sewing up the lips of another Louise,*
                who is also riddled with knives
        We know
        that you
        let

your daughter
smother
in the grave while you clawing through the dead and
    dying climbed out

OTHER LOULIS   *hitting other Louises*
              That you
              sold
              your wife and children
              to be
              assassinated
              a few hours – that's still something – later

ALL THE LOULIS
              That doesn't mar
              the meaning
              of the words
              love family humanity
                      The Loulis pushing away the Louises
              they complain
              they're still being exterminated
              but have they stopped spoiling
              the faith we have in our own charity

LOUISE   *to Louis, showing the Little Louise in black*
              There she is
              the one I killed
              the one I never was
              you could have
              loved her
              not me
              a murderess
              cannot be loved in place of the girl she killed
                      All is torn, forming walls, corridors of
                      Louises. Louise and Louis are separated.

THE LOULIS   *going in all directions, talking in waves,*
                      each to her Louise.
              You lost your holiness when the Time called for it
              Night will be total it's the Prince of Drink who
                  governs
              A dog–faced generation is risen
                      The Louises and Loulis hit each other
                      with pieces of the Tables of the Law.

THE LOULI—CORRIDORS

in waves
Mother of flames
devoured by sadness
you persist
in defending
that which leaves you
to your distress
don't say these are Holy Wars
but
last Convulsions
you can no longer stop crushing yourself to bits
dove
your head is read with your own blood
look at your nails
eagle claws
have grown there

A beat. Each Louli disappears with her
Louises into a corridor that becomes
increasingly narrow, made of flesh and
stone.

THE LOULIS

soft, sad
The little dead girl
named Celeste
didn't stay with impunity
trapped in your secret dungeons

Louise is pushed against a wall of
Louises riddled with knives.

THE LOULIS   She's grown fat
formless
fulvous
cut—throat
little pink men
with pig shoulders
lie there in ambush

A beat. They push Louise, as though she
were an animal, from corridor to
corridor. They become ever lower and
narrower.

THE LOULIS   *in waves*
                    Every night
                    they
                    throw me
                    in corridors
                    enclosed under roofs
                    made of knives
                    people
                    are no longer
                    people
                    but
                    precise
                    intentional
                    lightning bolts
                    I'm not dreaming
                    it's all true
                    even if
                    certain nightmares
                    aren't
                    happening now
                              the corridors grow more cramped, close.
                    Louise
                    we're going
                    to be
                    walled in
                              A beat. Everything is closed.

THE VOICES   *ironic, light*
                    Your family
                    who love you
                    lock you up
                    Palace
                    without master
                    stone
                    among   echo
                    stones

THE LOULIS   I went mad when outside
             and now it's terrible to enter
                        a beat
             If at least I could cry
                        *She throws herself against a wall made
                        of Tables.*

313

But I hum
before the Door
unable
to find myself though I'm walled in
    They scream, in eternal distress, against
    the wall.

LOUISE   *trying to move Louli-of-the-Swamps' carriage*
Louli
speak to me
help me
the little time I have
to confront
the horror
not of dying
that I can't escape
I'm sick to the stones
but at dying badly
without finding the joy
that within me
is true
    a beat

LOUISE   *feverish, remembering*
The carriage of flames and voices
Louli help me get in
    Louli-of-the-Swamps moves her lips, no
    sound comes out. Suddenly the Louises
    and Loulis are pulverized by The Voices,
    which are mute. Twisting, they look
    like flames, they are "The Little
    Carriage of Flames and Voices." Louise
    looks at them. During the Vision,
    Louli-of-the-Swamps keeps moving her
    lips.

THE VOICES   *sick with nostalgia*
The beginning of the Vision is lost like Prehistory
what she remembers starts with the Door
she
outside
watching
what goes on in the room

it's an
enormous
Trough
the Baker
doubtless a prince
has just kneaded his bread
it's a woman
modest
serene
he loves her you can feel it in his Hands

> *The Loulis and Louises, kneaded now,*
> *turn slowly, in ecstasy. In the middle*
> *of the group, Louis contemplates a new*
> *Louise, very beautiful, molded from the*
> *soft part of the bread.*

THE VOICES She
looks
at the door
she hurts
but jealousy yields
this woman is so beautiful
eternal, immutable, lacerating
beauty

> *A beat. Louise, standing apart, watches.*
> *Louli erupts in hoarse cries, like those*
> *of mules or mutes.*

THE VOICES Suddenly the Prince is sorry
they've stolen her from him
he cries
"she's not complete
she can't
walk"

LOUISE *getting into the "Carriage," that is to say*
rejoining the Louises and Loulis
Your assistants have hidden her
to play a joke on you
you'll find her
that's for sure
I'm going to help you

THE VOICES   They're searching
              he increasingly concerned
              she increasingly relentless maternal
              they don't see the sun rise and re—rise
              the assistants started the Kneading but can't stop
                 it

LOUIS   *being mocked*
              She's a woman whose beauty cannot fade
              I knew the Times and the Measures when I made her
              but they've stolen her from me

THE DEMONS   *screaming, striking*
              My ass they have
              all dough rises
              to swell
              aggravate

LOUISE   She existed I saw her I was at the door
              she was beautiful
              a perfect beauty
              that cannot fade
              no I can't prove it
              I can't prove anything
                    a beat

THE VOICES   The assistant with the fattest neck
              the smallest eyes
              takes power
              becomes Prince of the Bakery
              the Dough swells more and more monstrous Mother of
                 Anarchies
              millions of agglutinant people rise
              in loaves
              scream
              blend
              are thrown into the pit
                    *A fairly long moment during which the
                    Louises and Loulis whirl about, a living
                    forest pursued by a demented autumn. A
                    deluge of indistinct words and cries.*

316

THE DEMONS   *dominating The Voices*
              Nothing germinates in its time
              there is no law
              Disorder
              is king
              copulate

LOUISE, LOUIS, THE VOICES
              There are Times and Measures
              I have created the work that can endure
              you have stolen it from me cries the old man
              they don't hear him he's only a shadow
              he himself has forgotten the golden number
              and they've ruined the Work
              even absent forgotten it was ruined
              for Thieves here you can no longer arrest them
              you'll vanquish them but after the Massacre
              we must suffer it all
              you can no longer stop them
              you can only harden them with your weakness in
                 their eagerness to rip each other apart
              great is your strength for birds of prey can only
                 consume themselves in their rage

LOUISE   *in the melee, astounded, amazed*
              Great is your strength for birds of prey can only
                 consume themselves in their rage
              I'm crying for joy though I can't breathe
              between Teeth already clenched
              cry
              cry
              the Door of Tears is never closed
                     They cry. One part of the Wall sinks,
                     disappears. They're no longer walled in.

              GREEN DEATH OR THE BEGINNING OF THE SEVENTH PATH

LOULI—OF—THE—SWAMPS
                  mechanical, halucinatory voice
              The Seventh Millenium has already begun

unknown to many for Time was falsified
the Bread fermented
there's no longer real Bread nor real Men they
were refined But
the Good will triumph
we've been gathered into Hands
that I know reveal to Me by the Supreme Path
that the Green Death has begun

> *The Loulis and Louises are snatched*
> *up by Green Hands coming up through*
> *the earth.*

LOULI-OF-THE-SWAMPS
The roots are swollen
they're going to
snatch and smother
no one escapes even in the cities where nothing was
   growing
some suffer a long time trying to understand
others fight sinking lower
some heads transcend all that
crowning with their sorrow this living forest
buried
by waves

> *Everything sinks*

LOUISE
Even lost I rise up to sing
illumine
be this corner of light that cannot
at the height of the Eclipse
be Eclipsed

> *Louise takes up the melody She sang*
> *earlier in the Garden of the Wise,*
> *disappearing*

LOUISE
> *disappearing*

The light was will be is

> *She repeats the last phrase several*
> *times. The syllables begin to sound*
> *like nonsense. The Voices are quiet.*
> *The Louises and Loulis keep moving*
> *their lips.*

LOULI—OF—THE—SWAMPS
also sinking
Those from Elsewhere are amazed by such silence
A moment during which the Louises and
Loulis, mute, disappear.

I would like to return to trouble to haunt
one never mourns me enough
then your children call you've forgotten them
you ascend particles of sun neither rolling nor
    flying
as it is said morning doesn't last but in the end
    it triumphs
opening the doors
of long corridors where the drowned surface
        Numerous green Louises come out onto the
        Seventh Path, while the last Louises and
        Loulis, calmed, keep sinking.

The suns of madness yield their depths to the seven
    heads of the world
beneath the blast one consoles the other
the Seventh has not yet been touched
for a thousand years you'll be able to breathe
    beneath real trees
recalling This as you go to Museums in graying
    weather
        A few pieces of the Skyscrapers and
        Tables driven into the earth, museum or
        cemetery remain, The Voices among the
        green Louises who keep climbing,
        undulating.

Translated by Marguerite Feitlowitz

with poetry

and reflections

SHELLEY EHRLICH

NAAMAH AND THE ARK

1   *Dreaming the Ark*

Instructions reach Naamah
in sleep – winging, vanishing
like moths through dreams. Mornings,
awakening beside Noah, she listens
to the doomed world rustle its leaves,
to the four–note call
of the mourning dove and its mate.

In Noah's ear the Voice chants
a litany of lists, each detail
as precise as a kernel of corn.
One list Noah hands her consumes
Naamah for weeks: "construct containers
for wheat, figs, oil, five million
living insects for the birds."

She blazes in the faithfulness
of work, listens to how air rings –
saw, hammer shaping wood.
Neighbors wave, snicker behind their
hands. Evenings, chores done, her body
glows – the embers warming her into
sleep, Noah's breath across her cheek.

Alone, she stands inside the landlocked
ark. Its virgin stalls, bins, fragrant
as a forest floor. Framed within,
one room for the human family –
eight beds, eight chairs, a kitchen table.
"Home for a year," she thinks and wakes,
quivering like a hooked fish.

She knows that beast, fowl, reptile,
insect will survive intact. Noah sees to
food, to rain being funneled in and stored.
The Voice readies him for the day
and night creatures, for cleanliness. But
vital matters are being left to her
alone, through dreams and something more.

She probes past the code of
righteousness she shares with Noah.
To begin, she studies what she handles
daily: spoon, kettle, needle. Their
forms stir her like a Sabbath candle.
From there, her mind leaps — intent,
curious, uncertain of its landing.

Solitude, memory, privacy, play. Words
collect like buttons in a basket, each
shape unique, explosive. Stitching words
into the cloth of dreams, she discovers
what the ark needs from her. Nothing
she chooses is on Noah's list: fern,
flute, fabric. Unrecorded, she gathers in.

The Spirits flashed
their histories,
then withdrew.

Giraffe becomes
my neighbor.
Chimpanzee,
a passerby
nibbling food.

Dusting my home
I sway now —
water lily
on a stem.

Among feather,
fur and song,
the small comforts
of family,

I'm burrowing
in. O Angel,
whisper, whisper!
Quicken me
with dream.

Looking Outside

Grey waters lap
grey wood.

Scattering seed
each day,
I look for light —
rain ended.

But He has banished
sun, moon, stars
for this voyage.

Where pearly horizons glowed,
nothing.

Where colors were,
His eraser.

Missing the Trees

How the willows
held up twilights
with the seamlessness
of lovers embracing.

I traveled branches,
riverbeds, inlets
of sky.

Longing is
a paddle,
a language.

Awaking

How the scant
needs of life

welcome me
back. Rising,

I bless what
is, saying —

"shawl, plum, ark."

Traveling

Sitting still
before the Flood —
handling peas, needle
at cottage window —
I paddled out

to stars, clouds,
branches, barley spikes.
Now endless water,
the only vista.

Now warblers flocking
over wildebeests
create a meadow.

Oh worlds, worlds
to discover.

The olive leaf signals us back,
hints at the lives
we'll inherit. "Dove and bitter
olive," I'm saying. Noah frowns,
limps away. Sickened by
the smell of panthers, tigers,
he's at the window searching
for dry patches. Listening
for the Voice, he turns from
the ark history.

Yes, I want earth, sunshine,
grandchildren. But to leave
the ark is to enter the unknown.
Together for a year we fed
owl, weasel, elephant. Stroked
the homesick and forlorn.
Shovelling out the stalls,
the well brother took over
his sick brother's chores.
A mother of sons, I learned
how to dance with daughters.
The marriage bed forbidden,
each flame burned low, but
burned. No humans ever worked
so hard, harming so little.

And when we disembark?
Dispersed, all the creatures.
Noah will limp toward
planting his vineyard. And me?
Looking at my family, knowing
we'll replenish the world,
I tremble. Always, the memory
of balancing on water.

NELLY SACHS

O the chimneys

And though after my skin worms destroy this
body, yet in my flesh shall I see God.
                              — Job, 19:26

O the chimneys
On the ingeniously devised habitations of death
When Israel's body drifted as smoke
Through the air —
Was welcomed by a star, a chimney sweep,
A star that turned black
Or was it a ray of sun?

O the chimneys!
Freedomway for Jeremiah and Job's dust —
Who devised you and laid stone upon stone
The road for refugees of smoke?

O the habitations of death,
Invitingly appointed
For the host who used to be a guest —
O you fingers
Laying the threshold
Like a knife between life and death —

O you chimneys,
O you fingers
And Israel's body as smoke through the air!

O the night of the weeping children!

O the night of the weeping children!
O the night of the children branded for death!
Sleep may not enter here.
Terrible nursemaids
Have usurped the place of mothers,

Have tautened their tendons with the false death,
Sow it onto the walls and into the beams —
Everywhere it is hatched in the nests of horror.
Instead of mother's milk, panic suckles those little ones.

Yesterday Mother still drew
Sleep toward them like a white moon,
There was the doll with cheeks derouged by kisses
In one arm,
The stuffed pet, already
Brought to life by love,
In the other —
Now blows the wind of dying,
Blows the shifts over the hair
That no one will comb again.

Now Abraham has seized the root of the winds

Now Abraham has seized the root of the winds
for home shall Israel come from the dispersion.

It has gathered wounds and afflictions
in the courtyards of the world,
has bathed all locked doors with its tears.

Its elders, having almost outgrown their earthly garb
and extending their limbs like sea plants,

embalmed in the salt of despair
and the wailing wall night in their arms –
will sleep just a spell longer –

But youth has unfurled its flag of longing,
for a field yearns to be loved by them
and a desert watered

and the house shall be built ·
to face the sun: God

and evening again has the violet–shy word
that only grows so blue in the homeland:
Good night!

If the prophets broke in

If the prophets broke in
through the doors of night,
the zodiac of demon gods
wound like a ghastly wreath of flowers
round the head –
rocking the secrets of the falling and rising
skies on their shoulders –

for those who long since fled in terror –

If the prophets broke in
through the doors of night,
the course of the stars scored in their palms
glowing golden –

for those long sunk in sleep –

If the prophets broke in
through the doors of night
tearing wounds with their words
into fields of habit,
a distant crop hauled home
for the laborer

who no longer waits at evening –

If the prophets broke in
through the doors of night
and sought an ear like a homeland –

Ear of mankind
overgrown with nettles,
would you hear?
If the voice of the prophets
blew
on flutes made of murdered children's bones
and exhaled airs burnt with
martyrs' cries –
if they built a bridge of old men's dying
groans –

Ear of mankind
occupied with small sounds,
would you hear?

If the prophets
rushed in with the storm-pinions of eternity
if they broke open your acoustic duct with the words:
Which of you wants to make war against a mystery
who wants to invent the star-death?

If the prophets stood up
in the night of mankind
like lovers who seek the heart of the beloved,
night of mankind
would you have a heart to offer?

In the Land of Israel

I do not want to sing you battle hymns,
brothers and sisters, outcasts standing before the doors of the
     world.
Heirs of the redeemers of light, who tore out of the sand
the buried rays
of eternity.
Who held in their hands
sparkling constellations as trophies of victory.

I do not want to sing you battle songs,
beloved,
only stanch the blood
and thaw out the tears
which froze in the death chambers.

And seek the lost memories
which smell prophetically through the earth
and sleep on the stone
in which root the flowerbeds of dreams
and the ladder of homesickness
which transcends death.

This land

This land
a kernel
on it carved

His name!

Star—toothed sleep holds him fast
in the hard apple—flesh of earth
with buds of psalms
he taps out resurrection.

This land
and all its paths
blossoming blue
with timelessness

all tracks run outside —

Sand trembling volcanically
shoveled from the dream
by rams' horns.

The hour of the prophets hastened
to peel the corpse—skin from the dead
like dandelion seed
but winged with prayer
they traveled home —

Women and girls of Israel,
the land sown with the bush of sleep
is broken open by your dreams –

In the kitchen you bake the cake of Sarah
for something else is always outside waiting! –
Weigh what reasons have weighed before

mix what was mixed by constellations
and what the yeoman completed.
The longing of earth reaches for you

with the scent of the opened shrine of spices.
Mandrake in the cornfield, which, since Reuben
found it, had grown into invisibility,

reddens again with your love.

But the desert, the great bend in the road to eternity,
which had already begun to fill with its sand
the hourglass of lunar time,

breathes above the filled-in footsteps
of those who go to God, and its parched veined springs
fill with fertility –

for your shadow, women and girls of Israel,
swept across its golden topaz face
with the women's blessing –

We mothers

We mothers,
we gather seed of desire
from oceanic night,
we are gatherers
of scattered goods.

We mothers,
pacing dreamily
with the constellations,
the floods
of past and future,
leave us alone
with our birth
like an island.

We mothers
who say to death:
blossom in our blood.
We who impel sand to love and bring
a mirroring world to the stars —

We mothers,
who rock in the cradles
the shadowy memories
of creation's day —
the to and fro of each breath
is the melody of our love long.

We mothers
rock into the heart of the world
the melody of peace.

O you animals!

Your fate turns like the second—hand
with small steps
in the unredeemed hour of mankind.

And only the cockcrow,
wound up by the moon,
knows perhaps
your ancient time!

As if covered with stones
is your violent longing to us
and we do not know what bellows
in the smoking stable of parting
when the calf is torn
from its mother.

How does the fish, struggling between water and land,
keep silent in the element of suffering?

How much creeping and winged dust
on the soles of our shoes,
which stand like open graves at evening?

Oh, the horse's war—torn body
where flies without question sting
and the wildflower grows through the empty eye socket!

Not even Balaam, prophet of the star,
knew of your secret
as his ass
beheld the angel!

Franz Marc

The Blue Rider has fallen, a Moses descending Sinai, the aura of
Eden still around him. Over the landscape he cast a blue shadow.
It was he who could still hear the animals talk; it was he who
transfigured their unintelligible souls. From the Front, the
Blue Rider reminded me over and over: it is not enough merely to
be kind-hearted to human beings, for whatever consideration you
give to the horses, who suffer so indescribably on the battlefield, that is the kindness you show to me.

He has fallen. Mighty angels up-lift his great body to God, who
holds in His hand his blue soul, a beacon of light. I recall a
talmudic story which a priest once told me: how God stood with
the people before the destroyed temple and cried. For wherever
the Blue Rider walked he bestowed the heavens. Myriads of birds
fly through the night, still able to play and catch the air, but
we no longer know anything about this down here. All we can do
is hack each other up or pass each other by, uncaring. In this
barrenness a bloodmill will arise, menacingly, and all of us will
be ground to death. Walking endlessly over the waiting earth.
The Blue Rider has reached his end. He was too young to die.

Never has a painter painted with more holy seriousness and tenderness than he. He called his animals "Lemon-Oxen" and "Fire-
Buffaloes," and a star shone from his temple. Even the wild
animals became plant-like in his tropical hand. Tigresses were
magically transformed into anemones, leopards he adorned with
the jewels of the lotus flower; his painting spoke of the pure
death, as when the panther snatches the gazelle from the rock. A
young Adam in Eden was he, a lovely Jacob, a prince from Cana.
Around his shoulders he wildly flung the thicket, his beautiful
face was mirrored in the spring; over the fields he carried,
like a sleepy little boy wrapped in hide, his awed but tired
heart, home.

All that was before the war.

Pharaoh cast out his flourishing women;
They wafted into Amon's garden.

Fragrant as grain, his royal head
Rests on my shoulder.

Pharaoh is fashioned of gold.
His eyes ebb and flow
Like scintillating waves of the Nile.

But his heart lies in my blood;
Ten wolves thirsted after my well.

Pharaoh always remembers
My brethren,
Who threw me into the pit.

In sleep his arms become pillars,
Threatening!

But his dreamy heart
Ripples in my depths.

And my lips form
Glorious sweetsounds
In the wheat of our mornings.

Boaz

Ruth searches everywhere
For golden cornflowers,
Passing by the grainkeeper's huts –

Bringing sweet storm
And glittering games
To Boaz's heart,

Which sways so high
In his corngarden
Toward the fair corncutter.

Ruth

And you seek me by the hedges.
I hear your step sighing
And my eyes are dark heavy pools.

Your glances flower sweetly in my soul
And fill themselves,
As my eyes wander into sleep.

At the well of my home
Stands an angel,
Singing the song of my love,
Singing the song of Ruth.

Jerusalem

God formed out of his spine: Palestine
Out of one single bone: Jerusalem.

I wander as through mausoleums –
Our holy city turned to stone.
Stones lie along the bed of her dead waters
Instead of the water–silk at play: flowing and ebbing.

Transfixed by earth's cold stare,
The wanderer founders in the starry chill of her nights.

There is a fear I cannot overcome.

Were you to come . . .
Wrapped in a snow bright Alpen–coat
And take the twilight of my day –
My arm would encircle you, framing a holy image.

As once, when I suffered in the dark of my heart –
There were both your eyes: blue clouds.
They took me from my melancholy.

Were you to come –
To this ancestral land –
You would reproach me like a little child:
Jerusalem, arise and live again!

We are greeted by
Living banners of the One God,
Greening hands, sowing the breath of life.

To My Child

You will die again and again to me
In each departing year, my child,

When the leaves scatter
And the boughs grow thin.

With red roses
You tasted death bitterly,

You were not spared
One single withering beat.

Thus I cry so, eternally . . .
In the night of my heart.

The lullabies still sigh from me,
That sobbed you into the sleep of death,

And my eyes no longer turn
Toward the world;

The green foliage blinds them.
– Yet the eternal lives in me.

My love for you is the sole image
of God a human is allowed.

Through my tears in the wind and hail,
I also saw the angels.

They hovered . . .
In heavenlike air.

When the moon is in flower,
My child, it resembles your life,

And I do not want to see
The butterfly – light–giving and care–less – float.

ELAINE STARKMAN

A Town That Has No Night Or Day
after M. Kulbak (1896-1940)

In the Home for the Jewish Aged, Eva stares from the window
pressing pre-war pictures of Vilna to her withered ear,
her mind half silenced from too much medicine.

"Senile dementia," writes the doctor.
"Old Jew," confirms the nurse.

She wheels onto the porch,
pinches down thin hair, twists strands with bird hands
while her grandkids stand and state:

"It wasn't true, Grandma;
You don't remember right."

Bands of marching music storm her brain;
she spits on the railing
as the grandkids shrink from her wasted body.

"Don't remember right?
Six million a lie?
At school you don't learn?"

She sucks in lips, smoothes down thin whiskers,
points a trembling finger at the oldest.

"That was a long time ago, Grandma;
there's been other wars since then."

"Thirty years is long?
Ohter wars make this one less?"

339

She wheels away from their blonde faces
flesh of her own American—born flesh
with good jobs and paid vacations.

Away from them and this Home
to a little town inthe picture
that has no night or day and
can't be clicked off giant clocks in polished hallways.

Softly she moans, bangs fists on the tray
until the nurse shoots Valium.

and Vilna is a psalm, an amulet, a silenced prayer
that lies at the end of the hallway
waiting for the machines to mop up memory,
waiting for the grandchildren to go.

"*Just One Hour And You Have Come So Far?*"
Massada, 1978

From window of the white Fiat
this road a trail to the moon
crazy—cratered, stars strung inside out.
Sky black—tongued eating up earth
as Gush Etzion & Kiryat Arba spring
oases from the ground and
spurt forth blond—*kippaed*
hitching soldiers.

They could be your brothers
or at least cousins
from long—ago *shtetls;*
their feisty Hebrew
bumps on the back seat
dissonant and sweet.

Then swells into another sound
carried on white and black robes
that circle Arab villages without exits;
mustached policemen waving,
        "*Salaam, Salaam.*"
Stone houses, aqua—painted porches
guard against gold—eyed mountains
silent as sulphur and mystic secrets.

Now you are nowhere in the desert
        ready to ascend.
Quiet fear dries inside your mouth
as a grizzled man with cigarette dangling
shakes a crooked finger, shouts:
        "Take water to the top.
        Water!"

You start up vast sand and rock.
Heat hums across its tabletop,
across your forehead,
waiting for the onslaught of day
as Herod waited for wadis to fill;
winter waters to fall into cisterns
lest the zealots born after him
die before their suicides.

Each drop of blood and rain
sing slogans down centuries
   960 times.
   "Never again Massada,"
   "Never again!" echoes above.

You stagger up pre—dawn light,
pains in chest panting:
   Speck of dust;
   Too soon to blow away!

Your hands feel an urge to unhinge
from the ramps and feet ache to drop below
ending all questions about god,
but they keep climbing pink layers
to greet the swift sun while your eyes
span the Dead Sea
salt—white on its soundless shore.

Here at the top
   Forget your name.
   Forget who you are.
Look for skull and hair in the *mikvah;*
listen to prayer in the synagogue:
   Better to die a Jew
   Than live a Roman!

Touch her ancient sandals on mosaic floors;
catch her tears on frescoes,
Roman fire after her feet,
grain in the storeroom,
lots cast on the ground,
time twisting about her heart
and hurdling itself at you.

Don't delay. Ten minutes for the palace.
Nothing to see. Scrolls & *shekels* cleared away
        for reconstruction.
Only rubble & tourists under this copper sun.

A new day has begun.
And Jerusalem awaits.
Knees shake all the way down
to the Fiat where the grizzled man
squats, puzzles, and asks:
        "Just one hour and
        you have come so far?"

down interstate five

teary because
for three days we
leave our kids who
wave last-minute demands
from the door as concrete road
a work of work not art grabs us
curbed cement made by mexican hands
to connect this long golden state ginsberg-
lamented and tourist-praised

a lonely
two-lane road
spilling forth bored
drivers who play pass as
an old okie thumbs south to
l.a. where fat motels waste water
cleaning sheets, dumping untouched dishes
and bankamerica eats eyes of our hearts

here sky
grows black with
progress and we nod no
to nasty third fingers
wagging us down this gray ghoul
that moves time and space/where wire
and haze are strung-up harps/and metaphors
fly from fingertips/or slip from skulls wobbling
images of sky and mountain that beat on windshields

bang rhythm
to the one named
The Name, Holy One
who transcends all news
on cbs & nbc, forgive us our
trespasses, deliver us from smog,
do not forget us as we have forgotten
You

RAQUEL JODOROWSKY

The sea offers up
flowers of glass
like thick light.
They are transparent landscapes.
Men say
they are like animals
and give them bitter names.
Out of the middle of nowhere
the sea offers
a garden of petals
flesh of hard water.
Men tear these underwater eyes
to pieces
in the sand
drive sticks
into deep purple roses
liquid rocks
destroying at its foundation
a city of the universe
reflected.
Man heart of an idol
feet of concrete
does not see.
How can he claim to give
if he does not know how to receive?
The sea
all its blue, lode of silver!
gathers up its vestiges
of splendor
unraveled on the shore.
It retreats
with its broken harvest
and renders to men
in silence
a morning that wars
with the soul.

THE POWER OF MAN

When the force of man
calms down
stops its machines
puts away arms
A silence swells
in which I hear
the light of the Moon.
A chemical silence
in which I see sounds
from the beginnings of Earth.
In this, I feel growing
the spine of time
crackling like broken insects.
These are hours
apart from the hours
when I start to balance myself
on the horizon.
On the edge of the planet
I capture poetry
dictated in other orbits.
It is not the stillness of nature
It is the silence of the mind to each other.
that leads us
to the magic of the World.

SONG FOR VOCAL CORDS AND INSTRUMENTS OF ELECTRONIC CRYING

Sound of the universe flowing in my intestines
Sounds of machines chewing up men
Sounds of clothes annihilating bodies
Sounds of boots kicking in eyes that dream
Sounds of heroes dressing in their enemies' skin
Sounds of children devouring grandparents
Sounds of microbes battering livers
Sounds of throats trying to sing while waiting
    in the electric chair
Sounds of white hunters of black heads
Sounds of pins deflating stomachs of 200 pound
    bankers
Sounds of fingernails scaling prison walls
Sounds of penises breaking drums
Sounds of rain rain rain falling falling on a
    body that is bleeding without help
Sounds of writers gnawing writers
Sounds of priests smothering spirits
Sounds of politicians being preserved in saliva
Sounds of geniuses being drained in compounds
Sounds of hunger howling in the solitude of hospitals
Sounds of criminals that went to heaven immortalized
    on posters
Sounds of poems burned by the state
Sounds of families that were separated searched for each other
    called to each other swallowed their unanswered echoes
    inside crematories
Sounds of teachers' books announcing the advances of
    civilization
Sounds of my eyes following me in the darkness
Sounds of sounds of sounds circling in the vacuum in
    the silence in the vacuum.

(Translated by Pamela Carmell)

347

TIANANMEN SQUARE
June 4, 1989

Karl Marx, take your time,
looming over Highgate on your plinth.
Snow's falling on your beard,
exiled, huge, hairy, genderless.
Terminally angry, piss—poor,
stuffed on utopias and cold,
cold as iron.

I'm thinking of your loving wife,
your desperate children and your grandchild
dead behind the barred enclosure of your brain.
Men's ideas the product, not the cause
of history, you said?

The snow has killed the lilacs.
Whose idea?
The air is frozen with theory.

What can the man be doing all day
in that cold place?
What can he be writing?
What can he be reading?
What big eyes you have, mama!
Next year, child, we will eat.

I'm thinking of my middle—class German grandmother
soft as a pigeon, who wept
when Chamberlain declared a war.
Why are you crying, grandma?
It's only the big bad wolf, my dear.
It's only a story.

There's no end to it.
The wolves have come again.
What shall I tell my grandchildren?

No end to the requiems, the burning trains,
the guns, the shouting in the streets,
the outraged stars, the anguished face
of terror under ragged headbands
soaked in death's calligraphy.

Don't turn your back, I'll say.
Look hard.
Move into that frozen swarming screen.
How far can you run with a bullet in your brain?

And forgive, if you can, the safety of a poem
sharpened on a grieving night.

A story has to start somewhere.

CAROL ADLER

Shoreline

far out
there was nothing but more of the same
indiscriminate grayish–white

but close–up
orbiting at our feet
tiny galaxies of grass poking
out of the sand

each pooled by its own
nimbus made by the wind
you said as it twirled them around
forcing them to mark
their own perimeters

far out
nothing
and close–up only
the pin–and–chalk
of our marked destinies

plant me in the sand i said
so i can wait for the wind to
show me

then stretch the string
beyond each point

so that when you and i
walk the shore
and look out

each day will be a marked
event circled by more
of the same
nothing visible far out
and close–up
only what you and i
can see

Markings

It rained last night
and when I went out
before dawn

even though there was no
moon and the stars
were covered

I found my way
by following
the hollows where the
water had been trapped.

Black on black
they shone as if
with a light of their own.

But when I came to the
spot of the Broken Heart
it was totally dark

and there was nothing
to follow
but a yellow line

and the silvered scars
on the bark of a tree:

Nothing to follow
but a map of pain

that guided me
with certainty.

Night Blizzard

at 3 a.m.
hardly awakened
by the plow;

for it was the silence
of the falling snow
that had alerted us

for the harsh grating
of those blades.

Warning us to clear the streets
we tried.

But the streets filled up
too fast with all the warnings

and the snow came
predictably too soon.

Stranded,
should we atone? --

For according to the Almanac
we should never have
set out

and according to the
traffic
even from the start
we were doomed.

After Wallace Stevens

Sunday
leafing through the papers
and studying photographs of
flowering bougainvillaea:

while the snow outside
leaps against the wall

and the dancer down the street
choreographs obscenities
(only last week
another poet turned on the ignition
and today
the neighbors having risen early
discovered to their chagrin
that the church had blown away)

we couldn't help feeling somewhat
victimized
either by the elements
or the unnatural condition
provoking this unnaturalness
yet calling it natural,

while in Florida at that moment
the retired general was
squeezing himself a fresh glass
of orange juice and clearing the table
from his last campaign --.

There were whole lists of shrubberies
we'd never heard of,
or if we had, here
sheathed in their Latinate
taking on an aura as plastic as a plastic orange

orange related to cockatoo or mandarin
so did not exist,
the choice
became ours.

Closing our eyes and jetting down to Florida
where lying on the sands
we could justify what we laughed at (stripping
the names, stripping those ruins) --

because how could a church simply blow away,
and why for the poet
must inanition be sin
(while the ordinary meateating competitor
who greets each day with a grin--)

Yes.
It should be
the other way around,
a gamble at least
or a jest
for the one-in-residence
radiant and free.

So we deliberated. Fig trees
from Teheran
or a miniature bonsai shipped
directly from Japan;
the regularity of a hedge
or trees grown tall
that might structure something else
besides a wall
(poplars, the spires of a church
beech the back of a brow-beaten
philosopher)
enclosing what was as foolish as it was impractical,
meaning what?

And that evening
as the snow crashed against the pane,
as the crystals built infinite cathedrals
and we listened to the 2nd Brandenburg
we added six forsythia
four pin oaks
and a scarlet weigela. Who could be blamed?

It was a kind of build-up of hysteria
low pressure at a high scream
once wrote D. H. Lawrence
that could not be combatted by anything
but art,
or sex.

So it was still snowing when they came,
somewhere at the end of March
or was it already April; –

dumped by the door
with the rest of the mail
and a package of socks
ordered the day before from the local
department store.

A package no bigger than a broom
containing "forty-eight trees"
read the label.

According to the Almanac

this was supposed to be the mildest
winter in history;
and in Florida said the paper
the first alligator was getting
a heart transplant, somewhere
in the Keys.

Tomorrow, I whispered.
Tomorrow we'll put on the Mahler 5th
and dig forty-eight holes.
And as soon as we've listened
to the entire Symphony

48 times
we'll fuck,
just as many. Forty-eight
fucks under six dozen willows
six dozen pines
three thousand silver maples
and a flowering bougainvillaea––

Proving to
the dancer and the poet
and even to that old Floridian general
that nothing and everything
is not un–
related to a certain Sunday desperation
causing us to order
what we didn't want.

MELONS PEACHES AND CORN

for the Sweeneys

When winter's moon hangs in the sky
orange and succulent
and over the snow
the ears of early morning light
fill out with yellowing kernels

when the down of the sun takes on a
rosy blush

letting the juice dribble
from my chin
and sweeten the ground
like the freshest dew.

until there seems to spring
from hidden sources
golden fruit.

These visions
harvesting from frozen fields
memories of tomorrow's yield.

WIRES TELEPHONIC (SQUIRREL GAZING)

After Richard Eberhart

Whirling in the cornucopia of the invisible
ear's trumpeting

he was oblivious to his own expertise
so in a sense superior;

and although these wires were meant
neither for humans nor squirrels

it was for each indubitably
the neatest way to cross the street.

Yet if I were he,
even if licensed I know I would not risk it,

at least without a net.

Nor would I dare the go—between
of any trafficked height

not so much I think for the danger of it
as for the spectre
of myself floating above the cement
giving all who chanced to look up
adequate reason for comment.

Then there is always the end ——
Who could tell what would happen

once the gossip having finished
and some argument begun: invading the wrong
peripatry ignorant or ill—advised
the very sky would seem to hum

Are those wires strong enough
or would they snap? -- And what if
some storm grabbing hold of them
would chew them off,

leaving me there dangling mid-air,
again open for pedestrian fare.

Yet to a squirrel
if a squirrel can master parallels

we would probably seem equally ridiculous,
deliberately shooting ourselves off
wireless

or, scampering back and forth
between two poles discovering ourselves

too late ensnarled in the wrong extreme.

So what do squirrels and humans share
but a harlequin faith

meant neither for them or us
nor for anyone else who might be

slightly Messianic . . .

on love,

sex,

& marriage

in the

sixth millennium

NAOMI DOUDAI

THE MYTH OF THE MORNING OF THE WORLD

Except for the stewardess and a lady in a sari, they were
the only two on the plane – Hugo, a Hollander he said, and she,
– had seen it on her bags – from the Antipodes, a lady on her
own in the exotic East. "And not afraid?" She was from Christ-
church, she corrected him, did not dislike being on her own, nor
was she afraid. Not of anything, not even of this flight, she
told herself, alone aloft an inland line somewhere south of the
equator, alone with this beautiful blond Dutch boy whose hair
and eyes reminded her of something, some stuffed, straw-haired,
calico doll – a doll she had disliked? Hugo was, however, rub-
bery, and had blue eyes that smiled. No, she repeated, not afraid,
not her, no way. "You are so downright, all of you from down-
under. Ach, but it is admirable," his blue eyes glittered. "It
is what I like." This time she did not correct him though again
she had half understood: for downright was different, different
to direct. She spoke out straight because she saw things straight,
so said them straight which was not the same as being downright,
which was only being direct. He had not understood her direct-
ness. Later, she thought vaguely, later he will.

The plane was comfortless, said Hugo, a ramshackle relic of
World War Two. Several of the seats were cluttered with his
camera gear because the hostess – (she sat apart admiring the
pink points of her polished nails, brown seductive, in a ravish-
ing batik sarong) – had not troubled to stow them away. He was
here, he said to take pictures for Garuda with which he had
flown in. The big brother airline, they called themselves. Pulling out a brochure he pointed to the picture on the cover, a
mythical bird, symbol of safe carriage, that carried people to
far off lands in search of new excitements and adventures. That,
he sighed, that was Garuda. "All you've got to do is catch it.
Go catch a Garuda!" Now he sneered more than he sighed. She
didn't like it when he sneered. Somehow it surprised. He's not
so nice, she thought, not when he sneers. He was on his way

359

back from the islands, he was going on, was now bound further
east. And she? In search of what — excitement, adventure, the
exotic East? On the contrary, she answered, it was the West
that she was after, was on her way out West for this, her first
trip far from home. At which he pretended relief, that it was
the West she wanted, ach, admirable, ya, to prefer the West. His
lips retracted, thinning to a taut, tense smile in which the
sneer, she thought, was still incipient. She frowned, since for
a moment she had wondered — yes, it had really crossed her mind
— that this might just be all the West that she was looking for.
"We have to get out," she said taking refuge in her teacher's
tone, "to collect our cultural quota, where and when we can, we
who are the educators, on intermittent but long leaves. New
Zealand has a lot, but lacks." "Of what?" he said still smiling.
"Scenery . . ." she said uncertain, "mountains, sheep, Scottish
dancing. My father like his father plays the Scottish bagpipes,
plays them splendidly, for the Highland dancing. Weird, well
isn't it? Weird and wonderful, what a weird, wonderful world."
"What kind of world are you looking for?" he said, blue eyes
suddenly deprecating. I know what he is getting at, she thought,
but is all wrong, I'm not all that naive: nor is it to escape
that I am here. My windows look out on a wider world. She knew
for certain he was wrong and told him too. Again he feigned
relief. He understood, of course. Even in Paradise, he said,
there are those who must get out, escape through windows,
especially and on account of windows, because windows imprison
them. He pointed to the tiny squares of sky where daylight
entered the plane. The windows on this plane were grilled, had
she not noted? Yes, this pane had been a transport plane used
to transport prisoners. Then she had never heard of them, the
prisoners of Buru? The ten thousand with their poets, professors,
and politicos, in for life without a trial? He had just come
from them, from their island, had photographed them in a party
of pressmen permitted to view moral rehabilitation as practised
in the East. Ach, then she had not heard? "Flying, you forget.
When you fly you're free." He was sneering once again.

As their plane touched down, a military craft taxied to a
standstill alongside, cracked open down the centre and disgorged
its load; one shot, said Hugo, he really would have liked to
have, the strong men of the South China Sea, gorillas dressed as
generals, clothed in jungle green. And sneered once more. What

did it give, all this sneering? Satisfaction, maybe? The idea
surfaced in her mind but was at once dismissed. She would not,
could not, dislike Hugo. He was smiling now without the sneer,
a human straw-haired doll. The run from Seremban to Jokga, he
was saying, was long and dusty. So better, if more bumpy, to go
by bus. Ach, but she had just got in, had not yet dreamed of
dust, did not yet know what it was to lick the lava. But soon
she would, he said, no one could escape it, a cultural quantity
that seeped through outer clothing, outer skin, into the deep
dark places of the soul, percolated into places otherwise
insensible to dark or light. Lava was the loveliest and last,
maybe the most sinister, of all terrestrial quantities, until
the atom bomb. "How I love it," he was saying, "Its volcanic
aridity. Yes I love it, I love lava."

At customs there was a form to fill in, mainly items they
prohibited. "Weapons, narcotics, phornography . . ." he read
out, sneering at the misprint, ". . . dogs, cats, monkeys, ah,
and exposed films. And what is for pornography in their local
lingo?" He searched his travel brochure for a Malay phrase.
". . . jabber jabber, barang barang, jabber jabber . . ." he
read out, and shrugged. "None of them," he said, "suggestive.
Not for tourists, eh? Perhaps you think their culture clean of
it? No pornography, yes? I promise you I find some." When he
saw she was embarrassed he at once desisted. This is courtesy,
she thought, true innate courtesy, what one would expect of the
cultured West. At the edge of the airstrip a young man was
waiting. He wore European dress and a wide, tourist-turned
smile which he switched off from the lady in the sari who had
eluded him, and onto them. He was, he said, a student cultural
guide, also good English speaker. He could show — rhythmically
he reeled them off — Javanese Classical Dance, Javanese Self-
defense, Wayang Kulit Shadow Play, Gamelan music: or maybe it
was temples that they wished to visit? Did they know who was
Arjuna, what batik was made of, also where to see a genuine
Javanese wedding? And had they heard of the Horse Trance
Dance? "Wait!" said Hugo, "Horse Trance Dance you say . . ."
Then stopped himself abruptly. "His English," he turned to the
girl, "how is his English?" the other, unasked question still
lingering in his eyes. "Quaint," the girl said as though she
had not noticed. "Not more? Language lab level, I think, at
least," returned Hugo studying the student's face. "This gentle—

man commands a cultured English, no?" "Yes," the student stammered, "also culture, cradle of our culture. Central Java, yes,
indeed, the cradle of our culture. So, too, the Horse Trance
Dance, you want to see?" Hugo now rejected the suggestion.
What they wanted now, he said, was a place to stay. Some kind of
reasonable hotel. "So let's go," said the student in the same
lab-drilled tone. He would take them to the Surabaya Palace, a
hotel fit for a sultan built with the best modernity in the shade
of the Sultan's Kraton by the Japanese. "The active Merapi volcano which is standing beautifully behind the hotel," Hugo read
from the brochure, "is blowing its smoke all the time." The girl
grinned. "By which they mean," continued Hugo, "that when you
wake up in the elegance of your equatorial suite, a volcano will
be puffing there outside your window, blowing on an archetypal
landscape. In Java the collective unconscious is what confronts
you. It is that, the unconscious memory of all mankind that you
find there." Hugo's English was marvellous. She marvelled at
his English. "Yes," he said, "thank you. My excellent English.
And now for a room with a view, that is what you must demand, a
room with an archetypal view." The student, they discovered,
was still with them, had something he was trying hard to tell.
An automobile, he was explaining – our limousine, he called it –
at the disposal of the visitors, to take them to the Surabaya
Palace or wherever they commanded. Hugo bowed but waived the
offer. "We walk," he said. "We see the city. Or better still,
take a bejak, a cart-cum-bicycle, in which the feet keep clear
of lava." But when they climbed inside the vehicle the lava
dust was there as everywhere. They trod it underfoot, wiped it
from their eyes, breathed it in, for the air hung heavy with it,
yellow as the sky. The girl sneezed. "I'm choking," she said.
"No," he said, "You mustn't! You don't choke on it, you eat it.
You like lava, you love it, you have to." And fondly let his
fingers run through the abrasive air. From the moving bejak he
drew tracks along the dust with a stick that he had picked up on
the way. "Cradle of our culture," he was muttering, "Cradle of
our culture. . . of the Horse Trance Dance. . ." He stopped again
abruptly, for the words had slipped out accidentally. "The Sur-
abayá Palace," he said reverting to a tourist tone, "would probably be air-conditioned. A tourist temple complete with bar,
barber, beauty shop, florist, druggist, private bath and radio
in every room in addition to the private view of the active
volcano." At the hotel they registered, and later found the
student in the lobby waiting. Hugo bowed again, craved her

consent to send the fellow packing till the morrow, when, with
her permission, he should wait upon them as their joint guide.
"To the Horse Trance Dance?" she asked on a sudden impulse.
His smile frosted in his face. "As Madam desires," he bowed in
reply. Outside her room he bowed once more. "Remember the landscape, ya? Oh yes, and there is nasi goreng or, if you prefer
it, gado gado for your dinner . . . ."

She slipped between iced sheets and slept, but only fitfully,
words jingling in her ears . . . volcanic . . . equatorial . . .
archetypal . . . . Suddenly she wakened to a cold clutch of the
heart, to a sense of horrid heat and the sight of her own body
stretched before her naked. The air-conditioning had stopped.
She got up and staggered to the window, pulled the curtains open.
An enamel, green-glazed sun beckoned from the pool. When she
got down she found Hugo at the bottom of the steps waiting, as
if he knew that she must come. "Their ancient gods," he said,
pointing to the grotesque stone statues that surrounded them,
then, looking not at her nor them but at their reflections in
the water, moaned, "a graveyard of gorgeous gods. Shall we swim?"
Together they slipped underwater, never touching, separate, in
silence, while the gods humped in strange stone shapes, looked on.
From the pool, the garden with the gods seemed remoter, full of
shadow; the gods themselves had started sneering, scorning the
intrusion of their green liquid shrine. Their sneers perturbed.
She shivered, started out of the water and left the pool by the
stone steps. Hugo followed soundlessly. As they sat, the good
warm stone against their backs sucking off the drops of water,
the sense of horror vanished. She even smiled again, relieved,
and would have taken hold of one of Hugo's hands but for a
strangeness that, with shock, she noticed in his fingers: then
she recognised the motions, in the finger-play the collings and
contortions of the snakes that circled the bare feet of the grinning gods. "So this isn't it?" Hugo broke the silence, "Not
the world you were looking for. . . ." The implicit sneer was
obvious now. Sneering at her, at her supposed quest, when he
for his part had not once confided what he was looking for, had
not been straight nor even sincere with her. So let him sneer.
He faced her then, eyes lit with a peculiarly intense passion
that was neither lust nor love, she reckoned, but hunger of
another kind, written there inside his eyes if you could read
it. But she couldn't. Nothing there that gave a clue. Whatever

it might be she didn't have it, that was clear, for suddenly he rose and calling, "It's enough," left her to ruminate the meaning of his swift departure. He was not finding her so admirable after all.

After breakfast they collided with the lady in the sari, spitting all about her in excitement. Where had they been? She had lost sight of them ever since the airfield, yes, indeed, but now, please – ah, they must permit her, she tendered a card – Mrs. or, Professor, well in point of fact preferred plain Doctor, Chandri, on the way back from a conference in Australia and none too happy, oh dear no, travelling alone in this poor place, all the dust and the live volcano, too distressing, yes indeed, she did not like the landscape, not in the least. She was coming from Calcutta herself, she said and they? Supposed they too would do the sights. There was fine sightseeing, but the rest so very disappointing. Such a poor place, so primitive also the people. "The Capital, Madame," Hugo pointed out politely, "the Capital of Central Java." Yes, yes, yes indeed, she said, but a poor place just the same. Notwithstanding which there were the shrines, holy Hindu shrines, which they would visit, oh yes, surely. "Possibly," said Hugo, "with a guide." No need, said Mrs. Chandri spitting, no indeed, none at all. Not to put themselves to the expense. They must permit she offered them her humble services instead, for if a nuclear physicist, a pious Hindu too, so they must go with her to see the shrines. She begged to let her show them over Borobodur. Hugo bowed and thanked her. They had arranged to see the Horse Trance Dance today, he said. He must now go and try the student's number for he should have shown up by now. He tried. There was no answer. The number did not even ring. Out of order, offered Mrs.Chandri clucking consolation, or perhaps not plugged in. The student was not showing up? Then why not accompany her instead, come with her, she ventured to suggest, to see the Borobodur? Indeed, she had it calculated. They could cut the cost by hiring a car together. "I consult my friend," said Hugo. "It's okay," the girl whispered, "I'm for it!" She liked the lady in the sari, especially her wide white smile. "Magnificent!" exclaimed Mrs. Chandri as they approached the monument, "Magnificent!" And coaxed them out the hired car and up the stupa steps. Mrs. Chandri – from now on, please, plain Mrs., please to forget formalities – smiled her pleasure at the many-storied monument, at the little latticed stone umbrellas, at the unnumbered terraces and steps leading to the topmost stupa, the place, she puffed, a veritable wonder of the world, a sacred replica of the universe entire, and hoped they were in good condition for the climb.

The lowest terrace was already filling up with people, mainly local young men in rakish straw hats, square steel sunspecs and California-cut clothes. Mrs. Chandri snorted. Uncivilised, she called them, so-called students climbing all over her sacred shrine like a pack of monkeys chasing coconuts, Indonesians for sure. Her nostrils flared out in contempt. "You know what's wrong with them," Hugo whispered to the girl, "they're not Hindus, not even Buddhists. They're Muslims. In a Buddhist sanctuary. The very idea disgusts, their very touch total desecration." Manifest in the structure of these stupas was the law of Karma, the whole of Buddhist cosmology, Mrs. Chandri was reciting, her strong black eyebrows beetling as yet another bus released its load of screaming students down below. "A tranquil atmosphere," she snorted, "it is vital to the world of meditation. Instead of all this pagan revelry, agh! Vexing, very, yes indeed!" and went on to elucidate the one thousand four hundred and sixty scenes before them. Hugo sighed, almost imperceptibly but the girl noticed; Mrs. Chandri, spitting all about her, had not. He fretted at the tale of the princess with the beautiful bull, fidgeted all through the legend of Siva, but Mrs. Chandri carried on regardless. "Now we come to the reincarnation of the bodhis-attwa," she was moving on, "and the life-story of Buddha Gautama. Ah, and now to Queen Maya who dreams that a white elephant has entered her womb. There she is, the Queen. Do you see her standing, holding the branch of a tree to give birth to a son? Yes, and here the daughter of Mara is attempting to seduce the bodhisattwa with lustful dances and female allurements." For a moment Hugo gave her his attention, but desisted, disappointed, as she added, "All in vain." He smirked as she whipped past the frieze with the bare-breasted goddesses, had hoped, he said, to hear from Mrs. Chandri the secrets of Indian erotic art: a sug-gestion Mrs. Chandri amiably evaded leaving him to sneer again at what he styled the gap in her enlightenment, her flawed sophistication. Insincere once more, the girl noted in silence, for the sneer was aimed at something else, something written in his eyes if only you could read it. But, as before, she could not. It was a relief when it was over, Hugo thanking Mrs. Chandri for her efforts and erudite explanations. "The way to Nirvana," he said with fake gratitude, "is laborious and long, but in the end we made it, Madam, no?" Whereupon Mrs. Chandri mopped her cheeks and smiled with gratification.

Back at the hotel, they found the student waiting. "The Solo Family, Sir," he greeted them, "very strong stuff, Sir, much action, very much blood. Such strong stuff you find not in the West, not Starsky, not Hutch, not Kojak. The Solo Family, Sir, you like?" Mrs. Chandri frowned. Hugo, willfully ignoring her, replied, "Yes, we like, tomorrow morning early, and we like it prompt!" But the student reappreared that very evening. "To take you to my home, to the Horse Trance Dance," he said, holding out another of his tatty yellowed hand-outs. A quick consult, suggested Mrs. Chandri, would not be out of place. She had not changed for dinner, she wished to point out, was still in her sweat-stained sari — just a cheap one, you see, suitable for travel but for nothing more formal — and was altogether somewhat soiled from the day's endeavours, so begged to be excused. They must manage without her. The spectacle of the divinities that decorate the holy shrines had been rewarding, yes, of course, but felt she must deprive herself of more. "I retire to my room," she smiled. "I must say I miss it that there is no mosquito net — on account of the air-conditioning probably — so trust you two take your malarial pills." She gave another look at the tatty yellowed hand-out. "A kind of wayside circus," she suggested. "They eat chalk, ground glass and other tidbits. So a bit of a bore. Also as my stomach is not strong what with the dust and lava, so I shall not go. But you two, you who are so insatiable . . ." Hugo made her one of his enchanting European bows. "All she means by that," he said inside the student's limousine at last, "is that we're not too choosey. And that she's a snob. Is cognisant and contemptuous of what we are about to witness, disdains any culture closer to the archetypal than her own. So you have been warned, we are slipping, falling low. Not so? Ach, these Indian intellectuals with their cultivation and their culture." The girl could not but agree. Where Mrs. Chandri came from, people died like flies. "And the survivors?" Hugo sneered, "wash away their sins, no, in what is it they call it?" "The Holy Ganges," she suggested. "Holy, yes, wholly unsanitary — you allow me that I pun — so she suffers from a sensitive stomach. Despite which she supports the squalor of Calcutta, the beggars and the cholera, the rotting limbs and lopped-off legs, the sickness and starvation, the streets strewn with moribundi and the decomposing head. And yet, one whiff of old ape in her nostrils and she is all aquiver, she languishes, mein gott! Devils are disgusting. And decadents are not?" This time the sneer stretched out his face into a sardonic mask. "Ach, these high-

caste, high-strung Hindus," he was still denouncing, "best that
we forget them, better we go back, back to the morning whence
we all are sprung." He subsided after that, strangely silent
yet exalted, muttering still "The Myth," then "the myth of the
morning of the world, the ceremony you are soon to see."

Outside the Kraton the arriving tourists were welcomed by a
dowager dressed in a sarong kebaya richly hung with gold. There
was gold, too, inlaid in her smile. "His mother," Hugo whispered.
The student bowed them past her into an inner courtyard surrounded by high walls and paved in trodden mud, two stunted trees the
only vegetation. Inspecting, Hugo's eyebrows contracted in the
faintest of faint frowns. The student saw and stiffened. "The
Sultan," he said proudly, "commands his dancers still." "But naturally," Hugo smiled back, "and this is them, this family in all
its generations?" He pointed to the furthest corner of the courtyard where a troupe of ragged actors crowded under one of the
two stricken trees. "A circus, mused the girl, just as Mrs.
Chandri had predicted, low-class, lean and mangy, the youngest a
mere infant scratching at her sores. A small man with a whip
and clean white cotton gloves swaggered back and forth among
them pulling on a king-size cigarette. He wore a long-sleeved
red silk shirt, although the rest wore rags, odd unmatching items
of western wear pulled on over drab sarongs. "Aboriginals,"
exclaimed the Dutchwoman sitting next to them. She was breathing
heavily inside her floral frock, fat, embarrassed by the heat.
"Brutish, blunted creatures," she was gasping, "misérables, ach
mein gott!" "Look over there," Hugo interrupted, "look at her
legs!" A bare bulb had lit up under one tree trapping in its
light a woman with long livid scars bitten deep into her flesh.
"They're leper marks," said Hugo. The Dutchwoman looked, then
noting his excitement, pursed her mouth in disapproval. "Misérables," she repeated. "The Solo Family," a voice invisible announced. A second light switched on, catching the actors' upturned faces, vicious, rouged, and caked with powdered rice.
"Welcome visitors," the voice croaked again. "Welcome and please
to be seated." Hugo, though she nudged him, rose at once and
craned his neck to get a better view. He needed to be nearer,
he was saying urgently, much much nearer. The voice came on
again, and monotonous, insistent, "Visitors please to be seated.
Please to observe the menu. Broken glass, crushed coconuts,
and yams." The toddler in the frilly frock, one hand clutching a

367

pair of fancy nylon knickers, while the other held a tray of glass, coconut, and yams. A bamboo mask in the centre was held on high by the small man with the whip for all to see. "The Horse!" Hugo cried hoarsely, rising to his feet. "Visitors, please to be seated," the voice intoned again. The small man with the whip was showing off the mask, demonstrating how its mobile mouth could clack and grind as well as grin. A family of gum-chewing Americans clacked back. The horsehead grinned. As their cameras started clicking the small man obligingly moved forward and stepped beneath the light. It dripped like ketchup down his shiny shirt, glancing off his square steel sunspecs, his stainless Hong Kong watch, onto one white-gloved hand that now gave the signal to start. At which the lady with the leper marks came forward, chanting to the beat of kettle drums. She knelt next to the man. "Incantation!" cried the overheated Dutchwoman, as the leper lady lit a candle over a low altar. "She's the Chief Enchantress. She's invoking evil, and that's the sacrificial flame! Evil, I can sense it, I can feel it. Evil, I tell you, I smell evil everywhere!"

Next, four cobra-headed women, carmine lipped and wrapped in dull sarongs, clattered round the small man on their horseheads. The small man raised his whip. It came down with a crack like steel springs snapping, catching them over the eyes, the neck then lips. A shiver rippled through the audience. "No danger to onlookers," the hidden voice assured. The tourists shifted in their seats, embarrassed and uneasy nonetheless, all except for Hugo who, the girl noticed with a shudder, was salivating endlessly, sucking in his lips. "This is it," she heard him slobber, "the authentic archetypal myth. In the original. Undiluted, unadulterated, unabridged." And next thing had moved off, half-crawling, half-crouching between chairs, encumbered with his camera gear. Out there in front the whipmaster laid on, lashing out relentlessly at the women on their bamboo steeds, till rewarded by a chorus of shrill, horse-simulated neighs. The audience grew tenser. "Angry ape, lay off!" cried an American at the back. The disembodied voice came back on the air. "No danger to onlookers. The Kuda Kudang is performed by the Solo dancers frequently." By now a little monkey man had replaced the women on the horseheads. He stood in the centre underneath the light, jaw muscles exerted, masticating tidbits fed to him from off the toddler's tray. As he ate, the whip came stinging down across

his back, his eyes, and lips. The blood began to trickle. He
licked it off, voracious, gulped it down together with the vic-
tuals. "Bon appetit," the Dutchwoman said, "mein gott, he is insatiable. Like an insect. Look, he munches, munch, munch, he
must have mandibles." The Chief Enchantress now took up the whip
and the monkey man grovelled on the ground before her lapping
up the morsels that she tossed him. "Enough!" the American at
the back began to shout, "you angry ape you, it's been enough!"
"Stop them, then," the Dutchwoman screamed back. "Why do we let
them? Why do we? It's all abacadabra, primitive propitiation,
peace-offerings to their private gods. . . ." And seemed about
to swoon when a voice like velvet intervened. "And which of all
their gorgeous gods," it crooned, "would they be propitiating,
Madame?" It was Hugo, briefly back beside them, camera still
clicking. He was sneering still. "No, Madame," he went on
sneering, "no propitiation. What you have before you here is
Shamanism, second century syncretism in its authentic, undiluted
unadulterated state." To demonstrate, he licked his lips in
imitation of the little monkey-man. "Satanism!" the Dutchwoman
hissed back, but Hugo had already left, camera aimed into the
air. He had started shooting madly, like a creature driven.
The girl started to shiver. If the Dutchwoman was right, if that
was what he was plugged into, she had never noticed, not till
now. Yet he – she saw it straightaway – had known all along.
After that she lost him all but for a second when it seemed he
might be signalling, trying to say something that she knew could
not be said. Yet the substance of the message came over, that
this was it, the thing he had been searching for and known he
would find. Had known all along, she had to tell herself again.

"Her turn now," shouted the Dutchwoman as the Chief Enchantress returned amounted on a horsehead too. The small man raised
his whip. When he brought it down across her face the saliva
oozed, red and runny, glittered on the ground in a pool of blood,
mud, and spittle that spread. Her sunspecs fell into the pool and
splintered. She laughed and trampling them underfoot, turned a
blood-smeared smile on her tormentor, laughing all the time.
"More!" the Dutchwoman cried, "She still wants more!" The American at the back called back, "Decadent, disgusting, it's enough!
The woman's drooling with delight." The girl looked round for
Hugo. What of him, and of his second century syncretism now.
She could hear his camera out there, shooting insatiably, turning

369

reels and reels of the revolting stuff. Camera-drunk, she thought, or crazy. "Scandalous," the Dutchwoman said, mopping her empurpled cheeks. The American answered, chewing like his kids on their everlasting gum. "It sure makes me sick," he called over, "but not him. Would you have a look at him!" It was Hugo he was pointing to, Hugo in a golden sweat, his eyes and hair aglitter, Hugo stockstill and enraptured watching the leper lady dance across hot coals into final trance. "Bravo, the show is over!" the Dutchwoman cried. "Finito la commedia, what a charming family ach mein gott!" She took out a cigarette. The American came over with a light. "So that was it," he said, hands trembling, "Me, you, all of us, the whole of mankind! Wasn't that the morale, I mean . . . Man's no more than an angry ape?"

"Angry apes!" Hugo exploded inside the student's car. "They didn't like it, uh?" The girl remained silent. "One little whiff of old ape in the nostrils, and modern man feels worthless, no? Yes, even you. You lost your sense of self-worth too." Now, the girl thought, it's now or never, now it must be said. Up till now he had not understood but now for once he should. The difference between direct and downright, he should have it now. "No," she answered, "nothing lost. And nothing gained." "Then what?" he said. "Disgusted, maybe?" "Disgusting, yes," she spoke slowly, "sheer sadism they said, a show of squalid sadism, that's what." "Shamanism," he corrected her, "and permit me that I undeceive you – it was self-disgust. How so? Allow me, I explain." He paused to moisten his lips. "Yes, we will take it back, first to the ancient myth, the myth of the morning of the world, we shall call it, yes? A mirror is held up to man in which, caught up in the myth, he sees himself distorted. Yes, in the mirror of myth man sees himself and discovers there a crack. The crack to his own image. Flawed, no longer faultless he finds he cannot take himself, cannot bear his own imperfections. So what to do? He has to escape himself, to sidestep despair, avoid the scourge of self-abusement. Yes, man must save himself from dissolution. To this end he resorts to self-disgust, yes that is it. I trust you like my explanation." Again the girl said nothing. The need to be articulate had left her. "No? You don't?" Hugo shrugged away her silence. "Nor did Mrs. Chandri. Spurned alas, so what to do?" "Spurn it too," she answered in a whisper. He heard her with a sneer. "On the contrary my darling, my plan is to espouse it. That, you see, is why I'm here. To make myself its master."

"Magicmaster of the West," the girl said. It was her turn to
sneer. "What can that give, ever?" "Once I have possessed myself
of it? Ach, but no end of valuable things," he said. "The power
to put people into trance, the power over personality. What cannot one do with a power as strong as that? Change the soul of
modern man, cure him of the sickness of his sick society. Yes,
that is it, cure the sick, empty the souls of the self-spurning,
charge them with a stronger, clearer spirit, that is what still
must be done, not that enough? No. You are still skeptical. Alas,
downright was better." For the girl, as he started glittering
all over again, had shrunk from him in horror. "No," she moaned,
"oh no, not you, not that, ever." "But why not me," he retorted,
"when what I offer is the same as peddled by your own head-
shrinkers, the Shamanists of the West that some call shams. You
appreciate it how I pun, I hope, in my so excellent English."

When they got back to the hotel there was a note from Mrs.
Chandri which Hugo read aloud. She had found a better hotel,
also cheaper, not so many big soft towels nor much modernity but
had a mousquetaire, a Dutch device, not unlike an aviary. "Or
maybe she means a monkey-cage," said Hugo once more subsiding
into sneers. "We are invited to inspect this singular equipment?
Come, I invite you to the pool instead." She went back to her
room to change, and sighting the ice-cold bed, flopped down and
fell asleep, and dreamed. In the dream she recognised the sequel
to the myth. They were in the pool, she and Hugo and the family
from Solo. She could hear them chanting and the beating of their
kettle drums. He was happy to be back with them, she knew, for
he had started laughing, a laughter that came muffled through the
water like the clacking of the horsehead masks. Suddenly he
turned to her in solemn earnest. The magic, he was saying, he
would try it out on her. He would bring her into trance, empty
out her soul, charge her with a clearer, stronger spirit, yes,
he would touch her finally with death and dissolution. . . . She
woke up screaming. She had been deep down behind his eyes and
had seen a hunger that she knew she could not satisfy, that no
one on this earth would ever satisfy, because it was, in truth,
insatiable. She had read it in his eyes at last. She rose and
had to retch. After, she went over to the window. Down below
the gods stared stony, grave, grinning still into the glass-green
pool. There was something there, something long and green floating near the bottom, an inflated plastic pillow, at first she

371

reckoned, but saw it was a man and screamed again. Then, without waiting to see if it surfaced, she began to run and kept on running till she reached Mrs. Chandri's cheap hotel, and had secured herself with her inside her cage. Mrs. Chandri rubbed her eyes at the intrusion. "What is this? Mosquitoes, eh?" She was crumpled, sleeping still in her soiled sari. "But no, a visitor? Indeed. How nice. Please be seated, tell me how your evening was, enjoyable, I trust." The girl tried to tell her, holding back the worst, but even as she spoke she saw that Mrs. Chandri's eyes were closing. Mrs. Chandri had dozed off. Asleep, the girl thought, she looks less friendly, less familiar, just a creature of the East. How should she mean anything to her, she thought, who I am, what I'm after, why I'm here. . . . "What kind of world are you looking for?" Hugo's question. It hit her suddenly again. What sort of world was she looking for? Here she was, fumbling to find it still, it hardly mattered where, though was it wise, she wondered to seek it in the East? Or in the West for that matter. Had she not had what could be expected of the West, and had she not, before she met with worse, best turn back?

Outside she caught a taxi on its way back to the big hotel. At the turning to Solo it overtook a lorry where she spotted a straw-haired figure curled up inside. It reminded her of something, some Dutch doll she had disliked. All but for the mouth, a red-painted mobile mouth masked in a familiar horse-like sneer. When she pondered it in passing, she saw she was mistaken. There was no mask, no horse-like sneer: no, no, nothing but a horse-trance smile and one that was no longer simulated.

CLARICE LISPECTOR

THE SMALLEST WOMAN IN THE WORLD

In the depths of equatorial Africa the French explorer, Marcel Pretre, hunter and man of the world, came across a tribe of pygmies of surprising minuteness. He was even more suprised, however, to learn that an even smaller race existed far beyond the forests. So he traveled more deeply into the jungle.

In the Central Congo he discovered, in fact, the smallest pygmies in the world. And — like a box inside another box, inside yet another box — among the smallest pygmies in the world, answering, perhaps to the need that Nature sometimes feels to surpass herself.

Among the mosquitoes and the trees moist with humidity, among the luxuriant vegetation of the most indolent green, Marcel Pretre came face to face with a woman no more than forty—five centimeters tall, mature, black, and silent. "As black as a monkey," he would inform the newspapers, and she lived at the top of a tree with her little mate. In the warm humidity of the forest, which matured the fruits quickly and gave them an unbearably sweet taste, she was pregnant. Meanwhile there she stood, the smallest woman in the world. For a second, in the drone of the jungle heat, it was as if the Franchman had unexpectedly arrived at the end of the line. Certainly, it was only because he was sane that he managed to keep his head and not lose control. Sensing a sudden need to restore order, and to give a name to what exists, he called her Little Flower. And, in order to be able to classify her among the identifiable realities, he immediately began to gather data about her.

Her race is slowly being exterminated. Few human examples remain of their species which, were it not for the subtle dangers of Africa, would be a widely scattered race.

Excluding disease, the polluted air of its rivers, deficiencies of food, and wild beasts on the prowl, the greatest hazard for the few remaining Likoualas are the savage Bantus, a threat which sur—rounds them in the silent air as on the morning of battle. The Bantus pursue them with nets as they pursue monkeys. And they eat them. Just like that: they pursue them with nets and they eat them. So this race of tiny people went on retreating and retreating until it finally settled in the heart of Africa where the fortunate explorer was to discover them. As a strategic defense, they live in the highest trees. The women come down in order to cook maize, grind mandioca, and gather green vegetables; the men to hunt. When a child is born, he is given his freedom almost at once. Often, one must concede, the child does not enjoy his freedom for long among the wild beasts of the jungle, but, at least he cannot complain that for such a short life the labor has been long. Even the language that the child learns is short and simple, consisting only of the essentials. The Likoualas use few names and they refer to things by gestures and animal noises. As a spiritual enhancement, he possesses his drum. While they dance to the sound of the drum, a tiny male keeps watch for the Bantus, who appear from heaven knows where.

This, then, was how the explorer discovered at his feet the smallest human creature that exists. His heart pounded, for surely no emerald is so rare. Not even the teaching of the Indian sages are so rare, and even the richest man in the world has not witnessed such strange charm. There, before his eyes, stood a woman such as the delights of the most exquisite dream had never equaled. It was then that the explorer timidly pronounced with a delicacy of feeling of which even his wife would never have believed him capable, "You are Little Flower."

At that moment, Little Flower scratched herself where one never scratches oneself. The explorer – as if he were receiving the highest prize of chastity to which man, always so full of ideals, dare aspire – the explorer who has so much experience of life, turned away his eyes.

The photograph of Little Flower was published in the color supplement of the Sunday newspapers, where whe was reproduced life size. She appeared wrapped in a shawl, with her belly in an advanced stage. Her nose was flat, her face black, her eyes deep-set, and her feet splayed. She looked just like a dog.

That same Sunday, in an apartment, a woman, glancing at the picture of Little Flower in the open newspaper, did not care to look a second time, "because it distresses me."

In another apartment, a woman felt such a perverse tenderness for the daintiness of the African woman that – prevention being better than cure – Little Flower should never be left alone with the tenderness of that woman. Who knows to what darkness of love her affection might extend. The woman passed a troubled day, overcome, one might say, by desire. Besides, it was spring and there was a dangerous longing in the air.

In another house, a little five-year-old girl, upon seeing Little Flower's picture and listening to the comments of her parents, became frightened. In that house of adults, this little girl had been, until now, the smallest of human beings. And, if this was the source of the nicest endearments, it was also the source of that first fear of tyrannical love. The existence of Little Flower caused the little girl to feel — with a vagueness which only many years later, and, for quite different reasons, she was to experience as a concrete thought — caused her to feel with premature awareness, that "misfortune knows no limits."

In another house, the consecration of spring, a young girl about to be married burst out compassionately, "Mother, look at her picture, poor little thing! Just look at her sad expression!"

"Yes," replied the girl's mother — hard, defeated, and proud — "but that is the sadness of an animal, not of a human."

"Oh Mother!" the girl protested in despair.

It was in another house that a bright child had a bright idea.

"Mummy, what if I were to put this tiny woman in little Paul's bed while he is sleeping? When he wakes up, what a fright he'll get, eh? What a din he'll make when he finds her sitting up in bed beside him! And then we could play with her! We could make her our toy, eh!"

His mother, at that moment, was rolling her hair in front of the bathroom mirror, and she remembered what the cook had told her about her time as an orphan. Not having any dolls to play with, and maternal feelings already stirring furiously in their hearts, some deceitful girls in the orphanage had concealed from the nun in charge the death of one of their companions. They kept her body in a cupboard until Sister went out, and then they played with the dead girl, bathing her and feeding her little tidbits, and they punished her only to be able to kiss and comfort her afterward.

The mother recalled this in the bathroom and she lowered her awkward hands, full of hairpins. And she considered the cruel necessity of loving. She considered the malignity of our desire to be happy. She considered the ferocity with which we want to play. And the number of times when we murder for love. She then looked at her mischievous son as if she were looking at a dangerous stranger. And she was horrified at her own soul, which, more than her body, had engendered that being so apt for life and hap-

piness. And thus she looked at him, attentively and with uneasy
pride, her child already without two front teech, his evolution
under way, his teeth falling out to make room for those which
bite best. "I must buy him a new suit," she decided, looking at
him intently. She obstinately dressed up her toothless child in
fancy clothes, and obstinately insisted upon keeping him clean
and tidy, as if cleanliness might give emphasis to a tranquilizing
superficiality, obstinately perfecting the polite aspect of beauty.
Obstinately removing herself, and removing him from something
which must be as "black as a monkey." Then, looking into the bathroom mirror, the mother smiled, intentionally refined and polished,
placing between that face of hers of abstract lines and the raw
face of Little Flower, the insuperable distance of millenia. But
with years of experience she knew that this would be a Sunday on
which whe would have to conceal from herself her anxiety, her
dream, and the lost millenia.

In another house, against a wall, they set about the exciting
business of calculating with a measuring tape the forty-five centimeters of Little Flower. And as they enjoyed themselves they
made a startling discovery: she was even smaller than the most
penetrating imagination could ever have invented. In the heart
of each member of the family there arose the gnawing desire to
possess that minute and indomitable thing for himself, that thing
which had been saved from being devoured, that enduring fount of
charity. The eager soul of that family was roused to dedication.
And, indeed, who has not wanted to possess a human being just
for himself? A thing, it is true, which would not always be
convenient, for there are moments when one would choose not to
have sentiments.

"I'll bet you if she lived here we would finish up quarreling,"
said the father, seated in his armchair, firmly turning the pages
of the newspaper. "In this house everything finishes up with a
quarrel."

"You are always such a pessimist, José," said the mother.

"Mother, can you imagine how tiny her little child will be?"
their oldest girl, thirteen, asked intensely.

The father fidgeted behind his newspaper.

"It must be the smallest black baby in the world," replied
the mother, melting with pleasure. "Just imagine her waiting on
table here in the house! And with her swollen little belly."

"That's enough of that rubbish!" muttered the father, annoyed.

"You must admit," said the mother, unexpectedly peeved, "that
the thing is unique. You are the one who is insensitive."

And what about the unique thing itself?

Meanwhile, in Africa, the unique thing itself felt in its heart – perhaps also black, because one can no longer have confidence in a Nature that has already blundered once – meanwhile the unique thing itself felt in its heart something still more rare, rather like the secret of its own secret: a minute child. Methodically, the explorer examined with his gaze the belly of the smallest mature human being. It was at that moment that the explorer, for the first time since he had known her – instead of experiencing curiosity, enthusiasm, a sense of triumph, or the excitement of discovery – felt distinctly ill at ease.

The fact is that the smallest woman in the world was smiling. She was smiling and warm, warm. Little Flower was enjoying herself. The unique thing itself was enjoying the ineffable sensation of not having been devoured yet. Not to have been devoured was something which at other times gave her the sudden impulse to leap from branch to branch. But at this tranquil moment, among the dense undergrowth of the Central Congo, she was not applying that impulse to an action – and the impulse concentrated itself completely in the very smallness of the unique thing itself. And suddenly she was smiling. It was a smile that only someone who does not speak can smile. A smile that the uncomfortable explorer did not succeed in classifying. And she went on enjoying her own gentle smile, she who was not being devoured. Not to be devoured is the secret objective of a whole existence. While she was not being devoured, her animal smile was as delicate as happiness. The explorer felt disconcerted.

In the second place, if the unique thing itself was smiling it was because, inside her minute body, a great darkness had started to stir.

It is that the unique thing itself felt her breast warm with that which might be called love. She loved that yellow explorer. If she knew how to speak and should say that she loved him, he would swell with pride. Pride that would diminish when she should add that she also adored the explorer's ring and his boots. And when he became deflated with disappointment, Little Flower would fail to understand. Because, not even remotely, would her love for the explorer   one can even say her "deep love," because without other resources she was reduced to depth – since not even remotely would her deep love for the explorer lose its value because she also loved his boots. There is an old misunderstanding about the word "love," and if many children are born on account of that mistake, many others have lost the unique instant of birth simply on account of a susceptibility which exacts that it should be me, me that should beloved and not my money. But in the humidity of the jungle, there do not exist these cruel refinements; love is not to be devoured, love is to find boots pretty, love is to like the strange color of a man who is not black, love is to smile out of love at a ring that shines. Little Flower blinked with love and and smiled, warm, small, pregnant, and warm.

The explorer tried to smile back at her, without knowing exactly to which charm his smile was replying, and then became disturbed as only a full-grown man becomes disturbed. He tried to conceal his uneasiness, by adjusting his helmet on his head, and he blushed with embarrassment. He turned a pretty color, his own, greenish pink hue, like that of a lime in the morning light. He must be sour.

It was probably upon adjusting his symbolic helmet that the explorer called himself to order, returned severely to the discipline of work, and resumed taking notes. He had learned to understand some of the few words articulated by the tribe and to interpret their signs. He was already able to ask questions.

Little Flower answered "yes." That it was very nice to have a tree in which to live by herself, all by herself. Because — and this she did not say, but her eyes became so dark that they said it — because it is nice to possess, so nice to possess. The explorer blinked several times.

Marcel Pretre experienced a few difficult moments trying to control himself. But at least he kept occupied in taking notes. Anyone not taking notes had to get along as best he could.

"Well, it just goes to show," an old woman suddenly exclaimed, folding her newspaper with determination, "it just goes to show. I'll say one thing though — God knows what He's about."

CLARICE LISPECTOR

THE DAYDREAMS OF A DRUNK WOMAN

It seemed to her that the trolley cars were about to cross through the room as they caused her reflected image to tremble. She was combing her hair at her leisure in front of the dressing table with its three mirrors, and her strong white arms shivered in the coolness of the evening. Her eyes did not look away as the mirrors trembled, sometimes dark, sometimes luminous. Outside, from a window above, something heavy and hollow fell to the ground. Had her husband and the little ones been at home, the idea would already have occurred to her that they were to blame. Her eyes did not take themselves off her image, her comb worked pensively, and her open dressing gown revealed in the mirrors the intersected breasts of several women.

"Evening News" shouted the newsboy to the mild breeze in Riachuelo Street, and something trembled as if foretold. She threw her comb down on the dressing table and sang dreamily: "Who saw the little spar—row . . . it passed by the window . . . and flew beyond Minho!" – but, suddenly becoming irritated, she shut up abruptly like a fan.

She lay down and fanned herself impatiently with a newspaper that rustled in the room. She clutched the bedsheet, inhaling its odor as she crushed its starched embroidery with her red—lacquered nails. Then, almost smiling, she started to fan her—self once more. Oh my! – she sighed as she began to smile. She beheld the picture of her bright smile, the smile of a woman who was still young, and she continued to smile to herself, closing her eyes and fanning herself still more vigorously. Oh my! – she would come fluttering in from the street like a butterfly.

"Hey there! Guess who came to see me today?" she mused as a feasible and interesting topic of conversation. "No idea, tell me," those eyes asked her with a gallant smile, those sad eyes set in one of those pale faces that make one feel so uncomfort—able. "Maria Quiteria, my dear!" she replied coquettishly with her hand on her hip. "And who, might we ask, would she be?" they insisted gallantly, but now without any expression. "You!" she broke off, slightly annoyed. How boring!

Oh what a succulent room! Here she was, fanning herself in
Brazil. The sun, trapped in the blinds, shimmered on the wall
like the strings of a guitar. Riachuelo Street shook under the
gasping weight of the trolley cars which came from Mem de Sá
Street. Curious and impatient, she listened to the vibrations
of the china cabinet in the drawing room. Impatiently she rolled
over to lie face downward, and, sensuously stretching the toes
of her dainty feet, she awaited her next thought with open eyes.
"Whosoever found, searched," she said to herself in the form of
a rhymed refrain, which always ended up by sounding like some
maxim. Until eventually she fell asleep with her mouth wide open,
her saliva staining the pillow.

She only woke up when her husband came into the room the
moment he returned from work. She did not want to eat any dinner
nor to abandon her dreams, and she went back to sleep: let him
content himself with the leftovers from lunch.

And now that the kids were at the country house of their
aunts in Jacarepaguá, she took advantage of their absence in
order to begin the day as she pleased: restless and frivolous in
her bed . . . one of those whims perhaps. Her husband appeared
before her, having already dressed, and she did not even know
what he had prepared for his breakfast. She avoided examining
his suit to see whether it needed brushing . . . little did she
care if this was his day for attending to his business in the
city. But when he bent over to kiss her, her capriciousness
crackled like a dry leaf.

"Dont paw me!"

"What the devil's the matter with you?" the man asked her in
amazement, as he immediately set about attempting some more
effective caress.

Obstinate, she would not have known what to reply, and she
felt so touchy and aloof that she did not even know where to
find a suitable reply. She suddenly lost her temper. "Go to hell!
. . . prowling round me like some old tomcat."

He seemed to think more clearly and said, firmly, "You're
ill, my girl."

She accepted his remark, surprised, and vaguely flattered.

She remained in bed the whole day long listening to the
silence of the house without the scurrying of the kids, without
her husband who would have his meals in the city today. Her
anger was tenuous and ardent. She only got up to go to the
bathroom, from which she returned haughty and offended.

The morning turned into a long enormous afternoon, which
then turned into a shallow night, which innocently dawned throughout the entire house.

She was still in bed, peaceful and casual. She was in love
. . . . She was anticipating her love for the man whom she would
love one day. Who knows, this sometimes, happened, and without
any guilt or injury for either partner. Lying in bed thinking
and thinking, and almost laughing as one does over some gossip.
Thinking and thinking. About what? As if she knew. So she just
stayed there.

The next minute she would get up, angry. But in the weakness
of that first instant she felt dizzy and fragile in the room
which swam round and round until she managed to grope her way
back to bed, amazed that it might be true. "Hey, girl, don't you
go getting sick on me!" she muttered suspiciously. She raised
her hand to her forehead to see if there was any fever.

That night, until she fell asleep, her mind became more and
more delirious — for how many minutes? — until she flopped over,
fast asleep, to snore beside her husband.

She awoke late, the potatoes waiting to be peeled, the kids
expected home that same evening from their visit to the country.
"God, I've lost my self-respect, I have! My day for washing and
darning socks . . . . What a lazy bitch you've turned out to be!"
she scolded herself, inquisitive and pleased . . . shopping to
be done, fish to remember, already so late on a hectic sunny
morning.

But on Saturday night they went to the tavern in Tiradentes
Square at the invitation of a rich businessman, she with her new
dress which didn't have any fancy trimmings but was made of good
material, a dress that would last her a lifetime. On Saturday
night, drunk in Tiradentes Square, inebriated but with her husband at her side to give her support, and being very polite in
front of the other man who was so much more refined and rich —
striving to make conversation, for she was no provincial ninny
and she had already experienced life in the capital. But so
drunk that she could no longer stand.

And if her husband was not drunk it was only because he did
not want to show disrespect for the businessman, and, full of
solicitude and humility, he left the swaggering to the other
fellow. His manner suited such an elegant occasion, but it gave
her such an urge to laugh! She despised him beyond words! She
looked at her husband stuffed into his new suit and found him so
ridiculous! . . . so drunk that she could no longer stand, but

without losing her self-respect as a woman. And the green wine from her native Portugal slowly being drained from her glass.

When she got drunk, as if she had eaten a heavy Sunday lunch, all things which by their true nature are separate from each other — the smell of oil on the one hand, of a male on the other; the soup tureen on the one hand, the waiter on the other — became strangely linked by their true nature and the whole thing was nothing short of disgraceful . . . shocking!

And if her eyes appeared brilliant and cold, if her movements faltered clumsily until she succeeded in reaching the toothpick holder, beneath the surface she really felt so far quite at ease . . . there was that full cloud to transport her without effort. Her puffy lips, her teeth white, and her body swollen with wine. And the vanity of feeling drunk, making her show such disdain for everything, making her feel swollen and rotund like a large cow.

Naturally she talked, since she lacked neither the ability to converse nor topics to discuss. But the words that a woman uttered when drunk were like being pregnant — mere words on her lips which had nothing to do with the secret core that seemed like a pregnancy. God, how queer she felt! Saturday night, her every-day soul lost, and how satisfying to lose it, and to remind her of former days, only her small, ill-kempt hands — and here she was now with her elbows resting on the white and red checked tablecloth like a gambling table, deeply launched upon a degrading and revolting existence. And what about her laughter? . . . this outburst of laughter which mysteriously emerged from her full white throat, in response to the polite manners of the businessman, an outburst of laughter coming from the depths of that sleep, and from the depths of that security of someone who has a body. Her white flesh was as sweet as lobster, the legs of a live lobster wriggling slowly in the air . . . that urge to be sick in order to plunge that sweetness into something really awful . . . and that perversity of someone who has a body.

She talked and listened with curiosity to what she herself was about to reply to the well-to-do businessman who had so kindly invited them out to dinner and paid for their meal. Intrigued and amazed, she heard what she was on the point of replying, and what she might say in her present state would serve as an augury for the future. She was no longer a lobster, but a harsher sign — that of the scorpion. After all, she had been born in November.

A beacon that sweeps through the dawn while one is asleep, such was her drunkenness which floated slowly through the air.

At the same time, she was conscious of such feelings! Such
feelings! When she gazed upon that picture which was so beautifully painted in the restaurant, she was immediately overcome by
an artistic sensibility. No one would get it out of her head
that she had really been born for greater things. She had always
been one for works of art.

But such sensibility! And not merely excited by the picture
of grapes and pears and dead fish with shining scales. Her sensibility irritated her without causing her pain, like a broken
fingernail. And if she wanted, she could allow herself the luxury
of becoming even more sensitive, she could go still further,
because she was protected by a situation, protected like everyone
who had attained a position in life. Like someone saved from
misfortune. I'm so miserable, dear God! If she wished, she
could even pour more wine into her glass, and, protected by the
position which she had attained in life, become even more drunk
just so long as she did not lose her self-respect. And so, even
more drunk, she peered round the room, and how she despised the
barren people in that restaurant, while she was plump and heavy
and generous to the full. And everything in the restaurant seemed
so remote, the one thing distant from the other, as if the one
might never be able to converse with the other. Each existing
for itself, and God existing there for everyone.

Her eyes once more settled on that female whom she had instantly detested the moment she had entered the room. Upon
arriving, she had spotted her seated at a table accompanied by a
man and all dolled up in a hat and jewelry, glittering like a
false coin, all coy and refined. What a fine hat she was wearing!
. . . Bet you anything she isn't even married for all this pious
look on her face . . . and that fine hat stuck on her head. A
fat lot of good her hypocrisy would do her, and she had better
watch out in case her airs and graces proved her undoing! The
more sanctimonious they were, the bigger frauds they turned out
to be. And as for the waiter, he was a great nitwit, serving
her, full of gestures and finesse, while the sallow man with her
pretended not to notice. And that pious ninny so pleased with
herself in that hat and so modest about her slim waistline, and
I'll bet she couldn't even bear her man a child. All right, it
was none of her business, but from the moment she arrived she
felt the urge to give that blonde prude of a woman playing the
grand lady in her hat a few good slaps on the face. She didn't
even have any shape, and she was flat-chested. And no doubt,

383

for all her fine hats, she was nothing more than a fishwife try—
ing to pass herself off as a duchess.

Oh, how humiliated she felt at having come to the bar without
a hat, and her head now felt bare. And that madam with her
affectations, playing the refined lady! I know what you need,
my beauty, you and your sallow boy friend! And if you think I
envy you with your flat chest, let me assure you that I don't
give a damn for you and your hats. Shameless sluts like you are
only asking for a good hard slap on the face.

In her holy rage, she stretched out a shaky hand and reached
for a toothpick.

But finally, the difficulty of arriving home disappeared; she
now bestirred herself amidst the familiar reality of her room,
now seated on the edge of the bed, a slipper dangling from one
foot.

And, as she had half closed her blurred eyes, everything took
on the appearance of flesh, the foot of the bed, the window, the
suit her husband had thrown off, and everything became rather
painful. Meanwhile, she was becoming larger, more unsteady,
swollen and gigantic. If only she could get closer to herself,
she would find she was even larger. Each of her arms could be
explored by someone who didn't even recognize that they were
dealing with an arm, and someone could plunge into each eye and
swim around without knowing that it was an eye. And all around
her everything was a bit painful. Things of the flesh stricken
by nervous twinges. The chilly air had caught her as she had
come out of the restaurant.

She was sitting up in bed, resigned and sceptical. And this
was nothing yet, God only knew — she was perfectly aware that
this was nothing yet. At this moment things were happening to
her that would only hurt later and in earnest. When restored to
her normal size, her anesthetized body would start to wake up,
throbbing, and she would begin to pay for those big meals and
drinks. Then, since this would really end up by happening, I
might as well open my eyes right now (which she did) and then
everything looked smaller and clearer, without her feeling any
pain. Everything, deep down, was the same, only smaller and more
familiar. She was sitting quite upright in bed, her stomach so
full, absorbed and resigned, with the delicacy of one who sits
waiting until her partner awakens. "You gorge yourself and I
pay the piper," she said sadly, looking at the dainty white toes
of her feet. She looked around her, patient and obedient. Ah,

words, nothing but words, the objects in the room lined up in
the order of words, to form those confused and irksome phrases
that he who knows how will read. Boredom . . . such awful boredom . . . . How sickening! How very annoying! When all is said
and done, heaven help me — God knows best. What was one to do?
How can I describe this thing inside me? Anyhow, God knows best.
And to think that she had enjoyed herself so much last night!
. . . and to think of how nice it all was — a restaurant to her
liking — and how she had been seated elegantly at table. At table!
The world would exclaim. But she made no reply, drawing herself
erect with a bad-tempered click of her tongue. . .irritated. . .
"Don't come to me with your endearments" . . . disenchanted,
resigned, satiated, married, content, vaguely nauseated.

It was at this moment that she became deaf: one of her
senses was missing. She clapped the palm of her hand over her
ear, which only made things worse . . . suddenly filling her ear-
drum with the shirr of an elevator . . . life suddenly becoming
loud and magnified in its smallest movements. One of two things:
either she was deaf or hearing all too well. She reacted against
this new suggestion with a sensation of spite and annoyance,
with a sigh of resigned satiety. "Drop dead," she said gently
. . . defeated.

"And when in the restaurant . . ." she suddenly recalled
when she had been in the restaurant her husband's protector had
pressed his foot against hers beneath the table, and above the
table his face was watching her. By coincidence or intentionally?
The rascal. A fellow, to be frank, who was not unattractive. She
shrugged her shoulders.

And when above the roundness of her low-cut dress — right in
the middle of Tiradentes Square! she thought, shaking her head
incredulously — that fly had settled on her bare bosom. What
cheek!

Certain things were good because they were almost nauseating
. . . the noise like that of an elevator in her blood, while her
husband lay snoring at her side . . . her chubby little children
sleeping in the other room, the little villains. Ah, what's wrong
with me! she wondered desperately. Have I eaten too much? Heavens
above! What *is* wrong with me?

It was unhappiness.

Her toes playing with her slipper . . . the floor not too
clean at that spot. "What a slovenly, lazy bitch you've become."

Not tomorrow, because her legs would not be too steady, but
the day after tomorrow that house of hers would be a sight worth

seeing: she would give it a scouring with soap and water which
would get rid of all the dirt! "You mark my words," she threatened
in her rage. Ah, she was feeling so well, so strong, as if she
still had milk in those firm breasts. When her husband's friend
saw her so pretty and plump he had immediately felt respect for
her. And when she started to get embarrassed she did not know
which way to look. Such misery! What was one to do? Seated on
the edge of the bed, blinking in resignation. How well one could
see the moon on these summer nights. She leaned over slightly,
indifferent and resigned. The moon! How clearly one could see
it. The moon high and yellow gliding through the sky, poor thing.
Gliding, gliding . . . high up, high up. The moon! Then her
vulgarity exploded in a sudden outburst of affection; "you
slut," she cried out, laughing.

Translated by Giovanni Pontiero

ANGELINA MUNIZ-HUBERMAN

JOCASTA'S CONFESSION

As he climbed the stairs of the palace, slow, straight, proud
in the certainty of his conquest, I knew that it was he. I did not
doubt it for a moment. His eyes and his mouth reflected my love,
my passion on the night that he was conceived. And I loved him
too: I loved his lithe, young body, the firmness of his muscles,
his sculpted head and perfectly proportioned limbs, like a colt
racing headlong toward the sea. I knew that it was he and yet I
said nothing: the prophecy was sealed. My desire for his body
and his lips, for his smile and the color of his eyes, his smooth,
burnished skin, his hard chest with its light covering of hair,
made me conceal what I ought to have revealed. I would not
reveal his identity, even though I knew his name from the moment
he set foot on that first step, his tense leg displaying the
hardness of his muscles, entering the main door as if the palace
belonged by rights to him, a hero and a liberator. He entered
through the great front door not because he was my son, but
because he had conquered the awful Sphinx. What he deserved by
birth he had won by deed. His pride invaded me doubly. In his
love, I saw the features of Laius, his father, and my own features as well. His love was also double. On that late afternoon,
the sun that was burning the clouds and the sky, reflecting
orange and black on water — river, sea, pond — was also illuminating the slow ascent of the stone stairs, the slow ascent of
someone whom I knew well. And yet I said nothing, as if to
avenge not my weakness but the cruel words of the prophecy, the
lewd voices of the priests, the accusing silence of the people.
Or perhaps it was to avenge my own weakness, which was again
compelling me to accept fate's design, even as I deceived myself
into thinking that I had made the decision. Who holds sway, the
gods or man? I couldn't pray to the gods because I was going to
be impure, but man, the man who slowly climbed the stairs, filled
me to overflowing: he returned to me because he had come out of
me, and I only awaited the moment when two pains — two pleasures
— would unite us again. But my desire was not impure: I wanted
to love both father and son again in one person. In that way, I

would deny the jealousy that I might once have been able to feel and I would have sons again by my own son. Halfway up the stairs, when he hesitated for a moment and when I could still have cried out, I did not encourage his hesitation but bit my tongue instead. He would reach the top of the stairs and I would be delivered to him. My hand in his, he would lead me to the bedroom of his origin and his downfall. He would not recognize me at all for I merely gave birth to him, although at times a certain flash of hatred would cross his eyes, earth—sea—blue. I dreaded the moment when he would speak and question me.

Every day that I said nothing the silence became more and more necessary. The silence was as still as stagnant water. The silence stung like sudden hailstones. The silence sowed doubt and created words which were never spoken. He asked me if I had had a son, he asked me if I had lost him. He asked me if I had wanted someone to die and he asked me what Laius was like. I sensed his jealousy, his despair, and his longing to be loved. His questions came afterwards, after we made love, when we lay beside one another, our bodies touching, our odors mingling, our spent but wondering hands still searching for sensations. I would sometimes forget who he was and would think that happiness would redeem my guilt and that, because I had respected the prophecy when I could have ignored it, I would someday be pardoned by some god. But I knew that I was deceiving myself. I didn't speak because I didn't want to waste our nights – each night, every night, eternity, drop by drop – when his body warmed mine and his arms held me. I had forgotten Laius. I had only hatred for him, the hatred and fear that he himself had felt when his son was born and he had sentenced him, indolently protecting himself by obeying the gods. It was Laius who had brought bad luck: his ignorance and his näiveté made him believe the ironic words of the priests. It was he who invented the prophecy when he saw me gaze with love at our son. So Laius is hidden in the black and forgotten reaches of my memory.

I believe in my son alone, in his unsatisfied and contradictory love, in his penetrating and futile gaze, in his body – statuesque perfection – that recognizes mine and loves me like a true lover, his mouth at my breast, seeking the pleasure that he did not know and that he had despaired of exchanging for the pleasure he is now experiencing. I wanted my milk to flow once again, milk that was never for him.

We have arrived at the point where neither law nor morality exists. I disregard the shadows and the remorse. At dawn, light enters my window, light and the sun. I contemplate his sleeping body, his lips that outline a smile. He is mine, all of him is mine, I possess him as no one ever has or ever will.

The suffering won't matter later. I had expected all of this from the moment that I saw him climbing the stairs, slow and sure. I knew that the river could dry up, that stone could be ground to dust and the color of the petal fade away. I also knew that he would suffer and his memories would torment him. For me, only death remained, and when I was at his side I could do nothing but await the final blow. Step by step up the stairs, night by night on my body, doom prowled, not knowing where to stop, but the wound already open and the blood flowering upon my skin.
Afterward, nothing would remain but chaos and darkness.

Translated by Lois Parkinson Zamora

NORA GLICKMAN

THE JEWISH WHITE SLAVE TRADE IN LATIN AMERICAN WRITINGS

Polaca ("Pole") was the generic name applied to all Jewish prostitutes in Argentina, whether they came from Poland, Russia, or Rumania. Between the 1880's and the early 1930's, a period when the country was undergoing vast waves of predominantly male immigration, the Jewish white slave trade was of great social significance in Argentina. While brothels were licensed, violations of the law were widely tolerated by corrupt officials in the police customs office. As Robert Weisbrot reports, "The lax atmosphere in which this trade flourished was most visible in the theatres, where hundreds of prostitutes nightly patrolled the balconies in search of customers."[1] In consequence of all these factors, white slave traders found Argentina to be quite congenial for their operations.

Despite all the publicity that the phenomenon of Jewish white slavery in Argentina has received, it is still not fully understood. Prostitutes were extremely reluctant to testify, for fear of reprisals from their slavers. The traffickers, for their part, did all in their power to keep their activities secret; and the laws protecting minors against the trade were seldom enforced. Statistical data on Jewish prostitution in Argentina are scant and unreliable.[2]

Since the white slave trade is, by its nature, clandestine, most authors who have written on the subject knew it only by hearsay or were able to gather just enough information to mention it in their stories without shedding any real light on the phenomenon. Some authors who claimed to be writing serious studies of white slavery actually relied mainly on their imagination, but even impressionistic accounts of this kind can sometimes enlighten us about the nature of historical events in ways that history cannot accomplish. Other authors, however, were more concerned with first-hand documentary evidence. Such is the case with Albert Londres and Julio Alsogaray.

Le Chemin de Buenos Aires (1928), by the French journalist Albert Londres, falls between the categories of documentary reporting and the novel.[3] Londres purports to be writing a factual account, but he appears to have filled some gaps in the narrative creatively. Hence one must exercise skepticism about his work.

Traveling as an investigator for the League of Nations, Londres followed the voyage of women who were destined for prostitution from their places of origin in Europe (Paris, Marseille, Warsaw), across the ocean to Buenos Aires. His account is valuable because he describes both the women "who do not die by it," and the men "who live by it" – the traffickers, or "caftens," who represent themselves officially as fur merchants; "Well," Londres remarks, "human skins are pelts too, I suppose!"[4] Most strikingly, Londres reports on the business terminology used by the secret gangs that recruited these women in Europe. The slavers' organization was known as "the centre;" the women were called "remounts" (a term meaning "fresh horses" and normally used for animals); underage girls were known as "lightweights," while those arriving in Buenos Aires without papers were known as "false weights."

Londres drowned while traveling in a French ship "that burnt in the Atlantic, as it was bringing a human shipment of 300 women destined to practice prostitution in this part of South America."[5] In the prologue to the Spanish translation of the book, the critic Andrés Chinarro suggests that the fire was of suspicious origin.

Londres is moralistic about this "old problem," which, in his view, began with hunger and poverty in Europe. In exposing these conditions, he goes down "into the pits where society deposits what it fears or rejects; to look at what the world refuses to see; to pass my own judgment on what the world has condemned."[6] Londres does not have much faith in repressive measures, such as official decrees and bans against the white slave traffic, for "they simply serve to absolve from responsibility the officials who are supposed to contend with it."[7]

Despite Londres' claim to inform the reader and to document with impartiality important details of this traffic, his portrayal of the Jewish pimp is a caricature:

> Those dark Levites, their filthy skins making the
> strangest effect of light and shade, their unwashed
> locks corkscrewing down their left cheeks, their

flat round caps topping them like a saucepan lid
. . . . I shuddered: I felt as though I had fallen
into a nest in which great mysterious dark birds
were spreading their wings to bar my retreat."[8]

Londres focuses chiefly on the non-Jewish *francesas*, or
French prostitutes, who were the most highly valued group of
prostitutes. But he also devotes significant sections to the
polacas, the Jewish prostitutes, and the *criollas*, the native
Argentinians. On the popular scale of values, French women are
the "aristocracy;" then come the *polacas*, and finally the lowest
social group, the "serfs" or *criollas*. What the customers did
with them seemed to follow a pattern: "Throw over the Creola,
sharpen their claws on the Polack, and try for the Franchucha."[9]

Londres aims to destroy the sentimentality usually associated
with prostitution. He sees the tragedy of this profession, and
he claims that the responsibility falls on everyone involved:
"Until recently it was maintained that these women were exceptional cases. Scenes from a romance; the romance of a girl
betrayed; an excellent story to make mothers weep: but merely a
story; *the girl who is unwilling knows where to apply* [emphasis
added]."[10] Londres is probably referring here to women's-assist-
ance institutions such as Ezrat Nashim, based in London, which
helped prostitutes who showed interest in rehabilitating themselves.

One factor which cannot be left out of account was the climate of hostility to the slavers and their women in the Jewish
community of Buenos Aires. Despite the pressure the slavers
exerted and their economic influence, Jewish institutions rejected them as *tmeyim*, or "impure ones," and thus they were
forced to create their own guild, the Zewi Migdal.[11] Those whose
families insisted on burying them in the Jewish cemetery were
placed alongside the suicides and the beggars, in a corner facing
the wall. The ostracism of the Jewish community made it harder
for Zewi Migdal leaders to conceal themselves when they were
under investigation.

Julio Alsogaray

The Jewish communal institutions by themselves could not have
eliminated the white slave trade, but in 1930 a major campaign
against the slavers was mounted by Julio Alsogaray, deputy com-
missioner of police in Buenos Aires. Alsogaray's efforts had a
great impact in terminating the trade. He then wrote a detailed

report, *Trilogía de la trata de blancas* [White slave trade tri-
logy] (1931), in which he defined his struggle as that of "a
Lilliputian against Hercules."[12] As a result of the police
crackdown, several hundred members of the Zewi Migdal were
arrested and convicted, and severe sentences were imposed by
the presiding judge, Manuel Rodriguez Ocampo. The testimony of
a victimized woman, Rachel Lieberman, was instrumental in Alsogaray's success. The Jewish community as a whole was legally
exonerated of blame.

Another factor of major significance was the 1930 coup
d'état, which brought to power a more conservative government,
led by General José F. Uriburu, which restricted immigration and
raised barriers against the naturalization of foreigners already
living in Argentina. Uriburu drastically restricted the slavers'
operations between Europe and America, forcing most of them out
of Argentina.[13]

This period was characterized by a general xenophobia directed against minority groups already living in Argentina. Even
before 1880, when the physical presence of the Jew was almost
nonexistent in Argentina, certain authors expressed exaggerated
fears of the dangerous influence of Jews in their country. Anti-
immigration conservative writers linked the white slave trade
with the corruption and debasement of Argentinian morality; they
vented their anger, not only against the slavers, but against
all Jewish immigrants. Some of their works give a distorted
picture of the Jew because of racial prejudice and the prevailing
Christian myths based on Judas and the Wandering Jew. The stereo-
types of wealthy bankers were influenced by anti-Semitic European
writings, such as the *Protocols of the Elders of Zion* and Edouard
Drumont's *La France Juive*.[14] As the critic Gladys Onega points
out in her book *La inmigración en la literatura Argentina:
1800–1910*, "xenophobia has served in our country . . . as a
pretext for the defense of the most conservative and antisocial
values and interests."[15]

Julián Martel and Manuel Gálvez

Juan María Miró (1867–1896), known by his pseudonum Julián
Martel, published in the major conservative newspaper *La Nación*
(August 19, 1891) a fictional account which he labeled a "social
study" and which later became the first chapter of his novel *La
Bolsa* [the stock exchange], now a classic of Argentinian literature. *La Bolsa* introduced an anti-Semitic theme which has influenced nationalistic authors up to the present day.

393

In Martel's view, the Jews embodied the faults and vices of all foreigners. They controlled the world of financial speculation. They were the "extortionists," the "vampires of modern society," who struck easy deals and reaped exorbitant profits, and who promoted corruption among "naive publc officials." The "diabolical" characters were, consequently, also responsible for the slave trade. Martel's Jewish figure, Filiberto Meckser, is an odious sterotype, both in his repulsive appearance and in his sinister character: ". . . dirty teeth, pale complexion, small eyes, lined with red filaments that denounced the descendants of Zebulun's tribe, a hooked nose as in Ephron's tribe, dressed with the vulgar ostentation of a Jew who could never acquire the noble distinction that characterizes Aryan men."[16] Posing as a jewelry dealer, Meckser manages "to cover up his infamous traffic and to give an appearance of respectability to his continual trips abroad."[17] The real purpose of these trips, the reader knows, is to procure prostitutes. Without mentioning its name, Martel refers to the Zewi Migdal, presided over by Meckser, as a "club of human flesh traffickers, located next to the police station, which the police had never dared distrub."[18] Martel's anti-Semitism, uninfluenced by contact with flesh-and-blood Jews, ignored the campaign launched by the Jewish community in Buenos Aires to wipe out the Zewi Migdal.

Other Argentinian authors, although as conservative as Martel, did not share his opinion of Jews. The most important of these was Manuel Gálvez (1882–1962), who, despite his reservations about Jewish immigrants, praised Jewish efforts to eradicate the bad elements from their midst by denying them entry into their synagogues and burial in their cemeteries.[19] In his novel *Nacha Regules* (1922), which depicts the miserable state of prostitutes in Buenos Aires, Gálvez's sympathies are obviously with the "*polacas . . .* who were sold in public auction, who were brutalized and deeply hurt."[20]

Samuel Eichelbaum and David Viñas

Ten or twelve years later, a more romantic view of the *polaca* emerged in the writings of liberal, socially conscious authors who showed the prostitute as a victim. These include Samuel Eichelbaum and Davis Viñas, whose sympathy for the *polacas* and sensitivity to anti-Semitism were probably associated with their own Jewish origins.

Samuel Eichelbaum's drama *Nadie la conoció nunca* [No one ever knew her] (1945) is, in a way, a criticism of the cultural attitudes of the privileged class.[21] It portrays the anguished life of Ivonne, a *polaca* crushed by society, a true victim of social circumstance, and an outcast. Ivonne hides her real identity behind a French name, which serves partly to improve her professional status as a prostitute and partly to protect her from persecution. The joviality of the first act of the play turns serious when Ivonne hears a group of young Argentinian aristocrats – her clients and her lover, Ricardito – boast of having shaved the beard of a Jewish immigrant, publicly degrading him.

In her own living room Ivonne witnesses a playful reenactment of the shaving, performed by the perpetrators. Responding to this racial insult, she strikes one of the offenders, thus demonstrating that she still retains some feeling for her origins. The realization that they had done this for amusement shocks Ivonne into recovering her Jewish identity. It also brings back memories of her father, murdered during the Tragic Week of 1919, when a pogrom broke out in the streets of Buenos Aires. Recalling similar pogroms in Russia, which had caused her to emigrate to Argentina, Ivonne expresses her remorse in a confession of her errors: "I am glad . . . that my father did not live to see me leading this life of debauchery. I thank my stars that I never had to face him looking like this. Even worse, today I feel the emptiness of my whole life, like a terrible revelation."[22] As a redeemed heroine, Ivonne sees herself as a representative of all Jewish women. She feels compelled to behave with dignity "because now, in each one of us, in our words and our deeds, the [Jewish] race prevails."[23] Her curse is that despite her understanding, she is too weak to change and will remain a prostitute.

David Viñas (b. 1929), like Eichelbaum, links violence with casual amusement. In his novel *En la Semana Trágica* [During the Tragic Week] (1974), he exposes the thoughtless brutality of the *guardias blancas* (white guards), who went on a rampage of murder and destruction against the Jewish community in 1919.[24] Violence that week was an entertainment for well-to-do youth, who alternated between whoring with *polacas* or *francesas* and beating up defenseless Jews.

In a later novel, *Los dueños de la tierra* [The owners of the land] (1974),[24] Viñas's protagonist, Vicente, remembers that he and his fellow law students used to leave the courthouse and amuse themselves "with the *polacas* or with the Jewesses, who after all were the same thing."[26] When he compares the different sorts of

whores he has encountered, Vicente finally decides that, contrary
to public opinion, "one Jewess is worth four Frenchwomen any-
time."[27] Significantly, both Viñas and Eichelbaum create male
protagonists who, despite their expressed hatred for Jews, eventually fall in love with and marry Jewish women; yet this resolves
none of their internal tensions.

Mario Szichman and Moacyr Scliar

During the 1970's literary accounts of Jewish prostitution
became more realistic, their scope more ambitious, and their
characters more three-dimensional. Cases in point are the Argentinian novelist Mario Szichman and the Brazilian Moacyr Scliar.
Szichman writes in a bitter, sarcastic vein. His autobiographical
novels, linked to his Jewish heritage, are cynical, less conciliatory than those of earlier authors. Dora, a continuing character
in several of Szichman's novels, is a hardened, resourceful, unscrupulous woman who becomes a prostitute in Buenos Aires to save
herself from starvation: "I discovered that the world belonged
to men, and since I could not conquer it with my head, I used my
tujes [backside]."[28]

In her Yiddishized Spanish, Dora does not make any distinction between obscenity and refinement, as long as she gets what
she wants. She has no qualms about openly acknowledging the link
between crime and prostitution: "There was a certain *polaca* who
whistled at the client, and lured him into the passage . . . .
there they would take away his ring, his watch, his wallet."[29]
Dora cynically models herself on the melodramatic heroines of
tangos and milongas, as she retells the story of her life: "I
don't go rolling around from here to there as I used to. There
is luxury in my room. I spend as much as I wish. And no one
reminds me that once upon a time I was the mud of the delta, the
easy ride who was mocked on nights of carousing and of cham-
pagne."[30]

Dora's determination to succeed as a madam is based on her
conclusion that prostitutes who are uncooperative and unenthusi-
astic about their work can never get ahead. "I knew what was in
store for me . . . and wasn't going to let myself fall just like
that . . . to be a *curveh* [prostitute] was just a step in the
business, to become what I am today."[31] Since she must be a
prostitute, Dora is determined to be a good one. Her cynicism
dominates her conversations with her clients, as she portrays
herself as a victim of corrupt social institutions while at the

same time she is performing her job. Dora claims that prostitution "is a monstrous slavery, tolerated by society, regulated by
the state and protected by the police." When one of her clients
warns, "They will infect you with their horrible illnesses, you
will fall ever lower . . . that is what awaits you if you don't
change your life-style," Dora replies, "Sí, sí . . . I want to
be different. And you will help me; you who are so good. How do
you prefer, up or down?[32]

Dora fully agrees with Ema, her friend and model of a madam,
that "we Yidn are not like goyim; there is always the *moral issue*."
The "moral issue" is not so much moral as it is a desire to maintain ethnicity – to maintain Jewishness in a Catholic world. But
as a madam, Dora does not pretend to be naive or even cynical
any longer. She judges harshly the institutions that publicly
absolve from responsibility those girls who consider themselves
victims of society.

> "They always talk of the losers," Dora thought, "but
> they forget the others. Just because we are just a
> few, maybe? But can all be generals in a battle? . . .
> I'd wish just one of them [women] would come to me
> and tell me she was forced to do it. Just one. They
> beg us to give them work. Sometimes they have to be
> kicked out. And what's worse, they always come back.
> They are all stupid and greedy. And they wear every-
> thing they own. They don't even have five *tzent.* One
> has to teach them how to walk, how to behave. How
> many come out of it married: Liars, selfish, unkempt.
> One has to watch them with everything. Or they get
> fat, or ill, or careless."[33]

Although Dora pretends to be indifferent to the rejection of the
polacas in the Yiddish theatre, and to their segregation in the
Jewish cemetery, she takes comfort in the fact that they are
still part of the Jewish community.[34]

Moacyr Scliar's novel *O ciclo das águas* [The cycle of
waters] (1976), like the rest of the literature reviewed here,
makes use of the historical data on the subject of prostitution
in Argentina as a point of departure.[35] Scliar sets his novel
in Porto Alegre, Brazil, where the white slave trade withdrew
after being driven out of Buenos Aires. In *O ciclo das águas*
Scliar presents nostalgic reminiscences of the shtetl existence:
the dire poverty of Polish families, and the naiveté of parents
who entrusted daughters to unscrupulous men, believing the
claims to orthodoxy and the false promises of marriage made by

the *caftens* and their agents. Esther Markowitz starts as an innocent child in Poland. After her arranged marriage to a Jew who turns out to be a pimp, Esther is introduced to the brothel life in Paris, where all her contacts and clients speak Yiddish, as well as French and Polish. She is first humiliated and then seduced by the wealth and the easy life that surround her. Scliar seems to follow Albert Londres' description in the unfolding of events, turning his euphemistic terminology into dramatic action: "A *husband* dies, his *widow* is doing well, he assigns her to one of his trusted lieutenants."[36] In this novel, when Mendele dies, his "widow" Esther is assigned to "Luis el malo," or Leiser, the Latin Amercian chief of the Zewi Migdal organization.

The title of the novel, which may be translated as "The Cycle of Waters," symbolizes the rebirth of Esther in her illegitimate son, Marcos. This parallel between the chemical composition of the waters and the human reproductive cycle runs through the novel, for it is through Marcos that Esther regains her respectability. She sends her son away from her "house" in order to have him brought up as a proper Jewish boy, has him circumcised, and sees that he attains Bar Mitzvah. It is through Marcos that Esther expiates her guilt for having been a prostitute and for having failed her father, a *mohel* (ritual circumciser) in Poland. Throughout her life, Esther learns to cope with the unjust, painful realities of the world. Whether she is portrayed as the victimized woman struggling for independence and respectability, as the attractive "Queen Esther of America," or as the Frenchified Madame Marc (née Markowitz), Scliar's heroine never completely loses her dignity. She emerges from her painful trials as a proud, sensitive woman.

The fetid waters drunk by the children of Santa Lucía, a slum in Porto Alegre, become a revealing metaphor for Scliar. Despite the danger of contamination, despite the infected environment, the children of Santa Lucía grow up healthy. Marcos becomes a professor of biology. Studying in his laboratory, he views the polluted waters through a microscope, discovering each impurity and reporting it to his students. Marcos himself, born of a woman infected with syphilis, escapes unscathed and free of disease.

Esther's illegitimate son stands as a spokesman for middle-class values and human rights. He is deeply concerned about the corruption of Brazilian politicians who neglect the poor, about the stagnant university system which does not educate, and about land speculators who trample on the weak and disenfranchised.

These social ills, in Marcos's opinion, are far worse than prostitution.

Conclusions

It is worth noting that with the exception of the journalistic reports presented by Albert Londres and Julio Alsogaray,
none of the writers mentioned in this study had first-hand
experience with the white slave trade. Their tales about prostitution reflect their personal ideological convictions. The
various approaches to the portrayal of the *polaca* show the
different perspectives that each author chose.

The figure of the *polaca*, used as a means of illuminating
social conditions in Europe, also appears in the writings of
several European Jewish authors: Isaac B. Singer, Sholem Asch,
and Sholem Aleichem.[37] In Old World settings these authors use
the *polaca* to illustrate the traditional dilemmas and paradoxes
of shtetl life, but they romanticize the prostitute when they
project her into the New World. Sholem Asch's prostitutes, for
example, imagine being married to black princes in Argentina.
Singer's characters, on the other hand, fantasize that these
women will pay for their sins with venereal disease.

It is in Latin American writings that one finds the most convincing and complete portraits of the *polaca* in all phases of her
career – from naive immigrant to successful society madam. A com-
posite picture of the Jewish prostitute emerges from these literary portrayals. The literature shows that there was triumph
as well as suffering, resilience as well as despair, among the
polacas.

Notes

1. Robert Weisbrot, *The Jews of Argentina* (Philadelphia: Jewish
   Publication Society, 1979) p. 59.
2. Ernesto Pareja, *La Prostitución en Buenos Aires; factores
   antropológicos y sociales; su prevención y represión;
   policía de costumbres* (Buenos Aires: Editorial Tor, 1937);
   Adolfo Bátiz, *La ribera y los prostíbulos en Buenos Aires*
   (Buenos Aires: Ediciones Aga Taura, 1961); Ernesto Bott,
   "Las condiciones de la lucha contra la trata de blancas en
   Buenos Aires," *Oceana* 9, 2 (1916); Luis Saslavsky,
   Psicoanálisis de una prostituta (Buenos Aires: Falbo, 1966).

3. Translated by Eric Sutton as *The Road to Buenos Aires* (London: Constable, 1928).
4. Ibid., p. 170.
5. Albert Londres, *El camino de Buenos Aires* (Buenos Aires: Ediciones Aga Taura, 1927), p. 7 (no translator's name given).
6. Ibid., p. 244.
7. Ibid., p. 245.
8. Ibid., p. 166.
9. Ibid., p. 241.
10. Ibid., p. 247.
11. Zewi Migdal, an organization composed of Jewish immigrants from Poland, was held responsible for the white slave trade. It was first called "Warsaw" but later took the name of its leader.
12. Julio Alsogaray, *Trilogía de la trata de blancas* (Buenos Aires: n.p., 1933).
13. Weisbrot, *Jews of Argentina,* p. 63.
14. Edouard Drumont, *La France Juive* (Paris: Margon & Flammarion, 1885).
15. Gladys Onega, *La inmigración en la literatura Argentina: 1800–1910* (Santa Fe, 1965), p. 132.
16. Julián Martel [pseud. of Juan Maria Miró], *La bolsa* (Buenos Aires: Editorial Huemul, 1951).
17. Ibid., p. 53.
18. Ibid.
19. Manuel Gálvez, *Amigos y maestros de mi juventud* (Buenos Aires: Editora Kraft, 1944), p. 180.
20. Manuel Gálvez, *Nacha Regules* (Buenos Aires: Centro Editor de America Latina, 1968), p. 28. The title of the book is the name of the protagonist.
21. Samuel Eichelbaum, *Nadie la conoció nunca* (Buenos Aires: Ediciones del Carro de Tespis, 1956).
22. Ibid., p. 56.
23. Ibid.
24. David Viñas, *En la Semana Tragica* (Buenos Aires: José Alvares, 1966).
25. David Viñas, *Los dueños de la tierra* (Buenos Aires: Editorial Librería Lorraine, 1974).
26. Ibid., p. 69.
27. Ibid.
28. Mario Szichman, *Los judíos del Mar Dulce* (Buenos Aires: Galería Sintesis 2000, 1971), p. 134.

29. Mario Szichman, *La verdadera crónica falsa* (Buenos Aires: Centro Editor de América Latina, 1972), p. 26.
30. Szichman, Los judíos del Mar Dulce, p. 136.
31. Mario Szichman, *A las 20:25 nuestra señora entró en la inmortalidad* (Hanover, N.H. Ediciones del Norte, 1981), p. 120.
32. Szichman, *Los judíos del Mar Dulce*, p. 135.
33. Szichman, *A las 20:25 la señora entró en la inmortalidad,* p. 33.
34. Ibid.
35. Moacyr Scliar, *O ciclo das águas* (Porto Alegre: Editora Globo, 1978).
36. Londres, *El camino de Buenos Aires*, p. 169.
37. Isaac B. Singer, *Passions* (Greenwich, Conn.:Fawcet Books, 1951), p. 14; Sholem Asch, *Motke the Thief* (New York:Putnam, 1935); Sholem Aleichem, "The Man from Buenos Aires," in *Tevye's Daughters* (New York:Crown, 1958).

FRAN KATZ

DINAH SHORE, WHERE ARE YOU NOW WHEN WE NEED YOU?

Oh, Dinah Shore, I cried last night. Oh, Dinah, how could you have left my screen, left me with the sop of the week that is Sunday? You packed your hundred beautiful gowns, dismissed the rows of violently happy dancing girls, called off your chummy harmony, and rode out of my life like the winged victory on the radiator cap of my father's Dusenberg.

I miss those Sunday nights. I do not know whether it's five years, or fifty years since we set the diaper pail outside the door, loaded the washing machine with week-end jeans, turned the three-way switch to dim, which obscured the pea pods congealed in soy sauce on paper plates and the rice stuck to the funnies. I'd sit close to my husband as he sat on the sofa, relaxed for a two-steps-at-a-time junior executive, and I'd lean against his shirt which was smoked with maple leaves. The children, much smaller then, were curled up on the floor like balls of yarn in soft pink pajamas. (The oldest — a girl — has cast her color, pink, upon her brothers.) Now and then, the grandparents snored on the Early American two-seater that doubled as a bed. With my head beneath my husband's unshaven Sunday chin, I watched while the world came up in living color.

7:00
This Sunday morning in October, I must fortify myself with black hot coffee, extra strong. I wait, scrambling my anxieties in an egg, for a phone call from my daughter who has been arrested. She was a demonstrator.

Last night while I was watching Spencer Tracy on the late movie make a princely surrender to the demands of conscience (he played a judge) the university my daughter attends in the city called to inform me that all members of CONTACT had been taken directly to the County Jail.

Her cat, Nefertiti, sniffs at the cracked egg shell that has just missed the waste basket where she's been sucking empty scotch bottles again. The degenerate.

I wander into my daughter's room, followed by the cat, who
has just finished my eggs. Nothing impairs her appetite. Gently,
I riffle my daughter's drawers, searching for that part of her
that has always somehow escaped me. She has left for me an empty
junior mints box, a pamphlet entitled, "How to Study," and another
pamphlet, mine, on oral contraception. I see her, from a distance,
holding her guitar like a shield, cross-legged, her head pressed
against the white posts of her bed.

<blockquote>

If I had a hammer
I'd swing it in the morning
I'd swing it in the evening . . .

</blockquote>

I hum her favorite song as I look for her in the bathroom,
in the mirror where she spent a thousand hours rolling her hair.
Part of her is in the bathroom, if it's here anyplace.
   I hum it at the piano, which is now quiescent (except for
the atonal chopsticks of her brothers), collecting a fine sedi-
ment of dust on the keyboard where she often played Debussy in
the style of Rachmaninoff to suit her mood.
   Through the window I look for her in the canvas chair she
sunned in all summer. The shape of her, where she read Valley
of the Dolls, The Prophet, Camus is still here.
   Last year, when she was still in high school, she left her
diary, leaking with information, underneath the dirty clothes
that she knew I would pick up.

Dear Diary,
   I do not want to marry some nice boy and go into the
suburbs and die. SHE would like me to buy my smile at
Saks Fifth Avenue like her friend's charming daughter –
in three styles; one for every occasion, hand washable.

All summer my daughter wanted to know what was it I was
afraid of? Who she was going to sleep with? She couldn't think
of any other freshman whose parents insisted they have dormitory
hours.
   "You put the emphasis on the wrong things, like appearances,"
she had said, swooping up her clothes off the floor with her bare
foot, like a circus performer. By the very clothes she chose,
she has often picketed around this town.
   One hot afternoon she called me out of the tub to read a
graduation poem her boyfriend had written. Wrapped in a towel
and dripping, I read it:

Listen, without you I could not have made it.
> Climbed the cliffs; icy, white
> Tunneled through the night; endless, black
> Told them I must know myself
Please, take this hand!

"He's trying to get it published," she said, watching my face. "I can communicate with everyone but you."

I felt that I must warn her. "Confession is not always honest."

"All you want to do is force your own tidy morality on me! What difference have you made in the world in your British Walkers and heather tweeds?" she cried and tossed her underwear to the cat.

"God, you think your sense of the order of things is truth!" she said.

"What is truth freedom from?" I asked her, unmasking the cat. I know she would like me better if I was her cat. I am too verbal. This may be her first time in jail, but I have been her training ground for non-violent resistance.

The phone rings, finally, and I run to answer it. My child and I are better friends on the phone. But it is my mother, telling me that she is getting a cold; she and Dad don't feel up to making the trip from the city today.

Would I, she asks (like the fading monarch requesting his son and heir to bring his trophies to his bedside), would I bring the boys and come to see her?

"I'll come," I tell her, although I am reluctant to leave the phone.

"If she calls I'll be at Mother's," I tell my sleeping husband, shaking him. He lifts his martini head and nods; then drops it to the pillow like an overripe apple.

The boys are sleeping off the late movie, and I decide against waking them.

9:00

The apartment hotel, where my parents live, awakens early. The tenants drift down to the lobby for the Sunday papers before they have changed their slippers or put in their teeth. Keening over their shoulders, they look to see if Mr. Grumbacher in 2D, with the heart condition, or Mrs. Morris in 5A (she had another sroke) has made it through the night. Sleep is their undeclared enemy.

404

The elevator man, in a worn lizard—grey uniform, his skin yellow as old photographs, takes me up.

"Look at the papers," he says. "There it is right there. Revolution. They make it clear. That's the only way you can figure these kids out today." He shakes the gold epaulets, which are heavy on his thin shoulders.

My parents have the door open, waiting, and I inquire along with their health if I have had any calls. I have never been able to fool my mother with bogus sunshine: she says, "What's the matter?"

To my mother, who has spent her life in the pursuit of clean-liness and kitchen—tested moderation, her granddaughter's arrest is prophetic of doom. She lists the most recent riots, the geo-graphically closest rapes, two attempted airplane bombings. She shakes her fingers, on which her rings rattle loosely.

"What did I tell you?" she says. "It's coming." She is fearful.

Another bell. I reach for the phone, but it is a neighbor in flowered robe and pink satin mules, who has come to borrow a stick of margarine. Her perfume fills the room like incense. She hopes, she says, that my mother uses margarine, because to give my father butter would be homicide.

My mother goes to the refrigerator, and my father and the neighbor woman check their cholesterol, their hearts, their blood pressure, and the stock market.

As the woman leaves, my mothers shoots a little deodorizer from a spray can. "The smell in the hall," she says. "It comes in under the door."

We sit around the rented hotel table, cheered by her familiar willow tree coffee pot, of which her blue veined hands have become an extension. We are united, not so much daughter—to—parent, but parent—to—parent, and we rub our hands and shake our heads like old men on a park bench. My mother reminds me that at least I had always phoned her — no matter where I was.

"Did she give you a minute's worry?" she asks my father.

In my own time, I'm nominated for sainthood.

Promising I will call them as soon as we hear any news, I start to leave, but my mother presses something into my hand wrapped in a handkerchief. It is the key to their safe deposit box. "Please," she begs, "keep it. You never know."

12:00

With his raincoat over his arm, my husband is waiting for me in the driveway. He hurries me into the car. "She called," he says. "We can bail her out."

"Is she all right? How does she sound?"

"Like the Maid of Orleans, after a weekend in the tower," he answers.

Which I remind him was a luxury hotel compared to the County Jail.

He has to be on the 6:00 o'clock flight for Seattle. He checks the black—faced watch, without numbers, that I gave him for his birthday. "I'll arrive 6:00 Pacific time. We have a conference at 6:30, cocktails at 7:30 with dinner following. You can reach me in my room after 10:00."

Time is his mistress. The corporation for which he works, indefatigably, to keep his place around the antique mahogany wake table, introduced them. He is habituated to her hot breath down his neck.

What was it he once said to me, a long time ago while we were parked down by the lake? "Stick with me, baby — I'm going to fly high."

Oh, fly me to the moon. The corporation will arrange the charter. But I will not go if I have to sit next to the second vice—president who pinches my thigh. Or is it the third? Just last winter we flew to the company's luxury resort, rising from a Caribbean isle. And we consumed huge buffets, shopped duty—free, shot dice, bet the wheel, were massaged and steamed in air—conditioned rooms under electric galaxies while sullen natives beat steel drums. From glass walls we saw endless carpets of golf courses, clear blue pools, and perhaps, a fringe of white dust, far in the distance. I cannot seem to remember the island.

Before the boys were born we planned a trip to Cape Cod. I don't want to go to the moon before I've been to the Cape.

The boys want to see the jail — not so much to see their sister brought to the bar of law and order, but for the opportunity to have a first—hand brush with crime, smell evil, and tell their friends about it. But they have agreed to stay at home if they can go to the airport later.

I slip over the car seat, while my husband moves behind the wheel. He moves swiftly, with economy, tips his hat old—college—boy style over his apple—wrinkled forehead, and fingers the dial of the radio until he picks up a ball game.

He has a yen, an itch for competition that causes him to take sides, count points, even when the battle is not his own.

Once it was. After two martinis he tells the story of the
Jap who surrendered to him in the Guam jungle, while he was
squatting in the latrine, carbine across his knees. He tells how
the bastard came out of the trees, arms over his head, and just
about handed him enough points to ship home.

Now he says to me, "If she's all right, maybe it's the best
thing that could have happened. These kids have to learn you
can't have democracy without. . . ."

"But they want to contribute," I interrupt him.

"We contributed," he says. "We fought. Didn't we?"

"It's different," I reply. But silently I rake up my
daughter's charge. "You wrote down your idealism in an essay
final for intellectual history. The blue book is still in your
hermetic drawer smelling of lavender."

"You read it?" I had said, only half in anger, like an old
spy acknowledging the virtuosity of a younger one.

"It's no different," replies my husband, shaking me out of
my digressive tree. "Who wants to get their ass shot off?"

He is defensive and a little chagrined, as if I had disparaged
his commanding officer, his father, both long dead, and with
whom he had little empathy. His pupils recede into tiny outposts
in the whites of his eyes, and he grips the steering wheel like
a loyal memory that has been, for years, his security. No comfort
to find that you've fought for nothing.

He cites the armies of unkempt heads and dirty feet, marching
through the city with their bed rolls under their arms, burning
draft cards like sparklers, and repeats, "Nobody wanted to get
their ass shot off."

The Bears are on the scrimmage line: Kowalski has the ball.
"He kicks it," screams the sportscaster and my husband says,
"Damn those Bears. They should have passed . . . . Let her
contribute her tuition," he adds impatiently like the sovereign
who said, "Let them eat cake."

He is losing the girl whose heart belonged to Daddy. And he
can't fight back, because he thinks his seniority puts him out
of the action. I sense his frustration as we drive down the
highway and into a sky that has become, it seems, a hood for
Sunday bonfires.

1:00
Through the grated window in the door that separates us, I
pick out my girl at once; pale face, long unravelled hair. The
stony jail seems to have made the hostility of generations
concrete this afternoon.

I look to see if she is bruised or sick, and as our eyes
meet, I feel she is saying, "Isn't this where you've always
wanted me?" I imagine that she is telling her friends, "Underneath the country camel's-hair coat beats the heart of a warden
– her keys are in the patched pocket."

The guard unlocks the heavy doors of the prison day room,
and parents who have come to claim their children file into the
white-walled cavity. It is barren except for tables and chairs
on which the inmates sit staring or sleeping with their unkempt
heads on the tables. I am aware of a strong smell of disin-
fectant. The matron, a large woman in a frog-green uniform, her
short hair razor-bobbed, tells us that visitors are not usually
admitted here. "We are not equipped. . . ." she says, but she
is interrupted by a hysterical, piercing laugh from the tier of
cells that gape above our heads like a row of teeth. It seems
to be directed at someone in our group who strikes the laugher
as hallucinatingly funny. We look from one to another but are
not sure for whom the outburst is meant.

"Where's Dad?" asks my daughter.

"Bailing you out," I answer. Her white forehead is damp;
the room is overheated like the inside of a public swimming pool,
and the letters C-O-N-T-A-C-T on her sweat shirt limp across her
chest.

I am anxious to hear what happened, but she wants me to meet
her friends.

"They're different from the kids at home," she says. "We
relate to one another as human beings. We're all disenfranchised."

"Sarah, meet mother," she says with her lisp that suggests
innocence. She has had it since she was small.

We shake hands. Sarah has a large bandage, wrapped Crimean
War-style around her black forehead. She holds her head high,
as if she bore a stigma as well as a wound.

My daughter explains that Sarah was hurt trying to save Adam
and Eve, the plaster corpses, side by side in the flower-covered
coffin that they were pulling across the campus to the steps of
the law library. "It was all truth and beauty until the crowd
went wild," she said. "Eve was smashed to pieces, but we hid
Adam under the fountain."

Sarah said they couldn't have done it without my daughter,
who knows where it's at and how to get it there.

I put my arm around my child. I want her to believe that
part of me is still young, believes in justice; but she draws
away, as if I would contaminate her nobility. She thinks action

is with the mob, pulsating, accompanied by music that is rock-soul—rock.

"Do you think I can get my guitar back?" she asks.

An inmate whose age and sex are blurred by alcohol pokes her head out of the shell that is her body and says, "Don't you bother them none — these are my girls." Then, she snaps her head back, like a turtle.

A parent says in a voice loud enough for anyone to hear, "That one over there looks exactly like the cleaning woman that agency sent me last week. My God, if they all don't look alike!" She checks the clasp on the bright red bag that matches her shoes, and Sarah shifts her weight, nervously, from foot to foot like a batter.

My husband motions to us from the door that we are free to leave.

"Phase out," screams a voice from the tier above, and another hoots, "Yeah, come back when you can't stay longer."

A waft of steam from the women's laundry room fills the day room, carrying with it the institutional smell of stew. It escapes out the door with us.

As we reach the front of the building, a young man with my grandfather's mustache and wearing a World War I army jacket, clerical collar, and white workman's gloves, is shouting directions. "Everybody from CONTACT, please use the main exit: follow Washington Boulevard to the corner — a bus will have you back at the dorm in forty minutes."

It's Wendell Hale! The students scream, open—mouthed, laughing with acknowledgement.

It is, I think, the same resourceful young man who signed the letters that read, "Send your student a box of candy during exams and remember your son or daughter with his own personalized birthday cake. Show him you care."

Everyone is going back on the bus. She wants to go with them. I beg her to come home, but she says I always want her to be different.

A long time ago, when I wore saddle shoes and pulled my sweater down over my hips that swung to Moonlight Serenade in broad daylight, I used to say with bravado, "C'est la guerre."

I fasten my safety belt (I'm not so brave now). The bus moves away, increasing the distance between us.

She has promised to call as soon as she gets back to the dorms. She and I know that over the phone we can communicate.

4:00

On the ride home I fall asleep and dream that I am cooking
stew in the large copper kettle in which my mother used to boil
her wash. But it is boiling over the top of the pot. Frantically
I twist the dials on the stove, turn off the gas — but it is no
use. I'm helpless. The stew multiplies by gallons. It pours down
the stove, gushes across the counter tops and over the floor.
Like a huge wave, it sweeps out the kitchen and through the
house, carrying with it, chairs, tables, china — even the telephone. I see a man float into the kitchen in a raft, wearing
boots and a double-breasted rain coat, with button-down pockets.
His hat is over his eyes; I'm not sure if it is the second or
third vice-president. But he is carrying a little black box
that looks like an old fashioned grinder except for the compasses,
top and bottom, whose needles move beneath glass faces. A gift
from Cape Canaveral to the corporation. With it, he can save
me, my house, my kitchen — all that I possess — if I will simply
jump into his inflated raft. I have only to stretch out, next
to him. And as the water swirls around my knees, I awake.
Sweating.

At home I hang my coat outside the door, but I'm certain the
smell of the jail will cling to it forever. The boys are waiting
to go to the airport.

5:00

I taste his whiskey kiss at the departure gate, brush his
cleanly shaven cheek with my lips. He disappears into the wind,
his ears pink from rushing, his belt swinging from the metal
loops of his black raincoat.

"I want to see where Daddy is sitting," says his son.

"Can I take a picture inside the plane?" asks his brother.

"Hurry," I tell them.

A flock of young, springy-kneed stewardesses click their
plastic heels past me. Now, running from window to window,
eager to see the giant plane move down the runway, the boys are
lost in a family of many children, in which the girls wear red
coats two years too long and saggy socks that lop over their
Sunday patent leathers. I find them standing on either side of
an older sister who is holding a toddler by one hand while with
the other she balances in place a pair of glasses with a single
earpiece. When the plane is out of sight, I snatch those waving
arms that belong to me and look with empathy at the strained
mother of all the children giving the baby a bottle and smoking
a cigarette.

We want to be home in time for Mission Impossible, my boys
tell me. They tell me their daddy's going to have lobster
tempura for dinner with wine and the stewardesses change into
kimonas and slippers when they serve dinner. Let him have all
his meals in the air, I think, remembering the shrinking roast I
have in the oven.

7:00
At the dinner table the boys want to know why we don't have
chop suey anymore.

"I made a roast," I reply. "Chew your meat or you'll get
indigestion."

"What happens if you have to go to the bathroom on the
plane?" says my second son.

"I saw the door," he replies, "but I mean, what happens. . ."

"Eat your supper; you'll miss your program," I remind him.

Extempore they are Boeing 707's scooting on their bellies
down the throwrugs in the hallway. Perfect runways.

"Not after you eat," I warn, but the overload of fuel does
not hamper them. They buzz off and land in front of the television set. Will the enemy get the secret formula tonight from
the slick girl Friday pouring drinks?

Running the water in the sink, I don't hear at first the
phone baying like a neglected dog. I pick it up with wet hands.

"Mom, listen!"

It is my daughter.

"Are you listening?" she repeats.

The double admonition always prefaces a question that wants
approval.

"After they told us no more meetings on this campus, I had
this really cool idea." Her voice is breathless, husky, urgent.

"Listen, I want to bring the kids home next weekend. It's
not just because we don't have a place to go. It could be a
sleep-in for all of us. Rock and smooth the way. You never had
a chance to know us. It's important, Mom."

The soap bubbles on my hands are dissolving. They are cold
and sticky. My heart slaps against my chest like stiff bass
strings.

I have to give her an answer; decide yes, or no; risk her
disbelief.

"These are the people I live with, Mom," she said. "I want
you to know me as I am at school. I don't want to live a lie!"

I could see suspicious eyes peering at me through tinted

411

glasses, cigarette makings ground into the rugs. They would make love on every piece of furniture.

I hear my falsetto, starchy voice say, "No argument. You can bring them very soon. But right now — I don't think we are equipped for all your young people. Dad is going to panel the basement, add a shower. Then, bring them all."

I do not hear the voice on either end of the line because I am not listening. I am afraid.

Of what? Is that the question?

Is it death, like my parents, or terror of life that is changing? Will my husband return on the 5:45 and be, somehow, different? No, I might be different. Which is it?

I think I'm afraid that if I let them come, I will hear them chanting, "Who has lived the lie?" forevermore, on empty Sunday evenings, accompanied by my daughter's guitar.

And I will protest. "Not true. It is not me. I am aware, without illusions, that I know good from useless — love from contentment."

Drawing my country–garden chintz curtains, I listen to the sneaky wind that will decapitate the last of the flowers and to the hose hissing left–over water. Come back, Dinah. Come back with your camaraderie, your optimism. Bring back the time when nothing could go wrong behind the wheel in a three–way bucket seat.

And what makes me think of the portrait of the royal family, in the days before the revolution, picnicking in the park of the summer palace? The young princess, who later vanishes, is in the foreground.

TERESA PORZECANSKI

DYING OF LOVE

"She's dying because of love" they said. Letting herself
practically go on account of a ghostly man, surely unkempt, he
was killing her, not ony accepting her adoration with complacency,
but with cautious cruelty, while she, they said, agonized every
afternoon. She barely complained from within the depths of her
silent love, and if it wasn't exactly as I've said it was, it really
doesn't matter because her expressive figure could be seen, upon
entering the joint, leaning against the wall, bluegreen and
shadowlike, as a Viking goddess in all her glory.

Not knowing what to say I suddenly found myself alone in conversation, thinking about her, eternal lady, shedding her plumage
for the barren desire of the desert. Someone said, "She's mad.
All she can think about is that barren love. That's all she talks
about." And I recreated her faded petticoat and her veils, and
I recreated her, descending majesty of multiple stairs, in a
castle of unknown ancestry, unfathomable and solid – invulnerable
castles – resembling tombs, inviting tombs.

In other lives, it must have been in others, in this she's
next to nothing, she was a Duchess of abolished lineage, of obsolete stock, lady of passionflower gardens, romantic and sublime
lady seated at the right angle of a stone gardenbench. Then,
what riddles could comfort her? What schemes of adorned courtiers
would console her? What deeds of adventures untold? What sacred
liturgy? And from which cathedral?

One would have thought her of porcelain when the brim of her
old fashioned hat loomed over her face lost in thought. Her un-
seeing gaze, her sculptured torso concealed the resigned fate
violated by the cursed fervor of love and anguish.

Nobody dies for love nowadays I thought, one dies I told myself of extreme unction of hunger of separation of torture in
your gut blood I thought and murder and prison I mean solitude
and even madness injustice I thought persecution stigmas. We died
of irrefutable causes but, her death sentence was much older
than ours, after all ridiculous and inadequate because she was
dying for what flowed from within her.

Ethereal and fickle the old woman would stoop to each afternoon over the same table in the bluegreen space, to bear and better her own ghostly figure, devout and overdue in its splendor. The faded black satin was interrupted by strands of pearls – artificial and opaque – curving and terrified at the many ivory cracks embedded in her neck. And her fragile hands resembled unrequited signs, gestures closeted long ago, speaking from the dark background of the table, each one of them a question mark.

I drew closer to speak to her: "How is it really to die for love?"

She stared at me with her besieged eyes imprisoned in their sockets.

"Have you" – she answered in a weak voice – "ever died this kind of death?"

I could not answer for suddenly an aborted past opened up to the present and from within, unfolding comically at my feet came forth a most terrible silence. I had let so many passions dissolve in the clumsy intentions of the mornings, in my own forgetfulness, in the willingness to view ourselves as living without hope. "Then you have no right to ask," she responded as her eyes emptied themselves without pause. "Don't ask. Stop wondering what it's like over here on this side."

"On this side," I repeated. What would it be like to give in to that passionate death of love, that ultimate surrender, to give up that last resort of our body to the other that kills us? It was then that I was able to see her as she really had been – I'm talking about a woman who was dying – her long neck was tattooed by lines that formed designs, scars. Some were deep cracks; others minor scratches of dried secretions. The bones of her skull were visible through the translucence of her skin. Nothing remained immune. No one untouched. Her passing was felt everywhere.

Finally, I learned that there are differences of choice selecting the many deaths that are available to us: a fatal hypnosis, a somewhat sweet rupture, and the invention of a monster that would eliminate us successfully. She had chosen to die for that unexisting, lost man, and she was redeemed, overwhelmed and totally immersed in that hot and sticky totality of life, perturbing as it may be. The corpses that we will become, knocked on our doors from beyond the past like ghosts reclaiming their rights. And no one answered. From within that barrenness only she dared, sustaining the world, to die for love.

"You," – she concluded in her weak voice. "You neither have passion nor propriety. You have become hardened. Go in peace like the rats."

No one noticed us at that table in the imaginary bluegreen café, when suddenly, I swear, I heard my own deluded scream, which wasn't mine but burst out of me, a brutal howl slashing the space in half like a sword, forcing my balance at last, tearing me into strewn pieces, dispersing themselves in confusion like colts searing the placentas that imprisoned them. It was then that I knelt before her in worship, ancient nymph of light.

Translated by Patricia Greene

NADINE GORDIMER

SINS OF THE THIRD AGE

Each came from a different country and they met in yet another, during a war. After the war, they lived in a fourth country, and married there, and had children who grew up with a national patrimony and a flag. The official title of the war was the Second World War, but Peter and Mania called it 'our war' apparently in distinction from the wars that followed. It was also a designation of territory in which their life together had begun. Under the left cuff of the freshly-laundered shirt he put on every day he had a number branded on his wrist; her hands, the nails professionally manicured and painted once a week with Dusty Rose No. 1, retained no mark of the grubbing — frost-cracked and bleeding — for frozen turnips, that had once kept her alive. Neither had any family left except that of their own procreation; and, of course, each other. They had each other. They had always had each other, in their definitive lives — childhood that one has not grown out of but been exploded from in the cross-fire of armies explodes, at the same time, the theory of childhood as the basis to which the adult personality always refers itself. Destruction of places, habitations, is destruction of the touchstone they held. There was no church, schoolhouse or tree left standing to bring Peter or Mania back on a pilgrimage. There was no face in which to trace a young face remembered from the height of a child. Unfurnished, unpeopled by the past, there was their life together.

It was a well-made life. It did not happen; was carefully constructed. Right from the start, when they had no money and a new language to learn in that fourth country they had chosen as their home, they determined never to lose control of their lives as they had had no choice but to do in their war. They were enthusiastic, energetic, industrious, modestly ambitious, and this was part of their loving. They worked with and for each other, improving their grasp of the language while they talked and caressed over washing dishes or cooking together, murmuring soothing lies while confessing to each other — voices blurred by the pillows, between love-making and sleep — difficulties and loneliness encountered in their jobs.

She was employed as an interpreter at a conference centre. He lugged a range of medical supplies round the offices of city doctors and dentists, and, according to plan, studied electronics at night school in preparation for the technological expansion that could be foreseen. When the children were born, the young mother and father staggered their hours of employment so that she would not have to give up work. They were saving to buy an apartment of their own but they had too much loss behind them to forego the only certainty of immediate pleasures and they also kept aside every week a sum for entertainment.

As they years went by, they could afford seasonal subscriptions to the opera and concerts. They bought something better than an apartment – a small house with a basement room they rented to a student. Peter became an assistant sales manager in a multi-national company; Mania had opportunities to travel, now and then, with a team of translators sent to international conferences. Their children took guitar lessons, learnt to ski, and won state scholarships to universities, where they demonstrated against wars in Asia, Latin America, the Middle East and Africa they did not have to experience themselves. These same children came of age to vote against the government of their parents' adopted country, which the children said was authoritarian, neo-colonialist in its treatment of 'guest workers' from poorer countries, and in danger of turning fascist. Their parents were anti-authoritarian, anti-colonialist, anti-fascist – with their past, how could they not be? But if a socialist government came to power taxes would be raised, and so they voted for the sitting government. Doesn't everyone over forty know that it is not the real exploiters, the powerful and the rich, but the middle class, the modest planners, the savers for a comfortable and independent retirement who suffer under measures meant to spread wealth and extend justice?

There were arguments around the evening meal, to which those children no longer living at home often turned up, with their lovers, hungry and angry.

'You never would have been born if it hadn't been for the decent welfare and health services provided for the past twenty years by this government.' Peter's standard statement was intended to be the last word.

It roused outcry against self-interest, smugness, selling-out. Once, it touched off flippancy. The darling, blonde, only daughter was present. She peered from the privacy of her tresses, cuddling her breasts delightedly between arms crossed over her T-shirt.

'So you lied about how babies are made, after all, Mama!' Mania supported Peter. 'It's true — we couldn't have afforded to bring you up. Certainly you wouldn't have been able to go to university.'

Even at the stage when one's children turn against one, at least they always had each other.

Mania's work as an interpreter had taken her to places as remote from their plans as Abidjan (Ivory Coast, WHO conference on water—borne diseases), Atlanta, Georgia (international congress of librarians) and, since the '70's, OPEC gatherings in new cities she described in long letters to Peter as air—conditioned shopping malls set down in the desert. But she also had been sent many times to Rome and Milan, and Peter had joined her by way of an excursion flight whenever her period of duty was contiguous with a long weekend or his yearly holiday leave. Then they would hire a small car and drive, each time through a different region of Italy. They felt the usual enthusiasm of Northerners for Tuscany and the South; it was only when, from Milan one year, they took a meandering route via the Turin road to Genoa through the maritime alps that this tourist pleasure, accepted as something to be put away with holiday clothes for next time, changed to the possibility of permanent attachment to a fifth country.

At first it was one of those visions engendered, like the beginning of a love affair, by the odd charm of an afternoon in the square of a small Piedmontese town. They had never heard of it; come upon it by hazard. They sat on the square into which mole—runs of streets debouched provincial Italians busy with their own lives. Nobody touted or offered services as a guide. Shopkeepers sent shutters flying as they opened for business after the siesta. Small children, pigeon—toed in boots, ate cakes as they were walked home from school. Old women wearing black formed groups of the Fates on corners, and slowly climbed the steps of the church, each leg lifted and placed like a stake. At five o'clock, when Peter and Mania were sitting between tubs of red geraniums eating ice—cream, the figure of a blackamoor in doublet and gold turban swung out stiffly under a black—and—gold palanquin at the top of the church tower, and struck the hour with his pagan hand. Nobody hawked postcards of him; at six, when Peter and Mania had not moved, but moved on from ice—cream to Campari and soda, they saw local inhabitants checking their watches against his punctual reappearance. There was a kind of cake honouring him, the travellers discovered later; round, covered with the bitter-sweet black chocolate Mania liked best, the confections were called 'The Moor's Balls,' and these were what good children were rewarded with.

Peter and Mania found a *pensione* whose view was of chestnut woods and a horizon looped by peaks lustred with last winter's snow, distant in time as well as space. They shone pink in the twilight. Peter spoke 'Wherever you lived, round about here, you'd be able to see the mountains. From the smallest shack.' Mania had acquired Italian, in the course of qualifying for advancement in her job. She got talking to the proprietor of the *pensione* and listened to his lament that land values were dropping — the country people were dying out, the young moved away to Turin and Milan. When Peter and Mania returned the following year to the town, to the square with *il moro* in his tower, to the same *pensione*, the proprietor took them to visit his brother-in-law in a little farmhouse with an iron gallery hung with grapes; they drank home-made wine on yellow plastic chairs among giant cucurbits dangling from a vine and orange mushrooms set out to dry.

That same year Mania was again in Milan, and when she had a free weekend took a train and bus to the town; just to sit among the local people on the square and let the moor mark the passing of time (she would be retiring on pension in a few years), just to spend one evening on the balcony of the now familiar room at the *pensione*. Middle age had made it difficult for her to see without glasses anything close by. She was becoming more and more far-sighted; but here her gaze was freed even as high and far as the snow from the past that would soon weld with the snow of winter ahead. In his usual long account of family misfortunes, the proprietor came to the necessity to sell the brother-in-law's property; that night Mania sat up in the *pensione* room until two, calculating the budgets and savings, over the years, she had by heart. When she got back home to Peter, she had only to write the figures down for him, and how they were arrived at. He went over them again, alone; they discussed at length what margin in their calculations should be allowed for the effects of inflation upon a fixed income. In his late fifties he had grown gaunt as she had padded out. Dressed, his were the flat belly and narrow waist of a boy, but naked he looked closer to the other end of life, and he was getting deaf. His deepened eyes and lengthened nose faced her with likenesses she would never recognize because no photographs had survived. But she knew, now, what he was thinking; and he saw, and smiled: he was thinking that there was not one habitation, however small, from which you wouldn't have the horizon of alps.

They raised a mortgage on their house and bought the farm-house in Italy. It was not a dream, a crazy idea, but part of a perfectly practical preparation for retirement. The Italian property was a bargain, and when they were ready to sell their house they could count on making sufficient profit both to pay off the mortgage and finance the move abroad. Living was cheap in that safe, unfashionable part of Italy, far from political kidnappings and smart international expatriates. Their pensions (fully transferable under exchange control regulations, they had ascertained) would go much further than at home. They would grow some of their food and make their own wine. He would smoke trout. In the meantime, they had a free holiday house for the years of waiting – and anticipation. Once they had dared buy the farmhouse they knew that, from the afternoon they had first sat in the square of *il moro*, this had become the place in the world they had been planning to deserve, to enjoy, all their life together. The preparation continued with Detto, the *pensione* proprietor, and his wife looking after farmhouse and garden in return for the produce they grew for themselves, and Peter and Mania spending every holiday painting, repairing and renovating the premises. By the time Peter's retirement was due, Mania had even retraced, in fresh colours, the mildewed painted garlands under the eaves, with their peasant design of flowers and fruit.

Peter's retirment came eighteen months before Mania's. They had planned accordingly, all along: he would move first, to Italy, settle in with the household goods, while she sat on in inter-preters' glass booths hearing – each time néarer the final time – the disputes and deliberations of the world that had filled her ears since the noise of bombs ended, long ago in the country where she and Peter began. She saved money in every way she could. She worked through that summer. He was chopping wood, he said over the telephone, for winter storage: he had found there was a little cultural circle in the town, and had boldly joined in order to improve his Italian. She was sent to Washington and wrote that she thanked god every day it was the last time; the heat was primeval, she wouldn't have been surprised to see crocodiles slothful on the banks of the Potomac – 0 for the sky lifted to the alps! He wrote that the cultural circle was putting on a Goldoni play, and – he wasn't proud – he was a stage-hand along with kids of fifteen! It is always easier to give way to emotion in a letter than face-to-face – the recipient

doesn't have to dissimulate in response. She wrote telling him
how she had always admired him for his lack of pretension, his
willingness to learn and adapt.

She knew he would know she was saying she loved him for these
things, that were still with them although she was thick-ankled
and his pliant muscles had shrunk away against his bones.

After Washington it was Sydney, and then she went back to
autumn in the room she was occupying in her daughter's basement
apartment, now that the city house had been sold. She scraped
off the sweet-smelling mat of rotting wet leaves that stuck to
the heels of her shoes: this time next year, she would be living
in Italy. In old sweaters, she and Peter would walk into town
and drink hot coffee and wait for the moor to strike twelve.

That evening she was about to phone the *pensione* and leave a
message for Peter to say she had returned (they didn't yet have
a phone in the farmhouse) when he walked into the apartment.
Mother and daughter, like two blonde sheepdogs, almost knocked
him over in their excitement. How much better than a phone-call!
Husband and wife were getting a bit too middle-aged, now, to
mark every reunion with love-making, but in bed, when she began
to settle in for a long talk in the dark, he took her gross
breasts, through which he used to be able to feel her ribs, and
manipulated the nipples deliberately as a combination lock calculated to arouse both him and her. After the love-making he fell
asleep, and she lay against his back; she hoped their daughter
hadn't heard anything.

In the morning the daughter went to work and over a long
breakfast they were engrossed in practical matters concerning
the farmhouse in Italy and residence there – taxes, permits,
house and medical insurance. The roof repairs would have to be
done sooner or later and would cost more than anticipated – 'A
good thing I decided to work this summer.' However, Detto had
made the suggestion Peter might do the repairs himself. Detto
offered to help – through his foresight, Peter had bought cheaply
and stored away the necessary materials. 'Leave it until next
year when I'll be there to help, too – so long as it won't leak
on you this winter?' 'Heavy plastic sheeting, Detto says, and
the snow will pack down . . . I'll be all right.' And while she
washed her hair Peter went off into the city to enquire about a
method of insulating walls he couldn't find any information on,
in Italy – at least not in the region of the moor's sovereignty.

Mania was using the hair-dryer when she heard him return.
She called out a greeting but could not catch his reply because

421

of the tempest blowing about her head. Presently he came into the bedroom with a handful of brochures and stood, in the door-way. He signalled to her to switch off; she smiled and did so, ready to listen to advice he had gleaned about damp rot. What he said was 'I want to tell you why I came.'

She was smiling again and at once had an instinct of embar-rassment at that smile and its implication: to be here when I came back.

He walked into the room as if she had summoned him; Mania, sitting there with her tinted blonde hair dragged up in rollers, the dryer still in her hand.

'I've met somebody.'

Mania said nothing. She looked at him, waiting for him to go on speaking. He did not, and her gaze wavered and dropped; she saw her own big bosom, rising and falling with faster and faster breaths. The dryer began to wobble in her hand. She put it on the bed.

'In the play. I told you they were putting on a Goldoni play.'

Her brain was neatly stocked with thousands of words in five languages but she could think of nothing she wanted to say; nothing she wanted to ask. She slowly nodded: you told me about the play.

He was waiting for *her* to speak. They were two new people, just introduced with the words *I've met somebody,* and they didn't know what subject they had in common.

He struggled for recognition. 'What do you want to do.' He made it a conclusion, not a question.

'I? *I* do?'

She had pushed up one of the metal spokes that held the rollers in place and he saw the red indentation it left on her pink fore-head.

He insisted quietly. 'All the things are there . . . furn-iture, everything. The property. The new material for the roof.'

'You want to go away.'

'It's not possible. The person – she has to look after her grandmother. And she's got a small child.'

Mania was breathing fast with her mouth open, as she knew she did, now that she was fat, when they climbed a hill together. She also knew that when she was a child tears had followed deep, sharp breaths. Before that happened, she had to speak quickly. 'What do you want me to do?'

'It's so difficult. Because everything's been arranged . . . so long. All sold up, here.'

Their life had come to a stop, the way the hair–dryer had been switched off; here in a room in her daughter's life she would stay. 'I could bring things back.'

He was looking at the quarter–inch of grey that made a stripe below the blonde in hair bound over the rollers. 'I don't take her to the farmhouse.'

Mania had a vision of him, as she knew him, domestically naked about the bedroom; his thin thighs – and for the first time, a young Italian woman with black hair and a crucifix.

'Where does she come from?'

'Come from? You mean where does she live . . . in the town. Right in town.'

Oh yes. Near the square – the moor struck again and again – all those little streets that lead to the square, one of those streets off the square.

Suddenly, Mania forgot everything else; remembered. Her face swelled drunk with shame. 'Why did you do that . . . last night. Why? Why?'

He stood there and watched her sobbing.

She did not tell the daughter. Discussions about the farm–house, the property in Italy, continued like the workings of a business under appointed executors after the principals have died. Some crates of books were at the shippers; so was Mania's sewing machine – one could not stop the process now. Damp rot could not be left to creep up the walls of the house, whatever happened – there are already some brown spots appearing on your frieze, Peter remarked – and he took back with him the necessary chemicals for injection into the brick.

His letters and hers were almost the same as before – an ex-change of his news about the farmhouse and garden for hers about the grown–up children and her work. They continued to sign them-selves 'your Peter' and 'your Mania' because this must have become a formula for a commitment that had long been expressed in ways other than possession and meant nothing in itself. She postponed any decision, any thought of a decision about what she would do when her retirement came. A year was a long time, the one friend in whom she confided kept telling her; a lot can happen in a year. She was advised according to female lore to let the affair wear itself out. But just before the year was up she came to a decision she did not confess. She wrote to Peter telling him she would come to Italy as planned, if he did not object, and he could continue seeing ('being with' she phrased it) the person he had found. She would not reproach or interfere. He wrote back and rather hurtfully did not mention the person, as if this were so private and precious a matter he did not want to approach that part of his life even with tolerant words. He phrased his consent in the form of the remark that he was satisfied he had got everything more or less organized: she could count on finding the house and garden in fair order.

Mania knew she was sufficiently self-disciplined – held herself, now in a particular sense like that of a military bearing or a sailor's sea-legs – to keep her word about reproaches or interference. Once she was living with him in the farmhouse she realized that this intention had to be extended to include glances, pauses of a particular weight, even aspects of personal equanimity – if a headache inclined her to be quieter than usual, she had best be careful the mood did not look like something else. Peter did not make love to her ever again and she didn't expect it. That time – that was the last time.

She presumed he had a place to meet the person. Perhaps Detto, simple good soul, and a man himself, of course, who had become such an understanding friend to the foreign couple, had put Peter in the way of finding somewhere, just as he had put them in the way of finding the farmhouse to which the remote exaltation of the alps was linked as domestically as a pet kept in the yard. Peter must have found some place, if the person had the grandmother and a child living with her . . . but pious old women in black, children with fat little calves laced into boots – these thoughts were out of bounds for a woman standing ground where Mania was. She did not allow herself, either, to look for signs (what would they be? all had black hair and wore crucifixes) among the young women who carried shopping-bags, flowering magnificent vegetables, across the square of the moor.

Peter went with her on shopping trips into the town. A pleasant, unvarying round. The post office for stamps, and the bank where a young teller sleek as the film stars of their youth counted out millionaire stacks of lire that paid for a little fruit from the old man they always patronized in the market, and bread from the woman with prematurely grey hair and shiny cheekbones who served alongside her floury father or husband. It was autumn, yes; sometimes they did go on foot, wearing their old sweaters. They drank coffee at an outside table if the sun was shining, and got up to trudge back at the convenient signal of *il moro* striking his baton twelve times. But Peter did not go out alone, and for the first few weeks after her arrival she thought this was some quaint respect or dutiful homage: when she had settled in and he knew she did not feel herself a new arrival in her status as resident, he would take up again – what he had found.

He seemed reluctant, indeed, to go anywhere. Detto came by to invite him to go mushrooming, or hunting boars in the mountains, something Peter had talked about doing (why not?) all the years of anticipation; he yawned, in his slippers, looking out at the soft mist that wrapped house and alps in a single silence, and watched the old man disappear into it alone. One of their retirement plans had been to do some langlauf skiing, you didn't have to be young for that, and there was a bus to a small ski resort only an hour away. The snow came; she suggested a day trip. He smiled and blew through his lips, dropping his book in his lap at the interruption. She felt like child nagging to be taken to the swings. They stayed at home with the TV he kept flickering, along with the fire.

It was true that he had got everything more or less organized, on the property. When she asked him what he planned to do next – plant new vines, build the little smoke–house they'd talked of, to smoke the excellent local trout – he joked with her, apparently: 'I'm retired, aren't I?' And when spring came he did nothing, he still watched TV most of the day. 'It improves my Italian.' She busied herself making curtains and chair–covers. She would wrap up for a walk and when she came home, expect he might have taken the opportunity, gone out. Even before she entered the house, she would see through the window the harsh barred light that flowed on the black–and–white television screen, a tide constantly rising and falling back over the glass. He was always there.

She found minute white violets in the woods. She went up to him that day, sitting in his chair, and held the fragile bouquet under his nose, cold and sweet. He revived; met her eyes; he seemed to have come to in a place as remote as the peaks where the snow never melts.

She made coffee and he raked up the fire. They were sitting cosily drinking, she was stirring her cup and she said, 'I shouldn't have come.'

He looked up from the newspaper as if she had passed a remark about the weather.

It was an effort to speak again. 'You can go out, you know.'

He said from behind the paper, 'I gave up that person.'

She felt herself being drawn into a desolation she had never known. She got up quietly, tactfully, and went into the kitchen as she might to some task there, but whatever she did, that day, the sense of being bereft would not leave her. She did not think of Peter. Only that Peter, in spite of what he had just told her, could do nothing for her; nothing could be done for her, despite the coming about of the prediction of female lore. She carried on with what she had planned: finished the curtains and fitted the chair-covers, and a day came when she was released by what had seized her and she hadn't understood, and she went to Detto's wife to learn, as promised, how to fry pumpkin flowers in batter. A stray dog adopted Peter and her, and joyously accompanied her walks. It was no use trying to get Peter to come; he stayed at the farmhouse while a contractor repaired the roof, and listened to Detto's stories while Detto planted the new vines and tended the garden. They did go into town to do the household shopping together, though, and sometimes, in the summer evenings would sit in the square until the moor swung out to strike nine. One evening the woman from the baker's shop passed, carrying two ice-cream cones. 'That was the person,' Peter said. She didn't have black hair or wear a crucifix, she was the tall one with the shiny sad cheekbones and prematurely grey hair cut page-boy style. They had been into the baker's shop together – Peter and Mania – day after day, and taken bread from her hands, and there had never been a sign of what had been found, and lost again.

Contributors

CONTRIBUTOR NOTES

HANNAH ARENDT (1906-1975) was born in Germany and emigrated to the United States in 1933. She was a renowned philosopher, particularly known for her discerning studies of totalitarianism. BERNICE RUBENS lives in London. Her novel, Brothers, won the Booker Prize for Fiction, and her novel, I Sent a Letter to My Love, was made into a film starring Simone Signoret. FREDELLE BRUSAR MAYNARD (1922-1989) was born to the only Jewish family in Foam Lake, Saskatchewan. She went to the Universities of Manitoba and Toronto, and received a Ph.D. from Harvard. An authority on child care and family life, she wrote the controversial book, The Child Care Crisis, in addition to fiction. ANZIA YEZIERSKA achieved fame during the 1920's. Bread Givers was published in 1925 and is among the earliest fiction dealing with Jewish womanhood in the modern world. SHULAMITH HAREVEN was raised in Jerusalem. The author of eleven books, including the recently published novel, The Miracle Hater, she is the only woman member of the Academy of the Hebrew Language. AMALIA KAHANA-CARMON was born in Kibbutz Ein Harod and is an academic librarian. She has been a writer-in-residence at Tel Aviv University.

PEGGY PARNASS lives in Hamburg. Her articles appear frequently in anthologies, and her reports on Holocaust matters have been broadcast as radio dramas. Her column, "Judges and Other Sympathizers," became a successful film which won the Bundesfilmpreis award. MARIANNE WALTER was born in Hamm (Westphalia) Germany in 1910, and studied architecture in Hungary, but left for England in 1937, where she became the first architect to design school camps for evacuated school children (1938). FAY ZWICKY was born in Melbourne, Australia in 1933, and divides her time as a concert pianist and a teacher of literature at the University of Western Australia. She has edited Quarry: A Selection of Western Australian Poetry and Journeys: Four Australian Women Poets. ANGELINA MUÑIZ-HUBERMAN was born in France of Spanish parents, and has lived most of her life in Mexico City, where she is a professor of Spanish and Comparative Literature at the University of Mexico. BAT YE'OR was born in Egypt and now lives in Switzerland and is the author of many articles on non-Muslim minorities, an historical study of Egyptian Jewry (1971), and The Dhimmi. ESTHER CAMERON grew up in Madison, Wisconsin. She studied German literature at Berkeley, 1964-68, and reached Judaism by way of Celan, Buber, and Scholem. Her poetry, A Gradual Light (1983), was translated by Simon Halkin and won the Peter Schwiefert poetry prize in 1985.

EMMA GOLDMAN (1869-1940) came to the United States from Russia at the age of sixteen, and became feared and admired as an anarchist. She published an anarchist journal, Mother Earth (1906-1918), and was imprisoned during the first World War for opposing the draft. Deported to Russia in 1919, she fled to Paris, disillusioned with the Soviet system. NANCY KEESING was born in Sydney, Australia in 1923, and has had considerable literary influence there. She has edited innumerable anthologies, including History of the Australian Gold Rush, and Shalom, An Anthology of Australian Jewish Short Stories. In 1979, she was awarded the Membership of The Order of Australia (A.M.). CYNTHIA OZICK was born in New York City and educated at New York University. The author of six works of fiction, she is a pronounced stylist, and considered one of the leading writers in the United States. BARBARA MUJICA is a Washington-based writer whose articles concentrate on Hispanic and women's issues. She is the author or co-author of more than twenty books on Hispanic culture, and an Associate Professor of Spanish at Georgetown University. LUISA FUTORANSKY describes herself as a journalist, poet, and globetrotter from Argentina, who now lives in Paris. Her poetry has won several prizes. Son cuentos chinos is her first novel. Her translator, David Pritchard, translated A House In The Country, by José Donoso (Knopf, 1984), with Jill Levine, and contributed translations to A Longing For The Light: Selected Poems of Vicente Aleixandre (Harper & Row, 1979), the Nobel Prize Laureate. His translations also appeared in Echad One: A Literary Anthology of Latin American Jewish Writings. He is currently senior editor at Houghton Mifflin. SHIRLEY ESPAKA graduated from the University of Witwatersrand in South Africa in 1963, and now lives in London. Her fiction has appeared in many publications in England. Blood Fugue deals with the racial problem in Johannesburg society. EUGENIA GINZBURG (1906-1977), taught history at the University of Kazan, until her arrest in 1937. Her two memoirs of life in a Stalinist Labor Camp, were first circulated in typewritten sheets in Moscow. LILIANE ATLAN lives in France. Her plays have been performed in France, Austria, Belgium and Israel. In 1984, she was awarded the title of Chevalier de l'Ordre des Arts et des Lettres by the French government. Her translator, Marguerite Feitlowitz has translated such writers as Griselda Gambaro, Angelica Gorodischer, Ariel Dorfman, and Leopold Sedar Senghor. She was recently awarded a Fulbright Research Fellowship to Argentina.

SHELLY EHRLICH lived and worked in Massachusetts as a poet and psychiatric social worker. She combined both professions, using poetry to probe the meanings of dreams, fantasies, and death. She was afflicted with multiple sclerosis, and often translated her illness into poetic insights into our physical beings. Her talent and her courage will be missed. NELLY SACHS (1891-1971), wrought an extraordinary synthesis between the German romantic tradition in poetry and the Holocaust. She herself fled Germany in 1940, and lived in Sweden, but wrote in German. She shared the Nobel prize for literature in 1966 with S. Y. Agnon. Of ELSE LASKER-SCHÜLER, Gottfried Benn has said, "She was the greatest lyrical poet Germany ever had." She was born in Elberfeld, probably in 1869, a coal-mining region in West Germany. In 1939 she fled the Nazis and came to Jerusalem, where she died in 1945. She was famous for her flamboyant manner and glamorous poverty-stricken, bohemian life, even in old age. Yehudah Amichai described her as "the first hippie" he had ever seen. ELAINE STARKMAN lives in northern California as a poet, writing teacher, essayist, anthologist, wife and mother. Her writing has appeared in many literary magazines, and in The Woman Who Lost Her Names: Selected Writings of American Jewish Women. RAQUEL JODOROWSKY was born in Santiago de Chile in 1927 of immigrant parents, but now lives in Peru and is regarded as a Peruvian poet. She is also an artist and her work has been exhibited in Lima, Peru. CAROL ADLER describes herself as "an addict of Shakespeare sonnets, morning ten-mile runs, and ESM concerts." She has published three volumes of poetry.

NAOMI DOUDAI is the theater critic for The Jerusalem Post. She was born in Glasgow, Scotland, and received her Master's degree in English and history from the University of Glasgow. Her novel, Street of the Four Winds, was published in England. CLARICE LISPECTOR was born in the Ukraine and brought to Brazil at the age of two months. She became a journalist and a lawyer. The author of six novels and many short stories, within a decade after her death she was regarded as one of Brazil's prominent writers. NORA GLICKMAN was born in La Pampa, Argentina in 1944, and is now an Associate Professor of Latin American Literature at Queens College, New York. She edited Argentine Jewish Literature for Yiddish/Modern Jewish Studies (1990), Seven Argentine Jewish Dramatists: An Annotated Anthology, and co-edited with R. Di Antonio, Tradition and Innovation: Jewish Issues in Latin American Literature (SUNY Press). FRAN KATZ's work has appeared in many literary publications, and she was editor of Story Quarterly for eight years. She received an Illinois Arts Council Award for Fiction in 1976. TERESA PORZECANSKI was born in 1945, in Montevideo, Uruguay, of a father who came from Latvia in 1923, and a Uruguayan mother of Syrian Jewish descent. Her distinctive style of prose poetry has earned her several literary awards in Uruguay. Her translator, PATRICIA GREENE is currently conducting research on Gender and Exile in 20th Century Spanish Autobiography. She was born in Madrid, Spain and now teaches Spanish at Dartmouth College. NADINE GORDIMER was born in 1923 in the gold-mining area of South Africa. Her discerning fiction, critical of South Africa's apartheid policy, has won her an international reputation as well as innumerable literary awards. She has been called "South Africa's unchallenged First Lady of Letters."